Literacy Among African-American Youth

Issues in Learning, Teaching, and Schooling

SERIES ON
LITERACY: RESEARCH, POLICY AND PRACTICE

Series Editor:
Daniel A. Wagner

Associate Editors:
Richard L. Venezky and Vivian L. Gadsden

Editorial Advisory Board

The series is co-sponsored by the National Center on Adult Literacy at the University of Pennsylvania, which is part of the Educational Research and Development Center Program (grant No. R117Q00003) as administered by the Office of Educational Research and Improvement, U.S. Department of Education, in cooperation with the Departments of Health and Human Services and Labor. The findings and opinions expressed here do not necessarily reflect the position or policies of the Office of Educational Research and Improvement or the U.S. Department of Education.

Volumes in the series include:

Literacy Among African-American Youth (*Vivian L. Gadsden and Daniel A. Wagner, eds.*)

What Makes Workers Learn (*Donald Hirsch and Daniel A. Wagner, eds.*)

Forthcoming

Adult Basic Skills: Innovations in Measurement and Policy Analysis (*Albert Tuijnman, Irwin Kirsch, and Daniel A. Wagner, eds.*)

Adult Literacy Research and Development Vol. 1: Learning and Instruction (*Daniel A. Wagner, ed.*)

Adult Literacy Research and Development Vol. 2: Programs and Policies (*Daniel A. Wagner, ed.*)

Literacy Among African-American Youth

Issues in Learning, Teaching, and Schooling

Edited by
Vivian L. Gadsden
University of Pennsylvania

Daniel A. Wagner
National Center on Adult Literacy
University of Pennsylvania

HAMPTON PRESS, INC.
CRESSKILL, NEW JERSEY

Printed in the United States of America

Library of Congress Cataloging-in-Publication Data

Literacy among African-American youth / edited by Vivian L. Gadsden
    and Daniel A. Wagner
        p.   cm. -- (Literacy--research, policy, and practice)
    Includes bibliographical references and indexes.
    ISBN 1-881303-27-6. -- ISBN 1-881303-28-4 (pbk.)
    1. Afro-Americans--Education. 2. Literacy--United States.
I. Gadsden, Vivian. II. Wagner, Daniel A. III. Series.
LC2731.L58   1994
371.8'2996073--dc20   94-28878
                                                                  CIP

Hampton Press, Inc.
23 Broadway
Cresskill, NJ 07626

Contents

Series Preface

Daniel A. Wagner
National Center on Adult Literacy
University of Pennsylvania

Although most peoples and cultures today utilize literacy as a way to conserve cultural knowledge, imbue contemporary information through education, and enrich their societal heritage, literacy—as a set of learned skills for producing and comprehending written language—is poorly controlled by large segments of many societies across the world.

Once thought to be a fully literate country—with a 1990 UN "literacy rate" at nearly 98%—the United States, according to recent studies, now is believed to have a literacy rate at which between one-third and one-half of adults are "functionally illiterate"! Similar findings are coming in from around the world. Some specialists say that these discrepancies have more to do with changing definitions of literacy, whereas others say that previous claims were simply conjecture or based on poor methodologies for assessment. Both views are probably correct in part. What we do know is that changes in the globalization of economic exchange, industrial production, and worker retraining has put the acquisition of basic skills—of which literacy is clearly the most critical—at the center of national and international concern about education and development.

Through what I believe to be an historical quirk of academic scholarship and arbitrary disciplinary divisions, research on literacy has tended to fall into a variety of unconnected research and specialty camps. Thus, under the rubric of "literacy," we find books on adult learning and adult education, cognitive dimensions of reading acquisition in children, oral versus literate societies, orthographies and psycholinguistic processes, the role of literacy in cultural preservation, the impact of literacy on income and social mobility, and so on. These scholarly specialties are all valid, but they are remarkably insulated one from the other. Indeed, even the references utilized for these different approaches often take little note of what scholars have produced in other areas.

The present series, *Literacy: Research, Policy and Practice*, is one attempt to break down the walls that partition literacy into such separate intellectual territories. We will try to find interconnections not only among the three major segments of literacy specialists as denoted in the series subtitle, but also across the life span (children and adults) and across ethnic groups and cultures. This series, we hope, will provide an opportunity to make connections across various knowledge bases and expand the possibilities not only to achieve a better understanding of literacy in the past, present, and future, but also to lead to a future which is a more literate place to live.

Daniel A. Wagner
Series Editor, *Literacy: Research, Policy and Practice*
Philadelphia, PA

Foreword

Houston A. Baker, Jr.
University of Pennsylvania

A colleague of mine who possesses the most extraordinary sense of direction I have ever encountered arose and went for a jog on the first morning that our United States's delegation was in the old Moscow of 1983. As he and I ate an early morning breakfast, he described eastward and westward progressions, river turnings, the sights and sounds he had observed. There was in his voice and demeanor a sheer joy of both familiar recognitions and new discoveries.

Later in the week, the same colleague and I took a trip to the huge government shopping complex not far from Red Square where one is bowled over by the spectacular tomb of Lenin. I managed my souvenir purchases with the exuberance of universal consumers' sign language, pointing to items that I wanted to buy and holding up fingers to inquire "How much?"

Because my colleague had a conference session to attend at the Gorky Institute in the early afternoon, he asked if it would be OK for him to depart and leave me to finish my department store adventure. "No problem," I said, fingering one of the colorful Russian shawls so prevalent in the vast spaces of the government store. Off went my colleague.

When I departed with my multiple purchases and mementoes, I struck out confidently from Red Square and headed for the Gorky Institute where our conference was being held. The day was sunny; I was a successful shopper, and the way home was but a 40-minute walk.

But after briskly starting out and putting on my tourist's game face to show all Muscovites that I really was hip to their culture—saluting now a somber woman and then a tactiturn man with energetic nods of my head—I realized that I was lost.

Not, mind you, slightly "turned around" or a "bit out of my way"—but lost. Looking in every direction, spinning around rather frantically, I tried to discover familiar landmarks.

There were none.

Old Boy Scout chestnuts about moss on the northern side of trees, or venerable African-American lore about following the drinking gourd or the North Star seemed curiously useless. Hence, my wife's standard travel strategy lept to mind. "Ah ha," I thought, "I will just ask someone for directions."

But how?

My colleague who possessed the keen sense of direction had actually prepared for our Moscow conference by learning a bit of Russian and perusing several guidebooks on the history and landscape of Moscow. Not I! Intrepid tourist that I am, I knew that I could always improvise.

Now, the first eight people—including a formidable policeman—whom I approached for directions and help, regarded me as though I were a dark mechanical invention sent by heaven knows what demonic forces to irritate their afternoon.

I looked desperately at street signs, shop inscriptions, and monument headings only to encounter the meaningless arabesques of the Cyrillic alphabet. There were *no* readable signs, possible conversations, or saving instructions or directions available to me. I was a baffled tourist—an illiterate person in a world rendered suddenly strange and frightening by the disappearance of basic symbolic skills and understandings that a particular class and cast of us like to think of as *everyman's property*. But here I was illiterate in the dominant codes, symbols, and conversations of culture, reduced quickly, decisively, and terrifyingly to the status of a confused tourist among the mighty—a person without a country, a man with no active symbolic citizenship.

Now I did get to the Gorky Institute—thank heavens—or I would not have the honor of writing this brief foreword. But I only got to the Institute by hailing a taxi whose driver lied to me in a hybrid gibberish of languages—French, English, Russian, Arabic, and others—that was nearly as pathetic as my own babbling attempts to communicate. Together, in a welter of tongues, we managed to luck upon the place that I was going. He was far more lighthearted about my situation than I, but he was a good guy for all that.

My story is perhaps amusing, but in the context of the present brilliant collection of essays, it is also painfully emblematic. It autobiographically represents a terrifying problem faced by millions of human beings the world over. The people I have in mind are those who exist without facility, politesse, or possibilities in the dominant codes—the regnant signs and wonders—of the worlds they inhabit, primarily as laborers, preeminently as New World Order accidental tourists at the mercy of the controllers of signs. Black, inner-city youth and adults are, far too often, representative of these legions. Our black urban population is tragically, in my view, too often subject to the unmercifulness of lying taxi drivers, brutal policemen, unscrupulous landlords, avaricious merchants—indeed, the complete, complex apparatus of state surveillance and control that relies precisely for its power over them on black adult and youthful illiteracy.

In the 18th and 19th centuries in the United States, African slaves realized that their only hope for liberation and citizenship lay in the achievement of literacy. To seize the Angloamerican word by hook or crook was their burning desire. As the scholar Henry Louis Gates has noted, the eighth wonder of the modern world might well consist of an entire population of enslaved Africans in this land writing themselves not only into freedom, but into *human beingness* itself!

However, in the violent and terrible world of the 1990s, the romantic history of the slave's quest for literate human identity seems almost a fantasy. At times, in fact, it seems almost pointless with respect to the huge task of bringing an indispensable literacy to *all* of those who gaze at American street signs and find no help in the Roman arabesques discovered there, or who find policemen and stern-faced bureaucrats instantly turning hostile (and smug) at the first hint of Black English Vernacular— no matter how *fine* that Burberry or Nicole Miller looks on our backs. Nevertheless, although the task of bringing literacy to the millions who *must* have it is in no way easy, still it has been energetically begun and set in motion in our era by teachers, scholars, educational researchers, humanists and social scientists alike. Some of these pioneer workers are represented in the present collection. And the task that they have begun is far more likely to succeed in urban settings such as Philadelphia where there exist such resources as the National Center on Adult Literacy.

To conclude these brief reflections, then, one might say that the collection of essays that you are about to enjoy and the amazing contributors who offer their insights in the following pages constitute a brilliant assemblage. I would like to think of the combined effort, in fact, as a magnificent traveller's aid for all those who *must* in the century facing us be able to travel with literate confidence in scenic and symbolic geographies of a New World Order.

The present collection, therefore, might be seen as a New World Baedeker—a powerful model and a formal, revolutionary revision of 19th-century German guidebooks that so easily led Americans by the word alone. Today our guides in literacy and literacy research are teachers and scholars, administrators and government officials, concerned citizens and academic mentors, student tutors, and a host of others dedicated to making sure that everyone reads both the signs in the streets and the writing on the walls.

About the Contributors

James D. Anderson is Professor of Education and Chair of the Department of Educational Policy at the University of Illinois, Urbana. An educational historian, he has written numerous scholarly articles on the education of African Americans. Among his publications are an edited volume (with Vincent Franklin) *New Perspectives on Black Educational History* and a 1989 publication, *The Education of Blacks in the South, 1860-1935*, which received the Outstanding Book Award from the American Educational Research Association, the Critics Choice Award from the American Educational Studies Association, and the Outstanding Book Award from the Gustavus Myers Center for the Study of Human Rights in the United States.

Houston Baker is Director of the Center for the Study of Black Literature and Culture, Professor of English, and Albert M. Greenfield Professor at the University of Pennsylvania. He has published a number of scholarly works including *Workings of the Spirit: The Poetics of Afro-American Women's Writing* and *Black Studies, Rap, and the Academy*. He is a published poet whose most recent volume is *Blues Journeys Home*. In 1992, he served as President of the Modern Language Association of America, the first black person to do so in the more than 100-year history of the organization.

Herman Beavers is Assistant Professor of English at the University of Pennsylvania. His research currently focuses on the construction of African American Masculinity in literature and popular culture. Beavers is the author of a forthcoming volume (February 1995), *Wrestling Angels into Song: The Fictions of Ernest J. Gaines and James Alan McPherson*, which will be published by the University of Pennsylvania Press.

Jomills Henry Braddock II is Professor and Chair of the Department of Sociology at the University of Miami. His research focuses on issues of equity and social justice in education and employment. Recent publications appear in the *Journal of Negro Education, Review of Research in Education, Education and Urban Society, Encyclopedia of Sociology*, and the *Journal of Intergroup Relations*.

Eric J. Cooper is Executive Director of the National Urban Alliance for Effective Education (NUA) and an Adjunct Professor within the Education Administration Department of Teachers College, Columbia University. His educational mission is to support the improvement of education for urban and minority students. In line with this mission he has worked on a restructuring project with Ted Sizer and the Education Commission of the States and has produced numerous educational documentaries, teleconferences, and talk shows. His publications include *Reading, Thinking, & Concept Development; Educating Black Children: America's Challenge; School Improvement through Instructional Design*; and "Addressing Urban School Reform: Issues and Alliances."

Linda Darling-Hammond is William F. Russell Professor of Education and Co-Director of the National Center for Restructuring Education, Schools, and Teaching at Teachers College, Columbia University. Her research and policy work focus on issues of teaching quality, educational equity, and school restructuring. Among her recent books are *Professional Development Schools: Schools for Developing a Profession; Authentic Assessment in Action: Studies of Schools and Students at Work*; and *A License to Teach: Building a Profession for 21st Century Schools*.

Patricia A. Edwards is Professor of Language and Literacy and Senior Researcher at the National Center for Research on Teacher Learning at Michigan State University. She is the author of two nationally acclaimed family literacy programs: *Parents as Partners in Reading: A Family Literacy Training Program* and *Talking Your Way to Literacy: A Program to Help Nonreading Parents Prepare Their Children for Reading*. Her research focuses on family/intergenerational literacy, emergent literacy, and home/school/community connections. Among her most recent publications is a book chapter "Responses of Teachers and African-American Mothers to a

Book-Reading Intervention Program" in David K. Dickinson *Bridges to Literacy: Children, Families, and Schools* and an article "Before and After School Desegregation: African-American Parents' Involvement in Schools" in the September 1993 issue of *Educational Policy*.

Deidre R. Farmbry is the Principal of Simon Gratz High School in Philadelphia, Pennsylvania and a doctoral candidate in the Graduate School of Education at the University of Pennsylvania. Over a twenty year period, she has been a student teacher and a department head at Gratz and has focused on the power of personal identity as it contributes to the development of school community.

Michelle Fine is Professor of Psychology at the City University of New York and Consultant to the Philadelphia Collaborative in the School District of Philadelphia. Widely respected for her activist research, Fine has published numerous articles. Among her recent publications are the volumes, *Framing Dropouts: Notes on the Politics of an Urban High School; Beyond Silenced Voices: Class, Race, and Gender in U. S. Schools* (co-edited with Lois Weis); and *Chartering Urban School Reform: Reflections on Public High Schools in the Midst of Change.*

Michele Foster is Professor of Education at the Claremont (California) Graduate School. A recipient of numerous fellowships, including the National Academy of Education/Spencer Foundation Postdoctoral Fellowship, her research interests include sociolinguistics, anthropology of education, and the social and cultural contexts of learning. Her research has appeared in *Language and Society, Equity and Excellence in Education, Urban Education,* and *Theory Into Practice.* Foster also edited the volume, *Readings on Equal Education: Qualitative Investigation into Schools and Schooling.*

Vivian L. Gadsden is Assistant Professor of Education and Associate Director of the National Center on Adult Literacy at the University of Pennsylvania. Her research focuses on family development and literacy across the lifespan, primarily on African American families and other families of color, families in poverty, and adolescent mothers and fathers. A former National Academy of Education/Spencer Foundation Postdoctoral Fellow, Gadsden has been conducting a multigenerational study with 25 African American families (four generations) originally from the rural south. Her recent work appears in *Teachers College Record, Urban*

Education, and *Theory Into Practice* (for which she was Guest Editor). A forthcoming book, *Passages in Time,* presents research from the multigenerational study.

Violet J. Harris is Associate Professor of Education in the Department of Curriculum and Instruction at the University of Illinois, Urbana. She teaches graduate and undergraduate courses in children's literature. A former National Academy of Education/Spencer Foundation Postdoctoral Fellowship, Harris' areas of expertise include children's literature, multicultural literature, historical issues in literacy, and issues related to the literacy of African Americans. She is active in the National Reading Conference, the National Council of Teachers of English, and the International Reading Association. She serves on the board of directors of NRC as well as the editorial boards of *Reading Research Quarterly, Language Arts,* and *The Reading Teacher.* She has published numerous articles on children's literature and is the editor of *Teaching Multicultural Literature in Grades K-8.*

William Labov is Professor of Linguistics at the University of Pennsylvania. He directed a research group on African American English in South Harlem from 1965 to 1968 and in Philadelphia from 1983 to 1986. A well-known linguist internationally, Labov's publications on African American English include *Language in the Inner Cities, Social Stratification of English in New York City,* and "De Facto Segregation of Black and White Vernaculars" in D. Sankoff (ed.), *Diversity and Diachrony.*

Susan L. Lytle is Assistant Professor of Education, co-holder of the Joseph L. Calihan Term Chair in Education, and Director of The Philadelphia Reading Project and the Graduate Program in Reading/Writing/Literacy in the Graduate School of Education at the University of Pennsylvania. Lytle's research focuses on the professional development of teachers, literacy learning in adolescence and adulthood, and alternative assessment. She is the co-author of *Inside/Outside: Teacher Research and Knowledge; Adult Literacy Education: Program Evaluation and Learner Assessment* (ERIC); and *The Pennsylvania Framework: Reading, Writing, and Talking Across the Curriculum,* as well as many articles on literacy, assessment, practitioner inquiry and teacher education.

John U. Ogbu is Alumni Distinguished Professor of Anthropology at the University of California, Berkeley. Prior to emigrating to the United States, he taught high school in Nigeria. Ogbu is author of several books, including *The Next Generation: An Ethnography of*

Education in an Urban Neighborhood; Minority Education and Caste: The American Cross-Cultural Perspective; and *Minority Status and Schooling: Immigrant v. Involuntary Minorities* (with M. A. Gibson). He has published over 90 articles and book chapters, including "Black Students' School Success: Coping with the Burden of 'Acting White'" (with S. Fordham) and "Understanding Cultural Diversity and Learning." Ogbu is currently conducting a comparative study of "Community Forces and Educational Strategies" among African Americans, Chinese Americans, and Hispanic Americans in the San Francisco Bay Area in California.

Heraldo Richards is an Assistant Professor in the Department of Special Education at George Peabody College of Vanderbilt University. Before joining the Vanderbilt faculty, he served as a clinic supervisor in the learning disabilities clinic at Northwestern University. His research interests focus on cultural and linguistic issues related to the psychoeducational assessment of minority students.

Diane Scott-Jones is Associate Professor in the Department of Psychology at Temple University. Her research interests are in social development, family processes, and the development of African-Americans and other ethnic minorities. Her work has appeared in journals such as *American Journal of Education, Journal of Adolescent Research,* and *Phi Delta Kappan.*

Diana Slaughter -Defoe is a Professor of Education and Social Policy in the Human Development and Social Policy Program in the School of Education and Social Policy, Professor of African American Studies, and Fellow, Center for Urban Affairs and Policy Research, at Northwestern University, Evanston, Illinois. Slaughter-Defoe's research and writing center on study of the relationship between parental socialization and children's school-related behavior and achievement, and have included research into the parent involvement component of Head Start. Prior to publishing *Visible Now: Blacks in Private Schools* and *Black Children and Poverty: A Developmental Perspective,* Slaughter-Defoe served as a member of the Governing Council of the Society for Research in Child Development. In 1993, she was designated by the Committee on Public Interest Awards of the American Psychological Association to receive the Award for Distinguished Contribution to Research in Public Policy.

Dorothy S. Strickland is the State of New Jersey Professor of Reading at Rutgers University. Formerly the Arthur I. Gates Professor of

Education at Teachers College, Columbia University, she has been a classroom teacher and reading specialist. Her publications include *Family Storybook Reading; The Administration and Supervision of Reading Programs; Emerging Literacy: Young Children Learn to Read and Write;* and *Language, Literacy, and the Child.* She is the past president of the International Reading Association and a member of The Reading Hall of Fame.

Daniel A. Wagner is Professor of Education and Director of the National Center on Adult Literacy at the University of Pennsylvania. A cognitive psychologist, Wagner has published numerous professional articles and has received major research grants from the National Institute of Health, the National Science Foundation, the A. W. Mellon Foundation, and the MacArthur Foundation. His books include *The Future of Literacy in a Changing World; Towards Defining Literacy* (with Richard Venezky and Barbara Ciliberti); *Child Development and International Development* (with Harold Stevenson); a special 1992 issue of the *Annals of the American Academy of Political and Social Science* on the topic of "World Literacy in the Year 2000: Research and Policy Dimensions;" and *Literacy: Developing the Future*, published by UNESCO. His most recent work is *Literacy, Culture, and Development in Morocco*, published by Cambridge University Press.

Vanessa Siddle Walker is Assistant Professor at Emory University in the Division of Educational Studies. A former National Academy of Education Spencer Foundation Postdoctoral Fellow and recipient of the Young Scholars Award from the Conference of Southern Graduate Schools, Walker has focused her research most recently on a five-year study which has examined the nature of schooling in a "good" school for African-American children in the pre-integration south. In addition to talks and papers on the topic, she is the author of the forthcoming book, *Reaching Their Highest Potential*, which chronicles the case study.

Introduction
Literacy and African-American Youth: Legacy and Struggle

Vivian Gadsden
University of Pennsylvania

The problems of literacy education for African-American children have been chronicled in a variety of research and policy reports, ranging from the Coleman Report (1966) on educational equality to *A Nation at Risk* (National Commission of Excellence, 1983) and recently *America 2000* (U.S. Department of Education, 1991). These issues also have been the focus of classroom studies on literacy and of programs in school organization and restructuring. Despite seemingly widespread efforts and numerous studies conducted over the past 25 years, meaningful improvement in the literacy and school performance of African-American youth has been difficult to achieve. Comparative studies, such as the National Assessment of Educational Progress (1986), show only minuscule increases in test scores but substantial differentials between the performance of African-American youth and white youth. Literacy education and educational opportunity persist as elusive commodities to disproportionately high numbers of children and youth of African ancestry.

LITERACY IN THE AFRICAN-AMERICAN COMMUNITY: HISTORICAL PRECEDENTS

A young emigre, unfamiliar with American education, reading about literacy in the African-American community might well make two assumptions: (a) little tradition and valuing of literacy exist among African Americans and (b) urban schools, where high numbers of African-American and poor children are enrolled, are the sources of most of the problems facing American education (Holt, 1990). If the young emigre were of African ancestry and lived in an urban area, he or she would have little reason to sustain hope for his or her own future or to believe that academic success is achievable for most African-American children in the nation's schools. Add to that image references to the "permanent underclass" and dysfunctional families within urban contexts, and the future of African-American youth becomes hopeless and bleak. The young emigre might ask: Do African-American children and their families indeed lack interest in school-like learning? Do they not value literacy?

In the African-American community, views of literacy historically have been developed out of an intergenerational legacy of hope, valuing of education, and cultural uplift (Anderson, this volume; Gadsden, 1992; Harris, 1990, 1992). Because of slavery, segregation, and other societal obstacles, literacy has been envisioned as an empowering and liberating possession, sometimes obtained at great personal expense to the individual but imbued with possibilities for community improvement. In quotations representing four distinctive periods of American history, African Americans have expressed this valuing of literacy, schooling, and education:

Post-Slavery (1865):

There is one sin that slavery committed against me which I will never forget. It robbed me of my education.
(An ex-slave, shortly after being freed. Quoted in Anderson, 1988, p. 5)

It seemed to me that if I could learn to read and write, this learning might, nay, I really thought it would point out to me the way to freedom, influence and real secure happiness.
(Thomas Jones, a North Carolina slave who learned to read while hiding in his master's store)

Post-Reconstruction (1925):

I want to see the children of my grandchildren have a chance, so I am giving my all.
(An old Alabama ex-slave who in 1925 gave all of his life's savings to build a school for black children)

Civil Rights Era (1960s):

This movement [Civil Rights] won't make everything better, but it will be a start. Our children will know that they have rights—that they have the right to go to any school and be anything they want. The sacrifices of the movement are worth the inconveniences and the pain. Sometimes, I'm tempted, just as you, to go into the stores and hope no one sees me. Then, I think, why should I help somebody [white store owner] who doesn't care whether my children make it. If nothing else, I want my children and the children in this community to know that I believed in their future and fought so they would get a good education.
(Spokesperson at a South Carolina Civil Rights town meeting, 1962).

Post-Civil Rights (1990s):

You know, people say that the schools back then [1920s] didn't teach a lot, but learning to read meant everything to me. Of course, some children were better readers than others, and you had no time to waste. I didn't really know how far knowing how to read would take me, but I always thought it would take me far. So, when I didn't get it for myself, I got it for my children. All have a high school diploma and four of the six finished college. I depend on them, even when I know I can handle things. I want them to know that I respect what they know. Literacy, I guess, meant just knowing how to read at that time, and the people who learned to read and could stay in school, ...well they became some of our top people in this here community—the professors [local educators].
(83 year-old woman in South Carolina. Quoted in Gadsden, 1992, p. 11)

My son hates to read. He is only seven, and he hates to read! He cries when I tell him we are going to read books. I don't know why. He is going to learn to read. He needs to do well in school. I'm not sure what I need to do to help him, but I want him to make it.
(Young mother in search of help for her child. Quoted in Gadsden, 1993, p. 2).

Throughout our history, African Americans have sought literacy and have been willing to make sacrifices for the literacy education of their children. These sacrifices have been obvious in the development of community schools created as secret learning environments in places such as Savannah, Georgia and Natchez, Mississippi where slaves and ex-slaves learned to read and write. Later, normal schools across the South and parts of the North continued this tradition. These schools and the self-help educational efforts of African Americans throughout the South attest to the importance assigned to literacy learning as enlightenment and cultural uplift, encouraged through churches and other community institutions (Anderson, 1988). Similarly, the ability of African Americans to achieve high levels of literacy is demonstrated in the literary accomplishments and educational contributions of countless numbers of individuals. The best examples, however, come from the Thomas Jones' who used a little knowledge to create literacy opportunities for themselves and others in the face of human oppression and hardship. The power of literacy has been exclaimed throughout the African-American community for over 100 years, as James White, a black minister and union army veteran expressed, in order to "elevate [our] families" (Gutman, 1987, p. 260).

RECONCILING LITERACY WITH LIVING

Upon learning about the cultural history of African Americans, the young emigre might well question the paradox that appears to exist between this history and present-day perceptions of literacy's value. He or she might hear that many African-American youth and their families value literacy but see it as a struggle—to reconcile the ostensible advantages of literacy with the barriers to access, that is, day-to-day survival. He or she may be told that the barriers, real or imagined, sometimes predominate over the struggle.

Although there is enormous hope within many segments of African-American communities, there may be an equal level of pessimism and cynicism about the value of literacy in the lives of African-American youth and their families; occasionally, this hope and cynicism exist in tandem. The cynicism has been interpreted frequently as an internalization of oppositional beliefs and cultural norms about the importance of literacy and the relevance of education, seemingly developed out of an intergenerational transfer of distrust of schools and other societal institutions (Ogbu, 1987). In one interpretation of the schooling issues facing African-American youth, Weis (1985) notes that although African-American students in her study wanted to attend college and to "make it," they were skeptical that their sacrifices indeed would result in their making it. Ogbu (this volume) suggests that the relational factor which promotes school success among immigrant minorities is their acquiescence and trust with respect to schools and school personnel. This is not true of African Americans who, because of a history of inadequate or no rewards for educational achievement (e.g., jobs and social recognition), have come to see the inadequate and unequal reward of education as a part of an institutionalized discrimination against them which is not entirely eliminated by receiving an education. For African-American youth in these studies, access to literacy may appear to depend almost entirely on their willingness to replace their social and cultural values with those of institutional structures, without any assurance that those structures will accept them (Gadsden, 1990). The inertia around literacy that this research describes stands in stark contrast to the quotations presented in the previous section. Are the sentiments described those of only a select group of African Americans? Probably not. Just as the research of Erickson (1987), Fine (1987), Irvine (1990), Siddle-Walker (1993), and others suggest, many African-American youth and their families attempt to balance the desire to achieve literacy with mixed perceptions about the advantages of schooling. Their experiences reinforce the notion that children with literacy problems in school often are treated differently and more negatively by teachers than their more literate peers (Allington, 1983; Irvine, 1990); that schooling does not result necessarily in literacy (Fine, 1989); that their experiences as African Americans are not valued in schools (Asante, 1988); or that the social and employment opportunities in society may be prescribed, even when an African American has achieved high levels of literate competence (Berlin & Sum, 1988; Kantor & Brenzel, 1993). The perceptions, more often than not, have been supported by real-life experiences and by forces of segregation, racism, and unequal access to schools and teachers engaged in innovative and culturally-sensitive literacy practices.

Although overwhelming, these perceptions of societal inequities and real or subtle distrust throughout history have been as much a factor in the survival of African Americans (Foster, 1991) as they are a current-day impediment to literacy achievement. Rarely, however, have the problems associated with literacy for African-American youth appeared more debilitating than currently described in research and public discourse. Even for African-American youth who plan to use literacy as a means out of poverty, their goals may be offset by the problems of survival—poor housing, improper nutrition, crime-ridden neighborhoods, inadequate family incomes, and the degradation often incurred in seeking assistance for these problems (Edelman, 1989; Trotter, 1993).

The African-American youth of the 1990s have not lost the legacy of literacy publicly stated by ex-slaves in 1865, but they are in search of a way to reconcile the desire for literacy with the realities of living. The legacy demands much that current literacy practices in school and social conditions out of school can not ensure—cultural uplift, liberation, power, and community improvement. In attempting to live the legacy, African-American youth may find themselves in a quandary. After all, literacy was supposed to be accessible and success achievable, so the post-slavery legacy goes. One hundred years later, however, many obstacles to economic survival and success persist, the goals of students and schools often do not match, and literacy is perceived as inaccessible for high percentages of African-American youth. Despite these problems, many African-American youth in schools demonstrate their belief in the legacy and in the meaning of literacy when teaching enables them to expand their literary talents, to build their literacy ability, and to honor their homes and communities. In doing so, these youth begin to reconcile literacy with living.

LITERACY, TEACHING, AND SCHOOLING

Much of the current discourse about literacy and African-American youth focuses on the instructional and learning issues confronting teachers and children in urban schools. Although the issues identified in this volume reflect concerns about literacy for African-American youth in general, much of the discussion, in fact, focuses specifically on African-American youth in urban schools and from low-income homes. However, neither context (urban or rural) nor social class consistently overrides the prominence of race and culture as a factor in how African-American youth are perceived and how they perceive themselves in school and other contexts. As Irvine notes (1990), the problems of school failure are critical even for middle-class African-American children in suburban schools where social class differences may be obfuscated, but race is not.

Research on literacy over the past 10 years has attempted to examine the issues from multiple perspectives and to focus on the social and contextual nature of literacy across several cultures (Bloome & Green, 1987; Delgado-Gaitan, 1987; Heath, 1983; Paris & Wixson, 1987; Taylor & Dorsey-Gaines, 1988; Wagner, 1987; Weinstein-Shr, 1991). Implicit in this work is a way of thinking about learning and teaching that provides opportunities for researchers and teachers to examine critically not only how learners from different cultures acquire literate abilities but also when and under what circumstances and conditions. When assumed more broadly, the research has presented an opportunity for researchers to examine their own preconceptions and for teachers to analyze their own practices. It has reiterated, along several lines, what many researchers and teachers have long argued: first, learners do not develop knowledge and literacy exclusive of their social histories, cultures, and immediate contexts for using knowledge; and second, the presence of schools, classrooms, and teachers does not ensure necessarily that learners have access to literacy.

The chapters in this volume expand upon existing research in literacy and African-American education and discuss a range of literacy issues confronting African-American and other youth in and out of school. In examining issues of learning, teaching, and schooling, the chapters focus on the conditions, contexts, institutional constraints, and interpersonal factors that affect conceptions of literacy and educational practices within multiple settings. Several chapters stress the strengths of family and community contexts whereas others describe the structural obstacles to achieving literacy. Although the implications of the discussion may be most immediate for African-American youth and youth of color, they are also far-reaching for youth and families across a variety of cultures, ethnic groups, and backgrounds. In short, the issues are important for all youth learning literacy.

Most of the chapters in this volume were discussed at a conference that bears the title of the volume. The conference was sponsored by the Literacy Research Center and the Graduate School of Education at the University of Pennsylvania. The meeting brought together 75 specialists in literacy and related fields to examine access to literacy by African-American youth. Focusing on how home, school, and community contexts influence black youths' learning and use of literacy, discussions at the meeting revolved around appropriate learning models and issues to which future research should respond. The four themes in this volume reflect some of the critical domains of literacy research identified and discussed at the conference.

The chapters in Part I, "Access to the Word: Literacy in Historical and Contemporary Perspective," examine a sequence of issues in the historical development of literacy research and practice. In tracing the struggle for literacy among African Americans, James Anderson provides a compelling account of the social and institutional barriers to access from slavery to the segregated and unequal schools of the 1950s. He suggests that the issue of literacy for African Americans has been steeped historically in the economic and power shifts of the nation, resulting in a struggle for access that sets the stage for social protest. Labov's work complements Anderson's discussion by continuing the discourse of access and literacy through linguistic research from the 1960s to the present. Developed around research on reading and linguistic development of African-American urban youth, Labov's discussion links the literacy problems faced by many African-American youth to the isolation and separation of their communities—issues that have had social meaning and educational impact from the riots of the 1960s in Watts and Detroit to the 1992 riot in Los Angeles.

Strickland and Farmbry focus on the problems and successes in educating African-American youth as a national issue and from a classroom perspective. Citing national efforts designed to respond to the needs of African-American children, Strickland demonstrates how the problems of educating poor and low-income black children have framed the course of educational research, practice, and policy in and for schools, for example, Chapter 1 pull-out programs, add-on programs, in-class programs, and replacement programs. Strickland discusses the strengths and limitations of a few approaches and strategies developed over the past 25 years and presents several guidelines to assist practitioners in making decisions about literacy instruction in the classroom. In response to Strickland, Farmbry captures the classroom issues of literacy, to which Strickland refers, by locating the problems of literacy practice in the experiences and expectations of teachers. She proposes, based on her own experience as a practitioner working with African-American youth, that literacy instruction and classroom interaction must not only weigh but also integrate the realities of students' lives and their definitions of learning. Acknowledging the difficulty with which a practitioner approaches the problems facing her students, Farmbry encourages educators to build on the speech, linguistic, and literacy behaviors of their students and of the families and communities that nurture their growth.

The chapters in Part II, "Literacy in Home and School Contexts," focus on individual and group literacy issues in the two contexts in which youth are said to develop, sustain, or lose interest in literacy—home and school. In this section, the authors provide different perspectives on the common problems of literacy development within classrooms, homes, and schools. For example, John Ogbu examines literacy performance and educational achievement among African-American youth by focusing on the perceptions of access within the African-American community. Comparing the perceptions of literacy and trends in school performance of several "minority" groups, Ogbu attempts to explain how specific cultural beliefs have developed and why these beliefs persist in current educational settings. Diane Scott-Jones's discussion examines the multiple perceptions of literacy within African-American families. She describes the limitations of existing policies to help African-American families and youth improve literacy and provides recommendations for the implementation of alternative practices. Diana Slaughter-Defoe and Heraldo Richards discuss the effect of teacher perceptions and behaviors on black male children's literacy development in classrooms. Pointing to the difference in treatment of boys and girls generally, and of black boys and white boys, the authors contribute to a controversial discussion in literacy teaching, classroom studies, and school organization for African-American male children.

Part III, "Literacy, School Policy, and Classroom Practice," discusses the impact and implications of educational policy decisions and classroom interactions on the school lives of African-American youth. Linda Darling-Hammond develops a strong argument about the conflicting impact of educational policies intended to improve the teaching of literacy to African-American and other children in urban schools. She argues that popular state and local policies that remove certification requirements for teachers in school districts throughout the country are not always, or necessarily, advantageous for African-American or poor youth in urban schools, where literacy problems are said to be most pronounced. Jomills Braddock, building on his own research on tracking and desegregation, also reiterates findings by researchers such as Darling-Hammond (this volume) by highlighting the over-representation of African-American, Latino, and American Indian students in the lowest tracks in schools. He notes that the over-representation in the lower tracks is both a consequence and a contributor to the problems facing African-American youth, particularly those from low-income homes. Michelle Fine, whose work with high school students in urban schools demonstrates the "push-pull" attraction of literacy as a means to success, discusses how African-American youth are silenced through direct and subtle messages by teachers and school administrators. She suggests that these students eventually come to question the politics of literacy and whether or how staying with literacy will make a difference for them and their communities.

Each of the three chapters in Part IV, "Literacy Curricular Strategies," discusses highly visible issues in literacy instruction. Patricia Edwards describes the role of parents in children's early literacy development. Outlining some of the components of a program that she developed in rural Louisiana, Edwards provides useful information on the content, context, and conditions of literacy learning for African-American children and parents from low-income homes. Violet Harris's account of the development of literacy by African Americans is an interesting context in which to examine African-American children's literature. In describing the responses of African-American children to culturally sensitive literature, Harris discusses the relationships between children's prior experiences and their expectations of the literature. Eric Cooper encourages researchers and teachers to build instructional approaches that enable students to create effective learning strategies. He argues for effective coordination of the purposes for literacy teaching and assessment in American schools.

As the chapters in the volume suggest, African-American youth, despite a legacy of hope, often find themselves in a curious state—believing in the value of literacy but unable to attain it in the ways and for the purposes that they consider most important. The discussion in this volume reflects the intensity of the dilemmas facing many African-American youth who are learning literacy, who have lost interest in learning, or who aim to re-engage themselves in expanding their abilities. The question posed by a black youth in the 1930s, "What work can I get if I go through school?," has been reframed by youth of the 1980s and 1990s, "What difference will literacy make for me?" The response today may not be considerably more encouraging than the response of 60 years ago, however. These questions are at the heart of the struggle for literacy by African-American and other youth. The young emigre could be heartened to think that literacy research will continue to seek ways to remove the struggle from learning and that practice will contribute to ensuring that the struggle is transformed into literacy achievement for African-American youth. In focusing on these issues in this volume, we aim to present both the literacy problems facing African-American youth and the resources within the African-American community that may help ameliorate some of these problems. It is our hope that the volume explores these issues in a way that will contribute to serious discussions and promote action by researchers and practitioners to help reduce the struggle for literacy by African-American youth and provide a legacy for the future of all youth.

Vivian L. Gadsden
Graduate School of Education
University of Pennsylvania

REFERENCES

Allington, R. L. (1983). The reading instruction provided readers of different reading ability. *The Elementary School Journal, 83,* 549-59.

Anderson, J. D. (1988). *The education of blacks in the South, 1860-1935.* Chapel Hill, NC: University of North Carolina Press Press.

Asante, M. (1988). Afrocentricity. Trenton, NJ: Africa World Press.

Berlin G., & Sum, A. (1988). *Toward a more perfect union: Basic skills, poor families and our economic future.* New York: Ford Foundation.

Bloome, D., & Green, J. (1987). In search of meaning. In D. Bloome (Ed.), Literacy and schooling (Vol. 1, pp. 3-34). Norwood, NJ: Ablex.

Coleman, J. S. (1966). *Equality of educational opportunity.* Washington, DC: Government Printing Office.

Delgado-Gaitan, C. (1987). Mexican adult literacy: New directions for immigrants. In S. R. Goldman & K. Trueba (Eds.), *Becoming literate in English as a second language* (pp. 9-32). Norwood, NJ: Ablex.

Edelman, M. W. (1989). What can we do? In J. B. Allen & J. M. Mason (Eds.) *Risk makers, risk takers, risk breakers: Reducing the risks for young literacy learners* (pp. 314-318). Portsmouth, NH: Heinemann.

Erickson, F. (1987). Transformation and school success: The politics and culture of educational achievement. *Anthropology and Education Quarterly, 18,* 335-356.

Fine, M. (1989). Silencing and nurture: Voice in an improbable Setting. In H. Giroux & P. McLaren (Eds.), *Critical pedagogy, the state, and cultural practice.* Albany, NY: State University of New York Press.

Foster, M. (1991). Constancy, connectedness, and constraints in the lives of African-American teachers. *National Women's Studies Journal, 3,* 233-261

Gadsden, V. L. (1990). Minority access to literacy: An American case study. *Psychology and Developing Societies, 2,* 17-29.

Gadsden, V. L. (1992). Giving meaning to literacy: Intergenerational beliefs about access. *Theory Into Practice, 31,* 328-336.

Gadsden, V.L. (1993, April). *Literacy and the intergenerational culture of African-American women.* Paper presented at the annual meeting of the American Educational Research Association, Atlanta, GA.

Gutman, H. G. (1987). Schools for freedom: The post-emancipation origin of Afro-American education. In I. Berlin (Ed.), *Power and culture: Essays on the American working class.* New York: Pantheon Press.

Harris, V. J. (1990). African-American children's literature: The first 100 years. *Journal of Negro Education, 59,* 539-555.

Harris, V. J. (1992). African-American conceptions of literacy 1700-1990. *Theory into Practice, 31,* 276-286.

Heath, S. B. (1983). *Ways with words.* Cambridge, England: Cambridge University Press.

Holt, T. (1990). "Knowledge is power": The black struggle for literacy. In A. A., Lunsford, H. Moglan, & J. Slevin (Eds.), *The right to literacy.* New York: Modern Language Association.

Irvine, J. J. (1990). *Black students and school failure: Policies, practices, and prescriptions.* New York: Greenwood.

Kantor, H., & Brenzel, B. (1993). Urban education and the "truly disadvantaged": The historical roots and the contemporary crisis, 1945-1990. In M.B. Katz (Ed.), *The "underclass" debate.* Princeton, NJ: Princeton University Press.

National Assessment of Educational Progress. (1986). *Profiles of literacy: An assessment of young adults.* Princeton, NJ: Educational Testing Service.

National Commission on Excellence. (1983). *A nation at risk: The imperative for educational reform.* Washington, DC: Government Printing Office.

Ogbu, J. U. (1987). Variability in minority school performance: A problem in search of an explanation. *Anthropology & Education Quarterly, 18,* 312-334.

Paris S. G., & Wixson, K. K. (1987). The development of literacy: Access, acquisition, and instruction. In D. Bloome (Ed.), *Literacy and schooling* (pp. 35-54). Norwood, NJ: Ablex.

Siddle-Walker, E.V. (1993). The case of Caswell County training school: Relations between community and school. *Harvard Educational Review, 63,* 161-182.

Taylor, D., & Dorsey-Gaines, C. (1988). *Growing up literate: Learning from inner-city families.* Portsmouth, NH: Heinemann.

Trotter, J.W. (1993). Blacks in the urban north: The "underclass question" in historical perspective. In M.B. Katz (Ed.), *The "underclass" debate.* Princeton, NJ: Princeton University Press.

U. S. Department of Education. (1991). *America 2000: An education strategy.* Washington, DC.

Wagner, D. A. (1987). Literacy futures: Five common problems from industrialized and developing countries. In D. A. Wagner (Ed.), *The future of literacy in a changing world* (pp. 3-16). London: Pergamon Press.

Weinstein-Shr, G. (1991, April). Literacy and second language learners: A family agenda. Paper presented at the annual meeting of the American Educational Research Association, Chicago, IL.

Introduction to Part I
Access to the Word: Historical and Contemporary Issues

Herman Beavers
University of Pennsylvania

The hero of Zora Neale Hurston's most famous novel, *Their Eyes Were Watching God*, begins that book in what, today, would be considered a distressing set of circumstances. Janie, in the midst of being raised by her grandmother, who works for "quality white folks" (the Washburns), is the playmate of the employer's children. Since punishment and care are doled in equal portions to each child, Janie has no way to make distinctions between herself and other children. Totally unaware of how the social category of race affects her, Janie does not discover her racial identity until she attempts to locate herself in a photograph taken of her and the other children. Because she imagines herself to be white, the process of elimination leaves only a "real dark little girl with real long hair" to be identified. When the mother of the white children says to Janie, "Dat's you Alphabet, don't you know yo own self?" she responds, "Aw, aw, Ah'm colored."

I take time to recount this moment as a way of introducing the chapters in Part I largely because by examining it we can isolate the issues these chapters attempt to address. What is striking about the above exchange is that Janie's nickname, Alphabet, arises out of the fact that "so many people [have] named [her] different names." But, as the novel demonstrates, the more pertinent question is the one accompanying her nickname, that is "Don't you know yo' own self?" Clearly, Janie's lack of racial awareness—or more precisely, her inability to place herself within the racial category of blackness—signals a crisis of identity. Indeed, as Alphabet, Janie is associated with randomness and incomprehensibility. The key to *Their Eyes* lies in Janie's journey to selfhood, an enterprise that crystallizes as a viable undertaking because Janie dares to tell her story. As her adventures demonstrate, Janie's task is to extricate herself from the random and the incomprehensible in order to embrace eloquence.

What I propose is that Hurston's novel provides a moment in which we can interrogate the relationship between racial identity and voice. This correlation, as Hurston presents it, becomes clear when we note that Janie is disappointed at the news that she is, indeed, black and female. Although she is only a child, her utterance marks, at the very least, her awareness of racial hierarchy (with blackness holding the subordinate place). Moreover, as Alphabet, her presence is nullified because she is identified as a figure who exists outside the realm of meaning, occupying the more fundamental but less advantageous position of unintelligibility. Insulated from the more hostile world beyond the confines of the Washburn backyard, Janie is likewise prevented from grasping the complex set of social codes needed to maneuver in the Southern public sphere.

What links this discussion to the dialogue in this volume is that the three chapters in Part I so clearly present, in their respective fashions, the same issue confronted by Janie Starks in Hurston's novel: namely, the relationship between literacy and participation in, on one level, the educational sphere, but also in society at large. It is as children that we are prepared, given the necessary tools, to perform our duties as citizens. The African- American child, as the three chapters go to great lengths to describe, has been, and continues to be, in danger of being left behind, abandoned to the wages of randomization. The failures of public education to deliver, first, equitable educational resources, and second, to find ways to validate cultural difference, even as it enables students to straddle the necessities of different social arenas, form the concerns of this section.

Anderson's chapter, "The African American Struggle for Literacy and Education," is an excellent historical survey of the African-American experience as it relates to the expansion of literacy and education in American life from the 18th century onward. Anderson highlights the fact that universal literacy was the site at which American citizenship reached a kind of public fruition. However, as he takes great care to explain, the exclusion of African Americans from the question of American citizenship also meant that the debate over literacy was one that excluded them as well. This is an important discussion, especially when one considers that the African-American quest for freedom and literacy makes those efforts on the part of white settlers in the Midwest and state officials in the South to exclude blacks from receiving an education stand in even sharper relief. Indeed, the importance placed by African Americans on the acquisition of literacy, and along with it the right to participate in the workings of government as full-fledged citizens, functions in inverse proportion to the effort not only to limit the diffusion of literacy among Black Americans but also to create educational policy to derail any public initiative in this direction. By tracking the manner in which Southern states created two inequitable educational spheres by grossly underfunding black public education, Anderson concludes that the efforts to curtail the growth of a public school system in the South that would fund African-American educational equality continue to have an impact on the region and the nation.

In his chapter, "Reading Failure and Literacy: A Linguistic Approach," William Labov explores the relationship between the study of what he refers to as Afro-American Vernacular English (AAVE) and the attempt to improve pedagogical tools for the teaching of reading in inner-city schools in the United States. By examining the difficulties that pertain to the attempt to create useful strategies for the improvement of reading levels among inner-city youth, he proposes that the failure to understand properly the structure of Afro-American Vernacular English leads to more serious failure on the part of teachers, researchers, and educational policymakers to overcome what appears to be a conceptual gap between the rules of AAVE and those of what Labov refers to as "Classroom English." Labov's chapter assesses the BRIDGE program and its efforts to initiate an improvement in the reading scores of African-American students by utilizing vernacular strategies to introduce the students to standard English. However, the segregation that led to the poor material conditions that reinforce cultural isolation has worsened. As Labov correctly points out, there are actually several dialects spoken that fall under the larger heading of AAVE, particularly when one considers the category of class. As the black middle and lower classes have begun to diverge, not only geographically but also culturally and linguistically, race and class have come to represent dual sites of endeavor. Hence, societal energies in the form of a new awareness of the growing complexities in African-American speech must be brought to bear in order to assure that African-American children have the opportunity to engage in the project of advancing themselves through the medium of education, and thus propelling themselves into a more mobile—and participatory—orientation. At least a portion of this, Labov points out, must come through the realization that AAVE is a flexible, ever-changing dialect that calls for initiatives to mirror this characteristic and respond accordingly.

Dorothy Strickland's commentary and the accompanying response by Deidre Farmbry, "Educating Low-Income Black Children: National Issues to Classroom Practice," highlight many of the issues to which Anderson and Labov refer by examining the current context of educational practice and policy and their limitations in responding to the problems that many poor and African-American youth face. Strickland reminds us of the changes that have occurred in educational practice as a result of federal programs designed to improve the reading abilities and practices of African-American children and the relative difficulty in identifying the success of many of the programs to respond to the children's needs. Her commentary reinforces the underlying messages of both Anderson and Labov's work by suggesting that isolation of poor and African-American children—through neighborhood polarization or classroom separation into pull-out programs—are major contributors to the problems that these students experience in gaining access to effective instruction and support. Farmbry responds to the issues raised by Strickland by contextualizing literacy for African-American youth within linguistic issues that arose in her classroom. By focusing on the disparity between her own experiences as an African-American learner and those of her students, she not only critiques her own practice but also asks us to focus on cultural and social issues outside of school settings that affect youth learning literacy within school contexts. Her examination of linguistic variability among her students and the relationship between their linguistic codes and their images of literacy make a case for an increased focus on the complexities of cross-cultural issues in classroom practice and the implications for learning and teaching youth who may have limited access to experiences outside their homes, school, and immediate communities. The seriousness of this isolation is heightened by the fact that learning is seen as a more global enterprise today than it was 20 years ago; yet, many of the youth whom Farmbry teaches do not have opportunities to participate in that global perspective.

Taken together the three chapters force us to recognize the task at hand. Anderson helps us to understand the inherent difficulties in the education of black children at present because he examines with such care the history of governmental policies designed either to ignore or undereducate children. Labov forces us to consider seriously the failure to develop a deep understanding of the African-American vernacular speech act: by not investigating the complex web of rules and patterns that inform these speech events, teachers and policymakers not only diminish the prospects of children learning to read but they also risk the continued institutional (and ultimately, societal) isolation of these children. Strickland and Farmbry ask us to reexamine issues of access, practice, and policy as they have been promoted in local and national contexts.

Janie's problem in *Their Eyes Were Watching God* is one, finally, of learning how to negotiate the chasm between action and speech, insight and eloquence. In the course of that experience, she moves from voicelessness to a prominent sense of her own capabilities. Ultimately, Janie's answer is, as these essays so strongly purport, our problem: in our efforts to understand better the relationship between literacy and citizenship and why so many of our children are eliminated from this nexus, randomized beyond recognition, the challenge both for Janie and for us is that we will have "to go there, to know there." These chapters help us to revisit the past and plot the course of the future in the ongoing struggle to reconfigure American life.

REFERENCE

Hurston, Z. (1937). *Their eyes were watching God.* Philadelphia, PA: J.B. Lippincott.

1

Literacy and Education in the African-American Experience

James D. Anderson
University of Illinois

The evolution and expansion of literacy in America from the Colonial era to the present is a complex and contradictory story. Some historians struggle to fit the African-American experience into the larger context of the formation and development of literacy in American social thought and culture; most regard it simply as an aberration of the larger experience and treat it as a separate and distinct story. The focus of this chapter is on the meaning of African-American literacy in American history, both with respect to its significance within the black community and its meaning to the broader development of literacy in the national experience. African-American literacy is at once distinguishable yet still a part of the American fabric. It has been inseparable from the larger context of American culture, and in many ways its peculiar history has shaped profoundly national attitudes toward questions of access to literacy and the means to attain literacy.

The standard story of literacy's diffusion in American culture is that it was magnified and multiplied because Americans were broadly committed to an ethos that prescribed the diffusion of knowledge as essential to the well-being of society. Literacy was widely diffused among the white population of the Anglo-American colonies in the early 18th century. Although there were regional differences, it appears that over half of the white male population was literate in the early 18th century. The gender gap among whites, which was considerable in 1700, all but vanished during the course of the 18th century. By the early 19th century the difference between white male and female literacy rates became negligible, mostly reflecting the continued presence of elderly women who could not write. Young white women, in a general population in which the median age was about 16, were just as literate as men: Both were approximately 90% literate by 1800 (Brown, 1989, p. 12). In public and private behavior there remained discrimination based on rank, wealth, and gender. There was, however, a fundamental shift from the early 18th-century ethos of rigidly constricted literacy to the 19th-century ideology of citizenship tied to universal literacy.

The African-American experience with literacy differed sharply from the white experience (Cornelius, 1991), placing the national experience in a very different perspective. Despite fundamental elements of truth in the standard story of literacy development in the United States, the story does not prepare one to understand the distinct experiences of African Americans or to gauge the impact of their experiences on the nation's complex and contradictory attitudes regarding the rights of individuals to literacy. The African-American presence played a significant role in shaping the popular and dominant class attitudes toward universal literacy in both the free and slave states.

The African-American struggle to acquire literate culture began at least in the 17th century. Various state histories record the earliest attempts by different agencies and individuals to spread literacy among ordinary African Americans. In South Carolina, around 1695, for example, the Reverend Samuel Thomas of the Goose Creek Parish began teaching African Americans (Gordon, 1971/1929, pp. 82-86). Soon efforts by individuals and organizations, such as the Society for the Propagation of the Gospel in Foreign Parts, produced a few slaves and more free persons of color who could read and write. Schools for the instruction of slaves and free persons of color were opened during the first half of the 18th century. By the mid-18th century, there were schools in Charleston with as many as 60 pupils in daily attendance. This progress appeared rapid and threatening to the slave-holding class. Consequently, in 1740, South Carolina enacted a law prohibiting any person from teaching or causing a slave to be taught or from employing or using a slave as a scribe in any manner or writing (Woodson, 1916, p. 34). The reaction of South Carolina to the spread of literacy among slaves in the mid-18th century foreshadowed the responses by both slave and free states during the early 19th century. Once the new nation was formed questions were raised throughout the individual states and at the federal level regarding the legal status of free persons of color. More specifically, the central question was whether free persons of color were entitled to the rights, privileges, and immunities of citizenship guaranteed by the U. S. Constitution.

Free African Americans had considerable reason to be concerned with this debate, not only because their rights under the Constitution hung in the balance, but also because the nation came to prescribe increasingly the diffusion of literacy, particularly the means to attain literacy through public schools as essential to citizenship. Were the nation or individual states broadly committed to an ethos that prescribed the diffusion of literacy as an inalienable human right in accordance with the natural rights philosophy, the question of citizenship would not have been linked so inextricably to the question of literate culture. Even when there was a general recognition of universal literacy as a necessity for socially responsible citizens, so long as African Americans were not regarded as citizens this ethos held out little hope for their children. Hence, from the framing of the Constitution in 1787 until the question was settled more precisely by the Fourteenth Amendment in 1868, the question of citizenship had a critical bearing on African-American access to literacy.

From its inception, the United States was characterized by an all but universal belief in white supremacy, including the widespread belief among legislative, judicial, and executive authorities, as well as ordinary white citizens, that African Americans, whether slave or free, were not citizens of the new nation. Reflecting the popular conception of the United States as a white man's country, the "founding fathers," meeting in the First Congress of the United States in 1790, limited naturalization to white aliens (Takaki, 1979, pp. 14-15). Although this action went a long way toward linking race to citizenship with respect to prospective immigrants, it did not resolve the question of citizenship for those who were already here when the nation was formed. This important question was worked out at the federal and state levels during the first half of the 19th century.

Whereas the federal government did not define precisely the legal status of African Americans until the Dred Scott decision of 1857, individual states in the North made their own decisions. By 1811, anti-African-American forces in the Indiana territorial legislature had passed laws preventing free persons of color from testifying in court against whites, excluding them from militia duty, and barring them from voting. Ohio in 1807 excluded African Americans from residence in the state unless they posted a $500 bond for good behavior (Gerber, 1976, pp. 3-5). In 1813, Illinois ordered every incoming free black person to leave the territory under penalty of 39 lashes, repeated every 15 days until the person left the State. Michigan and Iowa soon followed suit, and Wisconsin also joined them in denying African Americans the right to vote (Berwanger, 1967, pp. 33-41). Such anti-African-American activity intensified in the 1840s and 1850s when Illinois and Indiana wrote harsh free-person-of-color exclusion provisions into their constitutions. Horace Greely, echoing the growing anti-African-American sentiment, declared that the Middle West and West "shall be reserved for the benefit of the white Caucasian race" (cited in Berwanger, 1967, p. 131).

The attitudes and the laws developed in the Midwest became the models for the new territories further westward. In 1849, delegates to the Constitutional Convention of California voted without debate to adopt constitutional restrictions on free persons of color similar to those found in the Midwest (Berwanger, 1967, pp. 63-67). The California state legislature swiftly debarred African Americans from intermarriage with whites, and local authorities segregated them. The U. S. Congress, in 1857, admitted Oregon to the union as the only free state with a black exclusion clause in its original constitution. Oregon demanded that all free persons of color leave the state and subjected those who stayed to periodic floggings and later made them servants to whites. "Oregon is a land for the white man," said the Oregon *Weekly Times* (cited in Berwanger, 1967, pp. 94-95). In Kansas, three out of every four antislavery advocates voted to exclude African Americans from residing in the territory, demonstrating what historians have come to recognize: that the successful antislavery movement embraced anti-African-American followers and their white supremacy doctrines (pp. 111-112). Indeed, the antislavery movement in the Midwest and West triumphed over proslavery in the name of white supremacy, arguing specifically that these territories should be preserved for whites only. Thus, the antislavery heroes of the Midwestern and Western plains were among the leaders in voting to limit suffrage, office holding, and militia service to white men only. This behavior was replicated in Utah, Colorado, New Mexico, and Nebraska.

Because the Midwest and the West had such statistically insignificant African-American populations, historians have pondered over the source of the intense attitudes in the region toward African Americans. A common and very plausible explanation is that these territories were threatened at some time with the legalization of slavery. Consequently, antislavery forces sought to protect the new territories from the threat of slavery by avowing to preserve them for free white labor only, thereby merging both antislavery and anti-African-American attitudes into a single objective. Despite some fundamental elements of truth in this explanation, it fails to account for the diffusion of anti-African-American feelings throughout the free states, even when they were not threatened by slavery. In 1833, Connecticut's legislators, for example, formally agreed that an increase of the African-American population would not serve the best interests of the state. This action was taken in conjunction with a statewide campaign to repress the efforts of Prudence Crandall, a young Quaker white woman who established a high school in Canterbury for African-American females. Local authorities seeking to close Crandall's school took her to court on charges of violating the newly established Connecticut law which prohibited the establishment of any school, academy, or literary institution for the instruction or education of colored persons who were not inhabitants of the state. During the second trial (the first jury could not agree on a verdict), Chief Justice David Dagett ruled that African Americans were not citizens. "God forbid," the Chief Justice declared, "that I should add to the degradation of this race of men; but I am bound, by my duty, to say, they are not citizens" (cited in Litwack, 1961, p. 130). All the northeastern states had abolished or taken steps for the gradual abolition of slavery within their borders by 1804. It is very unlikely that they felt threatened by the legalization of slavery in the 1830s. Still, African Americans in the northeast were a despised, excluded, and ostracized class. Only five states with the most insignificant numbers of African-American residents, all in New England, permitted them to vote. New York had property qualifications that withheld the ballot from African-American men. The Pennsylvania legislature formally refused African-American men the vote in 1837 and at the same time seriously debated, though did not pass, a racial exclusion bill (Litwack, 1961, pp. 74-75, 84-87). Northeastern states demonstrated conclusively that free African Americans even when the question of slavery was not a threat, were denied the rights, privileges, and immunities guaranteed to American citizens by the Constitution (Greene, 1942, pp. 290-315).

The federal government, although at times inconsistent, demonstrated consistency by backing the states' denial of citizenship status to African Americans. Congress repeatedly approved the admission of states to the union whose constitutions severely restricted the legal rights of free African Americans. The legislative debates of 1820-21 on the admission of Missouri centered squarely on the question of African-American citizenship. Missouri's proposed constitution enjoined the state legislature to pass such laws as might be necessary "to prevent free negroes and mulattos from coming to and settling in this state, under any pretext whatsoever" (Litwack, 1961, p. 35). If Congress agreed to such a measure, argued Secretary of State John Quincy Adams, the article would deprive African Americans of their rights as citizens. Representative Charles Pinckney of South Carolina, however, saw no inconsistency between Missouri's proposed constitution and the guarantees of the federal constitution. A delegate to the Constitutional Convention in 1787, Pinckney assured his colleagues in 1820-21 that the framers of the constitution did not intend to include African Americans as citizens of the United States. As he put it:

> I perfectly knew that there did not then exist such a thing in the Union as a black or colored citizen, nor could I then have conceived it possible such a thing could ever have existed in it; nor notwithstanding all that is said on the subject, do I now believe one does exist in it. (Litwack, 1961, pp. 35-36).

On March 2, 1821, Congress voted to admit Missouri with the anti-African-American clause intact so long as it would not be construed to limit the constitutional rights of citizens. It evaded the question as to whether the framers of the Constitution intended to exclude African Americans from the rights, privileges, and immunities entitled under the constitution of the United States (Litwack, 1961, p. 38). Yet, in other actions the federal government demonstrated that it agreed with the assessment of Congressman Charles Pinckney.

The Attorneys General usually agreed that the Constitution did not confer citizenship on African Americans. Attorneys General William Wirt in 1821, Roger Taney in 1831, and Hugh Legare in 1843 ruled that the framers of the Constitution had not regarded free African Americans as citizens and that the current conditions of African Americans warranted no change in their legal status (Litwack, 1961, pp. 50-54). If there continued to be any doubts regarding the legal status of free persons of color, they were all put to rest by the Dred Scott decision of 1857. Early in the decision Chief Justice Roger Taney, former Attorney General, confronted the question of African-American citizenship. Can the descendants of African slaves, he asked, be entitled to the rights, privileges, and immunities guaranteed to American citizens? Not only had the first Congress restricted naturalization to "free white persons," observed Taney, but subsequent state and federal legislation and "the conduct of the Executive Department" confirmed his conclusion that the descendants of Africans, whether slave or free, "are not included, and were not intended to be included, under the word 'citizens' in the Constitution, and therefore claim none of the rights and privileges which that instruments provides for and secures to citizens of the United States" (Litwack, 1961, pp. 59-61). Robert Purvis, African-American abolitionist, noted that Taney's decision was "in perfect keeping with the treatment of the colored people by the American Government from the beginning to this day" (p. 63).

The Dred Scott decision was indeed the culmination of a longstanding drift away from the natural rights philosophy that seemed so apparent in the Declaration of Independence. It was "all men" and not a race or color that were placed under the protection of the Declaration. Further, natural rights philosophy contended that a "man's" rights were inalienable, not dependent on his color or race. The leaders of the nation from the early national era through the antebellum period rejected this egalitarian reading of natural rights philosophy and modified the philosophy to claim only rights derived from white citizenship. Hence, only those who enjoyed the full and equal privileges of white citizens in the State of their residence were entitled to the rights and immunities guaranteed by the federal constitutions. In short, only free white persons were citizens. This judgment would remain fixed in American law and custom until African-American citizenship was confirmed by the passage of the Fourteenth Amendment in 1868 (Litwack, 1961, p. 63).

As the federal and state governments abandoned natural rights philosophy with respect to the question of citizenship, state and local governments rejected natural rights philosophy as the basis for determining access to literacy. People, according to the natural rights philosophy, are endowed at birth with uniquely human potentialities of mind, body, spirit, and will. A person's right to knowledge is inalienable, and thus every human being has a right to the means by which knowledge is gained. This implied equal access to those schools, particularly public schools, through which state and local government sought to develop the human potentialities of the young for their sake and the sake of society itself. As local and state governments faced the question of African-American education from the late 18th century to the Civil War, they rejected the idea that African Americans had an inalienable right to knowledge. Rather, state and local governments maintained that it was the status of citizenship that entitled one to public education. Because African Americans were not citizens, as the federal and state governments made clear by their actions and legal decisions, accordingly they were not entitled to the benefits of public education. African Americans were to be treated on the question of education as they were on the question of citizenship; their "rights" were left to the benevolence of whites in the individual states. As a result, in some states African Americans were granted rights and privileges that in other states they found denied to them. Educational opportunities reflected their status within the respective states; in some states they exercised access to schooling that in other states they found to be illegal or impossible to exercise.

Historians who have studied the education of African Americans in the free states during the bellum and antebellum periods underscore both its important value within the African-American communities and the frequently violent protests by whites against the education of free persons of color. African Americans' access to literacy was very limited from the founding of the nation to the Civil War. Although some public schools in the free states admitted African-American children, most excluded them altogether or established separate schools for them. In New England, local school committees usually assigned African-American children to separate institutions, although there were notable protests against any education for free persons of color. Pennsylvania and Ohio required district school directors to establish separate facilities for African-American children whenever 20 or more could be accommodated. The New York legislature authorized local school districts to provide for racially segregated schooling. In the absence of legal restrictions, customary racism excluded African-American children from the schools (Litwack, 1961, pp. 113-123).

Proposals to educate African-American children, whether in racially integrated or segregated public schools, or even in private schools, invariably aroused bitter opposition in northeastern, midwestern, and western states. Northern whites were most opposed to "racial mixing" or integrated public schools. The objections to racial integration, however, extended beyond public schools to private academies and colleges. In 1835, the admission of African Americans into Noyes Academy in Canaan, NH exposed whites' belief that whites had as much right to regulate race relations in private schools as in public ones. The Academy's policy in 1835 was to admit qualified applicants regardless of race or color. Hence, 28 whites and 14 African Americans were admitted to the newly established school in March 1835. On July 4, 1835, a white mob intent on destroying the Academy approached the institution, but was dispersed by the local magistrate. Later that month an official town meeting voted to appoint a committee charged with the responsibility of abolishing Noyes Academy. On August 10, the committee proceeded with its assigned task; with nearly 100 yoke of oxen they removed the building from its foundations (Litwack, 1961, pp. 117-120).

Similar behavior was displayed in New Haven, CT when, in 1831, white abolitionists and African Americans jointly proposed to establish a private academy for the advanced education of free persons of color. In October 1831, a crowded New Haven town meeting, called by the mayor and aldermen, denounced the proposed school as "destructive to the best interests of this city." The meeting formally approved these sentiments by approximately 700 to 4. The proponents of the New Haven academy accepted defeat and abandoned the project (Litwack, 1961, pp. 123-124).

As described earlier, nowhere was northern white opposition to the education of African Americans more vivid than in the case of Prudence Crandall. A young Quaker white woman, she established, in 1831, a popular girl's boarding school in Canterbury, CT. A year later she agreed to admit one African-American girl. This action brought a storm of protests from the white townspeople, resulting in the withdrawal of most of the white students. Crandall then decided, with the support of abolitionists, to open a private school exclusively for African-American girls. A Canterbury town meeting convened on March 9, 1833 and voiced its "unqualified disapprobation" of the proposed school. One Canterbury town official asserted, "that nigger school shall never be allowed in Canterbury, nor in any town in this State" (Litwack, 1961, p. 128). Prudence Crandall and her backers, however, refused to abandon the school. The school was opened in April 1833 and it attracted African-American females from Philadelphia, New York, Providence, and Boston. By this time Ms. Crandall's school had also attracted the attention of Connecticut's state legislature. On May 24, the legislature adopted a measure that outlawed the establishment of any school for the instruction of persons of color who were not inhabitants of Connecticut. The State legislature had dealt a serious blow to Ms. Crandall's school, but she refused to close it. Local authorities then arrested her on charges of violating the new law. After two trials, she was found guilty, but an appellate court reversed the conviction on a technical point. In the long run the pressures proved to be overwhelming, and Ms. Crandall finally abandoned the school in September 1834 (Litwack, 1961, pp. 126-131).

In states further west delegates to the constitutional conventions debated various proposals to exclude African Americans from the newly established public schools. Ohio's first public school law was passed in 1821, and African Americans were taxed locally to support the public schools, but they were universally excluded from the state's new school system. No public provision was made for their education until 1829, and even then a general refusal by many local officials to create black schools under the law caused its repeal two years later. Even exclusively African-American schools, as was true of Ms. Crandall's school in Canterbury, CT, met with popular disapproval. In Ohio, for example, whites destroyed African-American schools and exposed their teachers to insults and violence. In Zanesville, OH, whites entered the African-American school building, destroyed the books and furnishings, and ultimately drove the institution from the town. In 1840, an Ohio newspaper reported that the residents of Troy had virtually demolished a school because it had been established for the instruction of African-American children. Legislation passed in 1849 finally obliged Ohio's township trustees to use a prorated share of the common school fund for the support of African-American schools. This legislation was supplemented in 1853 with a law providing guidelines for the creation of black school districts. Still, during Ohio's pre-Civil War history, most African-American children were educated in private academies, financed by private contributions, and often held in the back of churches or in crude shacks, or by individual private tutors (Gerber, 1976, p. 4, 190-191).

Illinois's constitution did not have an article devoted to education and the public schools until 1870. When in the Illinois constitutional convention of 1847 an education article was proposed for the new constitution, a majority of the delegates feared that such an article might bring African Americans into white schools. The proposition was voted down, and the Illinois constitution of 1848, in force until 1870, avoided the subject of public education (McCaul, 1987, pp. 4-5). Nonetheless, the state was willing to translate into statutes its values regarding the education of all children. The proceeds from the school funds were by law apportioned according to the number of white children of school age. School officials, if courageous enough to admit black children into the district schools, would not be reimbursed from the funds and would have to sustain the additional costs without aid from the state, county, and township. Consequently, most school districts would not admit African-American children to the common schools.

Various sources reveal that in the mid-1860s African-American children were being admitted to public schools in Alton, Decatur, Galesburg, Jacksonville, Peoria, Quincy, and Springfield. The total number of African-American children attending school in Illinois in1865-66 were 300 or 5% out of some 6,000 African-American children of school age. The number of whites attending were 614,000 or 80% of 759,987 school-age children (McCaul, 1987, pp. 44-46). In Illinois, as elsewhere in the free states during the pre-Civil War years, there was almost universal denial of public education to African-American children. One of the great ironies of this era was that white political leaders, including those who bitterly opposed educating African-American children, contended that widespread illiteracy in the African-American population prevented any extension of suffrage or other civil rights.

Although generally excluded from public schools and confined in other instances to separate public schools, African Americans gradually gained access to education. This was especially true of the larger urban African-American populations. Before the end of the 18th century the larger urban African-American populations had already begun to make communal efforts to obtain educational facilities for their children. This was often necessary even in cities that permitted African-American children to attend the regular public schools. The public schools in several major cities were not initially segregated by law, but the harassment of African-American students was so extensive and so intense that they were effectively excluded from racially integrated schools. In the face of such denial of public school facilities, African Americans used their newly established independent churches as educational societies and in the 1790s opened schools associated with them.

By the mid-1820s African-American Sunday schools taught basic literacy to thousands of pupils in cities throughout the North. In all of the northern cities the level of instruction available to African-American students was generally at the elementary level. With the exception of Gilmore's high school in Cincinnati, no institution of secondary education for African Americans existed in major cities in 1850. Still, African Americans made considerable sacrifices to provide their children access to basic literacy. The percentage of African-American children attending school in major northern cities during the 1849-50 school year ranged from a low of 38% in Cincinnati to 79% in Boston (Curry, 1981, pp. 166-170). Despite the powerful and persistent opposition by northern whites against the education of African-American children, parents and community organizations as well as white missionary societies never lost faith in the individual and collective value of education. Through private efforts and constant protest against public restrictions on the education of their children, free persons of color in northern states pressed for and received increasingly better educational facilities.

As the nation girded for war in 1861, most state constitutions refused to grant citizenship and equality to African Americans (Wood, 1968, pp. 82-88). In the Midwest, for example, Illinois and Indiana held no provisions for the education of African-American children. Iowa, Ohio, and Illinois excluded men of color from jury service. Exclusion laws carrying severe penalties prohibited African Americans from settling in Indiana, Illinois, and Iowa. As the war ended in 1865, every state in the Midwest denied African Americans the right to vote and barred them from the militia (Voegeli, 1967, p. 2, 166-172). African-American children were still excluded from the public schools of Indiana, were not provided for in the laws of Illinois, and were segregated into separate schools by statute in most parts of Ohio. All urban areas segregated African-American children into separate and unequal schools, and most rural districts refused to admit them to "white" public schools and failed to establish separate schools for populations that were often small and scattered across several school districts. For all practical purposes the questions of African-American citizenship and their rights to literacy and education rested until after the war. It was only then that state after state in the "free" territories began to eliminate wholesale their so-called "black laws" (Wood, 1968, pp. 157-169).

After the war, attention within the African-American community and throughout the whole nation shifted to the South as over 4 million slaves were emancipated as a consequence of the Civil War. Because more than 90% of African Americans lived in the former slave states, and more than 90% of them were illiterate in 1865, their condition was of the upmost concern to African Americans everywhere. The grassroots politics, culture, and general enthusiasm of the generations of African Americans who had endured slavery sparked the drive for literacy during the postwar period. Capitalizing on their newly acquired political power, and forming workable coalitions with some white republicans, the ex-slaves constituted the vanguard movement for public education in the late 19th century South.

Universal literacy was never favored by southern whites who believed that illiteracy among the slaves and free persons of color was essential to the well-being of society. This particular attitude toward literacy among African Americans constructed fundamental cultural norms that were hostile to the idea of universal literacy (Anderson, 1988, pp. 18-28). In its 1830-31 legislative session, Virginia, for example, prohibited under penalties the attempt to teach any slave or free person of color to read or write. The census of 1830 documents that Virginia's (Eastern District) population was comprised of 375,655 whites, 416,320 slaves and 41,005 free persons of color. When the state legally mandated illiteracy among its African-American population, it also enforced illiteracy among 55% of its total population. Hence, the antiliteracy laws aimed specifically at slaves and free persons of color constructed a larger environment that was hostile to universal learning and sought to restrict literate culture as the precious possession of the wealthy, powerful, or whites. African Americans were the primary force against this ethos during the postbellum years. From their use of political power in the state legislatures to create state systems of public education to their establishment of literacy schools in churches, they sought to make literacy a universal possession. Between the end of the war and the eve of the 19th century, African Americans made important strides toward eliminating illiteracy among their young.

By the turn of the century, African Americans found that education was one of the few areas in which they had concrete reasons to remain optimistic about the future. Despite the depressing setbacks in politics and economics that had been wrought by disfranchisement and the tenant farm economy, black southerners could look to education as an area of remarkable progress. By 1900 their postbellum campaign for free universal education was paying handsome dividends. Slightly more than half of southern blacks claimed to be literate, a remarkable achievement in light of conditions a generation earlier. The postbellum decline in illiteracy was larger among blacks than whites. However, even this portrayal does not tell the full story of the remarkable and rapid decline of the black illiteracy rate. The overall rate remained high because older blacks (virtually all of whom had been enslaved at birth) were highly illiterate during the immediate postbellum period and remained high as these cohorts aged. The literacy rate in 1900 for black males aged 10 to 14 was 64% and for black females aged 10 to 14 the rate was 71%. Whereas the high rates of illiteracy imposed by slavery continued to remain high among adults (in 1900, 64% of black men aged 45 to 54 were illiterate), African-American children were becoming literate at a very fast pace (Margo, 1990, pp. 6-9). The spread of literacy among southern blacks was a consequence of the acquisition of literacy by the young through school attendance. Because high rates of adult black illiteracy persisted into the 20th century, it seems apparent that the majority of black children did not learn to read and write at home. Rather, illiteracy rates declined rapidly among the young as school attendance rates rose over time. In 1900, about 65% of black children aged 10-14 attended school (pp. 9-12).

At the dawn of the 20th century black southerners seemed poised to achieve universal literacy and to increase their overall levels of educational attainment, particularly at the secondary and higher education levels. Having acquired a solid foundation of literacy among its children, African Americans only needed a decent system of public education in order to attain higher levels of educational advancement. It was at this point that the dominant white South mounted a campaign of massive resistance to the educational progress of black southerners. As with slavery when literate black persons were presumed to be discontented laborers or worse, potential trouble-makers, southern whites from the late 1800s to the early 1900s regarded educated African Americans as a threat to the region's social order. As Governor James K. Vardaman of Mississippi put it in 1899: "The negro isn't permitted to advance and their education only spoils a good field hand and makes a shyster lawyer or a fourth-rate teacher" (cited in McMillen, 1989, p. 72). William Dorsey Jelks, ex-governor of Alabama, concurred:

> The education of the negro has made him a burden, or, to express it differently, far less valuable as a citizen. The farm is the one opening for him, and this, when he has acquired a smattering of letters, he leaves. He congregates in the towns and leads for the most part an idle life, and in large numbers, a vicious life. Teaching him to read has thus far proven a curse to the material interests of the South, and this beyond the costs of the schools. The hope many had lay in the expectation that a second and third generation that could read would mark a distinct improvement on the first. We are yet to learn if this hope is ground-less. Books have given us a larger proportion of vagrants and a larger proportion of thieves as well. (cited in Jelks, 1907, p. 391)

To be sure, whites in the South responded to black public education in a variety of ways, depending upon particular configurations of class backgrounds and political and social interests. Whereas rural white planters in general staunchly resisted universal public education for black children, white urban industrialists supported a system of universal public schooling with clearly prescribed racial and class limitations. Further, there were some southern whites who supported black public education without prescribing a special kind of curriculum for African-American children. Most importantly, however, throughout the white South the most pervasive view of black public schooling at the turn of the century was the fear that educating black children would revolutionize the economic and social order (McMillen, 1989, p. 90). Neither the racially moderate views of particular southern white industrialists nor the support of a few white liberals could counterbalance the opposition of men like Jelks and Vardaman. Their views carried the day and were reflected in the policies and actions of state and county government. It was their kind of opposition to black public education that set the stage for the 20th century and reversed the pattern of advancement that had characterized black public education from Reconstruction to 1900. During the first half of the 20th century the dominant white South would use state power to repress the development of black public education, a process of repression so severe that it continues to affect the shape and character of black public education throughout the region.

In his brilliant essay in the inaugural issue of the *Journal of Negro Education*, Horace Mann Bond was among the first to document the dramatic shift in black public education from relative equality in the late 19th century to gross inequality during the "progressive" period of the early 20th century (Bond, 1932, pp. 49-51). It should be noted, however, that he was addressing only the question of common or elementary schools. Not even during the most progressive phases of the postbellum era did blacks achieve relative equality at the secondary and higher levels of education. Bond began by demonstrating that in the academic year 1889-1890, African-American children in Alabama received 44% of the school money appropriated in the entire state, although they were only 43.8% of the population. Forty years later, in the year 1929-1930, African-American children, then approximately 40% of Alabama's total school population, received only 11% of the school funds. Bond's point was significant not only for Alabama, but for other southern states; the pattern was the same throughout the region.

In 1890, black Mississippians received approximately 35% of the state's school fund. At the turn of the century, blacks comprised 60% of the state's school-age children, but received only 19% of the state's school funds. By World War II the gap had widened; blacks comprising 57% of the school population received only 13% of the total annual state school appropriation (McMillen, 1989, p. 73). In Mississippi, African-American children enjoyed relatively equal benefits from the school funds for 10 years after the close of Reconstruction, or from 1876 to 1886.

In Alabama they enjoyed this equal protection from 1875, the end of Reconstruction in that state, until 1890 (Bond, 1932, p. 50). The same pattern held in North Carolina where in 1890 black children received $7.75 per pupil and whites received $7.67 per pupil (Margo, 1990, p. 21). As earlier stated, these funds were intended to expand elementary education; there was gross racial inequality with respect to allocations for secondary and especially higher education. In sharp contrast to expenditures for higher education, the common school fund, during the late 19th century, was divided more or less equally between southern blacks and whites. By 1910, however, southern white school officials no longer divided school budgets equally between the races. The black-to-white ratio of per-pupil expenditures declined in every state between 1890 and 1910 (pp. 19-28).

The trend away from equality began in particular states in the late 1880s. Mississippi was the first state to bring about this condition of inequality. In 1886, Mississippi's legislature passed a law governing certificates that enabled local boards to grant salaries on the basis of the certificate held by the teacher. This law was framed in such a way that a school board could give a first-grade African-American teacher the minimum monthly pay of $25 and a first-grade white teacher the maximum of $55. South Carolina in its Constitution of 1895 gave the local school boards the power to discriminate in allocating the school funds between the races. Alabama changed the law in 1890 and substituted for the old system of relative equality one that allowed common school funds to be spent by local school boards as they saw fit (Bond, 1932, p. 50).

This heightened resistance to education for African-American children practically eliminated the concept of public education from southern state governments. Since the common school crusades of the 1830s, public education meant that the state should pledge itself to the education of all children, and the state's schools in a republic must diffuse virtue and knowledge. To achieve these goals the schools were to be made free to rich and poor alike. The free school system was to be financed by a tax on property and all property owners, irrespective of whether they had children attending the public schools, because everyone, it was presumed, derived political, civil, social, and economic benefits from the existence of free schools. The South inverted this democratic theory of public education and inserted in its place the theory that the state should pledge itself to the education of white children, even if this meant diverting to white schools the portion of school funds paid by blacks. The obvious corollary of this theory was that black southerners, despite being taxed for public education, would have to find other means to provide universal schooling for their children, or, as many white southerners preferred, have no schooling at all (Anderson, 1988, pp. 149-185).

In the end, discriminatory funding meant not only that black taxes were diverted for white school purposes, but that black schools were largely dependent on private philanthropy and what blacks called "double taxation," the practice of paying for their schools through voluntary contributions of land, labor, and money. In 1915, of 1,056 schoolhouses for black children in Alabama's "Black Belt," 426 or approximately 40% were publicly owned. This condition did not improve over the next two decades. In fact, it regressed. According to a 1938 school survey and school plant inventory, of all school buildings for black children in Alabama, there were 2,407 school buildings used for black children of which 730 or 30% were publicly owned (Knight, 1940, p. 12). The vast majority of schools for black children were held in churches or in buildings that were privately owned. Other southern states followed a similar pattern of making black education a private matter. In1940, roughly half of all black common schools in Mississippi still met in tenant cabins, lodges, churches, and stores—privately owned structures that under state law could not be improved with public funds. There were in 1940 some 90 black high schools in Mississippi, most of them either privately owned by blacks or built through grants from northern foundations. Further, a survey commissioned by the Sunflower County Board of Education reported in 1950 that the county had no publicly owned school buildings for black children (McMillen, 1989, pp. 84-85). By 1940, 66% of southern black children aged 5-9 were enrolled in elementary school, and 90% of those aged 10-14 were enrolled (Anderson, 1988, p. 181). Much of this enrollment, and in some states most of it, was made possible through private contributions. Southern states had yet to accept public responsibility for the most basic level of education—the common school. The conditions for public secondary and higher education, as one might induce from the conditions of the common schools, were even worse.

Because secondary education did not become an integral part of the public education system until the early 20th century, there was little state responsibility for it during the late 19th century. Although there were a few public high schools in the South during the late 19th century, the region, as the whole nation, had not come to view secondary education as a system that should be made free to all children. Both contemporary observers and later scholars agree that it was in the period 1880 to 1930 that the American high school was transformed from an elite, private institution into a public one attended by children of the masses. At the beginning of this era less than 3% of the national high-school-age population—either those aged 14 to 17 or 15 to 19—was enrolled in high school, and even fewer attended regularly. By 1934, the proportion of American children of high school age enrolled in public high schools had increased to 60%, and, including private school enrollments, it approximated 64% (Anderson, 1988, pp. 186-192).

The white South, in spite of its relatively impoverished economy, managed with the help of northern philanthropy to keep pace with the nation. In 1930 some 38% of the region's white children of high school age were enrolled in public secondary schools as compared with 47% for the nation as a whole. By 1934, for the nation as whole, 60 pupils were enrolled in public high school for every 100 children aged 14 to 17, inclusive; for every 100 white southerners of the same ages, 54 pupils were enrolled in public secondary schools. Thus, in the southern states the proportion of white children enrolled in public high school was 93% of that for the nation as a whole. In some southern states, notably Florida, Mississippi, Delaware, North Carolina, and South Carolina, the proportion of white children enrolled was equal to or greater than the national proportion of 60% (Anderson, 1988, p. 117).

African Americans were generally excluded from the southern transformation of public secondary education. In 1890, only .39% or 3,106 of the 804,522 black children of high school age were enrolled in high school, and more than two-thirds of them were attending private high schools. The proportion of southern black children enrolled in secondary schools increased to 2.8% by 1910, and the majority of these high school pupils were still enrolled in private schools. By 1930, the ratio of black public high school enrollment to school population reached 10.1%, and it jumped to 18% during the 1933-34 academic year. Even then it was 10% or less in Alabama, Arkansas, Georgia, and Mississippi. By the early 1930s, when rural whites, urban working-class whites, and the children of European immigrants had been brought systematically into the public high school, black children as a class were deliberately excluded (Anderson, 1988, pp. 187-200).

This pattern continued into the mid-century. On the eve of World War II, 77% of the black high-school-age population was not even enrolled in public secondary schools. The condition was even more dramatic in states with the largest proportion of blacks. In Alabama, Arkansas, Georgia, and Louisiana, more than 80% of the black high-school-age population was not enrolled in public secondary schools in 1940. More than 90% of Mississippi's black high-school-age population was not enrolled in public secondary schools. From 1940 to 1946 the enrollment of blacks in public secondary schools in the South decreased by 32.5%. By 1948 enrollment trends were again increasing, but more than two-thirds of the generation of 1950 was not enrolled in public high schools (National Education Association, 1954, pp. 35-37). Indeed, it was not until the 1960s that southern blacks could begin to regard public secondary education as universal.

Because they have had such high rates of illiteracy among older adults, historically, African Americans have relied heavily on schooling to eliminate illiteracy. Consequently, the denial of opportunities for schooling has translated into the denial of access to literacy. As African Americans fought and gained increased access to schooling their rates of literacy increased sharply. In 1870, shortly after emancipation, 81% of African Americans reported themselves to be illiterate, compared with 11% of whites. Although the the literacy rates for African Americans is higher today, there remain gaps in functional literacy among ethnic groups and classes. Further, there are significant inequalities in education that underlay differences in functional literacy. Jonathan Kozol's *Savage Inequalities* (1991) calls attention to the gross inequalities that exist in contemporary American education.

African Americans have struggled against such inequalities and outright denial of access to literacy and education since colonial beginnings. Currently, there is grave concern over the academic achievement of African-American children. Still, much has changed since the bellum and antebellum periods when African Americans, whether slaves in the South or free persons of color in the North, were virtually excluded from public and many private educational facilities and therefore denied access to literacy. The struggle for equal access to literacy and education continues, but as a consequence of the long war for education by generations of African Americans, it proceeds today on much different terrain.

REFERENCES

Anderson, J. D. (1988). *The education of Blacks in the South, !860-1915.* Chapel Hill: The University of North Carolina Press.

Berwanger, E. H. (1967). *The frontier against slavery: Western anti-Negro prejudice and the slavery extension controversy.* Urbana: University of Illinois Press.

Bond H. M. (1932). Negro education: A debate in the Alabama constitutional convention of 1901. *Journal of Negro Education, I,* 49-59.

Brown, R. D. (1989). *Knowledge is power: The diffusion of information in early America, 1700-1865.* New York: Oxford University Press.

Cornelius, J. D. (1991). *When I can read my title clear: Literacy, slavery, and religion in the antebellum South.* Columbia: University of South Carolina Press.

Curry, L. P. (1981). *The free Black in urban America 1800-1850.* Chicago: The University of Chicago Press.

Gerber, D. A. (1976). *Black Ohio and the color line. 1860-1915.* Urbana:University of Illinois Press.

Gordon, A. H. (1971). *Sketches of Negro life and history in South Carolina* (2nd ed). Columbia: University of South Carolina. (Original work published 1929)

Greene, L. J. (942). *The Negro in colonial New England.* New York: Columbia University Press.

Jelks, W. D. (1907). The acuteness of the Negro question: A suggested remedy. *North American Review, CLXXIV*, 389-395.

Knight, E. W.(1940). *A study Of higher education for Negroes in Alabama.* (Series 1, Sub-series 3, Box 384, Folder 4013, General Education Board Files). Pocantico Hills, NY: Rockefeller Archives.

Kozol, J. (1991). *Savage inequalities.* New York: Crown.

Litwack, L. F. (1961). *North of slavery: The Negro in the free states,1790-1860.* Chicago: The University of Chicago Press.

Margo, R. A.(1990). *Race and schooling in the South, 1880-1950: An economic history.* Chicago: The University of Chicago Press.

McCaul, R. L. (1987). *The Black struggle for public schooling in nineteenth-century Illinois.* Carbondale: Southern Illinois University Press.

McMillen, N. R. (1989). *Dark journey: Black Mississippians in the age of Jim Crow.* Urbana: University of Illinois Press.

National Education Association and the American Teachers Association. (January, 1954). *Progress of the education of Negroes, 1870-1950.* Washington, DC: NEA.

Takaki, R. T. (1979). *Iron cages: Race and culture in 19th-century America.* Seattle: University of Washington Press.

Voegeli, V. J. (1967). *Free but not equal: The Midwest and the Negro during the Civil War.* Chicago: The University of Chicago Press.

Wood, F. G. (1968). *Black scare: The racist response to emancipation and reconstruction.* Berkeley: University of California Press.

Woodson, C. G.(1916). *The education of the Negro prior to 1861: A history of the education of the colored people of the United States from the beginning of slavery to the Civil War.* Washington DC: The Associated Publishers.

2

Can Reading Failure Be Reversed: A Linguistic Approach to the Question

William Labov
University of Pennsylvania

For 30 years linguists have carried out extensive studies of the dialect that we now refer to as Afro-American Vernacular English (AAVE). As a result, we now know more about this dialect than any other form of spoken English. Yet, there has been little progress toward solving the problem that was the original motivation for this study: to see if more knowledge about the dialects spoken by Afro-Americans could be used to improve the teaching of reading in the inner cities of the United States, particularly in the face of recurring social protests in these communities over the past three decades. This chapter reviews the history of research on AAVE as it might bear on the problem of raising literacy levels and explores the issues associated with the problem within the context of social isolation and educational access for black children in school. The discussion focuses on the particular solution that appeared to be the most promising in the 1970s, examining in detail the strengths and weaknesses of this approach with an eye to future developments. The chapter then turns to the results of recent linguistic research on AAVE in the past decade and asks if this new knowledge can be applied to the problem of raising reading levels.

THE NATURE OF THE PROBLEM

To begin, it is necessary to accept certain facts about the failure to teach reading in inner-city schools. The problems that we face today are as great as or greater than those that we confronted 30 years ago. The nature of that problem, however, has never been clearly presented by the average reading scores given in the newspapers or scholarly articles. In New York City, in 1965, the black children of South Harlem were, on the average, two years behind grade level in reading. But that average disguised the fact that the school population was sharply divided into two populations. One, the minority of roughly 40%, consisted of isolated individuals who did not participate fully in the street culture of organized groups (Figures 2.1 and 2.2 show the disparity between the two groups). Figure 2.1 shows the learning path followed by this section of

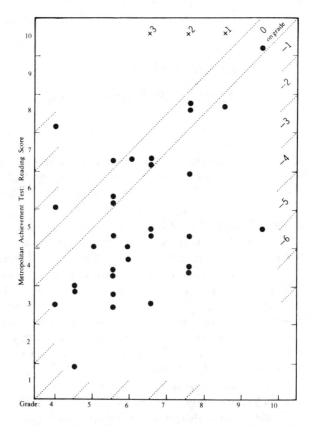

Figure 2.1. Grade and reading achievement for 32 nonmembers of street groups in south-central Harlem.

South Harlem students. The vertical axis is the reading score on New York City's standard reading scale, and the horizontal axis is age. It is clear that there is a general upward movement, one or two years behind grade level, and that learning is taking place. Figure 2.2 shows the contrasting pattern of the majority of the youth, members of established clubs or groups like the "Jets" and the "Cobras." Here the pattern is quite different. In place of a steady upward trend, there is a clear ceiling at a reading level of 4.9, which persists through the 11th grade. Furthermore, there is no correlation between the individuals marked for their verbal skills and success in reading.

This division in the population is of crucial importance in understanding the persistence of reading failure and the possible relevance of language differences. The division of the school population into two groups was made on the basis of research in the community, well outside of the school environment, in a milieu where the vernacular cul-

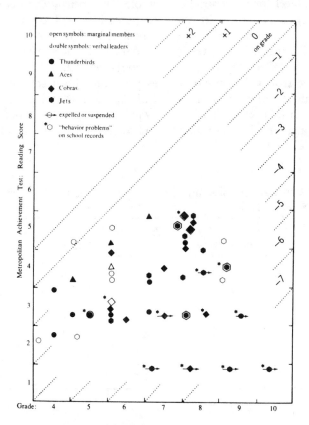

Figure 2.2. Grade and reading achievement for 46 members of street groups in south-central Harlem.

ture and value system could be freely expressed. In this environment, it quickly became apparent that the majority of Harlem youth were engaged in a cultural system that opposed the values of the school system, which was seen as the particular possession and expression of the dominant white society (Labov, 1972; Labov, Cohen, Robins, & Lewis, 1968). The situation in Harlem in the 1960s was more ominous in reality than the one that the teacher would have perceived, and forecast the situation in which the majority of the inner-city youth would remain at a flat level of functional illiteracy, in spite of various efforts to reinforce or reform the curriculum.

A similar situation existed in District 7 of North Philadelphia in 1976, 10 years later. Only 38% of the residents of Philadelphia were black; however, 62% of the students were black, the great majority located in racially imbalanced schools. The mean distribution on the California Achievement Tests for the city, including both math and reading, is shown in Table 1 for the district as a whole. The critical figure here is the number of students in the lowest 16th percentile on the national average—these are the students who are most clearly marked as suffering educational failure. The situation appears to be negative, but by no means desperate. In the elementary schools, only 22% of the students were in this group. The mean values for junior high schools show a decided shift downward at 33%, and at the high school level, we find almost 40% in this status. This downward trend is much more marked when we consider schools in the all-black working-class areas. The situa-

Table 2.1. 1976 California Achievement Test Scores for District 7 of the Philadelphia School District

| | PERCENTILES | | | |
	Below 16th	16th-49th	50th-84th	Above 84th
Elementary schools	22	36	29	13
Birney	31	42	21	6
Junior high schools	33	37	22	8
Cooke	50	41	9	0
Senior high schools	39	34	19	8
Franklin	75	20	5	0

Source: Philadelphia Inquirer, July 25, 1976

tion for one elementary school with which I am most familiar, the Birney School, shows figures considerably worse: almost one-third are in the lowest sixth, and 73% below the mean.When we pass to Cooke, the nearest junior high school in the district, one can see an even more rapid decline: 50% are in the lowest sixth, and 91% are below the mean. Finally, we pass to the nearest high school, Franklin, and find that 70% are in the lowest percentile. Because other figures show that verbal and mathematics scores follow the same pattern, this picture is roughly comparable to the one we saw in a closer view of the South Harlem schools in the 1960s.

Recent figures released by the Philadelphia Board of Education give mean reading scores for all schools, grouped into two categories: racially isolated and integrated schools (Philadelphia Inquirer, May 5, 1993). The 1991 mean reading scores for racially isolated schools, comparable to Birney, Cooke, and Franklin, showed only 9% in the highest quartile, 70% below the mean, and 40% in the lowest quartile. In the following year, 1992, there was a dramatic decline, with only 4% in the highest quartile, 83% below the mean, and 55% in the lowest quartile. The general pattern is continues: The relative position of African-American students declines steadily throughout the school process. This actually understates the problem considerably because the drop-out rate is also heavily concentrated in this population. The students who are experiencing the worst problems are removed from the scene, but the relative performance of the remaining group continues to deteriorate throughout junior and senior high school.

Positive Effect of Headstart and Other Intervention Programs.

The persistence of this pattern of educational and reading failure is alleviated by at least one positive finding in the efforts to improve education in the inner city. Long-term evaluations of early intervention programs such as Headstart have shown persistent positive effects (Clement & Weikart, 1984), and continued funding of these programs will undoubtedly have effects upon reading performance. Yet, the original research in South Harlem indicates that the major impact of these intervention programs will be on the minority of inner-city youth who are already detached from the main vernacular culture and that the majority will continue to follow a downward educational path.

The Social Dimension of Educational Failure.

The most important point that these figures indicate is that young children from the inner city do not start out with the grave handicap that they end up with. In the 1960s, efforts to explain reading failure concentrated on the concept of a cultural and verbal disadvantage that was the result of an impoverished home environment and a lack of motivation from the family. Yet, the overall picture is that young black children arrive at kindergarten full of enthusiasm for the educational adventure, with a strong motivation to succeed from their parent or parents. The pattern of reading and educational failure that follows is progressive and cumulative. Though it may be conditioned by early handicaps, it is largely the result of events and interactions that take place during the school years.

EARLY RESEARCH ON AAVE: EVIDENCE FOR CONVERGENCE

The original motivation for the research on AAVE was an effort to answer the question as to whether differences between this dialect and classroom English might be partly responsible for the reading problems of children in the inner city. At the time, there were two opposing views as to the nature of this dialect. Traditional dialectology held that the speech of blacks in the United States was no different from that of whites and that the blacks in the northern cities had simply carried with them the features of the Southern dialect in the areas that they had come from (Kurath, 1949, p. 6). This opinion was based on the finding of dialect geography that the sounds and the words used by black speakers were typical of the geographic regions of each area of the South, except for the coastal Gullah area of South Carolina and Georgia. On the other hand, linguists familiar with the Creole languages of the Caribbean came to the conclusion that AAVE was itself a Creole language, similar to the English-based Creoles of Jamaica, Guyana, and Trinidad (Bailey, 1965; Dillard, 1972; Stewart, 1967, 1968). Their position was based primarily on the absence of inflections and the copula and the presence of several preverbal aspect markers that were characteristic of Creole grammars, particularly the invariant particle *be*, signaling habitual aspect.

A number of sociolinguistic investigations were designed to give a more systematic view of the grammar of AAVE in a wide range of American cities, using quantitative measures of spontaneous speech, along with a number of experimental techniques (Baugh, 1983; Fasold, 1972; Labov, 1972; Labov et al., 1968; Legum, Pfaff, Tinnie, & Nicholas, 1972; Mitchell-Kernan, 1969; Wolfram, 1969). These studies showed a remarkably consistent grammar used by black inner-city youth in cities as diverse as New York, Washington, Philadelphia, Detroit, Los Angeles, and San Francisco. The relation of the AAVE grammar to other dialects was found to be intermediate between the extreme positions of the dialectologists and creolists. In at least five important respects, linguistic analysis showed repeatedly that AAVE was or had become close-ly aligned to other dialects of English:

- The plural -s inflection and concept of plurality was intact and even generalized to forms like *deers* that did not show a plural -s in other dialects.
- The possessive -s inflection was basically absent in attributive position, as in *my father house*, but was always present and even generalized in absolute position, as in *hers, John's*, and *mines*.
- The past tense was basically the same as in all other dialects, with a uniform use of the irregular past as in *went* and *told* and a somewhat greater rate of consonant cluster simplification of regular pasts than in other dialects.
- The copula and auxiliary *to be* was variably present, but showed a systematic relationship to the pattern of contraction in other dialects. Because AAVE showed deletion or contrac-tion only where other dialects showed contraction, it could be inferred that AAVE had the same underlying copula form as other dialects and that deletion of the copula was an extension of contraction.
- Almost all of the AAVE syntactic features, like double modals (*He might could do that*), multiple negation (*it ain't no cat can't get in no coop*), negative inversion (*Don't nobody know*), and inverted word order in embedded questions (*I asked Alvin could he play basketball*) were the same or extended versions of similar rules in colloquial Southern English.

In these respects, the AAVE grammar appeared to be a variant of other grammars, primarily differing in the rates of phonetic condensa-tion and deletion, but with the same set of underlying concepts and cate-gories. On the other hand, AAVE proved to be qualitatively different from other dialects in several respects:

- Subject-verb agreement was basically absent, except for the verb *to be*, and there was no systematic place in the grammar for the third-singular –s inflection.
- AAVE showed a number of preverbal aspect markers with syntax and semantics that are qualitatively different from other dialects: not only habitual *be*, but stressed *been* 'remote present perfect' (*I been know your name*), *be done* 'resultative' (*Get out the way or I be done go upside your head*), and *been done* 'past perfect' (*They been done did it*). These particles are not tied

to any particular time reference and do not show the syntactic behavior of auxiliaries that are subordinated to an inflectional node and follow the standard patterns of inversion, tag formation, and adverb or negative placement.

One of the subjects pursued most intently was the pattern of grammatical conditioning of the contraction and deletion of the copula. Holm (1984) and Baugh (1980) found that contraction and deletion were generally parallel, except for the effect of a following locative and adjective. The locative favored the contracted form, whereas the adjective favored the deleted form, which could only be explained by the reflection of an underlying creole grammar in which locatives always showed the copula, but adjectives did not.

A consensus that appeared to emerge among linguists in the late 1970s was summarized in the testimony of black and white linguists at the Black English trial in Ann Arbor (Labov, 1982; Smitherman, 1981). This case was initiated by the mothers of black children in a low-income housing project in Ann Arbor, MI, located in a middle-class white area. They sued the city and the state because their children were suffering educational failure, although they were of normal intelligence and ability. The school, the mothers argued, had failed to take into account their special cultural and linguistic background. Judge Joiner of the Federal Court found that the suit had merit under Title 20, Sec. 1703(f), which stated that no child should be deprived of equal educational opportunity because of the failure of an educational agency to take appropriate action to overcome linguistic barriers. The linguistic case for the plaintiffs was assembled by Geneva Smitherman; the testimony of linguists and psychologists established a position that eventually was adapted by Judge Joiner in his decision for the plaintiffs. In this testimony, AAVE was characterized by four propositions.

1. It is a subsystem of English with a distinct set of phonological and syntactic rules that are now aligned in many ways with the rules of other dialects.
2. It incorporates many rules of Southern phonology, morphology, and syntax; blacks in turn have exerted influence on the dialects of the South where they have lived.
3. It shows evidence of derivation from an earlier Creole that was closer to the present-day Creoles of the Caribbean.
4. It has a highly developed aspect system, quite different from other dialects of English, which shows a continuing development of its semantic structure.

The overall view of the relations between AAVE and other dialects was therefore one of *convergence:* AAVE had been much more different from other dialects in the past, and it was gradually becoming aligned with them, without losing traces of its Creole origins.

Some Linguistic Sources of Reading Problems

The study of structural differences between AAVE and classroom English showed a number of problems that might interfere with success in reading (Labov, 1966). The most obvious factors involved sound/spelling relationships. The differences between the written language and the spoken language were much greater for AAVE than for other dialects, primarily because the reduction of final consonants was much more extensive. Among young children this tendency of AAVE can lead to an extreme growth of homonymy and a great difficulty in recognizing distinctions that are obvious in classroom English:

1. Final consonant clusters were more widely reduced than with other dialects, so that AAVE children would more often pronounce *told* the same as *toll*, *mist* the same as *miss*, and *passed* the same as *pass*.
2. Final liquids /l/ and /r/ were vocalized to glides, and then often disappeared entirely, so that *told* and *toll* might be pronounced the same as *toe*, *four* the same as *foe*, and *help* the same as *hep*.
3. Single, final consonants also tended to disappear, although at a lower rate, so that *Boot* can sound like *boo*; *seat, seed*, and *see* may all be pronounced as *see*.
4. A number of mergers of vowels produce another set of homonyms: /e/ and /i/ are merged before nasals, so that *pin* and *pen* are always the same; /iy/ and /i/, /ey/ and /e/ often merge before /l/, so that *feel* and *fill*, *fail* and *fell* can be the same.
5. The Southern monophthongization of diphthongs is common in AAVE, so that *find, found*, and *fond* may be homonyms; *time* is not distinguished from *Tom*; and *boil* may equal *ball*.
6. The interdental consonants become labiodentals after a vowel, so that the *th* in *breath, mouth,* and *bath* is pronounced as /f/.

It is apparent that the relation between sound and spelling is far more abstract than with other dialects, and the difficult sound-spelling correspondences of English are even more difficult for AAVE speakers learning to read. Furthermore, these processes can interfere directly with the recognition of grammatical particles:

1. The contracted forms of the future are difficult to recognize because *you'll* may sound the same as *you*, and *I'll* is difficult to distinguish from *I*.
2. The copula or auxiliary forms of the verb *to be* may also be difficult to recognize on the printed page because of the high rate of deletion in many contexts.
3. The signals of the past tense may be difficult to recognize. Even though, from a linguistic point of view, AAVE has an underling past tense *-ed*, the high frequency of deletion apparently creates great difficulty for AAVE speakers in recognizing the *-ed* on the printed age as signifying past tense. Thus, in one experimental approach, AAVE speakers were able to transfer past-tense information to derive the correct pronunciation of *read* in *Last month I read the sign*, but not in *When I passed by, I read the sign* (Labov, 1972, p. 31).

The end result of these conflicts may be seen in the sharp reduction of those decoding skills that utilize the alphabet—a loss of confidence in the alphabet. All of the AAVE speakers studied in South Harlem had mastered the alphabet, no matter how poor their reading level, as far as the beginnings of words was concerned. Patterns of reading errors rarely showed mistakes in the identification of the first letter. Information theory would predict that errors would decline from the first to the last letter because each letter narrows down the range of possible words that might be chosen. In fact, the number of errors rose steadily from the first to the next to last letter. It is common to find words like *cold* misread as coop. The overall pattern is that AAVE speakers use alphabetic skills in attacking the first consonant, and the first letter of the vowel, but abandon such efforts beyond this point. This loss of confidence in the alphabet is a direct result of the very abstract relationship between the alphabet and the surface realizations of words in AAVE.

The Underlying Cultural Conflict

Although there were many points of structural conflict between AAVE and classroom English, the question remained as to whether these differences were large enough to account for the massive pattern of reading failure that we observed in the inner cities. The conclusion of most sociolinguists was that the semantic and structural differences between AAVE and other dialects were not great enough to be the primary causes of reading failure. Dialect differences affected education primarily as symbols of social conflict. Experimental approaches to the effects of speech on teachers' attitudes show that it is the most powerful single factor in determining teachers' predictions of student performance (Seligman, Tucker, & Lambert, 1972). The main effect of a child speaking AAVE was to affect teachers' attitudes toward the child, with a resultant negative expectation that affected teachers' behavior toward the child in many ways (Rosenthal & Jacobson, 1968). This was consistent with the pattern of Figures 1 and 2, showing that reading failure was associated with membership in groups that opposed the school culture, rather than with verbal skills.

There was strong evidence that such negative attitudes were created by the use of AAVE and little evidence of any mechanism that would lead to direct cognitive interference with reading. The outcome of the Ann Arbor trial was that teachers were given in-service training on the nature and history of AAVE in order to correct these negative attitudes. No changes in the actual reading curriculum were suggested to improve the teaching of reading. Later surveys showed that the teachers who had undergone such training did register more positive attitudes toward African-American language and culture, though there was no evidence that reading scores of the black students had improved.

THE APPLICATION OF LINGUISTICS TO READING PROGRAMS: THE USE OF BEV IN EARLY READING

Not all linguists believed that the main source of interference of AAVE on reading success was attitudinal. Those among the creolists who believed that the structure of AAVE was radically different from other dialects argued that the standard English of the classroom had to be taught by "semi-foreign-language" methods, and reading of that dialect was impeded by the cognitive gap between AAVE and standard grammar. It followed that instructional materials written in AAVE would be easier to read for black children, and that these might form a transitional path between the first stages of reading and the ultimate control of standard English. Stewart (1967, 1968) devised a series of dialect primers written in AAVE to test this hypothesis. However, the experiments that would confirm whether such primers were useful were never completed. Many teachers and parents reacted negatively to the idea that vernacular language was to be introduced into the classroom as part of a school program. Even though these materials were intended as the best means of transition to standard English, it was felt that their use in the curriculum amounted to an endorsement of the vernacular language.

Many people thought that such programs would actually be teaching children to speak AAVE rather than standard English.

The BRIDGE Program

By far the most important program for teaching reading in the inner city schools is BRIDGE, a curriculum written by two black psychologists, Gary and Charlesetta Simpkins, and a prominent educator from the Chicago black community, Grace Holt. As described in Simpkins and Simpkins (1981), this program is based on the method of "Associative Bridging," which was designed to overcome the cognitive problems faced by black youth in attempting to decipher the reading system in an unfamiliar linguistic code. *Bridge* was published by Houghton Mifflin in 1977 as a series of graded readings and cassette recordings that made use of the traditional folklore of African-American culture, moving in three stages from the vernacular to standard English. The program is introduced by a young black man on tape who serves as an intermediary between the culture of the classroom and the point of view of the black children of the inner city.[1]

> (1) What's happenin', brothers and sisters? I want to tell you about this here program called *Bridge*, a cross-cultural reading program. Now I *know* what you thinkin'. This is just another one of them jive reading programs, and that I won't be need no readin' program. But dig it. This here reading program is really kinda different. It was done by a brother and two sisters, soul folk, you know. And they put sump'm extra in it, they put a little taste o' soul. Matter of fact, a lot of soul. No jive, that's what they put in it, a little bit of soul, something you can relate to. And check this out, quiet as it's kept, you do need this here readin' program. If you be sittin' in this class, you don't be readin' any too cool. Now don't be lookin' around! I'm talkin' about you, here, right over right over there in the corner now, unless you the teacher, I'm talkin' 'bout you. Now I *know* what you gon' say. I don' need to be readin' no better, I get by! I don't *dig* no readin'. And they ain't nothin' I want to be readin' nohow. But dig! I know where you *been*, and I know where you comin' from too. When you was jus' startin' in school, readin' got on yo' case, now didn't it, got down on you, hurt your feelings. In the second grade, readin' jus' smacked you all upside yo' head, dared you do sump'm about it. In the third grade, hum, readin' got into your ches', knocked you down, dragged you through the *mud*, sent you home cryin' to yo' mama. Now, by the time you got to the fo'th grade, you

---

[1]The extracts to follow are my own transcriptions from the sample cassette designed to introduce BRIDGE to new users.

jus' about had enough of messin' around with this here readin' thing. And you said to yourself, I ain' gon' be messin' with this ol' bad boy no *more!* You jus' hung it up. But you had to keep your front So you say, I don' need no readin', it ain' nothin' I want to read nohow. And it wasn', you know, all front, cause that stuff was pretty borin'. So anyway, you stopped tryin', so you was just sick and tired of gittin' done in, bein' bored all the time by that readin' stuff. But dig! like I said now, this here program is kind of different. I want to hip you to that. It can help you git it together. You know, keep you from bein' pushed around by reading. And it ain't *borin'*. Cause it's about really interesting people. Matter of fact, it's about the most interesting people in the world, black people, and you know how interesting bloods can be.

It is clear that the speaker is addressing the target group of Figure 2.2—well-integrated members of the street culture, rather than the isolated individuals of Figure 2.1. It is not accidental that the person addressed is in the fourth grade (though the program, as we will see, was first tested with grades 7 to 12), since as noted above it is in the fourth grade that resistance to school instruction is first solidified by adolescent peer groups. *Bridge* directly attacks the problem of social conflict that was identified at the outset as the major obstacle to reading, and at the same time targets the problem of structural differences between the dialects concerned. Excerpt 1 shows many grammatical and lexical features of AAVE. To highlight the structural patterns that form the two ends of the continuum, items 2 through 8 are presented as alternating AAVE and standard classroom English (SCE) treatments of figurative language. In the AAVE version, italics indicate current black idiom and slang; the "[0]" symbols show the deletion of elements of the verb *to be* and other elements of the auxiliary; bold type shows positive features of nonstandard grammar, some common to other dialects, and others (like habitual *be*) specific to AAVE. In the SCE version, bold type indicates standard grammatical features that contrast directly with the AAVE norm, primarily in the use of third singular -*s*.

(2) AAVE: <u>What you [0] gonna learn.</u>
SCE: <u>What you will learn.</u>
(3) AAVE: To *dig* on talk that [0] saying more than **what** the words really mean.
SCE: To understand language that means more than the words themselves.
(4) AAVE: *Check this out.*
SCE: <u>Study the explanation.</u>
(5) AAVE: You [0] got what they call figurative language when you come across words that [0] saying something but ain't really saying

what it [0] saying.

SCE: Figurative language refers to a word or a group of words that describes something as though it were something else.

(6) AAVE: To understand this **here** figurative language thing, to really put it together, you [0] got to use a little taste of imagination. You can't **be using** the exact meaning of the words.

SCE: To understand figurative language, you can't use the exact meaning of the words. Instead, you must visualize the idea that the words suggest.

(7) AAVE: What you got to do is *trip* on the pictures that the words **be** painting for you.

SCE: You must allow words to paint pictures in your mind.

(8) AAVE: Now *dig* this: Suppose you **was** to hear two Brothers talking. And suppose one of them was to say to the other:

Man, that Billy, *he [0] fat as a rat in a cheese factory.*

Now, what [0] you think the Brother **be** saying 'bout Billy? Now you know that he **ain't** saying that Billy [0] overweight. And he **ain't** trying to *get down* on Billy by saying he [0] ugly as a rat eating cheese. What he [0] saying is that Billy **he** [0] got a lot of bread, or Billy *got over*, or that Billy [0] *got it made.*

SCE: A poet once advised,

Gather ye (your) rosebuds while ye (you) may

Old time is still a-flying

And this same flower that smiles today

Tomorrow will be dying.

What does the above example suggest to you? What advice do you think the poet is giving? Is he talking about picking rosebuds, or is he talking about people and life? To understand what the poet is talking about, you can't use the exact meaning of the words. If you allow the words to paint a picture in your mind, you will discover that the poet is talking about people and life.

The *Bridge* program was tested in five areas of the United States, with 14 teachers and 27 classes from the 7th through the 12th grades, involving 540 students—all but 10 of them black. The 21 classes who used the Bridge program showed a significantly larger gain in reading than the 6 control classes: an average gain of 6.2 months for 4 months of instruction as compared to 1.6 months for the control group (Simpkins & Simpkins, 1981). On the basis of this impressive finding, the program was marketed nationally by Houghton-Mifflin. However, the program encountered sociolinguistic obstacles. The publishers received enough objections from parents and teachers to the use of AAVE in the classroom that they ceased promoting it, and further development was shelved. The program is now being further developed by Gary Simpkins.

The initial success of the *Bridge* program in its primary function of improving reading scores is sufficient to warrant careful attention and a search for ways of developing its basic principles further. Its development has far-reaching implications for similar programs. Bridge appears to have four main strengths:

1. *General aims*. The program adopts as its goal the general aim endorsed by American education: to build on the resources that the child brings to school in order to achieve a mastery of the literacy skills needed in the general society. Simpkins and Simpkins point out that educational pedagogy shares an almost universal belief in the Dewey axiom, "Start where the child is" (Simpkins & Simpkins, 1980, p. 226). *Bridge* is a linguistic and cultural implementation of that axiom.
2. *Combined cultural and linguistic approach*. The *Bridge* program is so designed that it simultaneously operates on both social and cognitive dimensions: It reduces the cultural distance between the student and his or her first reading materials, and it also reduces cognitive impediments to reading. All of the research reviewed above points to the fact that such an approach should be initially effective in reducing the problems caused by types of factors.
3. *Approach to the vernacular*. The program was written by three authors who have a deep knowledge of vernacular culture and a keen sensitivity to the use of language across the entire range of Black English forms.
4. *Adaptation to the school environment*. The authors are thoroughly familiar with curriculum needs and have developed a program that fits into the classroom environment.

On the other hand, the program appears to have corresponding weaknesses that might well be remedied in a version that would have a greater impact on the reading problem of the inner-city schools:

1. *Sociolinguistic acceptability*. The presentation of the program to parents and teachers has not yet succeeded in connecting the use of AAVE in the classroom with the general educational axiom of beginning with the child's own experience and resources. Although many educators have come to realize that AAVE is a well-formed language with its own coherent logic, and extremely similar in all inner city areas, the general public still regards it as a form of slang or broken English. The program has not yet been presented in a way that counters the objection that it imposes and teaches a form of bad English that is not generally used by children.

2. *Mixed cultural and linguistic transition.* Because the program simultaneously varies on both the cultural and linguistic dimensions, it is not easy to evaluate which component is most effective in improving reading, and so it is not easy to improve or build on the positive results achieved. Thus strength (2) is also a corresponding weakness. Moreover, the programs show a shift of cultural content from vernacular culture to an elevated literary culture that is not necessarily—or fruitfully—associated with SCE. The example of SCE figurative language in item 7 above associates SCE with the romantic, poetizing stance of the end of the last century that may well be viewed as effeminate or inappropriate by male youth, black or white. Such a stereotype would not clearly motivate black youth to gain control of SCE.

3. *Temporal dating of vernacular forms.* Although the grammar and phonology reflected in the AAVE passages is still current, the vocabulary and idiom rapidly become dated. When I played the *Bridge* passage 1 to a group of 20 black college students in 1986, they heard it as authentically black vernacular, but comically old-fashioned. Idioms like *hip you to that, dig on, to be all front* were no longer possible for them, although *cool, check this out, trip, get over,* and *get down* on were still current. Because one of the important features of vernacular culture is the knowledge of what is current and what is not, a spokesperson for the program cannot afford to be heard as out of date. He (or she) will then be classified as someone who may once have been in touch with the street culture, but is no longer. For most youth, such a person is classified as a *lame*, whose advice is to be avoided.

The structural elements of AAVE do not change their status as rapidly, and all of the elements shown in the extracts are still characteristic of the vernacular. However, they are presented in a stereotyped form, without the variability that is characteristic of spontaneous speech. For example, there is no variation in the deletion of the copula in these extracts: Only zero forms appear in unstressed position, although in real life there is always a balance between full, contracted, and deleted forms. Thus, the program adapts the view that AAVE is an assembly of all those forms that differ from SCE, rather than reflecting the style of everyday speech. It seems more reasonable for the spokesman for AAVE to show the use of variables such as the copula in a realistic way. Any person in a cross-cultural environment would shift toward a more formal style within AAVE, which would show fewer deleted forms.

4. The problem of temporal dating just raised also raises the problem of fitting the *Bridge* program into the academic environment. *Bridge* is well designed to fit the pattern of a nation-ally distributed, printed curriculum, which is reasonably independent of local resources. Nationally distributed publications can undergo revisions, but cannot be revised as rapidly as popular idiom changes. It follows that the program must rely more on local resources, in which the main message of the program can be rewritten, or restated, in a more flexible form. The other option is to weaken the AAVE style by using a more general vocabulary, because it is not possible to predict which idioms and slang terms will remain fixed and which will become outmoded in five years time.

The balance of local and national resources raises the added problem of the relation between the teacher and the program, which is reflected in several of the problematic areas listed. Many black schoolroom teachers are capable of a wide range of style shifting, but many others are not. They are free to rely on the vernacular narrator as an intermediary between them and the students, in order to approach more closely the point from which the students start. However, this is equivalent to bypassing the teacher, and it is possible that such a step will reduce the teacher's authority. It might seem that the approach of *Bridge* should be modified to avoid any possibility of conflict between the two sources of information: the program and the teacher. The route toward resolving this problem may lie through a reconsideration of two concepts: the notion of *authorship* and the notion of a group decision.

First, in the case of authorship, the principle objection to the program stems from the notion that it appears to put the school system, as an institution, in a position of endorsing, promulgating, or even teaching AAVE. This is because the text, or the program, is incorporated into the curriculum without an explicit framing that separates the speakers, authors, or constructors of the program from the school. No such objection is raised when dialect is presented within a work of fiction, especially when authors frame the representation of dialect by prose that demonstrates their command of standard English. To find the most effective frame in which the male spokesman for *Bridge* and the vernacular culture will appear is not a simple matter. While he must appear as more than a casual visitor or guest in the educational process, the school as an institution cannot afford to incorporate him fully into its structure. The solution to this problem requires more than cultural insight—it demands social engineering.

Second, the notion of group decision begins with the communal view of learning in which the focus is on the group rather than the individual. Traditionally, the *old head* who advises male youth to pursue education is a person who could not or did not pursue that route when he was young, but came to appreciate its value too late to take full advantage of it. Late realization of the value of education occurs after he has emerged from the influence of the compelling forces of the lower class youth culture. As shown previously (see also Ogbu, this volume), the adolescent peer group of the black community rejects the school (but not education) because of its perceived identification with oppression and injustice. But the program as it is now constituted paints the rejection of education as the result of an individual failure, rather than as a group decision. It might therefore seem essential that the spokesman appears to be conscious of some of his own limitations, rather than appears as a full-fledged role model. Communication must be with the group, not the individual, because in the inner cities, the normal, socially adjusted individual will not decide to follow the educational route unless it is part of a group decision.

LANGUAGE ARTS IN THE INTEGRATED CLASSROOM

The approach taken by *Bridge* appears to be the most powerful way of attacking simultaneously the cultural and linguistic conflicts between AAVE and SCE. Given the high rate of residential segregation in the inner cities, programs must be designed for schools with close to 100% black enrollment, where students share a joint participation in the same language and culture. However, it is equally important to develop methods that will apply our knowledge to schools with mixed populations. If efforts to desegregate inner-city schools are to succeed, this will become even more important in the future. In such a situation it is not reasonable to assume a common starting point for all students.

One approach to a mixed situation is to bring to the forefront the actual differences between dialects, to endeavor to achieve a tolerance of dialect differences, and to use this knowledge to enroll all students in the acquisition of standard English. On the other hand, many educators consider this contrastive strategy counterproductive in two senses: (a) it emphasizes differences among students, and (b) it devotes time to talking about language that is subtracted from the process of learning to read and write. It might seem more helpful to use our knowledge of dialect differences to assist the teaching of reading without introducing this topic directly into the classroom. To date, I do not know of any program that has conveyed detailed and accurate linguistic knowledge about AAVE to the designers of reading programs in such a form that it can actually be used. The following suggestions for *Language Arts in the Integrated Classroom* are therefore put forward as a possible basis for such a program which has not yet been realized.

Most reading and phonics programs appear to be based on the assumption that all students have the same underlying forms for words and the same grammar. They are therefore optimally designed for those students whose mental dictionaries, grammars, and phonologies are closest to SCE: in other words, for those students who need the least help. It is not accidental that in the 1970s, the Philadelphia Board of Education engaged in a massive study to find which reading programs produced real improvement from the third to fourth grade. Only one program was found to produce a significant advantage and only for students who were at grade level or above. A program that would reverse this situation must be based on the axiom that *reading programs must be designed to give the most help to those who show the greatest need.* That is not to say that they will not also be helpful for those who are not suffering reading failure. The following suggestions are for ways to apply linguistic knowledge within the program that will give the maximum assistance to speakers of AAVE, Hispanic-influenced English, and other nonstandard dialects, without penalizing children whose home language is close to SCE.

Principle 1. Teachers should distinguish between mistakes in reading and differences in pronunciation. This principle can only be effected if teachers become explicitly aware of the patterns of AAVE pronunciation outlined above, so that they can focus their corrections on the important problem of deciphering meaning from the printed page. Although this principle has been widely discussed in the literature in the past two decades, no educational program has yet been developed to give teachers the information that they need to implement it.

Principle 2. Give more attention to the ends of words. The great majority of the phonics programs appear to give far more time and attention to initial consonants than final consonants. Some teachers avoid focusing on final consonants almost entirely, fearing that this might lead to such reversals as *was* for *saw.* This is, however, a trivial problem compared to the great difficulty that AAVE speakers have with final consonants and final clusters. It is therefore important to alter this normal procedure drastically to give even more attention to the ends of words.

Principle 3. Words must be presented to students in those phonological contexts that preserve underlying forms. For speakers of many dialects, this means presenting words in citation form—in isolation, or in the frame, "This is a ____." But it is in just this final position that AAVE words show the greatest reduction of their underlying forms. To help AAVE speakers grasp the correct relationship between words and their spellings, they should be presented in the most favorable environment when they are first introduced into the reading process:

- Words with final clusters like *test* should be presented as *test of* or *testing* rather than *This is a test.* Words like *old* should not be presented in the context *He is old,* but rather in phrases like *old eggs.* The same principle can also be applied to words like *bad* that have single final consonants: It is heard more clearly in *bad idea* than *He is bad.*
- The past tense *-ed* is best introduced in reading after words ending in /t/ or /d/. It is far easier for speakers of AAVE to recognize the past tense in *started, ended,* or *expected,* than in *passed* or *rolled.*
- The third singular *-s,* one of the most difficult concepts for AAVE speakers to grasp, is best introduced after verbs that end in a vowel, where it is realized most clearly as /z/. Thus, *John goes home* is to be preferred to *John walks home.* The application of this principle will radically reduce the number of cases where the AAVE speaking student perceives "silent letters," while the teacher does not.

Principle 4. Use the full forms of words and avoid contractions. As noted above, young AAVE speakers have great difficulty in recognizing the relationship between contracted and full forms, though both may be present in their speech. Full forms like *I will have gone* and *He is my brother* are quite natural, and indeed the most common form used by AAVE speakers, but contracted forms of *will* and *is* in *I'll be there* and *He's here* are often not perceived in speech or recognized in writing.

Principle 5. Grammar should be taught explicitly. Though AAVE and SCE share most rules of grammar, there are areas where young speakers of AAVE find no support in their underlying grammar that will help them interpret elements that appear in printed texts. Subject-verb agreement through third singular *-s* is the most striking example: It not only affects the regular verb, but affects the irregular verbs *have, do,* and *be.* The possessive *-s* in *John's idea* must be introduced with equal explicitness. Even the plural, which is securely in place for most AAVE noun phrases, must be taught explicitly with nouns of measure like *ten cents* and *five miles.* Direct instruction on such elements of grammar cannot harm speakers of other dialects and may serve many useful purposes in their later education. It is, however, essential if we are to reduce the mismatch between the printed page and the underlying knowledge of the AAVE speaker.

The application of these principles alone cannot reverse reading failure. I have summarized them here in order to outline the full range of possible applications of linguistic knowledge to the problem. Though they have not yet been implemented in any full-fledged reading curriculum, they should form an important element in such a program.

RECENT RESEARCH ON AAVE: EVIDENCE FOR DIVERGENCE

Let us now return to the field of linguistic research and inquire whether studies of AAVE since 1980 has added anything to earlier views. At the end of this period, at the time of the consensus of the Black English trial, it was generally agreed that in the 19th century, this dialect had been much more different from other dialects of English and was now gradually converging with them. In the years that followed, the evidence for this assumption was thrown into doubt, and new findings showed that the major currents of change were in the opposite direction. This is an area of research that now shows many disagreements; all that I can do here is to provide my own interpretation of the many new findings that have accumulated. Many of these interpretations are controversial: They represent only my best assessment of the available evidence.

FURTHER ARGUMENTS ON CREOLE ORIGINS

One of the crucial arguments on the origins of AAVE is that the repeated pattern of copula contraction deletion was best explained by a creole origin. The creole grammatical pattern referred to here is that noun phrases and the locatives show copulas and adjectives and that verbs do not. This is always a basilectal structure, typical of those speakers who are most remote from the superordinate colonial language. Unfortunately, the pattern found by Baugh (1980) and Holm (1984) has not been replicated in many other studies. Furthermore, Singler's study (1991) of Liberian Creole English showed that the route from the basilect to the acrolect lay through a mesolect, or middle form, where all copula and auxiliary forms of *to be* were absent. Indeed, Bickerton's work (1975) in Guyana which drew parallels with mainland AAVE did show that the zero form was most typical of the mesolect. Thus, it would seem unlikely that a basilectal copula structure could be transmitted to modern day AAVE by a process of decreolization.

In the study of Creoles, the concept of decreolization came into question. Attention to the social conditions that prevailed during the earliest period of creolization showed that the conditions for the continuum already existed at the beginning: that is, the plantation speech communities of the 17th and 18th centuries already had the full range of basilectal, mesolectal, and acrolectal forms (Alleyne, 1971). The arguments for decreolization had always had to cope with the fact that there is only indirect evidence for an earlier black Creole in the mainland United States, except for the surviving Gullah of the Sea Islands (Stewart 1967, 1968). But studies of the available direct evidence, the narratives of ex-slaves recorded in the 1930s, failed to show grammars with creole features similar to the Caribbean (Poplack & Tagliamonte, 1989).

Sociolinguistic studies of two outlying black communities, Samaná in the Dominican Republic and Nova Scotia, were carried out, yielding a view of the grammars of the descendants of blacks who had migrated from the United States in the early 19th century. Though one would expect many changes in the intervening period, it is always the case that such isolated speech communities preserve some of the features of the original settlers, because isolated linguistic groups rarely follow the same pattern of development as the parent community. Dillard (1971, 1973) referred to evidence for a creole grammar in the Nova Scotian black community, who arrived in Canada early in the 19th century. However, both of these communities show grammatical patterns very similar to those of early AAVE in the United States (Poplack & Sankoff, 1987; Poplack & Tagliamonte, 1991).

An increasing number of grammatical patterns of AAVE were found to be continuations of earlier patterns of English dialects. For example, the strongest conditioning factor in the deletion of the copula was that subject pronouns favored zero forms and full noun phrases favored full or contracted forms. This pattern of noun phrase marking was found to be a traditional characteristic of nonstandard English dialects (Bailey, Maynor, & Cukor-Avila, 1989). The end result of all this work is that the evidence for decreolization of AAVE has become increasingly narrow. In some respects, AAVE has converged with other dialects. The ex-slave narratives show less subject-verb agreement in the copula (high frequencies of *I is, we is, they is,* etc.), radically different patterns of pronoun use rarely found today (e.g., object *he*), and a steadily decreasing use of truncated forms like *bout* and *posed* (Vaughn-Cooke, 1986). But such converging trends did not characterize the major grammatical patterns.

EVIDENCE FOR DIVERGENCE

While the evidence for decreolization began to shrink, evidence of changes in the other direction began to appear. These new findings are reported in new and vigorous studies of AAVE aspect, especially the development of invariant *be*, and in new sociolinguistic investigations of

AAVE speech communities in the Dominican Republic, Nova Scotia, Philadelphia, and East Palo Alto, CA.

The Semantics of AAVE Aspect

Linguists had begun to find out more about the AAVE aspect particles like *be, been,* and *be done.* The more they were studied, it became clear that these particles had little connection with the finite auxiliaries of other dialects. Much of the evidence is drawn from the participant studies of Dayton (1992) in Philadelphia, who over four years accumulated many more examples than had been reported by all other linguists combined. These particles can be used in any time perspective—past, present ,or future—and shared none of the syntactic properties of other English auxiliaries. An increasing number of sentences of AAVE appeared to have no finite tense assignment. Though this development was typologically similar to Creole patterns, the actual semantics of these particles proved to be quite different from anything reported in the Caribbean or West Africa. Instead of showing characteristic aspectual features such as "perfect," "perfective," or "durative," they showed highly complex combinations of semantic features, with strong social affect more characteristic of modals than aspect. For example, AAVE stressed *been* in *I been own this* conveys the information that the statement has been true for a long time (psychologically speaking), that it is still true, and furthermore, that the addressee should have known this if he or she had been an accurate observer. In his study of the modal of moral indignation *come* (as in *He come comin' over here*), Spears (1982) shows that many new developments of AAVE are *camouflaged*; that is, they appear in forms that are so superficially similar to other dialects that they are accepted as slight variants of familiar grammatical forms.

The Recent Development of Habitual BE

The most frequent of these grammatical particles is the invariant *be* with a "habitual" meaning. It is the only specifically AAVE particle that is normally heard in the mass media, and it appears several times in the excerpts from *Bridge.* In a series of articles based on research in rural and urban areas of Texas, Bailey, (1985, 1987, 1989) and Maynor reported that this aspect marker was not characteristic of rural older blacks, who like the speakers of the ex-slave narratives, used invariant *be* as a simple alternant of finite *am, is, are.* They argued that the aspect marker is actually a product of a recent divergence of AAVE and other dialects and is found primarily among younger speakers in the inner cities where blacks had migrated from the rural South. In the black community of East Palo Alto, Rickford and his colleagues found a similar rapid development of invariant *be* (Rickford & McNail-Knox, in press). These findings agreed with the evidence cited in the previous section to indicate that the present-day AAVE structure is primarily a creation of the 20th century, rather than an inheritance of the 19th century.

Phonological Divergence

A second aspect of divergence emerges from the study of sound changes in progress throughout the United States. In a long series of studies of American cities—New York, Philadelphia, Buffalo, Detroit, Chicago, Los Angeles, and many others—it appears that local sound changes are developing rapidly, so that the dialects of these cities are now far more different from each other than they were 50 years ago (Bailey & Ross 1992; Eckert, 1988; Labov, 1980; Labov, Yaeger, & Steiner, 1972; Laferriere, 1977). In every one of these cities, this divergence is limited to the white community: Black and Hispanic groups do not participate at all in these sound changes. Instead, AAVE shows a gradual generalization of certain Southern features into a general northern black phonology.

In addition to the chain shifting of vowels, a number of mergers are rapidly expanding throughout the United States, and here again, a very different pattern is found among black speakers. For example, the expansion of the merger of long and short open o̱ in *cot* and *caught, Don* and *dawn*, and so on, has almost completed its expansion in the western United States, but the black community still shows a clear distinction (Veatch, 1992). These phonetic and phonological patterns have both a symbolic and a structural significance (Graff, Labov, & Harris, 1986). Studies of cross-cultural comprehension show that, in general, black speakers do not comprehend the new features of white speech as well as white speakers from the same community do (Labov & Ash, in press).

The Relation of Divergence to Social Networks

Earlier arguments for decreolization had been accompanied by the general understanding that blacks were making steady progress toward full membership in the rights and privileges of American society. This assumption is supported by progress in civil rights legislation and the upward movement of increasing numbers of black citizens out of the inner city. A more sober look at the position of the majority black community suggests that conditions for separation and divergence are more characteristic of the inner city. In the early 1980s, I participated in a study of the linguistic boundaries among black, Puerto Rican, and white speakers in Philadelphia. The results indicated that the inner city black speech community showed two radically different patterns. The central core of peer group members—young adults from 16 to 40 years old— had almost no contact with speakers of other dialects, and the AAVE features that they showed were far more extreme than any that had been reported before in the mainland United States. The use of verbal -s and possessive -s was close to zero. The deletion of subject relative pronouns, rare in other dialects, was close to 100%, especially in presentative sentences (*There's a man owns this store. . .*).

Within these close-knit networks we find the development of new grammatical analyses. The North Philadelphia core speakers showed very little verbal -s, but made a sharp contrast between narrative, in which verbal -s was used with considerable frequency, and nonnarrative, in which it was all but absent. Thus, grammatical reanalysis has not yet been found in other areas, but it marks a clear reversal of earlier patterns, even among blacks who use the historical present, which normally represents the importation of nonnarrative tense into narrative (Myhill & Harris, 1986).

On the other hand, a variety of black speakers in the same community, with the same superficial features of AAVE, showed the deep penetration of the grammatical features of other dialects. These were not speakers who "sounded white": They were fully integrated members of the community. But as musicians, political activists, or con artists, and through their occupations, legal or illegal, political or social, they had frequent face-to-face dealings with whites. Thus, the community was subtly divided into the majority who were diverging further from the pattern of the dominant society, and those who were converging with it (Ash & Myhill, 1986; Labov & Harris 1986).

It is important to observe that all of these speakers were exposed to standard broadcast or schoolroom English for many hours during the day. The crucial factor that distinguished them was whether or not they had frequent personal interactions with speakers of other dialects (white or middle-class blacks) on an equal basis. As other studies of the mass media show, they have little influence on the speech of those who listen to them, unless that influence is reinforced by face-to-face interaction.

Causes of Divergence

The Philadelphia situation shows more clearly than any other that the primary causes of divergence are the increasing residential segregation in American cities. The popular impression is that segregation is greatest at the time of in-migration and steadily declines as members of the new ethnic group spread out to other areas. However, Table 2 shows that in Philadelphia segregation of blacks has steadily increased over the past three decades (Hershberg, 1981). While these segregation figures are based on ethnicity alone, the linguistic segregation of the inner city is actually more intense than the residential segregation figures show. It is the increasing absence of middle class black speakers from the inner city that determines the high rate of isolation of AAVE and creates the conditions for further divergence.

THE EDUCATIONAL CONSEQUENCES OF DIVERGENCE FOR LITERACY EDUCATION

These new findings on the structure and directions of change in AAVE have not yet been applied to educational problems. Yet, it is not too soon to evaluate the suggestions developed in the section on the applications of linguistics to reading and literacy programs, in light of what has been learned to date. Let us accept the proposition that AAVE shows continued divergence from other dialects (though not without continuing tendencies to convergence in some areas of phonology and grammar). What are the consequences for the basic problem and for the various strategies outlined above? It is too soon to outline the possibilities in detail. However, some clear conclusions can be drawn, which can be summed up briefly in three ways.

Table 2.2. Residential Segregation of Blacks and Other Ethnic Groups in Philadelphia From 1850 to 1970

			Index of dominance				
	1850	1880	1930	1940	1950	1960	1970
Blacks	11	12	35	45	56	72	74
Irish		34	8			5	3
German		25	11			5	3
Italian			38			23	21
Polish			20			9	8

Source: "A Tale of Three Cities: Blacks, Immigrants, and Opportunity in Philadelphia, 1850-1880, 1930, 1970," by T. Hershberg, Philadelphia: Work, Space, Family and Group Experience in the Nineteenth Century, ed. T. Hershberg, 1981, Table 8, p. x. ©1981 by Oxford University Press. Reprinted by permission.

First, it is clear that the problem of continuing reading failure presented in the first section on the nature of the problem is one that would be predicted by the continued isolation and drift of AAVE in a context of increasing residential segregation. It is not simply that efforts to improve reading have been inadequate, but rather that the material conditions that created the problem have worsened.

Second, the need for a cross-cultural, cross-linguistic program like *Bridge* is even clearer. The problems that were addressed by *Bridge* have become steadily aggravated; the gap between the cultures has increased; and the cognitive problems created by linguistic divergence can only make the acquisition of reading skills more difficult.

Third, the need to develop language arts in the integrated classroom is even more evident. The fundamental finding of the Philadelphia and Texas studies of AAVE is that residential segregation is the primary cause of linguistic divergence. Any pattern of face-to-face interaction between speakers of different dialects—hostile or friendly—leads to a rapid reversal of that trend. A reduction in the basic causes of linguistic divergence can only be brought about by a reorganization of the residential patterns of large cities or a reorganization of the school system that brings speakers of AAVE into contact with speakers of other dialects. This means an integration of black lower-class youth with black middle-class youth as well as an integration of black and white youth.

If such integration can be achieved, to any degree, it is not a solution in itself. Speakers of the AAVE dialect will be at a great disadvantage in a classroom where the underlying assumptions, practices, and curricula are all designed for speakers of other dialects. An integrated classroom will then mean only another form of failure for children from the inner city. A reversal of reading failure is only possible if the curriculum is revised to provide help primarily for those who need it. The principles suggested in the third section deal only with the linguistic side of the matter. There are many oppositions of cultural patterns that concern the use of language in the classroom, patterns for dealing with authority, and cultural definitions of dignity and respect, which create hidden obstacles for the normal majority of African-American children in their dealings with the school system. The linguistic principles must be embedded in a larger perspective that recognizes these children as intelligent and well-adjusted products of their own culture. It is only in such a perspective that the standard language can be presented as an avenue towards educational advancement and the improvement of economic opportunity. Otherwise, it will continue to serve as an additional barrier to social mobility that will ensure further downward movement for black citizens of the United States.

REFERENCES

Alleyne, M. (1971). Acculturation and the cultural matrix of creolization. In D. Hymes (Ed.), *Pidginization and reolizatin of languages* (pp. 169-186). New York: Cambridge University Press.

Ash, S., & Myhill, J. (1986). Linguistic correlates of inter-ethnic contact. In D. Sankoff (Ed.), *Diversity and diachrony* (pp. 33-44). Philadelphia: John Benjamins Publishing.

Bailey, B. (1965). A new perspective on American Negro dialectology. *American Speech, 11,* 171-77.

Bailey, G., & Maynor, N. (1985). The present tense of BE in Southern black folk speech. *American Speech, 60,* 195-213.

Bailey, G., & Maynor, N. (1987). Decreolization? *Language in Society, 16,* 449-473.

Bailey, G., & Maynor, N. (1989). The divergence controversy. *American Speech, 64,* 12-39.

Bailey, G., Maynor, N., & Cukor-Avila, P. (1989). Variation in subject-verb concord in Early Modern English. *Language Variation and Change 1,* 285-301.

Bailey, G., & Ross, G. (1992). The evolution of a vernacular. In M. Rissanen, O. Ihalainen, T. Nevalaiene, & I. Taavitsainen (Eds.), *History of Englishes: New methods and interpretations in historical linguistics* (pp. 519-531). Berlin: Mouton de Gruyter.

Baugh, J. (1983). *Black street speech: Its history, structure and survival.* Austin: University of Texas Press.

Bickerton, D. (1975). *Dynamics of a creole system.* Cambridge: Cambridge University Press.

Clement, J.R.B., & Weikart, D.P. (1984). *Changed lives: The effects of the Perry Preschool Program on youths through age 19.* Ypsilanti, MI: The High/Scope Press.

Dayton, E. (1992). *Stativity: The semantic core of VBE invariant be.* Paper given at the annual meeting of the Linguistic Society of America, December, Philadelphia, PA.

Dillard, J. L. (1971). The West African day-names in Nova Scotia. *Names, 19,* 256-261.

Dillard, J. L. (1972). *Black English.* New York: Random House.

Dillard, J. L. (1973). The history of Black English. *Revista Interamericana/Interamerican Review, 2,* 507-520.

Eckert, P. (1988). Adolescent social structure and the spread of linguistic change. *Language in Society, 17,* 183-208.

Fasold, R. (1972). *Tense marking in Black English.* Arlington, VA: Center for Applied Linguistics.

Graff, D., Labov, W., & Harris, W. A. (1986). Testing listeners' reactions to phonological markers. In D. Sankoff (Ed.), *Diversity and diachrony* (pp. 45-58). Philadelphia: John Benjamins.

Hershberg, T. (1981). A tale of three cities: Blacks, immigrants and opportunity in Philadelphia, 1850-1880, 1930, 1970. In T. Hershberg

(Ed.), *Philadelphia: Work, space, family and group experience in the nineteenth century* (pp. 461-495). New York: Oxford University Press.

Holm, J. (1984). Variability of the copula in Black English and its creole kin. *American Speech, 59,* 291-309.

Kurath, H. (1949). *Word geography of the Eastern United States.* Ann Arbor: University of Michigan Press.

Labov, W. (1966). Some sources of reading problems. In A. Frazier (Ed.), *New directions in elementary English* (pp. 140-167). Champaign, IL: National Council of Teachers of English.

Labov, W. (1972). *Language in the inner city.* Philadelphia: University of Pennsylvania.

Labov, W. (1980). The social origins of sound change. In W. Labov (Ed.), *Locating language in time and space* (pp. 251-266). New York: Academic Press.

Labov, W. (1982). Objectivity and commitment in linguistic science: The case of the Black English trial in Ann Arbor. *Language in Society, 11,* 165-202.

Labov, W., & Ash, S. (in press). The cognitive consequences of linguistic diversity. *Language Variation and Change.*

Labov, W., Cohen, P., Robins, C., & Lewis, J. (1968). *A study of the nonstandard English of Negro and Puerto Rican Speakers in New York City. Cooperative Research Report 3288. Vols I and II.* Philadelphia: U.S. Regional Survey (Linguistics Laboratory, University of Pennsylvania).

Labov, W., & Harris. W.A. (1986). De facto segregation of black and white vernaculars. In D. Sankoff (Ed.), *Diversity and diachrony* (pp. 45-58). Philadelphia: John Benjamins.

Labov, W., Yaeger, M., & Steiner, R. (1972). *A quantitative study of sound change in progress.* Philadelphia, PA: U.S. Regional Survey.

Laferriere, M. (1977). *Consideration of the vowel space in sound change: Boston /æ/.* Paper given at the annual meeting of the Language Society of America, December, Chicago.

Legum, S., Pfaff, C., Tinnie, G., & Nicholas, M. (1972). *The speech of young black children in Los Angeles* (Tech. Publ. 33). Inglewood, CA: Southwest Regional Laboratory.

Mitchell-Kernan, C. (1969). Language behavior in a black urban community. *Monographs of the Language-Behavior Research Laboratory* (No. 2). Berkeley: University of California.

Myhill, J., & Harris, W. A. (1986). The use of the verbal -s inflection in BEV. In D. Sankoff (Ed.), *Diversity and diachrony* (pp. 25-31). Philadelphia, PA: John Benjamins Publishing.

Poplack, S., & Sankoff, D. (1987). The Philadelphia story in the Spanish Caribbean. *American Speech, 62,* 291-314.

Poplack, S., & Tagliamonte, S. (1989). There's no tense like the present: Verbal -s inflection in early Black English. *Language Variation and Change, 1,* 47-84.

Poplack, S, & Tagliamonte, S. (1991). African American English in the diaspora: Evidence from old-line Nova Scotians. *Language Variation and Change, 3,* 301-340.

Rickford, J. R., & McNail-Knox, F. (in press). Addressee- and topic-influenced style shift: A quantitative sociolinguistic study. In D. Biber & E. Finegan (Eds.), *Perspectives on register: Situating register variation within sociolinguistics.*

Rosenthal, R., & Jacobson, L. (1968). *Pygmalion in the classroom.* New York: Holt, Rinehart and Winston.

Seligman, C. R., Tucker, G. R., & Lambert, W. E. (1972). The effects of speech style and other attributes on teachers' attitudes towards pupils. *Language in Society, 1,* 131-142.

Simpkins, G., & Simpkins , C. (1981). Cross-cultural approach to curriculum development. In G. Smitherman (Ed.), *Black English and the education of Black children and youth. Proceedings of the National Invitational Symposium on the KING decision* (pp. 212-240). Detroit: Center for Black Studies, Wayne State University.

Singler, J. (1991). Copula variation in Liberian Settler English and American Black English. In W. F. Edwards & D. Winford (Eds.), *Verb phrase patterns in Black English and Creole* (pp. 129-164). Detroit: Wayne State University Press.

Smitherman, G. (Ed.). (1981). Black English and the education of Black children and youth. *Proceedings of the National Invitational Symposium on the KING decision.* Detroit: Center for Black Studies. Wayne State University.

Spears, A. (1982). The Black English semi-auxiliary come. *Language, 58,* 850-872.

Stewart, W. (1967). Sociolinguistic factors in the history of the American Negro dialects. *Florida FL Reporter, 5,* 1-7. (Reprinted in F. Williams (Ed.). (1970). *Language and poverty: Perspectives on a theme* (pp. 353-362). Chicago: Markham).

Stewart, W. (1968). Continuity and change in American Negro dialects. *Florida FL Reporter, 6,* 3-14. (Reprinted in F. Williams (Ed.). (1970). *Language and poverty: Perspectives on a theme* (pp. 362-376). Chicago: Markham).

Vaughn-Cooke, F. (1986). Lexical diffusion: Evidence from a decreolizing variety of Black English. In M. Montgomery & G. Bailey (Eds.), *Language variety in the South: Perspectives in Black and White* (pp. 111-130). Tuscaloosa , AL: University of Alabama Press.

Veatch, T. (1992). *Racial barriers and phonological merger.* Paper given at NWAVE XXI, October, Ann Arbor, MI.

Wolfram, W. (1969). *A sociolinguistic description of Detroit Negro speech.* Arlington, VA: Center for Applied Linguistics.

3

Commentary
Educating Low-Income Black Children

Dorothy S. Strickland
Rutgers University

The apparent problems of successfully educating poor and low-income black children have for some time been of major concern to American educators—so much so that, for many, these children's school achievement has become a template for the effectiveness of the public school system. It is important to be clear that although the educational problems of "black children" are commonly made the object of study, and data are often aggregated by race, not class, it is in fact the group of black children that experiences the socioeconomic problems accompanying poverty that is most at risk. Middle-class black children living in good neighborhoods do not have significantly more difficulty in school than do middle-class white children; instead, as the socioeconomic circumstances of middle-class blacks have improved, and those of poor blacks have worsened, so the gap between the educational achievement of these two economic groups of blacks has increased.

The largest and most far-reaching curricular reform aimed at disadvantaged children has been the federally funded Title I of the Elementary and Secondary Education Act (ESEA) initiated in 1965 and revised in 1981 as Chapter 1 of the Education Consolidation and Improvement Act (ECIA). Low-income black children became a primary target of this legislation as children from "disadvantaged backgrounds." Nearly three decades after the inception of ESEA the notion of compensatory education remains somewhat ambiguous. It is, however, arguably the most extensive and widely researched effort of its type. Moreover, the issues and problems associated with Title I/Chapter 1 typify those challenging the broader school community. For that reason, I have chosen to focus considerable attention on these reforms in an attempt to provide insight into what will and will not work with low-income black children.

Chapter 1 programs typically employ four basic instructional-organizational strategies. *Pull-out programs* provide instruction in locations outside the regular classroom. These programs have some unintended negative effects such as decreased instructional time due to time spent moving to the location of the compensatory services; fragmentation due to students' inability to make connections between the material covered in the compensatory setting and that of the regular classroom; the stigma attached to students who are pulled out of regular classes, resulting in lowered expectations for these students by the regular teacher; lack of communication and coordination between Chapter 1 instructors and the regular teacher; and segregation as minority students are pulled out of less segregated classrooms to receive Chapter 1 services in more segregated pull-out classrooms. These problems result from the lack of congruency between the regular and compensatory education classes.

Add-on programs provide instruction at times other than the regular school day or year and are most commonly used to provide prekindergarten instruction or to extend the kindergarten day. There appear to be significant, long-term achievement gains among poor minority children in enrichment programs according to Lazar and Darlington (1982), and early childhood programs have been considered the potentially most powerful intervention (Brown, 1978). Summer school, as an add-on program, does not seem to meet its goals of helping low-achieving students make up for academic deficits or to reduce summer losses, as students attending such programs did not differ in advancement from their peers who did not attend, according to a study by Carter (1985).

In-class programs that provide services to students within the regular classrooms, although relatively rare, may in fact be the best solution. Problems associated with time loss due to transportation, stigma, and the resulting lower expectations, fragmentation, and increased segregation could be theoretically solved by shifting compensatory education to the child's regular classroom. Although research is scarce in reference to in-class programs and their effectiveness, there is some evidence provided by Eubanks and Levine (1987) that improved performance by the lowest achievers has been attained through their placement in heterogeneous classes that emphasize individualized and small-group instruction.

Replacement programs that provide all the instruction in a given subject area, usually in a separate class including only compensatory education students, are extremely rare and only one such program has been evaluated. Regardless of the type of instructional organization offered, the need for instructional continuity for the student is crucial.

Reading and mathematics have dominated the content of compensatory education programs for poor black children and have emphasized the mastery of basic or foundational skills. Reading and mathematics are more likely to be targeted for testing than any other subjects and the results reported to the community, in those instances in which results are compared for relative achievement among schools. Unfortunately, Chapter 1 programs tend to rely heavily on programmed instruction and teaching to the tests with resultant higher test scores based on skilled feedback by students of bits and pieces of information. But, this kind of learning may be the least effective in truly enabling students to apply skills independently and purposefully. Although focusing attention on reading and mathematics as foundation skills is crucial to academic achievement, treatment of these areas apart from content of interest and importance to students can render them meaningless and dull.

Aspects of curriculum that have received some research attention are instructional organization, curriculum content, and instructional strategies. Active instruction is identified as a key link to the achievement gains of Chapter 1 students. It is characterized by the teacher's strong personal involvement in instruction in a business-like and task-oriented manner. Active instruction is designed to provide systematically low-income black children with the experiences that many middle income children gain simply by growing up with their parents. Cooperative learning strategies, based on the principles of team sports, reward helpfulness and sharing rather than competition and have been found to be highly effective in improving achievement among black students. Peer tutoring has, among its advantages, flexibility in allowing older children to tutor younger ones, or more advanced students at the same level to tutor their colleagues. Tutors often learn as much as those whom they are tutoring. Peer tutoring is an ideal strategy for heterogeneous student groupings because those who are knowledgeable are tutors for those who need to master the material.

There are several guidelines that help in making instructional decisions in the classroom. First, virtually all children come to school with a viable system of verbal communication which may differ from the school's expectations, but which is complete, not deficient as is so often claimed. Second, competence is not tied to a dialect or language. Users of any dialect differ in their language competence, which is more likely to be affected by the quality of verbal interaction at home, general intelligence, and the range of background experiences than the dialect spoken. Third, teachers need to know something about the language of the children they teach, no matter who they are. Knowing the source of divergence when children make errors in speech or reading will help the teacher know what, if any, corrective measures should be taken. Finally, black children need not have mastery of standard English to any specific degree prior to reading instruction. Many varied experiences listening and responding to literature coupled with the use of predictable stories, chants, and rhymes as beginning reading materials provide these children with a good start.

Although the school cannot rectify all of the social and economic problems associated with the low academic performance of poor black children, it can work towards enlightened policy both within and outside schools. Such an enlightened policy would weigh the effects of economic and academic issues as well as look at a child's functioning in the context of what is happening in his or her family and the family's fit with its surrounding community.

Over the years the focus of educational reform has evolved from the scientific challenge of Sputnik in the 1950s to concern for the failing poor in the 1960s and early 1970s. A return to concern for excellence in the technological world commanded our attention during the 1980s along with an intense interest in those schools that were the least successful. Presently we are emerging from a period in which it was assumed that schools could be changed merely by identifying certain positive attributes and then mandating them, and once again, there is a renewed interest in the problems of schools in which poor children are taught.

Throughout each wave of reform, the school curriculum has received a major share of attention. Looking back, perhaps a period of trial and experimentation was needed to establish what would and would not work. Perhaps also the new interest in the problems of at-risk students will bring about the needed reflection and wisdom as well as the will to generate new initiatives that benefit from what has been learned. It appears clear that any consideration of the kind of curriculum required for poor black children must take both policy and practice into account. School policy must seek to offset the negative impact of the social and economic problems described at the beginning of this discussion so that these children learn, and school practice must be based on a curriculum that allows them to learn.

REFERENCES

Brown, G. (1978). *Found: Long-term gains from early intervention.* Boulder, CO: Westview Press.

Carter, L.F. (1985). The sustaining effects study of compensatory and elementary education. *Educational Researcher, 13,* 4-13.

Eubanks, E.E., & Levine, D.U. (1987). Administrative and organizational arrangements and considerations. In D.S. Strickland & E.J. Cooper (Eds.), *Educating black children: America's challenge* (pp. 19-32). Washington, DC: Bureau of Educational Research, School of Education, Howard University.

Lazar, I., & Darlington, R.B. (1982). Lasting effects of early education: A report from the consortium for longitudinal studies. *Monographs of the Society for Research in Child Development* (47, Serial No. 195).

4

Commentary
Educating Black Youth: A Perspective From Practice

Deidre Farmbry
School District of Philadelphia

As a young, black teacher 20 years ago, assigned to an all black high school, I shared with all of my students the bond of ethnicity; I shared with some of them the bond of having been raised in a lower middle-class household. Despite these similarities, a major difference created a chasm between our worlds—my use of language.

All through childhood, I had been taught that education, with verbal proficiency being a subset, was the great equalizer. Yet, I found myself confronted by students who viewed my speech patterns, word choice, inflection and intonation as *different, foreign, correct, proper,* and most disturbing of all . . . *white.* Although they respected me, my accomplishments, and my earnest desire to help them do well, they persisted in denying me full claim to my proud assertion of being black because I did not talk the same as they did.

This was my first encounter with the relationship between language and self-image. It became clear to me that the preservation of a healthy self-image, particularly for young people groping for a definition of self, must be maintained as a high priority. I agree that the use of instruction that is experience-based is the most appropriate method for engaging students in discovering the value of multiple levels of literacy.

At first, my students adhered tenaciously to their right to the identity they felt their language validated. At the same time, they acknowledged the utility of my language as it facilitated professional, social, and economic mobility. I used this acknowledgment on their part as a wedge to pry them open to accepting the personal challenge of exploring other levels of literacy. I began by revealing that my identity as a teacher was one reason I felt compelled to speak a certain way in their presence, but my other identities—mother, wife, daughter, niece—elicited variations, although some more subtle than others, and to be honest, none too different from the way I spoke in the classroom.

I proceeded in this vein, based on my personal philosophy that one responsibility attendant with assisting students in becoming responsible for their personal growth is to guide them toward an understanding that the identity embraced today or at any given moment may not be the identity of tomorrow. Although I understood and appreciated the sacred relationship between language and identity, I felt compelled to get my students to project their multiple selves in relationship to time and to understand how the difference between the level of literacy one has achieved and the level of literacy one can achieve is the turnstile that enables the appropriate self to rise to the occasion. When it came to language, my students received a clear message: Loyalty to the present is foolish if it obstructs access to the future, and the challenge for students should be to attain a level of literacy high enough to equip them with the freedom and ability to have options.

Educators need to beware of trespassing on speech patterns shared by members of the students' nurturing base, for those early influences will most likely remain key components of self-identity, despite other manifestations that we, as educators, hope will evolve over time. A decade ago, the National Council of Teachers of English (NCTE) passed a resolution echoing this sentiment, which granted students the right to speak and learn in their own language. I adopted the three assumptions undergirding this resolution as my guide for instructional strategies. First, the sharing of experiences and role playing are better routes to flexibility and effectiveness than the emphasis on correctness. Second, grammatical drills seldom teach people to read and write; thus, I was free to abandon such drills and guide students through an examination of their own work and that of their peers. Even though it is true they were still "doing" grammar, it was the grammar of their design to be tailored for a better fit. The third assumption is simplistic and true: students are bombarded with home and neighborhood languages for longer periods of time than they are exposed to the language they encounter at school. While still wrestling with forming my own working philosophy of teaching, I encountered an article written by a black college student, Rachel Jones, who in recounting her own experiences as a bi-dialectical youth, came to understand that the ability to code switch skillfully and rapidly was an art practiced by famous black Americans who manipulate the language at will. She wrote: "Did Martin Luther King say, 'I has been to the mountain top and I done seen the promised land!'?" Enter laughter . . . exit opposition to my strategies. Enter the hope of students willing to try . . . exit the doom of a future bereft of options.

To adopt these philosophies is to adopt a commitment to change. Strickland (this volume) asserts that schools in poor neighborhoods, attended by the majority of black students most in need of literacy development, can make a difference if the principal is active, the teachers are committed, and the school climate is improved. There is a measure of humanism in this belief, for it places the onus for progress on both the student and the school, rather than placing all of the responsibility on students alone who often are too fragile to bear the weight of some of the burdens they bring. I assert, in conjunction with other researchers of a similar mind frame, that the true measure of the success of programs designed to enhance literacy is the degree to which students emerge able to travel the full range of life experiences. But as in most journeys, "home" should remain as a welcome point of return.

I believe in this. I conclude that the major challenge before us is to prepare students for the road while respecting the activity of the home, even if their home is not where your heart is.

Introduction to Part II
Literacy in Home and School Contexts

Emilie V. Siddle-Walker
Emory University

Clifton Collins, the 14-year-old African-American male who shared so freely his reservations, wishes, and disillusionments about English teaching with me (Siddle-Walker, 1992), has become over time my prototypical high school student. His description of "boring" teachers is refreshingly candid, and his unprompted reflective response to English class—that is, his desire to go to sleep—is insightful. Almost two years after our initial meeting, I had the opportunity to see him again. "How is English this year?" I asked. "Don't even ask," he told me with that shake of the head that is familiar in African-American communities as a sign of tolerated disgust. I concluded that Clifton's responses to school-imposed methods of literacy acquisition had not substantially improved.

The comments of this one young male and his self-described experiences, of course, cannot represent the aspirations and/or failures of the numerous other African-American students throughout the United States. However, what Clifton has become for me is research personified; he is the student behind the "studies." Bright, comical, a clear leader in his peer group, he is the one to whom we have attributed genetic deficiency (Jensen, 1969), lack of cultural synchronization (Hale-

Benson, 1986; Irvine, 1990;), low teacher expectations (Irvine, 1990), low student expectations (Ogbu, 1988), inadequate home environments (Scott-Jones, this volume), and peer pressure to shun academic success (Fordham, 1988; Fordham & Ogbu, 1986) as reasons why he, as an African-American student, might be expected to fail to succeed in school. Moreover, as the authors in this volume cite (Slaughter-Defoe & Richards, Scott-Jones), the statistics are voluminous, which suggests that the likelihood of his achieving, relative to the achievement that may be expected of his white peers, is slim.

In important ways, the chapters in this volume are really about Clifton. He is the student about whom the "young emigre, unfamiliar with American education" might read and conclude that there is "little reason .. . to believe that academic success is achievable for most African-American children in the nation's schools" (Gadsden, this volume). Indeed, the authors in the volume explore a range of issues that might help explain the likelihood, or unlikelihood, of the formation of a congruence of forces that would allow students such as Clifton to function as resourceful and economically independent persons in a democratic society.

More specifically, Part II, "Literacy in Home and School Contexts," explores the influence of home and community on academic achievement and thus the literacy acquisition of African-American students in school. The home and community of these children have generally been represented in two ways in the research literature, both oppositional. Either, as Scott-Jones (this volume) indicates, the influences out of school are characterized as strong and nurturing and help provide offspring with needed resources to function in an oppressive environment, or they are depicted as dysfunctional and debilitating—by extension, the primary cause of the failure of these children. In a second dichotomy of characterizations, African-American families and communities are assumed to be either uncaring and unsupportive in their interactions with school (Henderson, Marburger, & Ooms 1988) or, in fact, very caring, but misunderstood by the school systems with whom they need to interact (Chavkin, 1989; Siddle-Walker, 1993). In both representations, the experiences of the community affect the school performance of children.

The experiences of the home and community and the teacher/student/curricular interactions within the school are variables which are inextricably linked (Johnson, 1992). What happens in school influences community perceptions of school, thus creating the "mistrust" that Ogbu (this volume) describes as contributing to a cycle of perceptions that negatively influence each other. All the authors in this section acknowledge the important relationship between community and school in achieving literacy.

However, these authors also undertake the difficult task of untangling some of the school and community influences on schooling. Ogbu (Chapter 4) explores the wider context of achievement in the African-American community and its relationship to other communities, an assessment in which he considers the probable influence of "involuntary minority" status on African-American literacy acquisition. Slaughter-Defoe and Richards (Chapter 5) argue the importance of focusing specifically on African-American males in discussions of literacy and demonstrate through two cases the unlikely success that young males may be expected to experience in school contexts. Scott-Jones (Chapter 6) advocates the need to include adolescents, a developmental group which has been considered little, in discussions about barriers to literacy attainment.

The chapters provide several important contributions to our thinking about home and community contexts for literacy. First, they demonstrate the need to consider diversity, rather than single characterizations (e.g., "poor," "urban," "inner-city," "at-risk"), within the population of African-American students. Slaughter-Defoe and Richard's emphasis on exploring gender differences within the cultural group and Scott-Jones's argument for more attention to the needs of the adolescent (as distinct from the needs of elementary children) encourage academic explorations which include different research areas and concerns. Scott-Jones's further discussion of the ways community is created and sustained in suburban African-American families is another example of the diversity of exploration which is important in the research area, but which is, all too often, ignored as all African-American students are lumped into one category with one or two major "problems" which, if fixed, will solve the difficulties of the whole.

Second, the chapters provide an important range of issues about the likely effects of family and community on the schooling of African-American children. Breaking out of the oppositional ways in which families have been depicted, they collectively assess topics that range from the influence of cultural values on achievement to the question of why some children in some poor families achieve to a naming of aspects of family processes that may influence literacy. Taken together, the chapters allow for an important exploration of likenesses, as well as differences, in the cultural community. They provide a plethora of future research explorations for those considering studies in this area.

Perhaps most strikingly, the chapters issue a challenge. If, as Slaughter-Defoe and Richards argue, literacy with empowerment is the important outcome to be achieved in the schooling of African-American males and others, how can literacy with empowerment be achieved when many African-American children are victims of the attitudes associated with the involuntary minority—attitudes which, according to Ogbu, inhibit the attainment of powerful literacy? Should the responsibility to eradicate such attitudes be the school's? The community's? What are the collective responsibilities of the school to the community and of the community to the school? What is the responsibility of the United States's social and economic structure?

Such questions remain to be answered. Meanwhile, Clifton ends another year in school—oblivious to the research being done about how he can be helped to become a successful African-American male who is valuable both to the community and to the country. For his sake and for the sake of all the nameless other "Cliftons," I hope we succeed in answering the questions these chapters raise.

REFERENCES

Chavkin, N. F. (1989, Summer). Debunking the myth about minority parents. *Educational Horizons, 119*-123.

Fordham, S. (1988). Racelessness as a factor in black students' school success: Pragmatic strategy or pyrrhic victory? *Harvard Educational Review, 58*(1), 54-84.

Fordham, S., & Ogbu, J. (1986). Black students' school success: Coping with the "burden of 'acting white.'" *Urban Review , 18*(3), 176-206.

Hale-Benson, J. E. (1986). *Black children: Their roots, culture, and learning styles* (2nd ed.). Baltimore: Johns Hopkins University Press.

Henderson, A., Marburger, C., & Ooms, T. (1988). *Beyond the bake sale: An educator's guide to working with parents* (2nd ed.). Columbia, MD: National Committee for Citizens in Education.

Irvine, J. J. (1990). *Black students and school failure.* New York: Greenwood Press.

Jensen, A. R. (1969). How much can we boost IQ and scholastic achievement? *Harvard Educational Review, 39*, 1-123.

Johnson, S. T. (1992). Extra-school factors in achievement, attainment, and aspiration among junior and senior high school-age African-American youth. *Journal of Negro Education, 61*(1), 99-119.

Obgu, J. (1988). Cultural diversity and human development. In D. T. Slaughter (Ed.), *Black children and poverty: A developmental perspective* (pp. 11-28). San Francisco: Jossey-Bass.

Siddle-Walker, E. V. (1992). Falling asleep and African-American student failure: Rethinking assumptions about process teaching. *Theory into Practice, 31*, 321-327.

Siddle-Walker, E. V. (1993). The case of Caswell County training school: Relations between community and school. *Harvard Educational Review, 63*, 161-182.

5

Literacy and Black Americans: Comparative Perspectives

John U. Ogbu
University of California-Berkeley

INTRODUCTION

In contemporary urban industrialized societies, education for minority groups continues to be a problem relative to addressing the nature and quality of education, students' progress in school, and performance on achievement tests. Nondominant minority groups are often less advanced educationally in years of school completed and in their performance on measures of achievement, for example, standardized tests of academic achievement and cognitive skills. As a result, they are faced with the challenge of attaining educational parity with the dominant groups in pluralistic, urban industrialized societies. The tendency for children from minority groups in such societies to perform poorly in comparison with the dominant groups is worldwide (Ogbu, 1982d) and has been studied among minorities in Britain, Canada, Israel, Japan, New Zealand, Sweden, the United States, and West Germany.

In the United States, several explanations have been suggested for the educational disparities between the performance of minorities and the majority culture. Some theorists have insisted that the problems derive from a genetic deficit, concluding that minorities do not have the necessary genetic capability or "intelligence" required for qualitative educational performance (Jensen, 1969). Inadequate home environments and early socialization have been attributed by others as the reason that minority children do not perform well on intelligence measures and other standardized indicators of school success (Ramey & Suarez, 1985). According to class analysts, the lower socioeconomic status of the minority groups is responsible for their lack of educational parity (Bond, 1981).

Another pervasive belief is that the educational difficulties of minorities are caused by conflicts arising from differences in their language and culture. The proponents of this theory point out that differences in socially, ethnically, and regionally differentiated groups are demonstrated in the achievement test scores of many minority group populations. In accordance with this perspective, the performance of minority children in education is hampered by the fact that they are required to receive their education in a culture or linguistic learning environment that is unfamiliar to them. Under such circumstances, these children have difficulty acquiring the content and style of learning as presented to them in curricular materials and teaching methods (Philips, 1976).

That the aforementioned factors are sources of difficulty is not in question. Yet, none of these factors can explain the variability that one finds in cross-cultural research on minority education. For instance, those who posit the IQ factor as an explanation have not been able to account for the differences between the performance of black children and white children of similar ability. Or, consider the academic success of black children who are identified as "gifted" during the early elementary school years. Studies show that by the high school years the supposed high ability of these children is no longer reflected in their school performance (Commady, 1987; see also Fordham & Ogbu, 1986). Correlational studies using socioeconomic status (SES) cannot explain why black children from families with annual incomes of $50,000 or more score at the median of white children from homes with median annual incomes of $6,000 or less on SAT math tests (Slade, 1982). The cultural/language difference explanation is not supported by many instances in which minority groups who differ from the dominant group in language and culture do well in school (Ito, 1967; Ogbu, 1988).

Variability in school adjustment and academic performance of minority groups has been documented for the United States (Ogbu, 1974; Woolard, 1981), Great Britain (Ogbu, 1978; Tomlinson, 1982), New Zealand (Penfold, personal communication 1981), Malaysia (Wan Zahid, 1978), and Australia (Bullivant, 1987). In the United States, for example, a comparison of SAT and ACT test scores of minority high school college entrance examinees reveals that over a 5-year period there has been considerable variability in the scores of Blacks, Mexican Americans, American Indians, Asian Americans, and Hispanics. With the exception of Asian Americans, the test scores have fallen consistently below the scores of white students. The scores of Asian Americans, as noted above, have exceeded those of white examinees as well as those of the other minority groups. These data lead us to ask: How do we explain the differences in school adjustment and academic performance among the different minority groups, in particular, the literacy development and school success of black Americans?

PREREQUISITES FOR UNDERSTANDING WHY BLACK AMERICANS AND MINORITIES LAG IN THE ACQUISITION OF LITERACY

Black Americans are not just another minority group. They belong to a particular type of minority group. In this chapter, we suggest that a first step toward understanding the relative success or failure of minority groups in social adjustment and academic performance in school is to recognize that there are different types of minorities who experience and respond to schooling differently. For the purpose of this chapter, we classify minority groups into three types: autonomous, immigrant, and involuntary or castelike minorities.

Autonomous minorities, such as Jews and Mormons in the United States, are minorities primarily in a numerical sense. They may be victims of prejudice and pillory, but not of stratification. They usually have a cultural frame of reference that demonstrates and encourages academic success. Autonomous minorities are not the subject of this chapter.

Immigrant minorities are people who have moved voluntarily to the United States or to any other society, because they believe that such a move will result in improved economic well-being, better overall opportunities, and/or greater political freedom. The way the immigrants perceive and respond to their treatment by white Americans and institutions, such as schools controlled by whites, is influenced by the expectations the immigrants bring to the United States. The immigrants usually experience initial problems of adjustment in school, but they are not characterized by persistent problems of adjustment and low academic performance. The Chinese in Stockton, CA (Ogbu, 1974) and the Punjabi Indians in Valleyside, CA (Gibson, 1988) are examples of immigrant minorities.

The third type, involuntary minorities or castelike minorities, are people who did not initially choose to become members of American society. Rather, they were brought into U.S. society through slavery, conquest, or colonization. American Indians, Black Americans, Mexican Americans in the Southwestern United States, and Native Hawaiians are examples of involuntary minorities. Involuntary minorities exist in Japan, namely the Burakumin and Japanese Koreans. Involuntary minorities do not have the expectations of a better future that characterize the immigrants. On the contrary, they resent the loss of their personal freedom and interpret the social, political, and economic barriers against them as undeserved oppression. For them the future is grim with a struggle (Shack, 1970). This perspective influences the way involuntary minorities respond to white Americans and the societal institutions controlled by whites. In general, it is involuntary minorities who experience persistent problems in school adjustment and academic performance. The initial terms of incorporation of a minority group into American society or any other society affect the group members' understanding of their universe, that is, their "social reality" or their cultural model. This understanding affects both their general adaptation to minority status and their adaptation to schooling.

A second prerequisite is to recognize that the different types of minorities are characterized by different types of cultural and language differences. For example, black American cultural and language differences vis-á-vis white American mainstream culture and language are of a different order or type than the cultural and language differences of West Indian immigrants or Chinese immigrants vis-á-vis white American mainstream culture and language. The immigrants are characterized by primary cultural differences; involuntary minorities have secondary cultural differences.

Primary cultural differences are differences that existed before a group became a minority, that is, they existed before immigrants from China, India, or Latin America arrived in the United States. For example, before the Punjabi Indians in Valleyside, CA, arrived in the United States, they spoke Punjabi; they practiced Sikh, Hindu, or Moslem religion; they had arranged marriages; and the males wore turbans. The Punjabis also brought to America their own way of raising children. For example, they differ from white Americans in training children to make decisions and to manage money (Gibson, 1988). The Punjabis continue to adhere to these beliefs and practices in America. But, they also recognize the need to learn English or American language and other aspects of American culture that they think will help them achieve the goals of their emigration. They interpret the cultural/language differences they encounter in school and the workplace as barriers to overcome in order to achieve their goals.

Immigrants' perceptions and interpretations of their behavior in the area of cultural and language learning are similar to the perceptions and interpretations of Americans taking Spanish or French lessons when preparing for a vacation abroad. An American who is planning a vacation to Paris or another foreign country, but who has not yet learned the language of the country to be visited, realizes that in order to enjoy the vacation, he or she should study French or Spanish. The prospective tourist usually embarks on learning French or Spanish, and in the course of doing so, does not interpret the learning of the language as a threat to his or her cultural or language identity. The learner believes him- or herself merely to be acquiring a second language or an additional language to achieve a specific goal—to enjoy a forthcoming vacation. Similarly, the immigrant arrives in the United States with previously learned cultural values and acquired cultural ways of behaving and communicating, that is, he or she arrives with a different cultural frame of reference. Because the immigrant interprets previously learned cultural differences of the "homeland" as barriers to be overcome, he or she recognizes the need to learn aspects of the mainstream American culture in order to participate in the new society, that is, the necessity to participate in the cultural frame of reference of the dominant group or white Americans, without perceiving such participation as a threat to his or her own minority culture or language.

Secondary cultural differences, which characterize involuntary minorities, are different. These are differences that arise after a group has become a minority, such as after blacks were brought to America as slaves, or after an American Indian tribe was conquered, moved, and placed on a "reservation." This type of cultural difference is thus the product of a contact situation, one that involves the subordination of one group by another. At the beginning of the contact the dominant group and the minority are characterized by primary cultural differences. But, subsequently, the minorities develop new cultural features and reinterpret old ones in order to cope with their domination or oppression. Blacks, for instance, spoke numerous African languages and practiced a variety of primary African cultural patterns at the time of their arrival in America as chattels of dominant whites. However, due to the subordination and oppressive conditions of slavery, the indigenous languages and cultural patterns eventually were lost and replaced by new cultural forms.

These new cultural forms (including language), behaviors, and meanings become the minorities' cultural frame of reference or ideal way to guide behaviors. As a result, the minorities come to understand that there is a "white way" and an "Indian way, a "white way" and a "black way," or a "white way of talking" and a "black way of talking." Moreover, the minorities feel strongly that their way of talking, walking, or believing is an expression of their group identity.

The minorities who are bearers of secondary cultural differences do not interpret the cultural differences as barriers to be overcome. Rather, they see the differences as markers of group identity to be maintained. The cultural/language differences have become a part of a boundary-maintaining mechanism between white Americans and minorities. Unlike the immigrants, involuntary minorities may, perhaps unconsciously, perceive learning or speaking standard English and practicing other aspects of white middle-class culture as threatening to their own minority culture, language, and identity. Consequently, those who try to cross cultural boundaries may experience social or psychological pressures not to do so.

A third prerequisite is to recognize that voluntary or immigrant minorities and involuntary or castelike minorities interpret and respond to instrumental barriers, such as employment barriers, differently—a difference of no small significance for schooling. The difference between the two groups arises in part from the fact that voluntary minorities have a positive dual frame of status comparison; whereas involuntary minorities have a negative dual status frame of comparison. The immigrants tend to compare their situation in the United States with that of their former selves or with that of their peers "back home." When they make such comparisons, they find encouraging evidence to believe that they have more and better opportunities in the United States for themselves or for their children. Involuntary minorities, such as Mexican Americans or black Americans, do not have a "homeland" situation to compare with their situation in the United States. Consequently, they do not interpret their menial jobs and low wages as "better."

The immigrants may more easily perform tasks that could be considered status dystonic because they are strangers in a new world and not "at home." They lose no status because they are not around their peers "back home." For example, many black Americans find it very difficult to use the term "Sir" to address a white American male because they perceive that doing so is to concede continued servility and subordinate status. Immigrants, on the other hand, who have had no previous contact experience of status domination and subordination in America, consider such linguistic symbolism as a gesture of politeness and respect.

Instead, American Indians and blacks, for example, and other similar minorities compare their present status with that of their white peers, and when they make such comparisons, they usually conclude that they are worse off than they should be. They attribute this lack of access primarily to the discrimination and racism waged against them by the dominant group and to their subordinate minority status. Involuntary minorities also do not interpret their situation as a temporary one as the immigrants do. Quite the contrary, after having experienced discrimination over many years and generations, the involuntary minorities tend to interpret such discrimination against them as more or less permanent and institutionalized.

The immigrants differ from involuntary minorities by their folk theories of getting ahead in America, which affect their perceptions of and response to schooling. The immigrants appear to interpret, as noted already, the social, economic, and political barriers they encounter as more or less temporary problems or as problems they will overcome or can overcome with the passage of time, with hard work, or with better education. Furthermore, the immigrants may interpret their exclusion from better jobs as "understandable," given the fact that they are "foreigners," that they do not speak the English language well, or that they were not educated in the United States. Given the instrumental goals that motivated their emigration, the immigrants tend to adopt what appears to be the white mainstream folk theory of getting ahead, and they behave accordingly in the face of discrimination and other barriers.

In their own folk theories of getting ahead in America, involuntary minorities often desire to accomplish this through education and ability in the same way that their white peers do, but until recently they faced many barriers to their progress. It also seems that in the course of many generations of barriers to opportunity structures, they came to realize that advancement in this society requires more than education and more than individual effort and hard work to overcome the barriers to upward mobility. Involuntary minorities developed a folk theory of getting ahead that differs significantly from white middle-class American folk theory. Blacks, for example, developed a parallel culture in response to various forms of discrimination, slavery, and ghettoization. The parallel culture consisted of traits from the original African culture patterns and new traits acquired from contacts with Europeans and assisted in the survival of blacks in response to their isolation (Slade, 1982). The folk theory of involuntary minorities stresses collective effort as providing the best chances for overcoming barriers to get ahead.

Because involuntary minorities have no confidence that the societal rules for self-advancement work for them as they do for white Americans, they try to change the rules, in contrast to the immigrants who try to follow the rules. For example, involuntary minorities may try to change the criteria for school credentialing and for employment. They also develop "survival strategies," including "collective struggle" or civil rights activities and clientship to cope with the lack of opportunities and other perceived forms of domination or exploitation. Regardless of their intent to overcome and eliminate barriers to advancement and opportunity structure, ironically such collective strategies increase the chances of claiming "racism" for obstacles whether the racism is real or imagined.

The last prerequisites to be discussed are differences between immigrant and involuntary minorities in the degree of trust they hold for white Americans and societal institutions such as the public schools that the latter control. The issue of trust is important because it is difficult to acquire literacy or to learn other knowledge from people and institutions when there is no trust. The immigrants appear to acquiesce and to rationalize the prejudice and discrimination against them as described in previous sections of this chapter. Involuntary minorities distrust white Americans and their institutions to a greater extent than immigrants. In fact, some involuntary minorities, such as blacks, have experienced many events in their history that have led to their distrust of white Americans and their institutions. Unlike the immigrants, involuntary minorities find no justification for the prejudice and discrimination against them other than the fact that they are members of nonwhite minority groups. Furthermore, unlike the immigrants, involuntary minorities have come to interpret the prejudice and discrimination against them as institutionalized and enduring.

Many who study literacy and numeracy problems among black children and similar minorities focus on what goes on within and across schools, classrooms, or families. The assumption of this chapter is that in order to understand the proportion and persistence of the literacy problems of blacks and similar minorities, we must go beyond the events and situations in the school, the classroom, and the home and examine the historical and structural contexts in which these events and situations occur. More specifically, we must consider the nature and implications of the initial terms of incorporation of minorities into American society, their subsequent treatment by white Americans, and the minorities' collective interpretations of and responses to these events in their history. By doing so, we gain a better understanding of their case by comparing them with voluntary minorities.

To summarize, immigrant minorities and involuntary minorities differ not only in their initial terms of incorporation into American society, but also in reference group comparisons. These differences are embedded in the present status and future possibilities in folk theory of getting ahead, especially through education; in collective identity; and in cultural frames of reference for judging appropriate behavior and affirmation of group membership and solidarity. The groups also differ in the degree to which they trust white Americans and the institutions, such as schools, controlled by whites. These distinguishing beliefs and practices affect the knowledge, attitudes, and behaviors that minority children bring to school. Thus, children interact with school factors that influence their social adjustment and academic performance. We call the school factors "the first half of the problem." "The second half," or "community forces," consists of the cultural knowledge, attitudes, and practices that minority children bring to school. In the remainder of this chapter, we summarize the first half of the problem—the school factors—and examine the "community forces," or the second half. We focus on the community forces because we want to explain why some minority groups perform relatively better in school than other minority groups, in spite of facing similar cultural, language, economic, and other barriers.

SOCIETAL AND SCHOOL FACTORS

Before 1960 most societies did not provide their minorities with equal educational opportunity (Ogbu, 1978). Even now, minorities do not necessarily have equal educational opportunity, partly because of vestiges of past discriminatory educational policies and practices. Although in some instances significant improvements have been made and efforts are being made to equalize the education of minorities with the education of the dominant group, many traditionally or historically negative features of minority education persist in various countries throughout the world.

There are three ways in which minorities are denied equal educational opportunity. One is the denial to equal access to desirable jobs and positions in adult life. This was the experience of generations of black Americans denied equal opportunity in the job market through job ceilings (Ogbu, 1978). Blacks who qualified educationally were not given the opportunity, as their white peers were, to use their education meaningfully and were not rewarded with jobs and wages commensurate with their training and ability. Other American minorities have also had similar experiences (Ogbu, 1978). By denying minorities the opportunity to enter the labor market and advance according to their educational qualifications and abilities, and by denying them adequate rewards for their educational efforts in terms of wages, American society probably discouraged minorities from investing time and effort into the pursuit of education and into increasing their educational accomplishments. The experiences also appear to have discouraged minorities from developing a strong tradition of striving for academic achievement.

A second way is to deny minorities equal access to good education. Before 1960 blacks were channeled into inferior education by formal statutes in the South and by informal practices in the North. Their schools were characterized by inadequately trained and overworked teachers, different and inferior curriculum, inadequate funding, and poor and limited facilities and services. In the South, the school terms of blacks were shorter than the school terms of whites. Although formal aspects of unequal educational opportunity have been abolished by law, recent desegregation cases continue to reveal that minority and majority education in the United States are not equal. Inferior education ensures that blacks and other minorities do not qualify at the equivalent rate of whites for desirable jobs and other positions in adult life which require good education and in which education pays off. More importantly, minority children receiving inferior education cannot learn as much or test as well as white children who have access to superior education.

A third way is to lower expectations and limit support within classroom settings. Minority children also receive inferior education through what goes on inside the schools and classrooms themselves. Among the mechanisms that have been found to affect minority education adversely are lowered teacher expectations and the labeling of minority children as having educational "handicaps." Because of this a disproportionate number of minority children are channeled into special education and other forms of student containment or custodianship. There are also problems that arise from cultural and language differences that may not be attended to adequately. For example, the failure of school personnel to understand the cultural behaviors of minority children often results in conflicts that affect children's adjustment and learning. We should add, however, that minority children have an obligation to understand and relate to the culture and language of the school in order to adjust well in school and in mainstream society; the interaction must be reciprocal.

COMMUNITY FORCES

The complex and interlocking forces which affect the social adjustment and academic performance of black American and other minority children are not limited to those of the wider society or the school and the classroom. They also include those from the minority communities themselves. These "community forces" are different for immigrant and involuntary minorities, and they interact differently with school factors and achieve different educational results. We discuss the influence of the community forces under three classes: instrumental, symbolic, and relational. We first consider why the community forces promote school adjustment and academic success among the immigrants; then we show why the instrumental, symbolic, and relational classes function differently among involuntary minorities.

The Immigrants

Instrumental factors which encourage striving in school are derived often from immigrants' dual status mobility frame of reference, and their folk theory of getting ahead in America. These factors stress the importance of school success, of adopting appropriate academic attitudes, and of working hard and persevering at academic tasks in order to achieve school credentials for desired future jobs and other immigration goals. As we have already noted, the immigrants tend to believe that they have more and better opportunities to succeed in the United States than in their countries of origin and, indeed, they may have come to the United States precisely to give their children an "American education" so that the latter can get ahead in the United States or "back home," if they choose to return to their homeland. Immigrant parents, therefore, stress education for their children and take steps to ensure that their children behave in a manner conducive to school success. For their part, the children—whether they are Chinese, Central or South American Latinos, Cubans, Koreans, Punjabi Indians, or West Indians—appear to share their parents' attitudes toward "American education," to take their schoolwork seriously, to work hard, and to persevere. Immigrant minority parents usually do not want their children to regard them as role models because the parents want their children to be different and to succeed according to the mainstream system of status mobility; nor do the children want to be like their parents, who are often employed in menial jobs (see Gibson, 1987, 1988; Suarez-Orozco, 1987, 1989).

Symbolic factors also promote striving in school and success among the immigrants. The fact that the social identity and cultural frame of reference of the immigrants are different but not necessarily ambivalent or oppositional facilitates their ability to cross cultural and language boundaries in the school context. It also enables the immigrants to distinguish what they have to learn in order to achieve the goals of their immigration, such as the English language and expected school behaviors and attitudes, from other aspects of white American culture that may threaten their own minority culture, language, and identity. We have already pointed out that immigrants perceive and interpret the language and cultural features necessary for school success—the language and cultural differences they encounter in school—as barriers to be overcome in order to achieve their long-range goals of future employment, economic well-being, and other benefits. The immigrants do not go to school expecting the school to teach them in their native language and culture. Instead, they expect and are willing to learn the English language and standard school behaviors and attitudes. We are not suggesting that immigrant minority children do not experience language and cultural difficulties. The point is that the children, their parents, and their communities perceive language and cultural conflicts as problems they have to overcome with appropriate school programs as well as their own effort and perseverance.

The relational factor which promotes school success among the immigrants has to do with their acquiescence and trust with respect to the schools and school personnel. There appear to be three reasons for the acquiescing and trusting relationship. One is that the immigrants often consider the schools in the United States to be better than the schools of their homeland. Their comparative frame of reference is the school they left behind, not the school in American white suburbs. Another reason is that the immigrants think that they are treated better by public school personnel in the United States than by the school personnel of their homeland. Immigrant parents often speak favorably of the public schools in the United States; they do not have to pay school fees and their children are given free textbooks and supplies (Suarez-Orozco, 1987, 1989). A third reason is that the immigrants tend to rationalize the discrimination and prejudice against them in a way that does not discourage striving for academic success. Punjabi parents, for example, impress upon their children that as "strangers" or "foreigners" they may have to tolerate prejudice as the price to pay in order to achieve their immigration goals; they hold the children responsible for doing well in school (Gibson, 1988). The overall impression gained from ethnographic studies is that immigrant minority parents teach their children to acquiesce or trust their relationship with schools and school personnel. They teach them to accept and follow school rules and standard behaviors or standard practices for good social adjustment and academic success. It appears that immigrant minority children, more or less, do so.

Involuntary Minorities

The instrumental factors do not appear to function for involuntary minorities such as black Americans, Native Americans, and Mexican Americans in the same way that they function for voluntary minorities. In the first place, the dual-status mobility framework has been influenced by years of experience with discrimination and inequality of opportunity in the labor market and in the quality of education. On the one hand, while the folk theory of the group for getting ahead stresses the importance of education, studies show that quality-controlled returns to years of schooling differ considerably for involuntary minorities and whites (Slaughter-Defoe & Richards, this volume). In fact, for involuntary minorities, the attainment of education has often had an inverse effect on their economic position. For example, the literature on occupational income data suggest that the more years of schooling that a black person has, the more discrimination he or she encounters in the labor market (Berlin & Sum, 1988). Such data show that for most education levels, blacks earn lower returns than whites at the same level, lending support to the suggestion that differences in the occupational, unemployment, and income data of blacks relative to whites can be accounted for in terms relative to discrimination.

Although it must be recognized that there are regional, political, and social class differences among involuntary minorities and within each minority group, such experiences have not tended to support the norm of placing value on education as the means to achieve success among involuntary minorities. Because voluntary minorities have had no such long-term inverse experiences in their new homeland, such experiences can have little or no effect on their dual-status mobility frame of comparison. Involuntary minorities, on the other hand, do not have a former "self" or peers back home with whom to compare their present status, those links having long ago been lost. As such, many often compare themselves to the white middle class, a process that facilitates the development of an inverse dual-status mobility frame of comparison brought about by experiencing the barriers and inequality that exist against them in America and not "back home" as in the case of the voluntary minorities. Thus, for many sectors of involuntary minorities, such inverse relationship experiences among education, employment, and income appear to have enhanced the development of an ambiguous role for education as the means for shaping their advancement in society (Ogbu, 1982).

The folk theory of involuntary minorities for getting ahead stresses the importance of education, but this verbal endorsement is frequently not accompanied by the necessary effort. This is probably because involuntary minorities historically were not rewarded adequately for their educational achievement in terms of jobs, wages, and social recognition. Such experiences have often promoted the development of survival strategies that are incongruent with strategies required for school success. Researchers have pointed out that although the parallel culture developed by black Americans has been effective in social relations, this culturally specific strategy differs from the one that is required for success in the typical educational setting (see Slade, 1982). Furthermore, minorities may come to see the inadequate and unequal reward of education as part of an institutionalized discrimination against them that is not entirely eliminated by an education (Ogbu, 1982). The folk theory of many involuntary minorities stresses the use of means other than schooling to get ahead under such circumstances. These alternative or survival strategies appear to affect the pursuit of education adversely. For example, there is a tendency for many involuntary minority youth to divert their time and efforts from schooling into nonacademic activities such as sports and entertainment.

Symbolic factors often do not encourage striving for school success among many involuntary minorities. As noted before, many of the cultural and language differences they take to school and use in society are seen as markers of group identity to be maintained, not as barriers to be overcome. They also appear to think that learning certain aspects of white culture or behaving according to a white cultural frame of reference in certain domains is detrimental to their own minority culture, language, and identity. What further complicates these perceptions and interpretations is that many involuntary minorities, unlike immigrants, do not usually make a clear distinction between what they have to learn and do in order to enhance their school success, such as learning to use standard English and the standard behavior practices of the school, and the white cultural frame of reference. Frequently, some members of the involuntary minority groups who are themselves educators complain that the school curriculum and the school language of instruction are "white."

Such a rejection of the dominant group's cultural frame of reference must be considered from the historical context out of which it developed, that is, the aversion and treatment accorded the nondominant groups by the dominant group. Such social aversion led involuntary minorities to develop a cultural frame of reference that is in opposition to the white cultural frame of reference. However, equating standard English, the school curriculum, and the standard rules of school behavior with white American culture can lead to conscious or unconscious opposition or ambivalence toward learning and using these essential tools at school. Some involuntary minority students who adopt the attitudes and behaviors conducive to school success, those who speak standard English and behave according to standard rules of school conduct and practices, are often accused by their peers of "acting white" or, in the case of black students, of being "Uncle Toms" (Fordham & Ogbu, 1986; Petroni, 1970). They are often accused of being disloyal to the cause of their group, and they risk being isolated from their peers.

Even in the absence of peer pressures, as DeVos (1967) has observed, many involuntary minority students appear to avoid adopting serious academic attitudes and persevering efforts in their schoolwork, partly because they have usually internalized their groups' beliefs that attitudes and behaviors are "white," and partly because they are not certain that they would be accepted by whites if they succeeded in learning to "act white" and subsequently lost the support of their own groups. This state of affairs results in "affective dissonance" (DeVos, 1984) for individual minority students.

DeVos (1967) also suggests that the lack of serious effort in academic performance can be attributed to an involuntary minority group's perception of the group's performance abilities in relation to socially acceptable activities. If there is a widespread perception among group members of low-level academic ability or performance capability in some skill area, for example, the acceptance of this belief can affect the amount of effort individuals of the group put into activities in the skill area, resulting in a less than optimal effort. Many involuntary minority students such as black students, for example, often avoid taking advanced-level science, math, and foreign language courses because they often do not see other black students in such classes. This situation has given rise, in many areas of the United States, to a misconception among many black students that advanced-level mathematics, science, and foreign language courses are too difficult for black students and should be avoided. Often the myth is perpetuated from generation to generation by many involuntary minority parents who themselves had similar experiences. From this perspective, it can be seen that the lack of serious effort in such academic courses by involuntary minority students can result from a collective group perception of low esteem and low-level group performance and can serve as a catalyst for low-level individual as well as low-level group performance and achievement rates and expectations in such courses. Additionally, such a misconception can be reciprocal in that the misconception may be known and accepted by those who are not members of the involuntary minority group, such as educators who may consciously or unconsciously lower their expectations of performance of involuntary minority students in such academic courses.

Petroni (1970) is correct in stating that older involuntary minority students face a dilemma in schooling: They have to choose between academic success and maintaining their minority identity and cultural frame of reference, a choice that does not appear to arise for immigrants and for white students. Under the circumstances, many involuntary minority students who want to achieve academic success are compelled to adopt strategies that shield them from peer criticisms and ostracism (Ogbu, 1989).

The relationship among involuntary minorities, the public schools, and those who control the schools is no help in promoting academic success among the minorities. For example, the notion of replacing a Eurocentric curriculum in the schools with an Afrocentric or culturally diverse curriculum for the benefit of the education of African-American children as well as other minorities emanates from the involuntary minorities' distrust of the public schools and their personnel, and from the belief of the proponents of Afro-centric education and cultural diversity that the traditional mainstream American educational process has been dysfunctional for minority children. These proponents point out that the high rate of poor achievement and low performance among many minority children is reflective of the attitudes of many of the adults in the black community who are consciously or unconsciously rejecting traditional routes to achieve upward mobility; they perceive the traditional system to be alien to their cultural frame of reference. Adult members have turned to alternative survival strategies to achieve their economic goals because they do not trust the system as the means to arrive at their goals. So it appears that many may have transferred such perceptions of distrust to their children who do not strive for high academic achievement in school.

Moreover, minorities compare the schools in their neighborhoods to those in the affluent white suburbs and conclude that the education provided to their own children is inferior to that provided to the children of the dominant group. Where the schools are integrated, the minorities have noted that there is often a tracking system within the schools and classrooms. They believe that a disproportionate number of their children have been designated as "high risk" or "mentally retarded" and that these practices promote the acceptance of low levels of achievement and low-level goals, such as minimum competencies instead of excellence and positive ethnic identity. Because they do not trust the schools, many minority parents and adults in the community are skeptical that the schools can provide their children with good educations. The adult perception is communicated to the children through family and community discourse and public debates about specific issues relating to education. Black and Mexican-American students in Stockton, CA expressed skepticism about what they were taught in school, and they questioned the "relevance" of a high school history textbook, The Land of the Free, to their indigenous experiences (Ogbu, 1977).

CONCLUSION

Throughout this chapter we suggest that immigrant minorities are relatively more successful in school than involuntary minorities because the status of the former as voluntary minorities generates for them certain community features that enhance the attitudes and behaviors conducive to literacy development and school success. This does not mean that all immigrant minority students succeed and all involuntary minority students do not succeed in school. What has been described are what appear to be the dominant patterns of academic adaptation for the two types of minorities. Within each type, there are several culturally available strategies that enhance school success. But the two types of minorities differ in the degree of support, especially peer support, for individuals utilizing the strategies that enhance literacy and school success.

REFERENCES

Berlin, G., & Sum, A. (1988). *Toward a more perfect union: Basic skills, poor families, and our economic future.* New York: Ford Foundation.

Bond, G. C. (1981). Social economic status and educational achievement: A review article. *Anthropology and Education Quarterly, 12,* 227-257.

Bullivant, B. M. (1987). *The ethnic encounter in the secondary ethnocultural reproduction and resistance: Theory and case studies.* London: Falmer Press.

Commady, R. (1987). *Underachievement in Black gifted adolescents: An exploratory study.* Special project, School of Education, University of California, Berkeley.

DeVos, G. A. (1967). Essential elements of caste: Psychological determinants in structural theory. In G. A. DeVos & H. Wagatsuma (Eds.), *Japan's invisible race: Caste in culture and personality* (pp. 332-384). Berkeley: University of California Press.

DeVos, G. A. (1984). *Ethnic persistence and role desegregation: An illustration from Japan.* Unpublished manuscript, Department of Anthropology, University of California, Berkeley.

Fordham, S., & Ogbu, J. U. (1986). Black school success: Coping with the burden of "acting White." *The Urban Review, 28,* 176-208.

Gibson, M. A. (1987). The school performance of immigrant minorities; A comparative view. *Anthropology and Education Quarterly, 18,* 262-275.

Gibson, M. A. (1988). *Accommodation without assimilation: L Punjabi sikhs in an American high school and community.* Ithaca, NY: Cornell University Press.

Ito, H. (1967). Japan's outcasts in the United States. In G. A. DeVos & H. Wagatsuma (Eds.), *Japan's invisible race* (pp. 200-221). Berkeley: University of California Press.

Jensen, A. R. (1969). How much can we boost IQ and scholastic achievement? *Harvard Educational Review, 39,* 1-123.

Ogbu, J. U. (1974). *The next generation: An ethnography of education in an urban neighborhood.* New York: Academic Press.

Ogbu, J. U. (1977). *Racial stratification and education: The case of Stockton, California.* ICRD Bulletin, 12, 1-26.

Ogbu, J. U. (1978). *Minority education and caste: The American system in cross-cultural perspective.* New York: Academic Press.

Ogbu, J. U. (1982). Cultural discontinuities and schooling. *Anthropology and Education Quarterly, 13,* 290-307.

Ogbu, J. U. (1987). Variability in minority school performance: A problem in search of an explanation. *Anthropology and Education Quarterly, 18,* 312-334.

Ogbu, J. U. (1988). Diversity and equity in public education: Community forces and minority school adjustment and performance. In R. Haskins & D. McRae (Eds.), *Policies for America's public schools: Teachers, equity and indicators* (pp. 127-170). Norwood, NJ: Ablex.

Ogbu, J.U. (1989). The individual in collective adaptation. In L. Weis (Ed.), *Dropouts from schools; Issues, dilemmas and solutions*. Buffalo: State University of New York Press.

Petroni, F.A. (1970). Uncle Toms: White stereotypes in the Black movement. *Human Organization, 28*, 260-266.

Philips, S.U. (1976). Commentary: Access to power and maintenance of ethnic identity as goals of multi-cultural education. *Anthropology and Education Quarterly, 7*, 30-32.

Ramey, C.T., & Suarez, T. M. (1985). Early intervention and the early experience paradigm: Toward a better framework for social policy. *Journal of Children in Contemporary Society, 7*, 3-13.

Shack, W. A. (1970). *On Black American values in white America: Some perspectives on the cultural aspects of learning behavior and compensatory education*. Paper prepared for the Social Science Research Council, Subcommittee on Values and Compendatory Education, 1970-1971.

Slade, B.J. (1982). Afro-American cognitive style: A variable in school success. *Review of Education Research, 52*, 214-244.

Suarez-Orozco, M. M. (1987). Becoming somebody: Central American immigrants in U. S. inner-city schools. *Anthropology and Education Quarterly, 18*, 287-299.

Suarez-Orozco, M. M. (1989). *Central American refugees and U. S. high schools: A psychosocial study of motivation and achievement*. Stanford, CA: Stanford University Press.

Tomlinson, S. (1982). *Sociology of special education*. London: Routledge and Kegan Paul.

Wan Zahid, N. M. (1978) *The Malay Problem: A case study on the correlates of the education achievement of the Malays*. Unpublished doctoral dissertation, University of California, Berkeley.

Woolard, K.A. (1981). *Ethnicity in education: Some problems of language and identity in Spain and the United States*. Unpublished manuscript, Department of Anthropology, University of California, Berkeley.

6

Families, Communities, and Schools as Contexts for Literacy and Learning

Diane Scott-Jones
Temple University

INTRODUCTION

How do individuals acquire the skills necessary for successful adult functioning in a technologically advanced society? This difficult question becomes exceedingly complex in the case of African-American youth, who must achieve high levels of literacy in a society in which African Americans are a subordinate or castelike minority, experiencing disproportionate levels of poverty and related social maladies. In spite of a long history of working to improve education, African Americans as a group currently present a mixed picture of educational accomplishment and educational failure.

The educational achievement of African Americans and other minorities is of grave concern to the entire society, given the recent growth of minority populations. In 1986, minorities were almost 30% of the public school population (Baker & Ogle, 1989). Projections based on fertility and immigration trends indicate that, by the year 2030, approximately one-third of the population in the United States will be African

American, Hispanic, and Asian (Select Committee on Children, Youth, and Families, 1985). Although the increase in minorities in the last decade is accounted for mainly by Hispanic and Asian populations, African Americans remain the largest minority group. If African Americans, or any large segment of the United States' population, are poorly educated, the society as a whole cannot prosper. The amelioration of educational problems experienced by African Americans, and the consolidation of African Americans' educational achievements, must be high on the national agenda.

Plans for enhancing the academic achievement of African-American youth require close attention to the specifics of formal education: curriculum, instructional materials, teacher training, standardized tests, and structural arrangements such as tracking. Also critical is the broader social context in which the developing individual obtains a formal education. Families and communities, in addition to schools, are important contexts in which individuals grow and develop. These three developmental contexts—families, communities, and schools—are interconnected and embedded in the larger economic, institutional, and ideological patterns of society (for extended discussion, see Bronfenbrenner, 1979, 1986; Epstein, 1987, 1990; Epstein & Scott-Jones, in preparation).

The impact of the multiple influences of family, community, and school changes during the course of an individual's development (Scott-Jones, 1988). In addition, diversity exists within African-American families and communities (Scott-Jones & Nelson-LeGall, 1986). Therefore, a *developmental* and *differentiated* approach is necessary to understand the conjoint influences of family, community, and school on the literacy development and educational achievement of African-American youth.

Research and practice, however, have focused on the preschool period in efforts to improve educational opportunity and literacy development among African Americans. Head Start and other comprehensive early intervention programs for predominantly low-income African-American children, families, and communities have resulted in many positive outcomes (Lazar & Darlington, 1982; Levenstein, 1988; Scott-Jones, 1992; Slaughter, 1983; Slaughter, Washington, Oyemade, & Lindsey, 1988; Washington & Oyemade, 1987). In follow-up studies of program participants who had reached adolescence, the lasting positive effects of the intervention were reduced retention in grade and reduced enrollment in special education programs. Program participants, however, did not maintain their gains on measures such as standardized reading achievement test scores (Lazar & Darlington, 1982).

The latter outcome is very likely due to the paucity of intervention programs for older school-aged children (Ramey, 1982). Many early intervention programs were guided by strong assumptions regarding the existence of early critical periods in development. A common belief was that intelligence grew very rapidly until children reached 4 to 6 years of age and remained relatively stable during the remainder of the lifespan (e.g., Bloom, 1964). Successful interventions early in life, it was believed, were irreversible; the interventions "inoculated" the individual against later problems.

Longitudinal research, however, indicates that change in measured intelligence is common from the preschool years through late adolescence (McCall, Applebaum, & Hogarty, 1973). Further, an alternative theoretical view to early critical periods is that individuals have a high degree of responsivity or plasticity early in development but retain at least a moderate degree throughout the entire lifespan (Lerner, 1986). This theoretical view leads to an optimistic perspective on intervention: Change may be easier to effect in the early years, but the individual's capacity for change is not lost with advancing age.

Undoubtedly, the preschool years are important in development. Problems arise when researchers, policymakers, and program developers assume this is the *only* time that intervention is needed or is effective. Maintaining the effects of an early intervention may require a "booster" (Caldwell, 1987) or a "reinstatement" (Wachs, 1986), that is, the periodic and partial repetition of the early experience. Reinstatements may occur naturally if children, parents, or teachers engage in behaviors that essentially keep the intervention going. The Follow-Through programs established for children who completed Head Start are examples of the planned repetition of an intervention. Continuous attention to children's needs is necessary throughout infancy, childhood, and adolescence (Stipek, Valentine, & Zigler, 1979).

Chapter 1, the major federal source of funding for compensatory education, has concentrated on younger children, in grades 1 through 6. Although those funds are inadequate for even the younger children, twice as many fourth graders as eighth graders receive services under Chapter 1. In 1988, a new authorization which focused on adolescents was added to Chapter 1. The new program provides funds for dropout prevention and basic skill improvement beginning in the seventh grade (August, 1988).

In addition, the capabilities and needs of adolescents are noted in the Carnegie Council on Adolescent Development's recent report on the education of American youth (Jackson, 1989). The report calls for major changes in schools as contexts for adolescents' development and education; it also included schools' connections to families and communities as essential features of improved schooling for young adolescents.

The purpose of this chapter is to describe families, communities, and schools as contexts for literacy and learning among African-American adolescents. Because of the relative inattention to older children and adolescents in the past, this age group, which includes middle school and high school grades, is the focus of discussion. Adolescence is an important period to understand. Many adolescents make decisions and engage in behaviors that have lasting effects on their adult lives. Continued engagement in school at this time is critical for later educational success and for the prevention of social problems, such as unplanned adolescent pregnancy and drug abuse, that currently plague American youth. The focus of this chapter is not solely on literacy per se, but on education and achievement more generally. Because adolescents reach the legal age at which they can discontinue their schooling, the challenges facing schools, families, communities, and society are great. Adolescents need meaningful, engaging experiences in school and in out-of-school settings. A brief description of the current levels of literacy and educational attainment among African-American adolescents and young adults is presented, followed by discussions of family, community, and school contexts. The chapter ends with suggestions for future research, policy, and practice.

LITERACY AND EDUCATIONAL ATTAINMENT IN ADOLESCENTS AND YOUTH

African-American young adults, like their white counterparts, tend to possess basic literacy skills and to be high school graduates. The percentage of African Americans having basic reading and writing skills has increased during this century (Kaestle, 1985). Similarly, the percentage of African-American youth having completed high school has increased steadily. Among youths 20 to 24 years old, 81% of African Americans have completed high school, compared to 85% of whites and 62% of Hispanics (Baker & Ogle, 1989). At the next step in the educational pipeline—higher education—22% of all African-American 18-to25-year-olds were enrolled in 1986. In comparison, 28% of whites and 18% of Hispanics in this age range were enrolled (Baker & Rogers, 1989).

Although the majority of African-American young adults have completed high school, only 24% of African-American graduates have completed the number of English, social studies, science, and mathematics courses recommended by the National Commission on Excellence in Education. This percentage is greater than that of Hispanics (18%), somewhat less than that of whites (30%), and only half that of Asians (48%). The percentage of African Americans having completed the recommended number of courses has more than doubled since 1982, however, from 10% to 24% (Baker & Ogle, 1989).

A small proportion, 18%, of African-American 21-to 25-year-olds cannot read at a fourth-grade level; only 4% of whites in this age group have such low reading skills (Kirsch & Jungeblut, 1986). In addition, African-American young adults in the 21-to 25-year age range scored significantly lower than whites on three scales used by the National Assessment of Educational Progress to measure performance on everyday literacy tasks of the sort needed for successful adult functioning (Winfield, 1988). The scales measured prose literacy, such as reading and answering questions about newspaper articles; and document literacy, such as locating information in a bus schedule; and quantitative literacy, such as completing an order form and balancing a checkbook. Among the African-American young adults, females were more likely than males to be high-literacy proficient, that is, to score above the 75th percentile in the distribution of scores for African-Americans.

The National Adult Literacy Survey, conducted in 1992, also found that young adults have difficulty with prose, document, and quantitative literacy. In this survey, most of the adults who demonstrated low levels of literacy indicated that they could read and write "well" or "very well." Thus, adults seemed unaware of their own literacy problems. As in other similar surveys, the average performance of African Americans and Hispanics was lower than that of whites (National Center for Education Statistics, 1993).

Average scores on standardized tests of literacy are lower for African Americans than for whites at the high school, junior high school, and elementary school levels. In the 1986 National Assessment of Educational Progress for 3rd, 7th, and 11th graders in public and private schools, average reading proficiency scores of African-American and Hispanic students were lower than those of white students (Baker & Ogle, 1989). In the prior assessments conducted periodically since 1970, however, African-American students improved more than did White students. Thus, the African-American-white reading gap decreased but remains substantial (National Assessment of Educational Progress, 1985). Racial/ethnic differences in literacy typically are confounded with socioeconomic differences. Large socioeconomic status differences in reading proficiency were found in the eighth-graders assessed in the National Education Longitudinal Study (NELS) of 1988. With socioeconomic status taken into account, differences in reading proficiency between whites and African Americans, Hispanics, and Native Americans were reduced by 25-30% (Hafner, Ingels, Schneider, & Stevenson, 1990). Students with advanced literacy skills have distinct advantages over their less skilled counterparts. They are more likely to complete high school than those lacking such skills, and, once they complete high school, more likely to become employed (Berlin & Sum, 1988).

To summarize, only a small percentage of African-American adolescents or young adults is completely illiterate. These students need to acquire the rudimentary literacy skills of reading and writing. A larger percentage lacks the functional literacy skills needed to negotiate everyday life in a technological society. Functional literacy is essential for participation in American society. An even larger percentage of African-American youth may lack "empowering" literacy skills: the advanced literacy skills that enable individuals to comprehend complex ideas and phenomena and to engage in discourse on complex issues. It is this aspect of literacy—reading to master complex subjects—that poses the greatest problem in the United States today (Athey & Singer, 1987). Historical studies of literacy (Graff, 1986) and critiques of recent national reports of literacy (Rubin, 1986) emphasize the use of literacy in society. For African-American youth, proficiency in the use of literacy skills at the highest levels should be addressed, in addition to educational needs at the levels of functional and rudimentary literacy skills.

THE ROLE OF THE FAMILY IN LITERACY AND LEARNING

Diametrically opposed views of African-American families' roles in their children's academic achievement exist in the social science literature. At one end of the spectrum, the African-American family is seen as strong and inspiring. African-American families have nurtured their children through many obstacles in American society, from slavery to the present. High academic achievement has occurred in some African-American families who faced great difficulties. A strong family life is a prominent factor in the lives of African-American men and women of achievement described by Billingsley (1968) and in upwardly mobile middle-income African-American families studied by McAdoo (1981). Billingsley (1992) presents convincing evidence that the African-American family is resilient and adaptive. In marked contrast is the view of African-American families as weak and debilitating. Some researchers have concluded that African-American families are responsible for the poor school performance of African-American children, and ultimately, for the disproportionate poverty among African Americans (e.g., Coleman, 1987; Moynihan, 1965).

A second argument focused on the belief in genetic determinism and in the inherent inferiority of ethnic minorities that permeated American psychology in its early years and persists in some forms today (Scott-Jones, 1984). The role of genetic endowment in cognitive functioning cannot be denied; however, a broad range of reaction allows for considerable environmental influence on individual development (Lerner, 1992). Further, there is no convincing evidence of a genetic basis for observed group differences in intellectual and academic performance between African-American and white individuals.

In contrast to genetic explanations, environmental explanations of performance differences between African Americans and whites typically have been more positive, but can be as deterministic as genetic explanations. The belief that African-American children are irreparably damaged by poor family environments is as pessimistic, simplistic, and unsupported as the belief that African-American children possess an immutable, inferior genetic capacity for intelligence. The family environment is one of several factors affecting African-American children's achievement in a complex, dynamic manner.

Processes within the family may explain why some African-American children succeed in school; whereas other African-American children in ostensibly similar situations fail. Explanations of individual variation among African Americans, however, do not account for the fact that African Americans, as a group, remain substantially below whites in academic achievement. Society's institutions act to maintain the subordinate status of African Americans and the advantaged status of whites. Schools are geared toward middle-class white children and their families, not poor or African-American children. The problem appears to be a feature of the stratification system, not uncommon in other countries. Cross-cultural comparisons (Ogbu, 1978, this volume) indicate that castelike minorities in other countries, like African Americans in the United States, perform worse academically than the dominant group.

Family Status

Poverty is a status variable that is consistently associated with low educational achievement and low educational attainment. An alarmingly high percentage of American children grow up in poverty. Approximately one-fifth of children under 18 years of age live below the poverty level (Bane & Ellwood, 1989; Children's Defense Fund, 1990). Poverty rates for adolescents (considered separately from younger children) are similarly high; the proportion of adolescents living in poverty has increased steadily since the mid-1970s (Furstenberg & Condran, 1988; Sum & Fogg, 1991). If the "near poor" are included, approximately one-fourth of adolescents live in poverty. In addition, characteristics of the preteen population—children 7 to 12 years of age—suggest that the population of adolescents in poverty will increase in the 1990s (Sum & Fogg, 1991).

Although poverty is wide-ranging, affecting many white and two-parent working families (Bane & Ellwood, 1989), a disproportionate number of African-American children and children in single-parent families live in poverty. According to the Children's Defense Fund (1990), 44% of African-American children, 36% of Hispanic children, and 15% of white children live in poverty, and more than half (51%) of all children living in single-mother households are poor. Further, almost 60% of births to African Americans are to unmarried women (Cherlin, 1988). Low-income African Americans appear not to have benefited from the changes in the American opportunity structure that accompanied the Civil Rights Movement; overall, their economic situation has remained the same or has worsened over the last two decades (Ogbu, 1986).

Poverty is associated with low achievement. A nationally representative sample of poor 15 to 18-year-olds had median scores on the Armed Forces Qualification Test (AFQT) that were at the 18th percentile (Sum & Fogg, 1991). The basic academic areas assessed on the AFQT include work knowledge, paragraph comprehension, arithmetic reasoning, and numerical reasoning.

Some children from poor families perform well in school. In the National Longitudinal Survey of Young Americans, the majority of 14- and 15 year-olds who had inadequate basic skills were poor. Poor students with good basic skills, however, were no more likely to drop out of high school two years later than were their more affluent counterparts (August, 1988).

Children from poor families, on average, do not perform well in school, but some middle-income African-American children also have difficulties. Problems of racial identity may confront young middle-income African-American adolescents. Ambivalent feelings toward academic achievement may develop among middle-income African-American adolescents if their African-American peers typically do not perform well in school, are segregated in lower tracks, or attend separate schools. Banks's studies (1984, 1989) of middle-income African-American youth in predominantly white suburbs indicate that African-American parents provide contact with African-American institutions such as churches so that students maintain a positive African-American identity as they interact positively in predominantly white settings.

Structural changes in families, particularly the rise in single-parent households and in the employment of mothers outside the home, have been cited as reasons for the problems adolescents experience. The changes in families are interpreted as representative of a decline in parental commitment to children. Furstenberg and Condran (1988), analyzing data on family structure and on measures of adolescent well-being for African Americans and whites from 1940 to 1980, concluded that the empirical evidence does not support a link between family change and change in adolescent behavior during this time period. For example, the percentage of 18- to 24-year-old African Americans who graduated from high school increased as their family conditions were deteriorating. Further, the correlation between family change and change in adolescent well-being is lower for African Americans than for whites. There does not appear to be a clear, unequivocal relationship between family structure and adolescent achievement. The impact of status variables such as single-parent homes and maternal employment outside the home may be mediated by family processes and extrafamilial variables in communities and schools.

Family Processes

This section focuses on three aspects of family processes that may influence adolescents' literacy and learning: (a) parents as providers of literacy materials, (b) parents as childrearing strategists, and (c) parents as managers of their children's school careers.

Parents as providers. The foremost responsibility of families is to provide for the basic needs of children. Adequate food, clothing, and shelter are basic requirements of the developing adolescent. Epstein (1990) includes this basic obligation of families as Type 1 in her typology of parental involvement in education. Beyond their basic obligation, families also vary in the extent to which they provide material support for literacy and learning.

A study of 21- to 25-year-old adults suggests that different socioeconomic and ethnic groups had approximately equal access to literacy materials in their homes when they were in high school (Kirsch & Jungeblut, 1986). Respondents were asked whether, as high school students, they had access in their homes to six types of materials ranging in cost from a newspaper to a personal computer. The remaining four types were magazines, books, encyclopedia, and dictionary. Parental educational level was not significantly related to the number of types reported, and no significant differences were found among African Americans, Hispanics, and whites. When parental education and ethnicity were included in a model with other background variables, such as gender and parental occupation, to predict access to literacy materials in the home, there was a modest relationship between the set of background variables and access to literacy materials. Of the background variables, parental education contributed most to the relationship. With the effects of other background variables controlled, Hispanics reported having had access to fewer kinds of literacy materials in the home than did whites. African Americans' reported access, with other background variables controlled, was between that of Hispanics and whites and was not significantly different from either group (Kirsch & Jungeblut, 1986).

It should be noted that the dependent variable in this study (Kirsch & Jungeblut, 1986) was the number of types of literacy materials. Thus, the finding of no difference in these analyses does not necessarily mean that the respondents had the same literacy materials in their homes. One could argue that a personal computer has greater potential as a tool for literacy than do the other five types of materials. Future research should address in greater detail the utility of computers and other materials in the home in enhancing literacy in adolescents. Statements about access to literacy materials in the home and about ethic and socioeconomic differences in home environments need to be buttressed by some evidence regarding the relative value of various types of materials.

Parents as child-rearing strategists. As children enter adolescence, they view themselves as gaining in responsibility and independence (Pipp, Shaver, Jennings, Lamborn, & Fischer, 1985). Adolescents perceive their parents as gradually exerting less control over their behavior (Dornbusch, Ritter, Leiderman, Roberts, & Fraleigh, 1987; Steinberg, 1987). To some extent, parental influence becomes more indirect as adolescents internalize parental values and use those values when they have opportunities for independent decision making. Parental control is not relinquished entirely, however; parental control becomes increasingly domain-specific. For example, middle-class white 12- to 19-year-olds gradually gain control over their style of dress, but believe their parents retain the right to set standards for their school performance (Youniss & Smollar, 1985). Parents still may establish rules and monitor adolescents' behavior. Parents also may communicate with adolescents regarding important aspects of their behavior and development, encourage adolescents to express their own opinions and feelings, and respond to input from adolescents in setting and enforcing rules.

Students' school performance is positively associated with parents' exerting firm control, through clear standards for behavior, but also with parents' responding to adolescents' needs and desires, allowing them input into decisions and maintaining open communication (Dornbusch et al., 1987). In a long-standing typology, this parental style—appropriately high levels of both control and responsiveness—is labeled as authoritative (Baumrind, 1966, 1972, 1987, 1991). In contrast, authoritarian parents are high on control and low on responsiveness; permissive parents are low in control and high on responsiveness.

Ethnic differences may exist in these parenting styles. According to Dornbusch et al. (1987), Asian, African American, and Hispanic adolescents reported higher levels of authoritarian parenting than did whites. Furthermore, the positive relationship between authoritative parenting and school performance was greatest for white students. Adolescents from lower socioeconomic-status (SES) families rated their parents higher on authoritarian parenting than did middle socioeconomic-status (SES) adolescents.

An important feature of authoritative parenting is the responsiveness of the parent to the child. Responsiveness is a concept that can incorporate several bodies of literature and provide a link between families and school achievement. Conceptualized as a behavioral domain rather than as a specific behavior, responsiveness can be a generic construct that ranges across the life cycle (Martin, 1989). It includes the affective component of the social interactions in which teaching and learning occur. Responsiveness incorporates changes that must occur in parent-adolescent relationships, when parental behaviors that were appropriate for younger children may not foster adolescent development. Parental responsiveness may facilitate self-regulation, self-efficacy, security, motivation, or persistence in children. Responsiveness also may lead to parents' being more informed about and more sensitive to adolescent's developing skills and thus able to provide appropriate experiences. The responsiveness of parents to adolescents may be an important feature transcending many differences in observed childrearing strategies.

Control, the second component of authoritative parenting, also is important in school achievement. Clark (1983) provided case-study descriptions of high- and low-achieving African-American high school seniors, all from low-income single or two-parent families. Parents of high achievers appeared to exert control over their children and supervise them closely but not excessively. These parents believed that education was a means of social mobility; they monitored homework and interacted positively with the school. In contrast, low-achieving students' families appeared to be in a state of great despair. With fewer social and material resources than the families of high achievers, the families of low achievers struggled unsuccessfully for many years and appeared resigned to their economic conditions.

A study of African-American adolescent females enrolled in an academic enrichment program for high-achieving students found relatively high levels of parental monitoring and supervision (Scott-Jones, Turner, Davis, & Clemons, 1990). The adolescents reported that their parents almost always kept track of how well they performed in school, but the parents were less likely to check their graded assignments. The majority of these adolescents reported that their parents had rules for homework; the parents, however, explained these rules and allowed the adolescents to participate in rule making.

Measures of parental monitoring and control were used in a study of predictors of reading and mathematics achievement. Keith, Reimers, Fehrmann, Pottebaum, and Aubey (1986) defined parental involvement as students' perceptions of the following three aspects of parental monitoring and control: (a) whether parents usually knew where their adolescents were and what they were doing, (b) whether parents kept close track of how well their adolescents were doing in school, and (c) how extensively parents influenced adolescents' post-high school plans. The effects of parental involvement, time spent on homework, time spent watching television, and background variables on reading and mathematics achievement of seniors in the High School and Beyond data set were assessed. Using path analysis, Keith et al. concluded that the parental involvement variable had no direct effect on achievement. Television viewing had a small negative effect on achievement, whereas time spent on homework had a strong positive effect on achievement. Parental involvement was related to time spent on homework but the indirect effect of parental involvement on achievement, through homework, was small. Interestingly, more than half the students reported three hours or less of homework each week and almost half reported three hours or more of television viewing per weekday.

Attempts to understand the role of parental control and responsiveness in adolescents' academic performance must take into account the bidirectional influences in parent-adolescent relationships. Adolescents' behavior may affect parents' interactions in addition to parental behavior affecting adolescents' behavior. Furthermore, Ogbu (1981; this volume) has argued that parents' perceptions of the adult roles possible for their children guide parental childrearing strategies. Low-income African Americans' perceptions of a lack of adult opportunity may constrain their socialization practices.

Parents as managers. In addition to processes in the home, families' involvement in school activities may be important for adolescent achievement. Parents act as managers of their children's school careers when they are actively involved in schools, assist in decision making regarding courses and curricula, and assist in overall school policy. Parents represent students' interests in the connections between families and schools as institutions.

Parents of young children are more likely to become involved in school activities than are parents of older children. In a national sample of children 5 to 17 years of age, parent involvement, as rated by teachers, was higher for younger children (Stevenson & Baker, 1987). The decline in parent involvement occurs early in elementary school (Epstein, 1986). Many barriers to parent involvement exist in middle or junior high school. Extensive interviews of teachers and parents in two junior high schools serving low-income African-American populations indicated that teachers tended to blame parents for their children's problems. Parents admitted to some problems within themselves and their circumstances, but also cited teachers' attitudes and behavior as problems (Leitch & Tangri, 1988; Tangri & Leitch, 1982).

The organization of typical high schools also does not encourage a high level of parent involvement. High school teachers report only a little contact with parents, most of which is with parents of students with discipline problems or parents who have previously shown an interest in helping their children (Dornbusch & Ritter, 1988). In inner-city Catholic high schools, fewer than one-third of parents talked with a teacher more than twice during the school year (Bauch, 1988). Fewer than 20% of high school parents, however, expressed the belief that involvement in their children's education was no longer appropriate (Dornbusch & Ritter, 1988).

According to Baker and Stevenson (1986), parents must help their children advance through the organization of schooling successfully, in addition to helping children acquire cognitive skills. Baker and Stevenson interviewed mothers of eighth-graders who were making the transition from middle to high school. Mothers with higher education levels (race not specified) were more likely to select college preparatory courses, independent of the child's academic performance, to be able to name the child's teachers and to identify the child's best and worst subjects, and to have met with the child's teachers and attended school activities. Higher educated mothers whose children were performing poorly in school were more likely than any other mothers to take actions to prepare their children for the transition to high school.

THE ROLE OF COMMUNITIES IN LITERACY AND LEARNING

Influences external to the family also have an impact on adolescents' academic achievement. The family remains an important context, however, in spite of the changes in the parent-adolescent relationship and the increasing external influences on the adolescent. From many years of work on school reform, Comer (1993) concluded that families and schools need the support of the community to meet the educational and developmental needs of adolescents.

Nettles (1989) hypothesized that communities affect adolescents through four basic processes: *instruction, allocation* of resources and rewards, *mobilization* of people or resources for action, and *conversion* of one belief to another. According to Nettles, these community processes affect adolescents' investment behavior, that is, their decisions regarding activities that will bring the greatest return for the effort expended. Communities can influence adolescents to invest in constructive pursuits or, conversely, in harmful or illegal activities.

Community may be defined in several different ways. Community may refer to the physical neighborhood in which the family

resides. The many problems of poor urban neighborhoods are frequently described in media reports. Illegal drugs and associated violence create an unsafe atmosphere for families in these neighborhoods. Living in
such neighborhoods may affect parents' childrearing strategies and parents' and adolescents' aspirations for the adolescents' school achievement and future life. Although it may be assumed that families living in
such neighborhoods will acquire values consistent with the community
atmosphere, that is not necessarily the case. It seems inevitable, however, that families are placed at physical danger in these communities and
that developing adolescents are, at least, exposed to lifestyles that are
not conducive to high educational achievement. The family's socialization task is more difficult when the neighborhood has few elements that
value or require high educational achievement.

In attempting to understand the influence of neighborhoods on
adolescents, one can ask whether the qualities of the neighborhood actually affect adolescents and their families or whether families of a certain
type gravitate toward high-risk neighborhoods. According to Garbarino
and Sherman (1980), both processes occur. Garbarino and Sherman
assert that the neighborhood provides the ecological niche that "makes
or breaks" low-income families.

Urban African-American communities are often discussed in
terms of potential negative effects on African-American adolescents.
Earlier research (Billingsley, 1968), however, found that African-
American communities were important in augmenting the efforts of
African-American families to socialize their children toward achievement. African-American community members, in formal roles as teachers and ministers as well as in informal roles, provided models and
direct help for African-American youth. Billingsley (1968) singled out
the African-American church as having an especially positive impact on
African-American family life. The church may not necessarily be in the
physical neighborhood in which a family resides. *Community*, then, can
be defined by organizations chosen by families. The "church community," the "church family," and the "church home" may be important in
some adolescents' development.

Many African-American adolescents do not live in neighborhoods where there are African-American churches or other African-
American institutions. The "African-American community," therefore,
must be sought outside the immediate geographic area. Middle-class
African-American adolescents, in particular, may live in predominantly
white communities. Banks (1984, 1989) found that middle-class African-
American families living in predominantly white suburbs were successful in seeking out African-American individuals and institutions, particularly the African-American church and African-American social clubs.

Youth from these families developed a strong African-American identity, which may be related to achievement.

In addition to urban African-American neighborhoods and predominantly white suburban neighborhoods, African-American adolescents also live in rural neighborhoods. African Americans in rural areas are understudied, although they comprise one-fourth of the United States' African-American population (Lee, 1989). In some poor, rural areas in the South, African Americans are in the majority. In these communities, there are typically few financial resources for education and low levels of educational achievement. In addition, agricultural work and long bus rides may interfere with adolescents' schooling. According to Lee, however, the school, along with the church and the family, is an important institution in rural African-American communities. Rural adolescents engage in many social activities at the local junior and senior high schools. Extracurricular activities and athletic events may provide social outlets for the entire community as well as for adolescents.

In a study of African-American young adults, 20 to 25 years old, Winfield (1988) found that involvement in community organizations was associated with high levels of literacy. African-American young adults who scored high on literacy proficiency tests were more likely than low scorers to be involved in community organizations, although high and low scorers were not different in frequency of social activities. The effect of involvement in community organizations remained, even after the effects of other variables such as respondents' educational attainment, household income, and parents' education were taken into account. Winfield speculated that literacy skills are practiced and reinforced in community organizations' activities, such as voter registration drives and church programs.

In addition to the general functions and roles described above, communities may provide programs that focus specifically on literacy. Davidson and Koppenhaver (1988) concluded that good community literacy programs are important because some students may feel alienated from traditional school settings; these settings, therefore, may not be the best place for such students to learn. Community programs, especially those that provide individual attention and a relaxed atmosphere, may reverse the effects of students' negative experiences in schools. Community programs may create a context in which students feel a need to be literate, although these programs do not provide enough structured instructional time to compensate entirely for in-school programs.

Of the after-school community literacy programs studied by the Center for Early Adolescence (Davidson & Koppenhaver, 1988), some were sponsored by community agencies such as churches, businesses, and social service agencies. The researchers found few programs for early adolescents and, in most of these, young adolescents were the oldest eligible participants in programs designed for elementary school children. Examples of after-school community literacy programs include an East Harlem community literacy center for all ages and levels of readers, including adults, operated from a combination library-bookstore; an individual tutoring program developed in Chicago in 1965 by a corporation and a housing project; and a program in which college and high school students tutor younger Native American students. In addition to providing employee tutors, businesses can "adopt" a school by donating computers, or other equipment and supplies (Gibbs, 1989).

THE ROLE OF SCHOOLS IN LITERACY AND LEARNING

Schools are given the formal responsibility of producing an educated citizenry and remain an enormous influence on adolescents. They are the major providers of adolescents' literacy needs (Davidson & Koppenhaver, 1988) and the site where adolescents and peers interact most frequently. The popular belief that families are more influential or more responsible than schools for students' achievement is not supported by research. The high school curriculum is more strongly associated with educational attainment among African-American young adults than are family variables such as parental education, parental encouragement, and father presence (Wilson & Allen, 1987). Yet, high schools with predominantly minority and low-income student bodies have fewer advanced courses and more remedial courses. Of schools with 90% minority students, only half offer at least one section of calculus; whereas 80% of predominantly white schools offer calculus (Haycock, Alston, & Finlay, 1990). Further, poor and minority students attending predominantly white middle-class schools tend to be in the lower tracks (see Braddock, this volume, for a discussion of tracking).

Adolescents make an important transition from elementary to middle or secondary school. Many academic and adjustment problems, which may have had their origins in the earlier grades, become apparent or are exacerbated during this period (August, 1988). The typical elementary school organization, in which one teacher remains with students for the entire school day, is replaced by departmentalized instruction, with different teachers responsible for different subjects (McPartland, 1987; McPartland, Coldiron, & Braddock, 1987). Furthermore, there is a higher rate of teacher turnover in junior high than in senior high schools (Darling-Hammond, cited in August, 1988). In addition, African-American and other minority students may not be taught by minority teachers (King, 1993). Although the proportion of minorities in the student population has increased, the proportion of minorities in the teaching force has declined sharply. In 1971, almost 12% of teachers were minorities; by the year 2000, that proportion is expected to drop below 5% (Nicklos & Brown, 1989).

Schools can foster a sense of community and belonging among students. When the school is large and impersonal, the creation of "houses" and "teams" within the school can provide the adolescent with a stable group of peers and adults with whom to develop close relationships (August, 1988; Jackson, 1989). Further, schools can serve to organize and coordinate community and family efforts to enhance adolescents' literacy (Epstein & Scott-Jones, in preparation). The extension of the school day and the provision of summer programs for adolescents also have been suggested as a means of meeting adolescents' educational and developmental needs (Children's Defense Fund, 1987).

In addition to the transitions adolescents make from elementary to middle school and from middle to high school, an important transition occurs when adolescents complete or leave high school. High schools typically are geared to the needs of college-bound adolescents, leaving non-college-bound youth as the "forgotten half" (William T. Grant Foundation, 1988). In their report of a 2-year study of 16- to 24-year-old adolescents and youth, the Grant Foundation Commission concluded that whether they drop out or graduate from high school, the non-college bound are typically unprepared to be responsible citizens, to start new families, or to work at more than menial jobs.

FUTURE DIRECTIONS

A variety of strategies is needed to enhance literacy among African-American youth. A number of research initiatives is needed to provide the basis for intervention strategies. Unfortunately, the educational reforms proposed in the 1980s included very little that reflected the African-American experience (Billingsley, 1992). More research is needed that is based on a balanced view of African-American families. Reforms and interventions are more likely to be successful when they build on the strengths of African-American families.

The Carnegie Council report (Jackson, 1989), which called for many changes in school structure and school personnel, also concluded that family-school relations characterized by mutual respect, trust, and communication are necessary. In addition, community-school collaborations providing multiple sites and multiple methods for adolescents' learning are needed. Community service for adolescents is one such approach that also may improve adolescents' academic work. For example, in the Early Adolescent Helper Program, sponsored by the City University of New York in four cities, students work in child care centers, programs for latchkey children, and senior citizen centers while they participate in school seminars on human development (Haycock, Alston, & Finlay, 1990). The transitions from elementary to middle school and from middle school to high school may be critical points for adolescents. Recommendations for smooth transitions include improved communication between families and schools, communication between the faculty of the sending and receiving schools, and assignment of older students as "buddies" for new students (August, 1988).

We also need more appropriate program evaluation. The effectiveness of intervention programs for adolescents is difficult to judge by usual evaluation criteria. Typically, programs have limited funds that are used to provide services rather than to set up evaluations. Programs often must rely upon indicators such as anecdotal evidence and student attendance to document the success of their programs. Davidson and Koppenhaver (1988) concluded that no one program provided the "correct" design for literacy programs.

Finally, we need comprehensive policies and programs for families and children. Current policy for families and children is piecemeal and crisis-oriented. To prevent the problems African-American adolescents encounter, vast changes must occur in American society. Needed changes encompass almost all aspects of American life, including full employment, adequate health care, adequate housing, and adequate child care. Changes of this magnitude are unlikely, however (Gibbs, 1989). Programs and policies are likely to be more limited in scope and, therefore, less effective. Such programs and policies can result in small gains, as efforts to address the larger problems continue.

REFERENCES

Athey, I., & Singer, H. (1987). Developing the nation's reading potential for a technological era. *Harvard Educational Review, 57,* 84-93.

August, D. (1988). *Making the middle grades work.* Washington, DC: Children's Defense Fund.

Baker, C.O., & Ogle, L.T. (1989). *The condition of education 1989: Elementary and secondary education.* Washington, DC: U.S. Government Printing Office.

Baker, C.O., & Rogers, G.T. (1989). *The condition of education 1989: Postsecondary education.* Washington, DC: U.S. Government Printing Office.

Baker, D.P., & Stevenson, L.D.L. (1986). Mothers' strategies for children's school achievement: Managing the transition to high school.

Sociology of Education, 59, 156-166.

Bane, M.J., & Ellwood, D.T. (1989). One-fifth of the nation's children: Why are they poor? *Science, 245,* 1047-1053.

Banks, J.A. (1984). Black youth in predominantly White suburbs: An exploratory study of their attitudes and self-concepts. *Journal of Negro Education, 53,* 3-17.

Banks, J.A. (1989). Black youth in predominantly white suburbs. In R.L. Jones (Ed.), *Black adolescents* (pp. 65-78). Berkeley, CA: Cobb & Henry.

Bauch, P.A. (1988). Is parental involvement different in private schools? *Educational Horizons, 66,* 79-82.

Baumrind, D. (1966). Effects of authoritative parental control on child behavior. *Child Development, 37,* 887-907.

Baumrind, D. (1972). An exploratory study of socialization effects on Black children: Some Black-White comparisons. *Child Development, 43,* 261-267.

Baumrind, D. (1987). A developmental perspective on adolescent risk taking in contemporary America. *New Directions for Child Development, 37,* 93-125.

Baumrind, D. (1991). Effective parenting during the early adolescent transition. In P.A. Cowan & M. Hetherington (Eds.), *Family transitions* (pp. 111-163). Hillsdale, NJ: Erlbaum.

Berlin, G., & Sum, A. (1988). *Toward a more perfect union: Basic skills, poor families, and our economic future.* New York: Ford Foundation.

Billingsley, A. (1968). *Black families in White America.* Englewood Cliffs, NJ: Prentice-Hall.

Billingsley, A. (1992). *Climbing Jacob's ladder: The enduring legacy of African-American families.* New York: Simon and Schuster.

Bloom, B. (1964). *Stability and change in human characteristics.* New York: Wiley.

Bronfenbrenner, U. (1979). *The ecology of human development.* Cambridge, MA: Harvard University Press.

Bronfenbrenner, U. (1986). Ecology of the family as a context for human development: Research perspectives. *Developmental Psychology, 22,* 723-742.

Caldwell, B.M. (1987). Sustaining intervention effects: Putting malleability to the test. In J.J. Gallagher and C.T. Ramey (Eds.), *The malleability of children* (pp. 115-126). Baltimore, MD: Paul H. Brookes.

Cherlin, A.J. (1988). The changing American family and public policy. In A.J. Cherlin (Ed.), *The changing American family and public policy* (pp.1-29). Washington, DC: The Urban Institute Press.

Children's Defense Fund. (1987). *Opportunities for prevention: Building after-school and summer programs for young adolescents.* Washington, DC: Author.

Children's Defense Fund (1988). *Making the middle grades work.* Washington, DC: Author.

Children's Defense Fund (November, 1990). U.S. fails to reduce child poverty. *Children's Defense Fund Reports, 12*(3), 1, 10.

Clark, R. (1983). *Family life and social achievement: Why poor African-American children succeed or fail.* Chicago: University of Chicago Press.

Coleman, J.S. (1987). Families and schools. *Educational Researcher, 16,* 32-38.

Comer, J.P. (1993). The potential effects of community organizations on the future of our youth. *Teachers College Record, 94,* 658-661.

Davidson, J., & Koppenhaver, D. (1988). *Adolescent literacy: What works and why.* New York: Garland.

Dornbusch, S.M., & Ritter, P.L. (1988). Parents of high school students: A neglected resource. *Educational Horizons, 66,* 75-77.

Dornbusch, S.M., Ritter, P.L., Leiderman, P.H., Roberts, D.F, & Fraleigh, M.J. (1987). The relation of parenting style to adolescent school performance. *Child Development, 58,* 1244-1257.

Epstein, J.L. (1986). Parents' reactions to teacher practices of parent involvement. *The Elementary School Journal, 86,* 277-294.

Epstein, J.L. (1987). Toward a theory of family-school connections: Teacher practices and parent involvement. In K. Hurrelman, F. Kaufman, & F. Losel (Eds.), *Social intervention: Potential and constraints* (pp. 121-136). New York: DeGruyter.

Epstein, J.L. (1990). School and family connections: Theory, research, and implications for integrating sociologies of education and the family. *Marriage and Family Review, 15,* 99-126.

Epstein, J.L., & Scott-Jones, D. (in preparation). School-family-community connections for accelerating student progress in the elementary and middle grades.

Furstenberg, F.F., & Condran, G.A. (1988). Family change and adolescent well-being: A reexamination of U.S. trends. In A.J. Cherlin (Ed.), *The changing American family and public policy* (pp. 117-155). Washington, DC: The Urban Institute Press.

Garbarino, J., & Sherman, D. (1980). High-risk neighborhoods and high-risk families: The human ecology of child maltreatment. *Child Development, 51,* 188-198.

Gibbs, J.T. (1989). African-American adolescents and youth: An update on an endangered species. In R.L. Jones (Ed.), *African-American adolescents* (pp. 3-28). Berkeley, CA: Cobb & Henry.

Graff, H.J. (1986) *The legacies of literacy: Continuities and contradictions in Western society and culture.* Bloomington: Indiana University Press.

Hafner, A., Ingels, S., Schneider, B., & Stevenson, D. (1990). *A profile of the American eighth grader: NELS: 88 student descriptive summary.* Washington, DC: U.S. Government Printing Office.

Haycock, K., Alston, D., & Finlay, B. (1990). *An advocate's guide to improving education.* Washington, DC: Children's Defense Fund.

Jackson, A. (1989). *Turning points: Preparing American youth for the 21st century.* Washington, DC: Carnegie Council on Adolescent Development.

Kaestle, C.F. (1985). The history of literacy and the history of readers. *Review of Research in Education, 12,* 11-54.

Keith, T.Z., Reimers, T.M., Fehrmann, P.G., Pottebaum, S.M., & Aubey, L.W. (1986). Parental involvement, homework, and TV time: Direct and indirect effects on high school achievement. *Journal of Educational Psychology, 78,* 373-380.

King, S.H. (1993). The limited presence of African-American teachers. *Review of Educational Research, 63,* 115-149.

Kirsch, I.S., & Jungeblut, A. (1986). *Literacy: Profiles of America's young adults.* Princeton, NJ: Educational Testing Service.

Lazar, I., & Darlington, R. (1982). Lasting effects of early education: A report from the Consortium for Longitudinal Studies. *Monographs of the Society for Research on Child Development, 47* (2-3, Serial No. 195).

Lee, C.C. (1989). Rural African-American adolescents: Psychosocial development in a changing environment. In R.L. Jones (Ed.), *African-American adolescents* (pp. 79-98). Berkeley, CA: Cobb & Henry.

Leitch, M.L., & Tangri, S.S. (1988). Barriers to home-school collaboration. *Educational Horizons, 66,* 70-74.

Lerner, R.M. (1986). Plasticity in development: Concepts and issues for intervention. *Journal of Applied Developmental Psychology, 7,* 139-152.

Lerner, R.M. (1992). *Final solutions: Biology, prejudice, and genocide.* University Park: The Pennsylvania State University Press.

Levenstein, P. (1988). *Messages from home: The mother-child home program and the prevention of school disadvantage.* Columbus: Ohio State University Press.

Martin, J.A. (1989). Personal and interpersonal components of responsiveness. *New Directions for Child Development, 43,* 5-14.

McAdoo. H.P. (1981). Patterns of upward mobility in African-American families. In H.P. McAdoo (Ed.), *African-American families* (pp. 155-169). Beverly Hills, CA: Sage.

McCall, R.B., Applebaum, M.I., & Hogarty, P.S. (1973). Developmental changes in mental performance. *Monographs of the Society for Research in Child Development, 38* (Whole No. 150).

McPartland, J.M. (1987). *Balancing high-quality subject matter instruction with positive teacher-student relations in the middle grades: Effects of departmentalization, tracking, and block scheduling on learning environments* (Tech. Rep. No. 15). Baltimore: Johns Hopkins University, Center for Research on Elementary Schools.

McPartland, J.M., Coldiron, J.R., & Braddock, J.M. (1987). *School structures and classroom practices in elementary, middle, and secondary schools* (Tech. Rep. No. 14). Baltimore: Johns Hopkins University, Center for Research on Elementary and Middle Schools.

Moynihan, D.P. (1965). *The Negro family: The case for national action.* Washington, DC: U.S. Government Printing Office.

National Assessment of Educational Progress. (1985). *The reading report card: Trends in reading over four national assessments, 1971-1974.* Princeton, NJ: National Assessment of Educational Progress.

National Center for Education Statistics. (1993). *Adult literacy in America.* Washington, DC: U.S. Government Printing Office.

Nettles, S.M. (1989). The role of community involvement in fostering investment behavior in low-income African-American adolescents: A theoretical perspective. *Journal of Adolescent Research, 4,* 190-201.

Nicklos, L.B., & Brown, W.S. (1989). Recruiting minorities into the teaching profession: An educational imperative. *Educational Horizons, 67,* 145-149.

Ogbu, J.U. (1978). *Minority education and caste.* New York: Academic Press.

Ogbu, J.U. (1981). Origins of human competence: A cultural-ecological perspective. *Child Development, 52,* 413-429.

Ogbu, J.U. (1986). The consequences of the American caste system. In U. Neisser (Ed.), *The school achievement of minority children* (pp. 19-56). Hillsdale, NJ: Erlbaum.

Pipp, S., Shaver, P., Jennings, S., Lamborn, S., & Fischer, K.W. (1985). Adolescents' theories about the development of their relationships with parents. *Journal of Personality and Social Psychology, 48*(4), 991-1001.

Ramey, C.T. (1982). Commentary. *Monographs of the Society for Research in Child Development, 47,* 142-151.

Rubin, D.L. (1986). Achieving literacy: An essay review of two national reports on reading. *Metropolitan Education, 2,* 83-91.

Scott-Jones, D. (1984). Family influences on cognitive development and school achievement. *Review of Research in Education, 11,* 259-304.

Scott-Jones, D. (1988). Families as educators: The transition from informal to formal school learning. *Educational Horizons, 66,* 66-69.

Scott-Jones, D. (1991). African-American families and literacy. In S. Silvern (Ed.), *Literacy through family, community, and school interaction* (pp. 173-200). Greenwich, CT: JAI Press.

Scott-Jones, D. (1992). Family and community interventions affecting the development of cognitive skills in children. In T.G. Sticht, B.A. McDonald, & M.J. Beeler (Eds.), *The intergenerational transfer of cognitive skills* (pp. 84-108). Norwood, NJ: Ablex.

Scott-Jones, D., Turner, S., Clemons, T., & Davis, A. (1990). *Adolescents' perceptions of parents and peers: Implications for sexual activity and academic achievement.* Paper presented at the biennial meeting of the Society for Research on Adolescence, Atlanta, GA.

Scott-Jones, D., & Nelson-LeGall, S. (1986). Defining African-American families: Past and present. In E. Seidman & J. Rappaport (Eds.), *Redefining social problems* (pp. 83-101). New York: Plenum.

Select Committee on Children, Youth, and Families; U.S. House of Representatives. (1985, September 26). *Hearing summary, Melting pot: Fact or fiction?* Washington, DC: U.S. Government Printing Office.

Slaughter, D.T. (1983). Early intervention and its effects upon maternal and child development. *Monographs of the Society for Research in Child Development, 48* (Whole No. 202).

Slaughter, D.T., Washington, V., Oyemade, U., & Lindsey, R. (1988).

Head Start: A backward and forward look. *Social Policy Report, 3* (Whole No. 2).

Steinberg, L.D. (1987). Impact of puberty on family relations: Effects of pubertal status and pubertal timing. *Developmental Psychology, 23,* 451-460.

Stevenson, D., & Baker, D. (1987). The family-school relation and the child's school performance. *Child Development, 58,* 1348-1357.

Stipek, D.J., Valentine, J., & Zigler, E. (1979). Project Head Start: A critique of theory and practice. In E. Zigler & J. Valentine (Eds.), *Project Head Start: A legacy of the war on poverty* (pp. 291-314). New York: The Free Press.

Sum, A.M., & Fogg, W.N. (1991). The adolescent poor and the transition to early adulthood. In P. Edelman & J. Ladner (Eds.), *Adolescence and poverty: Challenge for the 1990s.* Washington, DC: Center for National Policy Press.

Tangri, S.S., & Leitch, M.L. (1982). *Barriers to home-school collaboration: Two case studies in junior high schools* (Final Report). Washington, DC: National Institute of Education.

Wachs, T.D. (1986). Understanding early experience and development: The relevance of stages of inquiry. *Journal of Applied Developmental Psychology, 7,* 153-165.

Washington, V., & Oyemade, U. (1987). *Project Head Start: Past, present, and future trends in the contexts of family needs.* New York: Garland.

William T. Grant Foundation. (1988). *The forgotten half: Pathways to success for America's youth and young families* (Final Report, Youth and America's Future: The William T. Grant Foundation Commission on Work, Family, and Citizenship). Washington, DC: William T. Grant Foundation.

Wilson, K. A., & Allen, W.R. (1987). Explaining the educational attainment of young African-American adults: Critical familial and extra-familial influences. *Journal of Negro Education, 56,* 64-76.

Winfield, L.F. (1988). *An investigation of characteristics of high vs. low literacy-proficient African-American young adults* (Final Report). New York: The Rockefeller Foundation.

Youniss, J., & Smollar, J. (1985). *Adolescent relations with mothers, fathers, and friends.* Chicago: University of Chicago Press.

7

Literacy for Empowerment: The Case of Black Males

Diana Slaughter-Defoe
Northwestern University
Heraldo Richards
Vanderbilt University

Literacy has been an enduring problem in the educational history of
African Americans, from the days of American slavery to the present
(Alkalimat & Associates, 1986; Anderson, 1988; Franklin & Anderson,
1978; Patton, 1981; Slaughter & Johnson, 1988). Each new generation has
struggled to confront this fundamental educational issue with only modest success, although each time better appreciating the complexity of the
problem. However, the problems associated with literacy for African-
American youth and for black males specifically have persisted and
have resulted in increased concern for the educational future of this segment of the American population.

By literacy for empowerment, we specifically refer to those
skills, both oral and written, that facilitate access to education and full
participation in the social, political, and economic benefits of society.
Literacy, in this vein, is seen as an instrument of self-determination and
self-control, which effectively creates options and opportunities for the

individual who possesses the necessary literacy skills. The acquisition of these skills has been elusive for large numbers of black males. The difficulty that black males experience in attaining these skills and achieving economic success has been the focus of much discussion. In this chapter, we examine the role of literacy as an instrument of power and empowerment and discuss the relative lack of such power for black males within classrooms and societal contexts.

The chapter is developed around two assumptions. The primary assumption is that literacy is the major form of individual, social, and personal empowerment in society. The renewed American interest in literacy that characterized the latter 1980s, and which continues into the 1990s, provides an opportunity to evaluate the status of African-American youth on this important educational outcome. The second assumption is that restricted access to literacy is tied to social control of black African populations, including African Americans, and historically has restricted significant numbers of these youth from achieving social and personal empowerment. In short, this chapter is predicated on the notion that literacy is power (Holt, 1990).

If literacy is power, then literacy becomes a valuable commodity in a competitive society; whoever has greater access to this commodity ultimately increases his or her power. Rarely has the black male been positioned to accrue the benefits of power resulting from literacy. Although all black youth are adversely affected by inadequate education, black males appear disproportionately affected (Ferguson, 1990). Given the importance of literacy in adulthood as a marketable tool for employment in the United States, black males, especially young black males, appear to be disadvantaged (Bowman, 1989, 1990). For black American males, in particular, the inability to use print as a means of gaining access to knowledge and information about the world is probably the very first developmental step toward educational disillusionment. For all too many, this leads to educational failure, school drop out, and marginal employment opportunities.

We begin our discussion by focusing on the current educational status of black, as compared to white, American males. Next, we discuss the problem of defining literacy as it affects black males. Having sketched these issues, we present a vignette to discuss the constraints to literacy development of two young black males in a classroom setting. We conclude with a discussion of the implications of literacy for educational programs and for support to families in meeting the literacy demands of our postindustrial, technological society.

BLACK MALES: CONTEMPORARY EDUCATIONAL STATUS

Despite increased participation in schooling, black males lag behind white males and females in both high school completion and employment (Berlin & Sum, 1988). After conducting a thorough review of the literature on the education and achievement of young black males in comparison to other gender, racial, and ethnic groups, Reed (1988) concluded:

> Black high school graduation rates have improved over the past two decades, and the gap between graduation rates by ethnicity has narrowed. Nevertheless, the gap remains. Black females complete high school at higher rates than black males, but it is clear that both groups complete high school at rates below those of whites. (p. 87)

Reed (1988) also stated that the mean scores for black students generally on the Scholastic Aptitude Test (SAT) and the National Assessment of Educational Progress at ages 9, 13, and 17 are considerably below those of other groups. Data on the literacy and reading skills of young adults, ages 21-24, reported in 1985 by the National Center for Education Statistics (NCES) support many of Reed's (1988) observations. NCES reported that three types of literacy—prose, document, and quantitative—were assessed in a national sample. Only 21.3% of blacks as compared to 63.0% of whites were able to locate information in a news article or almanac (prose literacy). Even fewer blacks (3.5% as compared to 24.3% of whites) were able to synthesize the main arguments from a lengthy newspaper editorial. In addition, only 20.1% of blacks, as compared with 64.1% of whites, were expected to be able to follow directions to travel from one location to another using a map (document literacy). Even fewer (2.2% of blacks versus 24.9% of whites) were capable of using a bus schedule to select the appropriate bus for departures and arrivals. Finally, only 21.4% of blacks, as compared to 62.9% of whites, were capable of entering deposits and checks to balance a checkbook (quantitative literacy). Considerably fewer (3.3% of blacks versus 24.8% of whites) were capable of determining the amount of a tip in a restaurant when given a percentage.

Although we might quarrel with these rather limited definitions of literacy, the data suggest that blacks, both males and females, are especially "at risk" with regard to those literacy skills associated with competent adult functioning in American society. The operational skills described are those that characteristically emerge during the elementary school years, years in which relationships between families and schools are particularly important for children's optimal learning and development. However, data from the NCES report suggest that African

Americans perform substantially below whites on several measures. According to the report, for example, high school graduation was the only indicator that African-American youth could complete the first of the two literacy skills mentioned in each of the categories—prose, document, and quantitative.

Literacy is the foundation for educational achievement, as measured by educational attainment, in American society. Educational attainment is highly correlated with successful labor-force participation, and, therefore, with the ability of black males to provide for themselves and their families. Available data on educational attainment and labor-force participation indicate the depth of this enduring problem confronted by many black males.

As part of a social profile of black males, Gary (1981) compared the educational status of African-American males to that of white males, using available statistical data from the late 1970s. He made three important points. First, if African-American males do not attend or complete college, they have few opportunities to participate fully in the labor force or to obtain jobs that are more than menial. Second, black and white males, at similar levels of educational and occupational attainment, typically have marked differences in income—differences that favor whites. Third, labor-force participation rates for black males 16 years and over dropped nearly 13 percentage points between 1959 and 1979 (from 83.4% to 71.9%); for white males, the comparable drop was 5.2 percentage points (from 83.8% to 78.6%).

In the late 1980s, statistics on black male educational status were moderately encouraging. Indications are, however, that black men continue to lag behind white men in educational attainment, although they have made modest improvement. In 1987, the median years of school completed by blacks was 12.4 years, as compared to 12.8 years for whites (U.S. Dept. of Commerce, Bureau of the Census, 1989). During the same period, 36.9% of black males aged 25 years and older had completed less than four years of high school, but the comparable figure for white males was 22.7%. Conversely, the percentage of black males aged 25 years and older with 4 years or more of college was 11.0%, compared to 24.5% for white males. If, as Gary (1981) indicated, college completion is essential for significant improvements in labor participation rates, then these gains in educational attainment over the past decade or so are necessary, but not sufficient, to change the quality of life for black men in America.

Although 1989 data indicate that the median years of school completed by both black and white males is equivalent to high school graduation, other data indicate that the December 1989 unemployment rates of the two groups are quite discrepant. For black males reporting school enrollment, ages 16-24 years, the unemployment rate was 25%, as compared to 10.7% for white males—nearly two and one-half times greater (U.S. Dept. of Labor, Bureau of Labor Statistics, 1989, p. 15). A similar profile is available for those not reporting school enrollment in this age category. The unemployment rate for these black males is 24%, as compared to 9.7% for white males (p. 16).

Given the known racial obstacles toward black adult males' full participation in the labor force, it is crucial for black boys to achieve in school and attain as much formal education as possible. Literacy provides the means for combatting these racial and related social status obstacles (Gadsden, 1991).

LITERACY: HOME, GENDER, AND SCHOOL

Definitions of Literacy

Attempts to define literacy have been as challenging as the efforts of blacks to achieve it (Venezky, Wagner, & Ciliberti, 1990). In a world of different and ever-changing societies, literacy universals prove elusive. Heath (1986) asserts that "literacy has different meanings for members of different groups, with a corresponding variety of acquisition modes, functions and uses" (p. 25). In other words, the meaning and importance of literacy directly relate to the functions and needs of a given population. Robinson (1987) adds: "Literacy is impossible to define, for whatever purpose, without reference to its nature and use in some one context—in some one delimited and clearly defined social context" (p. 345). For sure, delineating the parameters of literacy necessitates the consideration of a complex set of psychological, social, educational, political, and economic realities. The more the customs, practices, and technologies of one's society rely on the ability to communicate through written language, the greater the value of literacy; the more benefits realized by one's ability to read and write, the more literacy is prized. Because of the dependency on criteria and expectations exemplified in specific societal contexts, definitions of literacy are necessarily relativistic.

Stedman and Kaestle (1987) remind us of the multidimensionality of literacy; that is, literacy cannot be thought of as a single set of skills, but various skills by which a person may demonstrate different levels of competence. Characterizing someone as literate or illiterate raises the question of degree and type of literacy. A further distinction is made by Stedman and Kaestle between "reading achievement," or literacy skills which are directly nurtured and practiced in school, and "functional literacy," or skills exercised outside the school. This dichotomy rejects the notion that the ability to decode and encode information in a school text-book necessarily transfers to the practical application of literacy skills—or functional literacy.

Levine (1986) proposes functional literacy as "the possession of, or access to, the competencies and information required to accomplish transactions entailing reading and writing which an individual wishes—or is compelled—to engage" (p. 43). This proposition recognizes the application of literacy skills within the context of one's personal and social life for the purposes of empowerment. The ability to read and write is viewed as an enabling force without which the individual would not be able to realize certain goals. Moreover, when we consider the utility of literacy skills, at once the issue becomes one of power or the attainment of it. The possession of literacy skills is equated with power; conversely, the absence of literacy skills is equated with a lack of power.

The idea that literacy brings about social, political, and even economic power is eminently recognized by the nations of the world and is vociferously promulgated through organizations such as UNESCO (Levine, 1986; Stevens, 1988). Perhaps nowhere else is the power of literacy more strongly acknowledged than among Third World countries. In the midst of an Information Age in which access to knowledge—and ultimately power—is governed by the ability to send and receive information, the exigency of literacy is most keenly felt among fledgling nations seeking to assert themselves among powerful nations. For inhabitants of these countries, illiteracy is often seen as an impediment to self-improvement and enfranchisement. Adiseshiah (quoted in Stevens, 1988), writing on literacy and social justice among Third World countries, stated:

> Above all the functionality of literacy relates to the fight of the poor, illiterate, exploited and disinherited man who forms the 60 percent majority in the Third World countries, to organize himself and his fellow sufferers and fight against the existing power centers and decision-making processes, against the growing poverty he is living in, and for an equitable and just social and political order. (p. 7)

When describing the relationship between literacy and power, Robinson (1987) charges that "our first need in studying literacy, its uses, and acquisition is an ethnography of power and its uses, the kind of study that identifies agents and their actions rather than forces and their operations" (p. 350). We must, in fact, ascertain the controller of power and its related values and practices. In this chapter we attempt to look beyond the depressed literacy skills of black youth to also focus on the determiners and disseminators of literacy skills whom Robinson calls "the agents." By doing so, we acknowledge the importance of assisting black youth in overcoming deficient literacy skills demands by developing systematic programs for reading and writing, as well as for personal and career counseling. However, combatting the forces that *perpetuate* these problems among black males can only be understood and challenged within the context of social empowerment and its constraints.

We also assert that often unsuspecting families may lend support to, rather than buffer, the adversities experienced by many black boys—adversities that appear to be designed to render them powerless. The cultural contexts of both the home environment and the school frequently combine to exert an adverse impact on the early literacy development of black males. After an overview of available information about the possible contribution of families and home environment to literacy development in black males, we return to a consideration of the contribution of early schooling to this process.

Home Environment—Impact on Literacy

Despite the ambiguities associated with definitions of "literacy," researchers continue to observe the relationship between literacy and social and psychological variables. In the 1980s, a persistently positive and significant correlation between measures of familial social status and academic achievement in modern industrial societies (e.g., Stubbs, 1980; White, 1982) invited investigation and speculation as to the relationship between cultural-familial life styles and children's literacy development.

The research of Heath (1982, 1983), Taylor (1983, 1986), Teale (1986), and others point to the significance of the family environment to children's literacy. Most of these studies attempt to describe how cultural factors and social status are mediated by family processes. The researchers assume that children experience literacy in their home environment and that these experiences are complex and varied. Most of these experiences are assumed to be associated highly with social participation in family and community and to be relatively fleeting, casual events. However, some events, such as storybook reading in middle-class homes, are more enduring and regular and, therefore, somewhat more amenable to systematic study. The more naturalistic, graphic, humanistic, and highly idiosyncratic the research methods used (e.g., Leichter, 1986; Taylor 1986), the more compelling the finding of ties between the home environment and children's acquisition of literacy.

Anderson and Stokes (1984) argue that a family's disposition to certain types of literacy events, namely, interactions around schoolbooks and homework, are tied more closely to the constraints of socioeconomic status than to either cultural or ethnic variations in the number and types of exposure to literacy events. The views of Anderson and Stokes support our argument that social and personal empowerment is the major issue to be addressed in the discussion of black males and literacy.

The role and importance of the home and family on children's literacy and educational achievement have been chronicled in research by anthropologists, linguists, educators, psychologists, and sociologists. Slaughter and Epps (1987), in an overview of the literature on the relationship between black children's school achievement and the home environment, concluded that the home environment significantly affects children's achievements, particularly in preschool and elementary school. They described the impact of the home environment during the preschool years as demonstrably effective in the areas of language stimulation and development. In addition, student self-concept and motivation for school achievement are thought to be significantly influenced by the home environment (Slaughter & Epps, 1987). However, the evidence for a direct impact of the family and home environment is less compelling for secondary school, because the student's self-concept and perceived opportunity structure assumes such an important role during adolescence.

Surprisingly, the research literature on literacy, school performance, and related areas does not address gender effects within race. The research literature since 1980 does not address black males extensively, and when it does, typically not in comparison to black females or other racial/ethnic/gender groups. Much of the research that has been conducted has been framed around a sociological perspective. Hare (1985) and others (e.g., Gary, 1981; Hare & Castenell, 1985; Patton, 1981), for example, have suggested that black boys need to be highlighted in studies, and wherever appropriate, studied within a comparative framework. The literature available on black boys and school achievement in relation to the home environment is based on short case-study observations. However, one recently published longitudinal case-study conducted by Rashid (1989) is informative.

Rashid (1989) examined data on the lives of six young African-American males from their preschool years into their early 20s. At ages 3-4, all had been identified as "at risk" for later educational failure, given their low socioeconomic status, low IQ test scores, and the low level of their mothers' education. By age 23, two of the six males were incarcerated, and a third was on probation. However, three of the six males had no criminal record; one of these three was employed and pursuing a college degree, and two others had experienced steady employment (e.g., military, taxi driving, and auto mechanics). Rashid examined the extensive longitudinal data available on these men to ascertain what factors, over time, appeared to distinguish the two groups.

Rashid found that the extent of parental involvement in the early years of schooling was critical, including the preschool program in which the boys were initially enrolled. Specifically, mothers who were depressed, and fathers who worked long hours, if present in the homes, were least likely to establish and maintain persistent and personal contact with their children's preschool and primary grade teachers. While some parents saw the preschool experience as an opportunity to enhance their children's development and their own educative skills as parents, others saw it simply as a chance to get some free babysitting.

Rashid also reported that parental mediation of peer contacts and the availability of positive adult male role models were especially important to the lives of the males who, at 23, were more socially competent. In instances in which there was early delinquency and criminality as well as a history of school failure, parents' attempts to monitor and influence their sons' selection of, and interaction with, peers was either nonexistent or crisis-oriented. These men, from the beginning, seemed to have derived much of their sense of self from peer contact and from participation in peer-related activities, such as shoplifting.

Although Rashid did not focus on classroom observations of the six boys and the contribution of differential treatment from teachers, he did find that their teachers knew whether each boy had a supportive family environment. However, the teachers did not provide any special support to help the children from less supportive families adjust to early learning in school, or school life generally.

Kunjufu (1985, 1988) has been a consultant since 1974 to numerous schools, holding workshops with parents, teachers, and students, particularly black students. He believes that there is a "fourth-grade failure syndrome" and that black boys at this age are particularly at risk if they: are not on a school athletic team or come from a nonacademic household; come from lower income families and cannot afford private school or are nonreligious; demonstrate "macho" behavior; are exposed to an influential peer group, low teacher expectations, and no significant role models; use right-brain thinking; have African features; speak black English; and possess no societal survival skills. He emphasizes that the home environment has a major role in the early development of these children and suggests that few have role models who teach them to be responsible for their education, employment, and their overall skill development.

Kunjufu argues that responsibility training should begin with the child's learning in the family how to be responsible for personhood, belongings, and household chores. This also should include age-appropriate responsibility for siblings, allowances, sexual behavior, and spirituality, as well as academic studies. According to Kunjufu, a major contributor to the fourth-grade failure syndrome demonstrated by many black boys is the absence of early and ongoing home-based responsibility training. These experiences are further reinforced in primary-grade classrooms that are not staffed by concerned male teachers and teacher aides who are aware of the cultural or gender issues facing black males. Summating his position on this syndrome, Kunjufu (1985) comments that the fourth-grade year is a pivotal year in the "conspiracy" to destroy black boys:

> This transition from the primary grade to the intermediate and upper grades has many implications. The decline in male performance can be attributed to less-than-desired teacher competency in the primary division, few male teachers, parental apathy, increased peer pressure, and greater emphasis on mass media. The high performance level of Black boys in the primary division is not the result of quality teaching, but natural, raw ability. The poor development of this ability is illustrated in their lack of enthusiasm to learn, low self-esteem, and poor self-discipline, and is manifested—not created—in upper grades. (p. 15)

Because school is the child's "work," and the work in the preschool and primary grades essentially lays the foundation for early literacy development, the findings and observations of both Rashid (1989) and Kunjufu (1985, 1988) are highly pertinent to this discussion. Both parents and teachers are responsible for teaching young black boys how to "work" in school, including how to assume increasing responsibility for their own learning and development. Although we separate the discussion of the contributions of the home and the school environments for purposes of clarity in this chapter, our position is that cooperative/collaborative efforts between families and schools are essential for the early academic progress of these young boys.

Gender effects on literacy socialization is certainly not the only area of academic achievement research that has been neglected among black youth. Few studies of gender effects on any aspects of achievement aspirations, motivation, or performance among black youth have been conducted. Between January 1980 and May 1987, for example, the ERIC Document Reproduction Service listed only 48 such studies at any academic level. Typically, these studies simply reported gender differences and did not investigate behavioral patterns potentially linked to sex-role socialization experiences and family issues. However, a few studies were notable.

Flynn (1984, 1985) found lower income preschool boys were more likely, in comparison to girls, to show growth in their capacity to exercise self-control in response to a structured, compensatory preschool program. The observed sex differences over several affective variables suggested to Flynn that this arena could merit further investigation for the purposes of effective preschool curriculum planning.

Three studies examined differential attitudes and behaviors among minority youth. Jacobowitz (1980) investigated the career preferences of 261 black eighth graders in an inner-city school. She found gender to be the strongest predictor of science career preferences, with males more often selecting such preferences. Chester (1983) compared 127 black adolescent males and females attending two desegregated high schools (1 liberal arts, 1 vocational). Males at the liberal arts school, in particular, had significantly higher aspirations, self-esteem, and more positive, vocationally relevant concepts. Similar results were reported by Grevious (1985) with an urban black college-level population. However, Gupta's (1982) study of 125 low socioeconomic status (SES) and minority male and female adolescents indicated that all racial (white, black, and Mexican-American) and gender groups reported traditional family plans and little desire for, or expectation of, high-prestige occupations. Additionally, Dawkins (1980) reported no gender-related differences in aspirations and expectations for educational achievement among black high school seniors.

Denno (1983) reported a study of 987 black children, from birth through age 15. Sex differences in verbal/spatial IQ that emerged at age 7 were related to academic achievement at age 15. However, for black boys only verbal IQ, not spatial IQ, was significant. Further, for boys, but not girls, early environmental factors were particularly useful predictors of verbal IQ. However, for both sexes, the strongest environmental predictor was socioeconomic status.

In summary, available data suggest that black males may have higher vocational and career aspirations than black females. However, their verbal skills (cf. Slaughter & Epps, 1987) are more environmentally "at risk," and the social and affective dimensions of their earliest school experiences could be particularly informative about later school achievements. Early parental involvement, in the form of parental participation, in schooling is especially important, as these young boys learn how to be responsible about schooling and about themselves as learners. Nothing less than this broader perspective of the contribution of the home environment to early literacy is likely to enhance early literacy development. Black families must be educated to assist their children in overcoming the barriers incurred by lower social status and race in America.

AMERICAN CULTURE AND SCHOOLING:
ARE BLACK BOYS AT RISK FROM THE BEGINNING?

As the primary agent of the dominant culture, the school provides more than academic education; it inculcates dominant cultural values. Too often, these values conflict with the values of other cultures and are not always in the best interest of persons most different from members of the dominant culture. Particularly for black males, who are least likely to have appropriate role models in the preschool and primary grades, this incompatibility often translates into academic failure (Grant, 1985; Hare & Castenell, 1985).

Varenne and McDermott (1986) argued that the American public school system is designed to ensure that some children fail and others succeed. Measures used to assess school performance all make strong distinctions between high achievers and underachievers and between "winners" and "losers." Beyond the use of norms on standardized tests that dictate that 50% of the respondents will perform below average and 50% at or above average, teachers' grading practices encourage the identification of above- and below-average students. Furthermore, certain student behaviors are endorsed in school, for example, Standard English (Labov, 1969) and "topic-centered speech" (Michaels & Cazden, 1986). Moreover, the school not only reinforces the notion of a power structure in which selected participants are relegated to a higher status and others to a lower status, but, by its values and practices, also creates a system conducive to success by members of a particular group or social class— middle-class white students. For minority members, particularly blacks, whose historical circumstances produced cultural and social practices different from, if not antagonistic to, the dominant cultural values manifested by the school (Ogbu, 1988), success may mean reassessment of one's priorities, at best, and denial of one's social and cultural history, at worst. Hence, the school itself, more often than not, places black children at a disadvantage for educational success.

Recent research indicates that when a child's home-based interactive style differs from the teacher's style and expectations, "interaction between teacher and child is often disharmonious and not conducive to effective help by the teacher or learning by the child" (Michaels & Cazden, 1986, p. 132). The communication skills necessary for effective classroom participation in traditional schools are routinely cultivated and supported by certain home environments, but to a much lesser degree by others. Not surprising, the language style of the classroom teacher more closely matches that of the dominant home environment which, in America, is middle class and white. This disparity, relative to both socioeconomic status and racial background, further compounds the disadvantage of the black student, particularly black students from impoverished families. The evidence abounds of children who are competent but judged otherwise by the ethnocentric standards of an intolerant, monoculturally oriented classroom (e.g., Gilmore, 1986; Heath, 1982; Michaels & Cazden, 1986; Rist, 1973). In studying an all-black classroom, Rist (1973) drew attention to teacher's perceptions of children's ability based on perceived socioeconomic status. However, neither Rist's study nor other ethnographic and observational data explicitly focus on black boys. Two case studies that do are presented later.

Over a period of six months, the second author (Richards) made weekly visits to a preschool classroom in a small Midwestern community. Although student-teacher interaction was the primary research focus, an additional concern was the students' classroom adjustment and progress. As a participant/observer, the author became involved in classroom activities and focused observations on the behaviors and experiences of several black boys, two of whom are discussed. The case studies illustrate the potential for teachers' interaction with students to thwart the educational achievement of African-American male children as early as preschool. Teachers are not necessarily conscious of their roles in inhibiting, or even stifling, the achievement of black boys. Quite often, as products themselves of an educational system and a society in which middle-class white values are espoused and the devaluation and denigration of black youth are tolerated, teachers unwittingly promulgate such values.

In the classroom, Miss Moore, the teacher, is a white woman in her mid-20s. She holds a B.A. in early childhood education; however, this is her first year teaching and, although she is a native of the community who appears quite comfortable with the black children in the classroom, she expresses a desire to work with an older age group.

Cecil: The Quiet One

A shy, 3-year-old black boy, Cecil, rarely spoke in the classroom. He lives with his mother and father and a 4-year-old brother. Cecil's language behavior is especially interesting because his mother claims that he speaks at home "all the time" and "is more talkative and alert than his older brother." Efforts to get Cecil to speak in the classroom were rarely successful when initiated by the teacher or others. Even simple questions, such as "What is your name?" or "Which toy would you like to play with today?" would not evoke a response from Cecil. Thinking that it might make a difference, the teacher suggested that Cecil's mother visit the class for about an hour; this, however, did not make Cecil any more verbal. Strangely enough, however, Cecil did speak when least expected. One instance occurred with the teacher during lunch. The teacher, noticing that Cecil was not eating, inquired: "Cecil, why aren't you eating?" Much to her surprise, Cecil responded: "I ain't got no fork." Another unexpected reply came when the second author was helping Cecil get his coat on to go home. Somewhat distractedly, the second author asked Cecil, "Where is your hat?" He responded, "In my bag."

The birth of a new baby brother toward the end of the school year proved to be a highlight of Cecil's young life, spurring him to become more communicative in the classroom. Just after his brother was born, Cecil wanted to tell everyone about the new addition to his family. Indeed, whenever he was asked about his new brother, Cecil would volunteer the baby's name and proceed to describe how small the baby was and how much milk he drank. After the novelty of his new brother wore off, Cecil reverted to his quieter ways, although his occasional verbalization was more frequent.

Clearly, Cecil was capable of speaking. His occasional conversation as well as his mother's testimony attest to this. Why then did he choose not to speak? Possibly, Cecil had a difficult time adjusting to the structure and routine of the classroom, as well as to the teacher. Specifically, the linguistic as well as cultural environment of the classroom may have led to his reticence as a way of coping with the discomfort he experienced in school.

In the classroom Cecil was subjected to a totally unfamiliar figure, the authority of a white woman, with a different manner of speech from that of his parents. To compound his probable dilemma, the type of communication within the classroom required different verbal behavior (e.g., Does anyone know what this is? Now, it's time for . . . What do you think happened next? Tell Mr. Richards what we did yesterday.). As Heath (1982) suggests, the type of speech occurring in the classroom may often be so different from the speech in the child's home environment as to hinder the child's classroom adjustment and, ultimately, his or her academic achievement. Perhaps Cecil's transition to school would have been easier if the regular teacher had been black and, preferably, male. Whenever the author visited the classroom, Cecil was the first one to approach him. Cecil insisted on spending as much time with him as possible and became noticeably upset when he did not get to hold his hand on the way to the playground. His pleasure in having a black male adult in the classroom was obvious.

Cecil's language behavior was a primary concern because of the importance placed on oral communication within the mainstream classroom. An integral part of the American instructional system—verbal exchange between teacher and student—not only contributes to the educational process, but also provides for much of the perceptions teachers form about students. Furthermore, as evidenced in classroom oral activities such as Story Time in which the student tells the class about a personal experience, teachers often attempt to influence student language behavior and thinking by systematically amending students' speaking styles (Michaels & Cazden, 1986). The student who is noncommunicative without a specific disability, therefore, is viewed as resisting classroom socialization and becomes suspect by the teacher. By Cecil's limited verbalization, he is placed at risk for being ignored by the teacher, or worse, classified as verbally or mentally deficient. Indeed, his chances of becoming "invisible" in the classroom increases, and, with this invisibility, access to literacy decreases (Gadsden, 1991).

Cecil's refusal to speak in the classroom and the teacher's inability to rectify the problem provide an interesting example of early conflicts that could lead to long-term classroom maladjustment. Not finding his introduction to formal education especially comfortable, Cecil may come to regard school as a place where he is made to feel uneasy. The very avenue that we would argue essential for Cecil's full empowerment to shape his life may come to be viewed as a means of disempowerment. To be sure, unless Cecil eventually encounters a teacher who is able to bridge the gap between his home and school, his discomfort with the classroom setting will adversely impact on academic achievement throughout his school life.

In summary, we believe that cultural and linguistic style were importantly implicated in Cecil's school behaviors. Cecil did verbalize when he had the opportunity to bring some experiences from his home environment into the classroom with a positive reception, when he was asked a direct question to which he could give a direct reply (Heath, 1982), and when a culturally familiar person (i.e., a black man) was part of his academic environment.

Sam: The Talented One

A very talkative, personable, bright 3-year-old black boy, Sam appeared to thrive on the practices of the classroom. Very much involved in classroom activities, he demonstrated an eagerness to learn. Sam lived with his Jamaican-born father, his American mother, and a baby brother. His family appeared to play an active role in his school life, attending parent-teacher meetings and occasionally picking him up after school.

Sam's receptive and expressive language was good and appeared to be appropriate for his age. Whenever the teacher asked a question, Sam always responded, usually with the correct answer. He was often the one who answered when the children were asked what was done in the classroom on the previous day. Additionally, he was able to identify colors and shapes with reasonable accuracy, whereas many of the other children still lacked this ability. Finally, being relatively independent, he worked on a task when told to do so without becoming too distracted.

Sam was observant and learned quickly. For example, on a walk to the park, he noticed a statue of a man with an animal draped over his shoulder and exclaimed: "Look he has a snake around his neck!" All nodded in agreement. However, Sam continued to look back somewhat puzzled, as though he wasn't sure. On closer inspection, Miss Moore realized that what looked like a snake was really the neck of a duck, with its body hanging in back of the man. When Miss Moore correctly identified the animal, he appeared relieved and said, "Yes, I can see the other part of him." On that same walk, the teacher saw some birds pecking in the dirt and asked the class, "What do you think they're doing?" All but Sam looked questioningly at Miss Moore. Sam enthusiastically responded, "They're looking for worms to eat," as he proceeded to pantomime how birds dig for worms.

In spite of Miss Moore's acknowledgment that Sam appeared more advanced than the rest of the children, she still voiced reservations about his classroom progress. Despite praise for his demonstrated cognitive abilities, she felt, as the year progressed, that his maturity declined. She specifically referred to what she claimed was his need to be "teacher's pet." Citing Sam's attempt to monopolize her attention, Miss Moore expressed a desire to see him become less dependent on her. Taken at face value, this may appear to be a valid concern of the teacher. However, when considered in light of Sam's overall academic prowess, his behavior as compared to the other students, and his age, the validity of the teacher's comment becomes suspect.

If, in fact, Sam exhibited attention-seeking behavior, the teacher may have indirectly encouraged it by constantly demonstrating her pleasure with Sam's correct responses in class. Furthermore, at 3 years old, Sam's attachment to the teacher, whom he probably saw as a well of knowledge for his thirsty mind, could hardly be termed immature. Indeed, it may be that at such an early age Sam recognized the teacher and the knowledge she possessed as a source of power. His behavior demonstrated an awareness that the teacher's authority was supported by what she knew and what he did not.

In discussing the culture of power and education, Delpit (1988) submits that those with power are often ignorant of, or unwilling to admit, its existence; those with less power are often very cognizant of its existence. Furthermore, for the so-called radical or liberal teacher, it is most discomforting to be viewed as a member of the power elite. The dynamics of power described by Delpit may be applicable to the roles exhibited by Sam and Miss Moore. Whereas Sam readily acknowledged his teacher's power, the teacher may have felt uncomfortable with the power-elite role ascribed to her. As suggested by Delpit's argument, the teacher's discomfort with her membership in the culture of power may have prompted her to distance herself from Sam, whose adulating behavior constantly reminded her of her powerful status.

Other research suggests that factors outside of Sam's control may have been operating in the teacher's evaluation of him. Grant's (1985) ethnographic study of black boys, in comparison to white boys and girls and black girls in six first-grade classrooms, revealed that teachers of black students always identified one black male "superstar" among their pupils. However, Grant noted a recurrent disparity between the descriptions of black male achievers and their male counterparts of other races. In describing black male superstars, teachers used qualifications that denoted "the hint of some potential problem." Furthermore, teachers praised a black male student for his work but, at the same time, reminded him of the imperfection of his performance (e.g., "Good, but watch the spacing a bit more."). Grant (1985) concluded:

> [T]hese messages were consistent with teachers' mostly negative perceptions of Black males' academic skills. Such language might have conveyed to Black males, and to eavesdropping classmates, messages that these students' work needed careful supervision and usually fell short of first-rate standards. The patterns also were consistent with the teachers' perceptions that high academic performance was more difficult to achieve among Black males. (p. 15)

Teachers are not immune to enculturation by the values of the dominant culture. Consequently, attitudes that serve to buttress the power structure of the dominant culture are exhibited by teachers in their interaction with students. Black males are not expected to excel academically. Sam's teacher may have been evaluating him in the only way she knew how—praising him—with qualifications. Interviews with her indicated that she really believed she honestly gave Sam credit for his academic promise and that her admonishments about his behavior were intended to be constructive. However, because she did not unconditionally support Sam's academic self-worth, she actually may have helped to erode his confidence in his ability to be an active, responsible learner. Aware of their son's talents, and trusting in current feedback from the teacher, Sam's parents were probably unaware of this aspect of his early socialization into school.

The case of Sam illustrates that despite a bright and inquisitive mind, Sam is still at risk for not achieving his full potential. By denying Sam unequivocal praise when he is worthy of it, the school system, through the classroom teacher may, in fact, serve to stymie Sam's ambition. If the message he receives is that in school he can never receive full credit for his efforts, then there is little incentive to excel there. Most likely Sam thought he was doing everything possible to please the teacher, answering all her questions, seeking her assistance, and doing his classroom chores. It is doubtful that his young mind imagined that she would still find him lacking. However, she did. Hopefully, Sam will encounter future teachers who will recognize him without qualifications as a superior student.

Summary

Cecil and Sam provide interesting contrasts in classroom behavior. Cecil, the less verbal, did not appear to adapt to the classroom very well. Sam, the more verbal, appeared to thrive on the practices of the classroom. We could say that whereas Cecil was resistant to school socialization, Sam was highly amenable. Given the two personality profiles, if educators were asked to predict whether either was at risk for underachievement in school, the likely choice would be Cecil. However, we argue that Cecil and Sam are equally at risk; Cecil because of maladjustment, and Sam because of disenchantment. Without appropriate efforts by the school to accommodate Cecil, primarily by recognizing sociolinguistic conflicts between his home environment and that of the school (Heath, 1982, 1983, 1986; Smitherman, 1977), academic underachievement is highly likely. For Sam, knowing that his efforts are fairly rewarded by the school will bode well for his future academic achievement.

Many black boys in preschool and primary-grade classrooms present more complex portraits than those of Cecil and Sam. Both Cecil and Sam were accustomed to social order, family stability, and a degree of continuity between adult expectations at home and those at school. Both boys complied with teacher requests, and neither boy demonstrated behavior to suggest that he found compliance with a female and white teacher's preferences threatening (Paley, 1984).

Interdisciplinary perspectives are required to understand literacy as it influences black men, and, of course, developing black boys. We argued that the social and personal empowerment of these individuals is linked to literacy, and that because socioeconomic status is an integral feature of American culture, black males are particularly vulnerable to early socialization experiences that negate eventual empowerment. They are vulnerable because their families are more likely to be impoverished, with relatively little power and influence on other societal institutions such as schools, and because dominant cultural attitudes, particularly stereotypes about the intellectual and social inferiority of black males, still prevail. The functional value of these attitudes in the dominant culture is to retain power among members of the dominant group. Therefore, like others (e.g., Grant, 1985; Holliday, 1985; Rist, 1973), we perceive teachers as agents of the American cultural value system.

CONCLUSION

Although research in literacy has expanded significantly over the past few years, and despite a growing interest in the development of black males across disciplines, few research studies and programs of intervention examine these two issues within one context. An expanded definition of literacy permits the integrative, interdisciplinary research and intervention focus needed by black youth, particularly black males. Curricular interventions (e.g., Edwards, 1989, this volume, describes a very useful approach for the primary grades), although absolutely necessary, will not be sufficient to improve the educational prospects of black youth.

What is ultimately required is the institutional reevaluation and resocialization of individuals who encourage or tolerate negative attitudes and beliefs about black boys' educational potential. One way to honor that commitment is to influence the nature and content of teacher-training institutions (see Rist, 1973, for a thoughtful discussion of this point).

Second, a concerted effort should be made to increase the presence of black males in the educational life of black boys in the preschool and primary grades. For example, programs that involve fathers and other male kin in the school's life should be developed; more black male teachers and teacher aides should be trained in schools and colleges of education throughout the nation; more volunteer workers and presentations should be solicited by schools from black men in all walks of American life. The presence of these men would affirm the importance of formal education to developing black boys.

Third, a special appeal for heightened awareness of this issue needs to be directed to black families. The early socialization of black boys in America should not continue to be perceived by men and women as "women's work." Indeed, black families are charged with an enormous task—acting as change agents. What the schools threaten to usurp in terms of cultural identity, self-worth, especially academic self-worth, and even manhood, given the perceived close ties between education and work in American society, families must counter through consistent supportive, constructive efforts. Positive reinforcement for academic achievement, often denied at school, must be given at home; discipline and expectations for high achievement, too often denied at school, must be provided at home. Black communities, and society in general, must act to reverse the expectation of a "job ceiling" regardless of educational persistence, an expectation apparently often perceived by black adolescents (Ogbu, 1988) and corroborated in this chapter's discussion of available statistics on educational attainment and labor-force participation rates.

In the 1990s, we realize that black communities do not benefit from a societal climate that is conducive to the long-term effectiveness of specific intervention programs. Now we must think carefully about the environmental contexts in which such programs can realistically expect to be beneficial. This requires an ecological perspective, that is, the broadened definition of literacy.

Finally, we need more research into the course of development experienced by black youth in the diverse settings in which they are situated throughout the nation. The research should be designed and conducted to inform educational and labor-force policy making in the 21st century. To do less would be to break the social contract that this government has made with its people.

REFERENCES

Alkalimat, A., & Associates. (1986). *Introduction to Afro-American studies*. Chicago: Twenty-first Century Books and Publications.

Anderson, A., & Stokes, S. (1984). Social and institutional influence on the development and practice of literacy. In H. Gelman, A. Oberg, & F. Smith (Eds.), *Awakening to literacy* (pp. 24-37). Exeter, NH: Heinemann Educational Books.

Anderson, J. (1988). *The education of Blacks in the South, 1860-1935*. Chapel Hill: University of North Carolina Press.

Berlin, G., & Sum, A. (1988). *Toward a more perfect union: Basic skills, poor families, and our economic futures*. New York: Ford Foundation.

Bowman, P. (1989). Research perspectives on black men: Role strain and adaptation across the adult life cycle. In R. L. Jones (Ed.), *Black adult development and aging* (pp. 117-150). Berkeley, CA: Cobbs & Henry.

Bowman, P. (1990). Coping with provider role strain: Adaptive cultural resources among black husband-fathers. *Journal of Black Psychology, 16*, 1-22.

Chester, N. (1983). Sex differentiation in two high school environments: Implications for career development among Black adolescent females. *Journal of Social Issues, 39*, 29-40.

Dawkins, M. (1980). Educational and occupational goals: Male versus female Black high school seniors. *Urban Education, 15*, 231-242.

Delpit, L. (1983). The silenced dialogue: Power and pedagogy in educating other people's children. *Harvard Educational Review, 58*, 280-298.

Denno, D. (1983). *Neuropsychological and early maturational correlates of intelligence*. Washington, DC: Department of Justice, LEAA. (ERIC Document Reproduction Service No. ED 234 920)

Edwards, P. (1989, October). *Connecting Black parents and youth to the school's reading curriculum*. Paper presented at the conference on "Literacy Among Black Youth: Issues in Learning, Teaching, and

Schooling." Literacy Research Center, Graduate School of Education, University of Pennsylvania.

Ferguson, R.F. (1990). *Improving the lifes and futures of at-risk black male youth: Insights from theory and program experience.* Report to Rockefeller Foundation and the Urban Institute.

Flynn, T. (1984). Affective characteristics that predict preschool achievement in disadvantaged children. *Early Child Development and Care, 16,* 251-263.

Flynn, T. (1985). Development of self concept, delay of gratification and self-control and disadvantaged preschool children's achievement gain. *Early Child Development and Care, 22,* 65-72.

Franklin, V., & Anderson, J. (Eds.). (1978). *New perspectives on Black educational history.* Boston: G.K. Hall.

Gadsden, V. (1991). Trying one more time! Gaining and retaining access to literacy in African-American youth and adults. In M. Foster (Ed.), *Readings in equal education Volume 11: Qualitative investigations into schools and schooling* (pp.). New York: AMS Press.

Gary, L. (1981). A social profile. In L. Gary (Ed.), *Black men* (pp. 21-45). Beverly Hills, CA: Sage.

Gilmore, P. (1986). Sub-rosa literacy: Peers, play, and ownership in literacy. In B. B. Schieffelin & P. Gilmore (Eds.), *The acquisition of literacy: Ethnographic perspectives* (pp. 155-168). Norwood, NJ: Ablex.

Grant, L. (1985, April 1). *Uneasy alliances: Black males, teachers, and peers in desegregated classrooms.* Paper presented at the annual meeting of the American Educational Research Association, Chicago, IL.

Grevious, C. (1985). A comparison of occupational aspirations of urban Black college students. *Journal of Negro Education, 54,* 35-42.

Gupta, N. (1982). *The influence of sex roles on the life plans of low-SES adolescents* (Report No. EDN00001). Washington, DC: National Institute of Education. (ERIC Document Reproduction Service No. ED 235 434)

Hare, B. (1985). Reexamining the central tendency: Sex differences within race and race differences within sex. In H. McAdoo & J. McAdoo (Eds.), *Black children: Social, educational, and parental environments* (pp. 139-158). Beverly Hills, CA: Sage.

Hare, B., & Castenell, L. (1985). No place to run, no place to hide: Comparative status and future prospects of Black boys. In M. B. Spencer, G. K. Brookins, & W. R. Allen (Eds.), *Beginnings: The social and affective development of Black children* (pp. 201-214). Hillsdale, NJ: Erlbaum.

Heath, S. (1982). Questioning at home and at school: A comparative study. In G. Spindler (Ed.), *Doing the ethnography of schooling: Educational anthropology in action* (pp. 96-101). New York: Holt, Rinehart, & Winston.

Heath, S. (1983). *Ways with words: Language, life, and work communities and classrooms.* Cambridge, England: Cambridge University Press.

Heath, S. (1986). The functions and uses of literacy. In S. deCastell, A. Luke, & K. Eqan (Eds.), *Literacy, society, and schooling* (pp. 15-26).

Cambridge, England: Cambridge University Press.

Holliday, B. (1985). Towards a model of teacher-child transactional processes effecting Black children's academic achievement. In M.B. Spencer, G. K. Brookins, & W. R. Allen (Eds.), *Beginnings: The social and affective development of Black children* (pp. 117-130). Hillsdale, NJ: Erlbaum.

Holt, T. (1990). "Knowledge is power": The black struggle for literacy. In A. A. Lunsford, H. Moglan, & J. Slevin (Eds.), *The right to literacy* (pp. 91-102). New York: Modern Language Association.

Jacobowitz, T. (1980). *Factors associated with science career preferences of Black junior high school students.* Department of Educational Leadership, Montclair State College, Montclair, NJ. (ERIC Document Reproduction & Service No. ED 212 851)

Kunjufu, J. (1985). *Countering the conspiracy to destroy Black boys* (Vol. 1). Chicago: African American Images.

Kunjufu, J. (1988). *Countering the conspiracy to destroy Black boys* (Vol. 2). Chicago: African American Images.

Labov, W. (1969). The logic of nonstandard English. In J. Alatis (Ed.), *Georgetown University Monograph Series on Languages and Linguistics* (Vol. 22). Washington, DC: Georgetown University Press.

Leichter, H. (1974). *The family as educator.* New York: Teachers College Press.

Levine, K. (1986). *The social context of literacy.* London: Routledge & Kegan Paul.

Michaels, S., & Cazden, C. (1986). Teacher/child collaboration as oral preparation for literacy. In B. B. Schieffelin & P. Gilmore (Eds.), *The acquisition of literacy: Ethnographic perspectives* (pp. 132-154). Norwood, NJ: Ablex.

National Center For Educational Statistics (NCES). United States Department of Education. Office of Educational Research and Improvement. (1985). *Digest of Educational Statistics* (25th ed.). Washington, DC: U.S. Government Printing Office.

Ogbu, J. (1988). Cultural diversity and human development. In D. Slaughter (Ed.), *Black children and poverty: A developmental perspective* (pp. 11-28). San Francisco: Jossey-Bass.

Paley, V. (1984). *Boys and girls: Superheroes in the doll corner.* Chicago: University of Chicago Press.

Patton, J. (1981). The Black male's struggle for an education. In L. Gary (Ed.), *Black men* (pp. 199-214). Beverly Hills, CA: Sage

Rashid, H. (1989). Divergent paths in the development of African-American males: A qualitative perspective. *Urban Research Review, 12*(1), 1-2, 12-13. (Available from Howard University, Institute for Urban Affairs and Research, 2900 Van Ness Street, N.W., Washington, DC 20008.)

Reed, R. (1988). Education and achievement of young Black males. In J. T. Gibbs (Ed.), *Young, Black and male in America: An endangered species* (pp. 37-96). Dover, MA: Auburn House Publishing Co.

Rist, R. (1973). *The urban school: A factory for failure.* Cambridge, MA: MIT Press.

Robinson, J. (1987). Literacy in society: Readers and writers in the world of discourse. In D. Bloome (Ed.), *Literacy and schooling* (pp. 327-353). Norwood, NJ: Ablex.

Slaughter, D., & Epps, E. (1987). The home environment and academic achievement of Black American children and youth: An overview. *Journal of Negro Education, 56,* 3-20.

Slaughter, D., & Johnson, D. (Eds.). (1988). *Visible now: Blacks in private schools.* Westport, CT: Greenwood.

Smitherman, G. (1977). *Talkin' and testifyin': The language of Black America.* Boston: Houghton Mifflin.

Stedman, L., & Kaestle, C. (1987). Literacy and reading performance in the United States, from 1880 to the present. *Reading Research Quarterly, 22,* 8-46.

Stevens, E., Jr. (1988). *Literacy, law, and social order.* DeKalb: Northern Illinois University Press.

Stubbs, M. (1980). *Language and literacy: The sociolinguistics of reading and writing.* London: Routledge & Kegan Paul.

Taylor, D. (1983). *Young children learning to read and write.* Exeter, NH: Heinemann Educational Books.

Taylor, D. (1986). Creating family story: "Matthew! We're going to have a ride!" In W. H. Teale & E. Sulzby (Eds.), *Emergent literacy: Writing and reading* (pp. 139-155). Norwood, NJ: Ablex.

Teale, W. (1986). Home background and young children's literacy development. In W. H. Teale & E. Sulzby (Eds.), *Emergent literacy: Writing and reading* (pp. 173-206). Norwood, NJ: Ablex.

United States Department of Commerce. Bureau of the Census. (1989). *Statistical Abstracts of the United States* (109th). Washington, DC: U.S. Government Printing Office.

United States Department of Labor. Bureau of Labor Statistics. (1989, December). *Employment and Training Report of the President.* Washington, DC: U.S. Government Printing Office.

Varenne, H., & McDermott, R. (1986). Why Sheila can read: Structure and indeterminacy in the reproduction of familial literacy. In B.B. Schieffelin & P. Gilmore (Eds.), *The acquisition of literacy: Ethnographic perspectives* (pp. 188-210). Norwood, NJ: Ablex.

Venezky, R., Wagner, D., & Ciliberti, B. (Eds.). (1990). *Toward defining literacy.* Newark, DE: International Reading Association.

White, K. (1982). The relations between socioeconomic status and academic achievement. *Psychological Bulletin, 91,* 461-481.

Introduction to Part III
Literacy, School Policy
and Classroom Practice

Michele Foster
University of California-Davis

Over the past 30 years, educational researchers have advanced a number of theories to explain the academic failures and low levels of literacy attainment of African-American children. The most common of these theories include the cultural-deficit and cultural-conflict theories. Language and communicative patterns are central to both of these theories. According to the proponents of the first, African-American students perform poorly in school because their home and neighborhood environments do not adequately prepare them to succeed in school. Those who adhere to this theory argue that African-American parents do not expose their children to the kinds of language and communicative skills that are a necessary foundation for successful literacy learning. Conversely, proponents of the cultural-conflict view argue that the language and communicative skills African-American children master at home are not deficient, per se, but that these repertoires are in conflict with the communicative and linguistic patterns valued in school and those which African-American children bring to school (see Ogbu, 1987, and Erickson, 1987, for a comprehensive discussion of these positions).

Although home, community, and cultural factors are significant to the achievement of African-American students, a singular focus on these issues masks the institutional barriers and policy decisions which, although not always visible, seriously constrain African-American students' access to high-quality instruction. Each of the chapters in this section analyzes how educational policy decisions and institutional policies and practices result in differential access to school resources for African-American students, even when they attend the same school.

In Chapter 7, Darling-Hammond argues that a large part of the difference in school achievement between African Americans and other groups is the result of limited access to well-prepared and highly skilled teachers. After examining some of the reasons for the shortage of well-prepared teachers, she discusses why good teachers are unevenly distributed between poor and affluent communities, gifted and talented programs, and regular programs and high and low tracks. She argues that no matter how well intentioned, policies that promote alternate certification routes designed to address teacher shortages produce teachers whose classroom performance is less skilled than that of teachers prepared in more conventional programs. She contends further that this marginal classroom performance is evident in the language arts achievement of pupils. Despite being highly critical of the policies that place less qualified teachers in the classrooms of African-American pupils, she offers a number of policy recommendations—financial incentives, differentiated staffing, support for novice teachers, and improvement of the working conditions of urban teachers—that are not only necessary to make teaching into a full-fledged profession but also important to ensure that well-prepared, highly skilled teachers, including teachers of color, will be available to work with students who are currently least well served by public schools.

Complementing Darling-Hammond's analysis is Braddock's chapter (Chapter 8). Combining the data from several nationwide surveys, Braddock analyzes the patterns and trends in the tracking and ability grouping for African-American students and other students of color over 10 years, comparing these trends to those of white students. His discussion illustrates a pattern of pupil assignment in which African-American students are disproportionately placed in vocational and general programs over academic ones. Braddock concludes his chapter by presenting several alternatives to tracking and ability grouping. He cautions his readers, however, that viable options to current tracking and ability grouping practices are unlikely to occur without genuine investment in staff development.

In the final chapter of this section (Chapter 9), Fine considers how social policies and inequities in society are manifest in a particular set of administrative policies and classroom practices in one New York

City high school. Fine examines how administrative procedures and classroom discussions are intended to "silence"—by not naming the contradictions, complexities, and inequities that exist in students' day-to-day encounters in the larger community.

It is this very process of naming—of not silencing—that links the chapters in this section. By naming the educational policies that place better prepared and more highly skilled teachers in some classrooms and not others, we mask the structural inequalities that contribute to low literacy-achievement levels among African-American students. By naming the tracking and ability grouping patterns that give some students access to more privileged knowledge than others, we dispel the myth that the civil rights movement eliminated the last vestiges of the United States' caste society.

The strength of the chapters in this section is that they redirect our attention away from community, family, and cultural explanations of school failure to the educational policies and institutional practices that result in the inequitable distribution of educational resources. Some analysts have argued that access to better school resources will not automatically guarantee higher achievement or literacy levels. Whether this is true, we cannot ignore the fact that inequitable distribution and differential access to school resources illustrates how the caste system continues to operate in U.S. schools. At the same time that we push for more relevant curricula, more culturally responsive pedagogy, and improved home-school relations, we cannot lose sight of the fact that eliminating all traces of the caste system in society and schools should be the ultimate goal of our efforts.

REFERENCES

Erickson, F. (1987). Transformation and school success: The politics of educational achievement. *Anthropology of Education Quarterly, 18*(4), 335-356.

Ogbu, J. (1987). Variability in minority school performance: A problem in search of an explanation. *Anthropology of Education Quarterly, 18*(4), 312-334.

8

Tracking and School Achievement: Implications for Literacy Development*

Jomills Henry Braddock II
University of Miami

INTRODUCTION

Notwithstanding the growing national attention focused on problems of adult literacy, illiteracy is not the preserve of older Americans. Six percent of all 9-year-olds in the United States lack rudimentary reading skills. Forty percent of 13-year-olds have not mastered the reading skills necessary to perform at acceptable levels in the middle grades. By age 17, 16% of American youth who are still in school have not attained a level of literacy to be able to read for specific information, draw generalizations from a text, or make connections between their own ideas and the ideas in a text. At all three age-grade levels included in the National

*The author is grateful to Vivian Gadsden, John Hollifield, and Daniel Wagner for their helpful comments on earlier drafts of this manuscript. This research was supported by a grant from the Office of Educational Research and Improvement, Grant R117 R90002. However, the opinions expressed are those of the author and do not represent OERI positions or policy, and no official endorsement should be inferred.

Assessment of Educational Progress studies, African-American and Latino students performed worse than white students (National Assessment of Educational Progress, 1985, 1990).

Literacy among African-American youth, like among other young people in our society, is developed in large measure through learning experiences in schools. Notwithstanding the important roles played by families, communities, and other social institutions in literacy development, schools are the primary institutions in which literacy learning occurs. (For thoughtful discussions of the important roles of families, communities, and other social institutions, readers should pay special attention to the chapters in this volume by Scott-Jones, Slaughter-Defoe & Richards, and Ogbu.) Schools, which are the primary focus of this chapter, have failed miserably in providing even basic literacy skills to far too many of those they serve, especially young people of color (Venezky, Wagner, & Ciliberti, 1990).

Although American public education is based on a common school ideology, which purports to promote equal access to all learners, widespread and entrenched patterns of tracking and between-class ability grouping in our nation's schools often result in differentiated classroom learning opportunities for students. If students primarily learn what they are taught or are exposed to, these differentiated learning opportunities in schools have important implications for youth's literacy development. Research on reading instruction, for example, shows that classroom teachers teach good readers and poor readers differently in several important ways. Competent readers are assigned silent reading tasks more often and are monitored orally less often than poor readers. Because students who are reading silently spend more time engaged in reading than students who are involved in oral reading groups, the good readers actually receive more practice time than the poor readers (Allington, 1980). In addition, teacher interruptions of good readers are more often directed toward meaning and understanding, whereas their interruptions of poor readers are aimed at punctuation errors (Allington, 1980, 1983).

Studies of tracking and ability grouping have called attention to their potential harmful effects on African-American, low-income, racial, and ethnic subgroup students who are often overrepresented among the low tracks and classes (Oakes, 1985). Yet, very little is known about the prevalence of tracking and ability grouping in schools or about the actual dispersion of African-American, Latino, American Indian, Asian, and white students across school programs or classes of different ability levels. This chapter discusses student maldistributions across tracks and ability groups and the implications of these maldistributions for literacy development among African-American and other student subgroups.

These issues are addressed in this chapter using several different sources of large nationwide survey data to summarize current national profiles of school practices of tracking and ability grouping across the grades, to analyze recent trends in secondary-level tracking of African-American and other student subgroups, to discuss the implications of tracking for African-American and white students' educational outcomes such as adult literacy, and to consider alternative strategies that schools can use to address problems of effective instructional strategies for heterogenous classes and student diversity.

BACKGROUND ISSUES

In theory, schools use tracking or between-class ability grouping to accommodate instruction to the diversity of their student's needs, interests, and abilities. The assumption is that students will learn best when the instructional content is matched well to their current knowledge and abilities. Thus, it is necessary to divide students into homogeneous learning groups to have an effective instructional program. With homogeneous groups, a teacher can offer a lesson that no student finds too hard or too easy, which in theory should increase significantly each student's motivation and learning.

The arguments against tracking usually focus on the fact that tracking leads to unequal educational opportunities by distributing formal and informal educational resources unequally to different students (Darling-Hammond, this volume). The critics of tracking point out that lower track classrooms are usually assigned the least experienced teachers, even though they enroll the students with the greatest needs and who may be the most challenging to teach. Indeed, many districts and schools allow their most senior teachers to choose the tracks they wish to teach. The result is frequently the weakening of learning environments for students in the lowest tracks.

The most serious resource allocation problem involves the informal climate of the classroom, especially in terms of expectations for student achievement (Gadsden, 1991). Numerous case studies show that the lower track classes are often stigmatized by a general feeling that their students are not capable learners and cannot be expected to master the same kinds of skills that are demanded of other classes. When such negative images are shared by teachers and students in lower track classes, certain instructional consequences follow: fewer curriculum units are covered, the pace of instruction is slower, fewer demands are made for learning higher order skills, and test and homework requirements are taken less seriously (Oakes, 1985; Mitchell, Haycock, & Navarro, 1989).

Critics of tracking also describe a cumulative process through the grades that actually widens the gap in achievement between students in the top and bottom levels over time (Goodlad, 1983). Because the learning environments are weaker in the lower tracks, a student who is first assigned to a bottom class has an even poorer chance at the next grade level to move up to a higher class. So the effects of tracking produce slower and slower rates of learning for those at the bottom and fewer and fewer chances of receiving better track assignments. The cumulative effects are greatest when the tracking process starts in the early elementary grades.

Tracking can also undermine efforts to desegregate schools because students from poor socioeconomic backgrounds are most likely to wind up in low tracks (Epstein, 1985). Thus, in racially mixed schools, tracking usually produces a resegregation of African-American and white students into different classes within the school and fewer chances for minority students to progress to high school completion and college enrollment. Challenges to ability grouping have also become a key issue in a number of school desegregation cases (e.g., *Hobson v. Hansen*, 1967; *U.S. Department of Education v. Dillon County School District No. 1*, 1986).

There are recent signs that some of the problems of tracking may be finally addressed in practice (Braddock & McPartland, 1990; Slavin, Braddock, Hall, & Petza, 1989). As a result of major efforts for school restructuring recommended by both school practitioners and education policymakers, or often out of a concern for social justice, many districts have begun to reexamine their ability grouping practices. Nevertheless, it is also important to recognize that there are powerful forces at many schools and districts who perceive tracking to be in their own best interest. In particular, when the elimination of tracking is proposed, parents of the highest achieving students and teachers who can influence their own class assignments are often the most outspoken opponents of doing away with it. Many of the parents of high-achieving students designated as "gifted and talented" often worry that the quality of instruction their children receive in upper-level tracked classes will be seriously compromised if the student mix in classes becomes more academically heterogeneous, and they will fight hard against any attempts to do away with tracking. In addition, teachers in many districts who have obtained seniority rights to choose upper track assignments will act to protect the opportunities for job satisfaction and professional prestige that these assignments give them. Further discussion of the potential quality-equity tradeoffs of tracking can be found in McPartland and Crain (1987).

How pervasive are tracking and between-class ability grouping in the nation's public schools? To what extent are African-American, Latino, American Indian, and Asian students maldistributed across curriculum tracks and ability-grouped classes? We shed some light on these questions by, first, presenting descriptive profiles that show the status of high school curriculum tracking of race-ethnic student subgroups in 1982 compared to 1972, based on High School and Beyond (HSB) data and National Longitudinal Study of the High School Class of 1972 (NLS) data. Second, we present national distributions that show the overall prevalence of between-class grouping and curriculum tracking in American schools, based on data from the NLS, the HSB, and the Johns Hopkins University 1988 National Survey of Middle Grades Principals. Lastly, we use data from the 1986 National Assessment of Educational Progress (NAEP) Young Adult Literacy Survey to examine the effects of track placement on young adult literacy.

PATTERNS, TRENDS, AND INEQUITIES IN TRACKING AND ABILITY GROUPING: CROSS-CULTURAL COMPARISONS

High School Program Placement

Table 8.1 presents nationally representative data that show the status of curriculum track placement for African-American, Latino, American Indian, Asian, and white high school students in 1982 (HSB data, top panel) and in 1972 (NLS data, bottom panel). Descriptions of other societal norms and forces that create an inertia against changes in tracking can be found in Oakes (1989) and Slavin et al. (1989). These data allow us to examine two aspects of tracking: first, the recent status of tracking (in 1982) and the dissimilar distributions among the various student populations, and, second, trends in curriculum program tracking among these student populations during the 10-year period from 1972 to 1982.

We examine these data to compare the curriculum track status of African-American and Latino high school seniors with the curriculum track status of white high school seniors in 1982 and in 1972 and identify trends over the 10-year period for these populations.

We then report the status of American Indian and Asian subgroups compared to whites in 1982; no comparable 1972 data are available for these populations.

African-American students. The top panel of Table 8.1 shows that 36% of African-American high school seniors in 1982 were enrolled in academic programs compared to 41% of white seniors, 25% were in general education programs versus 30% of white seniors, and 39% were enrolled in vocational education programs versus 29% of white seniors. Thus, compared to whites in 1982, African-American students were sig-

Table 8.1. Curricular Program Enrollment of 1982 and 1972 High School Seniors by Race-Ethnic Group

Cohort and Curriculum Track	Race-Ethnic Category					
	Hispanic	American Indian	Asian	African-American	White	Total
1982 Seniors	(N=1759)	(N=198)	(N=178)	(N=1743)	(N=9503)	(N=13382)
ACADEMIC						
Percent	26.5*	18.8*	58.0*	35.9*	40.9	38.3
Parity Index	.65	.46	1.42	.88	1.00	
GENERAL						
Percent	29.6	48.8*	22.4*	25.5*	30.2	29.7
Parity Index	.98	1.62[a]	.74	.84	1.00	
VOCATIONAL						
Percent	43.9*	32.4	19.6*	38.7*	28.9	32.1
Parity Index	1.52	1.12	.68	1.34	1.00	
1972 Seniors	(N=631)	—[b]	—	(N=1594)	(N=3491)	(N=5715)
ACADEMIC						
Percent	28.1*	—	—	33.0*	52.5	44.3
Parity Index	.54	—	—	.63	1.00	
GENERAL						
Percent	42.4*	—	—	33.9*	28.2	31.3
Parity Index	1.50	—	—	1.20	1.00	
VOCATIONAL						
Percent	29.5*	—	—	33.1*	19.4	24.3
Parity Index	1.52	—	—	1.71	1.00	

Sources: Data for 1982 seniors based on first follow-up of sophomore participants in High School and Beyond Survey (HSB), U.S. Department of Education, National Center for Education Statistics. Data for 1972 seniors are drawn from base-year of the National Longitudinal Study of the High School Class of 1972 (NLS), U.S. Department of Education, National Center for Education Statistics.
[a]This can be interpreted as follows: "In 1982 the general education track participation rate for American Indian students was 62% higher than (or 1.62 times) the general track participation rate for white students;" [b]Insufficient sample sizes; *Represents significant difference from the white population at or beyond the .05 level.

nificantly overrepresented in the vocational education track and significantly underrepresented in the academic and general program tracks: African-American students participated in the vocational track at a rate 34% higher than the rate for white students. In contrast, the participation rate in academic programs among African-American students was 88% of the rate for whites, and, in the general track, the African-American student participation rate was 84% of the rate for white students.

The bottom panel of Table 8.1 shows that in 1972, 33% of African-American high school seniors were enrolled in academic programs compared to 52% of white seniors, 34% were in general education programs versus 28% of white seniors, and 33% were enrolled in vocational education programs versus 19% of white seniors. Thus, compared to whites, African-American students in 1972 were significantly overrepresented in the general and vocational education tracks and significantly underrepresented in the academic program track. African-American students participated in the vocational track at a rate 71% higher than the rate for white students and in the general track at a rate 20% higher than the rate for white students; in contrast, the participation rate in academic programs among African-American students was only 63% of the rate for whites.

Latino students. The top panel of Table 8.1 shows that in 1982, 26% of Latino high school seniors in 1982 were enrolled in academic programs compared to 41% of white seniors, 30% were in general education programs versus the same 30% of white seniors, and 44% were enrolled in vocational education programs versus 29% of white seniors. Thus, compared to whites, Latino students in 1982 were significantly overrepresented in the vocational education track and significantly underrepresented in the academic program track. Latino students were in the vocational track at a rate 52% higher than the rate for white students. In contrast, the participation rate in academic programs among Latino students was only 65% of the rate for whites.

The bottom panel of Table 8.1 shows that in 1972, 28% of Latino high school seniors were enrolled in academic programs as compared to 52% of white seniors, 42% were in general education programs versus 28% of white seniors, and 29% were enrolled in vocational education programs versus 19% of white seniors. Thus, compared to whites, Latino students in 1972 were significantly overrepresented in the general and vocational education tracks and significantly underrepresented in the academic program track. Latino students participated in the vocational track at a rate 52% higher than the rate for white students and in the general track at a rate 50% higher than the rate for white students; in contrast, the participation rate in academic programs among Latino students was only 54% of the rate for whites.

American Indian and Asian Students. The top panel of Table 8.1 shows that 19% of American Indian high school seniors in 1982 were enrolled in academic programs compared to 41% of white seniors, 49% were in general education programs versus 30% of white seniors, and 32% were enrolled in vocational education programs versus 29% of white seniors. Thus, compared to whites, American Indian students in 1982 were significantly overrepresented in the general education track and significantly underrepresented in the academic program track. American Indian students participated in the general track at a rate 62% higher than the rate for white students; in contrast, the participation rate in academic programs among American Indian students was only 46% of the rate for whites.

In the top panel of Table 8.1, the data show that 58% of 1982 Asian high school seniors were enrolled in academic programs compared to 41% of white seniors, 22% were in general education programs versus 30% of white seniors, and 20% were enrolled in vocational education programs versus 29% of white seniors. Thus, compared to whites in 1982, Asian students were significantly underrepresented in the general and vocational education tracks and significantly overrepresented in the academic program track. Asian students participated in the academic track at a rate 42% higher than the rate for white students; in contrast, the Asian participation rate in general education programs was only 74% of the rate for whites, and in vocational education programs the participation rate was only 68% of the rate for whites.

Summary. The distribution of program placements observed in Table 8.1 have clear implications for students' access to "learning opportunities" and for their future schooling and career options. Curriculum tracking, as traditionally practiced in American high schools, serves as an allocation mechanism that sorts students into vocational, academic, and general education programs. Vocational programs are designed to develop specific occupational skills that lead to direct entry into the labor market. Academic programs are designed to develop the more advanced academic skills and knowledge which are prerequisites for postsecondary schooling prior to labor-force entry, whereas general education programs lack the specialized focus of either the vocational or college preparatory curriculum and serve mainly as a holding pen prior to graduation or dropping out. Thus, tracking may be a key mediating mechanism in the link between education and adult career success.

Corporate leaders and educators have recently focused increased attention on the relationship between the level and type of skills American youth bring to the workforce and the content and quality of their high school courses and programs of study. Gamoran (1987) has noted that students' "opportunities to learn" and, consequently, their levels of academic proficiency are directly related to their course and track placements. According to a recent U. S. Department of Education report (National Assessment of Educational Progress, 1990), for example, high school seniors with higher reading proficiency scores reported being enrolled in academic programs and taking more rigorous course-work. The strong effects of tracking on adults' cognitive skill levels make it clear that if schools are to meet the requirements of our economy for a more highly skilled future workforce (especially in light of changing population demographics), public schools must provide more equitable access to "learning opportunities" that cultivate reasoning, inference, and critical thinking. Thus, there is a growing concern about the impact of tracking and other forms of educational stratification on workplace literacy and on the overall well-being of our national economy.

Trends Over 10 Years

The NLS data provide a snapshot of the status of program tracking for a nationally representative student sample in 1972; the HSB data provide a snapshot of the status of program tracking for a nationally representative student sample in 1982. Because these are nationally representative samples, we can compare the data and talk about "trends" that have occurred. We have no way of knowing, however, the real progression of any changes that have taken place, that is, whether changes occurred gradually over the time period or perhaps took place abruptly during a shorter span within the overall time period, or even whether changes occurred in one direction consistently or moved back and forth in various directions.

The major trend over the 1972-1982 period for both African-American and Latino students was to continue, compared to whites, to be overrepresented in vocational education tracks and underrepresented in academic tracks. The magnitude of the underrepresentation of both groups compared to whites in academic tracks had diminished by 1982—African-American representation was 88% of the white rate in 1982 compared to 63% of the white rate in 1972; Latino representation was 65% of the white rate in 1982 compared to 54% of the white rate in 1972.

On the surface, this looks as if African-American students have made substantial gains in representation in the academic track by their senior year of high school, and, in fact, they have, compared to white representation. However, the gain from 63% to 88% of the white rate was due mainly to a decrease in white students in the academic track (from 52.5% in 1972 to 40.9% in 1982). The same is true for the Latino gain from 54% of the white rate in 1972 to 65% in 1982—the gain is mostly accounted for by the decrease in white students in academic tracks from 1972 to 1982.

The actual percentage of African-American and Latino seniors in the academic track in 1972 and 1982 show clearly that, although these subgroups moved closer to parity with white students, they achieved no real gain in movement into the academic track. The percentage of Latino students in the academic track, in fact, decreased from 28.1% to 26.5%, whereas the percentage of African-American students in the academic track only increased slightly, from 33.0% to 35.9%. If the percentage of white students in the academic track had stayed the same from 1972 to 1982, the African-American student rate of representation compared to whites would be only 68% in 1982, compared to 65% in 1972. Similarly, the rate of Latino student representation compared to whites would be only 50% in 1982, compared to 54% in 1972. What these figures clearly show is that movement toward parity with white students by African-American and Latino students from 1972 to 1982 does not reflect that more of these students moved into the academic track in that 10-year period. Rather, it reflects the fact that white students shifted in substantial numbers from academic tracks to vocational, and especially general tracks, from 1972 to 1982.

We look briefly at the trends in representation in the vocational and general tracks from 1972 to 1982. Both African-American and Latino students continued to be overrepresented in the vocational track in 1982, compared to whites, and both had substantial increases in the percentage of students actually in vocational education programs—African Americans increasing from 33.1% in 1972 to 38.7% in 1982, and Latinos increasing from 29.5% in 1972 to 43.9% in 1982. The Latino students, despite their large actual increase in the percentage of students in the vocational track, remained at the same parity level with whites as in 1972 (represented at a rate 1.52 times that of white students) because white students also increased their actual percentage participation in the vocational track from 19.4% to 28.9% during the 10-year period. Similarly, although African-American students moved closer to parity with white students, going from a rate of 1.71 times to a rate of 1.34 times that of white students, this change came about because of the influx of a larger percentage of white students into vocational tracks, not because the African-American students decreased their own percentage in the vocational track.

Both African-American and Latino students decreased their actual percentage of participation in the general track from 1972 to 1982, and both went from being overrepresented in the general track compared to whites (1.2% and 1.5% of the white rate, respectively) to being slightly underrepresented in the general track compared to whites (84% and 98% of the white rate, respectively). Again, the move from over- to underrepresentation was influenced by an increased percentage of whites moving into the general track (28.2% in 1972 to 30.2% in 1982), but this time much of the shift was accounted for by actual movement out of the general track by the African-American and Latino students.

The data in Table 8.1 alone are insufficient to interpret the trends that we have reported. We can note that little change occurred from 1972 to 1982 in the percentage of African Americans and Latinos in academic tracks. Both these population subgroups remain underrepresented compared to whites in the track that leads to postsecondary education and better career opportunities. Also, both these groups increased their rates of participation in vocational education tracks substantially from 1972 to 1982, and both remain heavily overrepresented compared to whites in the track that, in theory, leads to employment directly out of high school.

We can comment on our findings regarding participation in the general track, which is acknowledged by most educators as being basically a "holding track" for students who otherwise would drop out. The substantial decrease in the percentage of African-American and Latino students in the general track is a positive change only if the vocational track, where most of them went, does indeed provide useful programs that lead to the acquisition of worthwhile and marketable skills and entrance into meaningful employment. At the same time, the fact that few of these students moved into the academic track is disquieting. It is very possible that the change out of the general track occurred because some high schools serving African Americans and Latinos simply eliminated the general track. The question then becomes whether the vocational track into which these students moved was broadened and expanded to provide them with a strong practical education, or whether it simply became the new holding arena.

MALDISTRIBUTIONS ACROSS ABILITY GROUPS AND TRACKING

Ability-Grouped Class Assignment and Curriculum Tracking

Our next sets of data pertain to the assignment of students to classes according to ability. Elementary school students often are assigned to high-, average-, or low-achieving self-contained classes on the basis of some combination of a composite achievement measure, IQ scores, and/or teacher judgment. They remain with the same ability-grouped classes for all academic subjects. In junior high and middle schools, ability-grouped class assignment may take the form of block scheduling, in which students are assigned to one class by ability and travel together from subject to subject, or students may be assigned by ability to each subject separately. Although high school students are usually assigned to academic, vocational, or general program tracks, they are also often assigned to separate ability-grouped courses within the curriculum tracks (e.g., honors or advanced placement, regular, and remedial courses).

Tables 8.2-8.7 report the prevalence of ability-grouped class and course assignment for African-American, Latino, American Indian, Asian, and white students at various grade levels based on multiple data sets. The Johns Hopkins University National Survey of Middle Grades asked principals whether they assign students to homogeneous groups on the basis of ability or achievement. Their responses, presented in Table 8.2, reveal several important differences in homogeneous grouping practices by subject and by school ethnic composition and "average" student ability.

Table 8.2 shows, for grade 7 students, the percentage of schools that use all homogenous grouping by subject. Analyses reported elsewhere reveal that roughly two-thirds of the schools report using at least some between-class ability grouping (Braddock, 1990; Epstein & MacIver, 1989). Across all types of schools, mathematics, reading, and then English are the subjects most often grouped by ability. Table 8.2 shows that the use of between-class grouping to create "all" classes homogeneous in ability is quite common in grade 7; roughly 1 of 5 schools report that their 7-grade classes are ability-grouped for each subject. This practice—homogeneous ability grouping for all subjects—is more often found in schools with sizable (more than 20%) enrollments of African-American and Latino students. As the bottom three panels of Table 8.2 show, this relationship between full-scale ability grouping and ethnic concentration holds even when schools are disaggregated in terms of principal reports of "average" student ability. The National Longitudinal Study of the High School Class of 1972 (NLS) also asked principals whether they assign students to homogeneous groups on the basis of ability or achievement and for which subjects. Principal responses to these questions in the NLS survey are presented in Tables 8.3 and 8.4. Table 8.3 shows the percentage of high schools that use homogenous grouping in all or some of their classes. Nearly all (92%) report the use of between-class ability grouping in some subjects. Where ability grouping is used, it typically applies to all students (57%). However, the use of ability grouping to create "all" homogeneous classes is somewhat more common for high-ability students (8%) than for low-ability students (5%).

Table 8.4 shows patterns of course tracking in high schools by subject. In grade 12, English (59%), mathematics/science (42%), and social studies (39%) are the subjects in which students are most often grouped by ability. English more often separates students into a larger number of groups (12% report 5 or more ability levels) than other academic subjects. Thus, Tables 8.3 and 8.4 show concurrently that course tracking,

Table 8.2. Ability Grouped Class Assignment in Public Schools Serving Early Adolescents by Selected Student Characteristics

All Schools	All Students	English	Mathematics	Reading	Science	Social Studies
All Homogeneous Classes	22.0	25.0	39.3	29.6	6.5	4.7
<20% Minority	20.0	25.2	40.6	30.1	5.9	4.3
>20% Minority	26.8	24.4	35.4	28.0	7.0	5.2
Schools where "typical" entering student is:						
Below Average						
All Homogeneous Classes	24.0	21.8	40.0	23.5	7.1	6.0
<20% Minority	23.5	20.8	39.9	23.2	6.8	5.8
>20% Minority	28.0	25.1	38.0	24.2	6.2	6.4
Average						
All Homogeneous Classes	20.2	30.0	40.7	35.2	5.2	2.6
<20% Minority	17.6	32.2	43.1	37.5	5.5	2.5
>20% Minority	28.0	23.5	32.8	27.4	3.3	2.4
Above Average						
All Homogeneous Classes	21.4	22.5	35.9	30.0	7.7	6.0
<20% Minority	15.5	18.9	35.0	30.3	4.1	4.5
>20% Minority	25.2	24.9	36.3	29.9	9.6	6.7

Source: Johns Hopkins University 1988 National Survey of Middle Grades Principals.

Table 8.3. Patterns of Course Tracking in Public Comprehensive High Schools for Different Types of Students and Schools

	All Subjects			Some Subjects
School Uses Between-Classes Ability Grouping	7.9			92.1
	All Students	High-Ability Students Only	Low-Ability Students Only	No Students
School Uses Between-Classes Ability Grouping (where applicable)	57.5	8.4	4.7	29.4

Source: National Longitudinal Study of High School Class of 1972.

Table 8.4. Patterns of Course Tracking in Public Comprehensive High Schools by Subject

	Subjects			
Tracking Patterns	English Language	Science/ Mathematics	Social Studies	Vocational Courses
School Uses Between-Class Ability Grouping	59.1	42.3	39.4	6.2
Number of Ability Groups (where applicable)				
Two	20.2	41.7	34.8	59.4
Three	46.2	40.0	41.4	12.2
Four	21.1	11.9	16.2	19.7
Five or more	12.5	6.4	7.6	8.7

Source: National Longitudinal Study of High School Class of 1972.

between-class ability grouping, is a prevalent grouping method in high schools, especially in major subjects. Patterns of course tracking by race-ethnic student subgroups (see Table 8.5) reveal some strikingly dissimilar distributions among whites and African Americans.

Similar patterns among African-American and white seniors are found in the top English (30% vs. 36%) and social studies (37% vs. 43%) classes of their schools. African Americans and whites in the general education and vocational education programs show few striking differences in top class participation patterns except for English in general education (6% vs. 14%) and science/math in vocational education (12% vs. 18%). Thus, overall differences between whites and African-

Table 8.5. Patterns of Course Tracking in Public Comprehensive High Schools by Subject Areas and Student Ethnicity

Subject and Ability Group	General African-American	General Hispanic	General White	Academic African-American	Academic Hispanic	Academic White	Vocational African-American	Vocational Hispanic	Vocational White	Totals African-American	Totals Hispanic	Totals White
Science/Mathematics												
Top Class	15.0	16.0	14.0	34.1	44.6	39.3	12.4	5.9	18.3	23.6	26.0	32.3
Second	55.3	59.0	58.5	40.5	47.8	49.6	49.6	39.5	56.2	47.0	50.2	52.1
Third	20.4	22.1	16.6	23.7	6.9	10.2	29.8	39.4	15.6	24.0	19.6	11.9
Fourth	4.7	1.1	5.9	1.7	.8	.5	4.2	11.6	4.1	3.3	2.8	1.9
Fifth or Below	4.6	1.9	5.1	—	—	.4	4.0	3.6	5.8	2.2	1.3	1.8
Mean	2.31	2.16	2.32	1.93	1.64	1.73	2.42	2.71	2.23	2.15	2.05	1.90
S.D.	1.03	.85	1.04	.80	.65	.71	1.03	1.01	.99	.95	.89	.86
English/Language												
Top Class	6.0	9.0	13.7	30.9	38.3	36.1	9.2	4.4	9.8	15.4	16.7	24.8
Second	47.2	48.7	54.8	42.5	47.4	50.1	49.6	43.4	50.0	46.5	47.7	51.5
Third	33.3	34.1	25.1	22.5	12.9	11.4	30.7	39.3	27.4	28.6	28.5	18.1
Fourth	9.3	4.4	3.3	3.3	—	1.6	7.9	7.8	10.3	7.1	3.8	3.9
Fifth or Below	4.3	3.7	3.1	.7	1.4	.8	2.6	5.1	2.5	2.5	3.3	1.7
Mean	2.60	2.47	2.29	2.00	1.79	1.82	2.47	2.67	2.46	2.35	2.31	2.07
S.D.	.93	.92	.92	.85	.77	.80	.92	.94	.91	.93	.95	.90
Social Studies												
Top Class1	3.8	12.6	17.7	36.9	46.6	43.1	11.1	11.4	12.8	22.1	22.3	30.3
Second	52.0	57.7	48.2	44.6	43.4	46.6	54.9	57.1	56.6	52.9	50.0	49.2
Third	26.1	28.0	26.6	17.3	9.0	9.9	27.9	25.7	20.5	22.6	22.7	16.3
Fourth	6.0	1.1	4.3	.6	—	—	4.1	5.9	7.5	2.0	3.7	2.6
Fifth or Below	2.0	.6	3.2	.5	—	.4	1.9	—	2.5	.3	1.4	1.6
Mean	2.30	2.20	2.29	1.83	1.61	1.68	2.32	2.26	2.31	2.05	2.12	1.97
S.D.	.86	.72	.98	.77	.65	.71	.83	.74	.91	.76	.84	.88

Source: National Longitudinal Study of the High School Class of 1972.

American student participation rates in top classes across core academic subjects are primarily linked to academic college preparatory programs.

Honors and Remedial Group Course Placements

How do student placements in "low track" remedial and special education courses versus "high track" honors courses differ by students' race-ethnic status? Based on data from High School & Beyond, Table 8.6 presents a summary of multiple regression analyses showing the effect of race-ethnicity on placement in special education courses and in remedial courses in English and mathematics of 1982 high school seniors with controls for sex, high school track placement, and school demographics (region, urbanicity, and size of 12th-grade class). Table 8.6 shows that, compared to white high school seniors, African-American seniors are significantly overrepresented in both remedial English ($b = .071$) and remedial mathematics ($b = .128$) courses. These effects are unstandardized regression coefficients and are the net of statistical controls for sex, track placement, and school demographics. In other words, African-American high school seniors are 7% and 13% more likely than white seniors to be placed in remedial English and mathematics, even after taking into account their track placement, sex, and selected school characteristics.

Similar results were found for American Indian and Latino students. American Indian seniors are also significantly overrepresented in remedial English ($b = .077$) and remedial mathematics ($b = .151$) courses,

Table 8.6. Effects[a] of Race-Ethnic Status on Special Education and Remedial English and Mathematics Course Placements among 1982 High School Seniors, Controlling for Students Background and School Demographic Factors

| | Race-Ethnic Group | | | |
Course Placement	African-American	Hispanic	American Indian	Asian
Special Education	.006	.014*	.008	-.001
Remedial English	.071***	.063***	.077*	.038
Remedial Mathematics	.128***	.131***	.151***	.018

Source: High School and Beyond
[a]Effects are unstandardized partial regression coefficients derived from multiple regression analyses in which course placement is regressed on race-ethnic group with controls for students' sex, curriculum track placement, and school demographic characteristics (region, urbanicity, and size).
*denotes direct effect is significant at .05 level.
**denotes direct effect is significant at .01 level.
***denotes direct effect is significant at .001 level.

compared to white high school seniors. Also, compared to white high school seniors, Latino seniors are significantly overrepresented in remedial English (b = .063), remedial mathematics (b = .131), and special education (b = .014) courses. In contrast, Asian seniors are not significantly overrepresented in remedial English (b =.038), remedial mathematics (b = .018), or special education (b = .014) courses, compared to white high school seniors. Table 8.7 presents a summary of multiple regression analyses showing the effect of race-ethnicity placement in honors (English and mathematics) courses for 1982 high school seniors with controls for sex, high school track placement, and school demographics. Table 8.7 shows that, compared to white high school seniors, African-American seniors are significantly underrepresented in both honors English (b = -.052) and honors mathematics (b = -.031) courses. Latino seniors, also, are significantly underrepresented in both honors English (b = -.031) and honors mathematics (b = .032) courses. However, neither Asian nor American Indian seniors compared unfavorably to white seniors. Asian seniors are significantly overrepresented in honors mathematics (b = .123) and are neither over- nor underrepresented in honors English (b = .039) courses, compared to white high school seniors. American Indian seniors are neither over- nor underrepresented in honors English (b = .001) nor honors mathematics (b = .008) courses, compared to white high school seniors.

These race-ethnicity effects are the net of statistical controls for sex, track placement, and school demographics—size, region, and urbanicity. The unstandardized regression coefficients shown in Table 8.7 indicate that the negative effect on honors English course placements of race-ethnicity is somewhat stronger for African Americans than for

Table 8.7. Effects[a] of Race-Ethnic Status on Honors English and Mathematics Course Placement among 1982 High School Seniors, Controlling for Students Background and School Demographic Factors

| | Race-Ethnic Group | | | |
Course Placement	African-American	Hispanic	American Indian	Asian
Honors English	-.052***	-.031**	-.001	.039
Honors Mathematics	-.031**	-.032**	.008	.123***

Source: High School and Beyond
[a]Effects are unstandardized partial regression coefficients derived from multiple regression analyses in which course placement is regressed on race-ethnic group with controls for students' sex, curriculum track placement, and school demographic characteristics (region, urbanicity, and size).
*denotes direct effect is significant at .05 level.
**denotes direct effect is significant at .01 level.
***denotes direct effect is significant at .001 level.

Latinos, whereas race-ethnicity has an equal depressing effect on honors mathematics course placements for both groups. However, the strongest net effect observed in these analyses is the positive effect on honors mathematics placement of race-ethnicity for Asian students.

The inequality of program and ability-group placements that we have described in Tables 8.1-8.7 have important implications for youth across cultural groups, particularly African-American youth. They suggest that students' access to learning opportunities in the middle grades and in high schools remain highly stratified, despite growing calls for school reforms and restructuring to develop critical thinking and problem-solving skills among our nation's youth, and despite continuing exhortations to ensure that all children are provided equal access to learning opportunities. Our next analyses examine the connections between restricted access to learning opportunities in high school and adult literacy outcomes.

TRACKING AND LITERACY

Despite some variations among race-ethnic subgroups and across different literacy domains, young adult literacy is strongly affected by high school curriculum track placements. This generalization holds even when levels of educational attainment and key social background factors are statistically controlled. Table 8.8 presents results from regression analyses based on the recent National Assessment of Educational Progress (NAEP) Young Adult Literacy Survey. These analyses compare the effects of high school curriculum track placement for African-American, Latino, Asian, and white students on three major dimensions of adult literacy: (a) prose skills and strategies needed to understand and use information from sources that are often found in the home or community, for example, a newspaper editorial; (b) document skills and strategies required to locate and use information contained in nontextual materials, including graphs, charts, indexes, tables, schedules, and the like; and (c) computational skills and knowledge needed to apply arithmetic operations in addition, subtraction, multiplication, and division (singly or sequentially) in combination with printed materials in tasks such as balancing a checkbook or completing an order form.

These analyses show that high school tracking alone (top panel) can be a substantial and statistically significant determinant of young adult literacy. For prose literacy skills, high school tracking accounts for between 5% (for African Americans) and 24% (for Asian Americans) of the total variation in young adult proficiency. A similar range of effects is observed for document literacy skills in which high school track place-

Table 8.8. Effects[a] of High School Curriculum Track Placement on Three Dimensions of Young Adult Literacy by Ethnic Subgroup with Controls[b]

Curriculum Effects (with and without controls)	Adult Literacy Domains											
	Prose				Document				Computational			
	White	African-American	Hispanic	Asian-American	White	African-American	Hispanic	Asian-American	White	African-American	Hispanic	Asian-American
TRACK (unadjusted)												
Metric	21.24	14.44	25.03	30.93	20.08	21.34	23.04	35.32	11.92	21.90	19.92	13.67
t statistic	24.12**	5.90***	5.99***	6.42***	22.70***	8.33***	4.42***	6.07***	12.93***	7.97***	4.34***	3.08**
Multiple R[b]	.11	.05	.09	.24	.10	.09	.05	.22	.03	.08	.05	.07
TRACK (+) (Social Background)												
Metric	14.37	7.01	16.29	28.13	14.46	15.65	11.26	29.48	6.93	14.91	11.15	12.41
t statistic	16.33***	2.69**	3.99***	5.37***	15.98***	5.54***	2.23*	4.85***	7.25***	4.97***	2.44**	2.55**
Multiple R[b]	.23	.19	.32	.28	.18	.17	.30	.32	.10	.18	.26	.11
TRACK(+) (Social Background + Education Level)												
Metric	5.64	-.92	1.72	20.99	6.79	9.63	-5.12	22.08	.48	9.30	-2.13	6.57
t statistic	6.76***	.40	.54	3.83***	7.66***	3.54***	1.22	3.44***	.50	3.17**	.53	1.28
Multiple R[b]	.38	.40	.62	.34	.30	.28	.56	.37	.18	.26	.48	.16

Source: National Assessment of Educational Progress 1986 Young Adult Literacy Survey.
[a]Effects are unstandardized partial regression coefficients derived from multiple regression analyses in which literacy outcomes are regressed on track placement controls; [b]Controls include respondents' education level, sex, age, parent education, region and county of birth. Note: The unstandardized partial regression coefficient can be interpreted as follows: Among Asian-American young adults, academic track participants score roughly 21 points higher on the prose domain of the NAEP literacy assessment battery than Asian-American nonacademic track participants, net of controls for educational attainment, sex, age, parents' education, region, and county of birth; *$p < .05$; **$p < .01$; ***$p < .001$.

ment accounts for from 5% (for Latinos) to 22% (for Asian Americans) of the variance in young adult proficiency levels. In contrast, although still statistically significant, the explanatory power of high school tracking is substantially less for computational or quantitative literacy skills, accounting for as little as 3% of the variance in young adult proficiency among whites and a high of only 8% among African Americans.

The middle and bottom panels of Table 8.8 show that, in general, high school tracking continues to exhibit a significant effect on young adult literacy proficiency, even when statistical analyses take into account social background and educational attainment indicators. Among white and Asian-American young adults, the net effect of high school tracking after controlling for social background and educational attainment remains substantial and significant for both prose and document literacy skills, but not for computational literacy skills. In contrast, among African-American young adults, the net effect of high school tracking washes away and is not significant for prose literacy, but remains significant and quite substantial for both document and computational literacy skill domains. For Latino young adults, educational attainment appears to wash away any influence of high school tracking on all three literacy domains. (This finding may be an artifact of the data, and further study is required.)

Overall, it appears that high school tracking effects on young adult literacy are stronger for Asian Americans and African Americans than they are for whites, with Asian Americans exhibiting the strongest effect among the ethnic subgroups examined. The net effects of track placement on young adult literacy shown in the bottom panel of Table 8.8 indicate that tracking exhibits a substantially stronger influence among African Americans than among whites on two of the three literacy domains examined: document and computational skills.

For document literacy skills the net effect of high school track placement is about 40% greater among African Americans, whereas the net track effect on computational literacy skills is nearly 20 times that observed for tracking on the quantitative proficiency of white young adults. For Asian-American young adults, the magnitude of the track net effect exceeds that of whites across all three literacy domains by an even greater margin, although among both groups it is statistically significant only for prose and document literacy. Our findings on the relationship between curriculum tracking and young adult literacy skills show clearly that placement in the academic track as opposed to placement in general and vocational tracks has substantial positive effects on prose, document, and computational literacy for young adults, whereas placement in general and vocational tracks has substantial negative effects on these literary measures. In general, because these effects remain after we con-some confidence that the tracking itself, over and above other factors, is responsible for a significant portion of the disparate outcomes among white, Asian-American, and African-American groups. To some degree this statement applies to the disparate outcomes for Latino young adults also, based on the fact that the effects remain significant for Latinos after we control for social background, although not when we control for educational attainment as well.

IMPLICATIONS AND CONCLUSIONS

Our findings on the maldistributions of groups of race-ethnic students in curriculum tracks and ability groups, and the effects of placement in those tracks and groups, have many policy implications for equity and excellence in American education. First, our clear findings on the effects of curriculum tracking and ability grouping indicate the need for changes in school organization and classroom practice. There may have been a time when curriculum tracking in schools did actually coincide with the needs of the society and the economy outside of schools. That is, a designated number of academically proficient students were needed to pursue further education and careers that depended on that education, whereas a number of nonacademically oriented students were needed to enter the workforce directly and perform the important and even well-paying jobs that required less education. This situation has changed dramatically, but curriculum tracking still exists and is widely practiced in American schools today. The effects of curriculum tracking and ability grouping are especially negative for African-American and Latino subgroups.

For both of these subgroups, our analyses show no real movement out of general and vocational track programs into academic programs over a 10-year period. African-American and Latino students constitute our largest minority populations, and the future economic health of the country depends on their access to a high-quality education. Further, the effects of tracking and ability grouping are also quite negative for American Indian subgroups. This is not a new concern. The historic ineffectiveness of American schooling for this disadvantaged population is well documented, and a significant amount of federal funds has been and is being directed toward this population, with few results so far. We badly need an accounting and synthesis of the educational programs that have been developed in our attempts to improve education for American Indians that will provide some basis for identifying and further developing programs that are actually effective.

The national media report that the success of Asian-American students in our curriculum-tracked schools is creating a social backlash against this population that bodes ill for their successful integration children into the fabric of American society. At the same time, the overall success of Asian-American students in tracked American high schools obscures the fact that some recent Asian-American immigrant subgroups are as educationally disadvantaged as the African-American, Latino, and American Indian subgroups.

Finally, there are some negative implications of our findings for white students as well. The decline of white students in the academic track between 1972 and 1982 (from 52.5% to 40.9%), coupled with the increase in the general and vocational tracks (from 28.2% to 30.2% and from 19.4% to 28.9%, respectively), could easily be viewed as a major shift from being advantaged to being less advantaged or even disadvantaged in terms of educational opportunities to learn. The maldistribution of students across tracks and ability groups and their effects on adult literacy outcomes presented in this chapter make it clear that if schools are to meet the requirements of our economy for a more highly skilled future workforce (especially in light of changing demographics), public schools must provide more equitable access to "learning opportunities" that cultivate reasoning, inference, and critical thinking. Accomplishing this important shift in educational policy will require major school restructuring efforts that encourage effective alternatives to tracking and between-class ability grouping. Whatever their achievement effects may be, ability-grouping plans in all forms are increasingly being questioned by many educators who feel uncomfortable making decisions about students that could have long-term effects on their self-esteem and life chances. In desegregated schools, the possibility that ability grouping may create racially identifiable groups or classes is of great concern (Epstein, 1985; Slavin, 1989). For these and other reasons, several alternatives to ability grouping have been proposed. An appealing alternative to ability grouping proposed by Oakes (1985), among others, involves cooperative-learning instructional methods in which students work in small, mixed-ability learning teams. Research on cooperative learning has found that when the cooperative groups are rewarded based on the learning of all group members, students learn consistently more than do students using traditional methods (Slavin, 1987a, 1987b). Thus, cooperative learning offers one plausible alternative to ability grouping that takes student diversity as a valued resource to be used in the classroom rather than a problem to be solved.

Braddock and McPartland (1990) describe several other possibilities, such as flexible grouping processes, which may include tracking only in math and/or English, but not in other subjects; using appropriate subject-matter tests to make student placements in the selected subjects; making all groups as heterogeneous as possible, even in tracked classes; and covering basic subjects (such as Algebra) at all levels. If there are 9 sections in 9th-grade math, for example, these sections can be subsumed under two or three broad groups, so there will be less stigma and more equitable access to learning opportunities for all students.

There are more ambitious alternatives—such as replacing tracking entirely in elementary and middle grades with the use of within-class grouping plus cooperative-learning methods, or with the use of competency-based curriculum in multigrade groupings, such as the Joplin Plan for cross-grade reading groups.

Effective and innovative responses to student diversity do not just happen. Educators and researchers agree that substantial investments by school systems in staff training may be required to substantially alter current patterns of ability grouping and tracking. Thus, if educators are to insure equal educational opportunities and to provide every student with opportunities to learn to their fullest potential, it is necessary to know more about both how to deal with student diversity and how to train teachers to do so.

REFERENCES

Allington, R.L. (1980). Teacher interruption behaviors during primary-grade oral reading. *Journal of Educational Psychology, 72*(3), 371-377.

Allington, R.L. (1983). The reading instruction provided readers of different reading abilities. *The Elementary Journal, 83,* 454-459.

Braddock, J.H. (1990). Tracking the middle grades: National patterns of grouping for instruction. *Phi Delta Kappan* (February): 445-449.

Braddock, J.H., II., & McPartland, J. (1990). Alternatives to tracking on the agenda for restructuring schools. *Educational Leadership, 47*(7), 76-79.

Epstein, J.L. (1985). After the bus arrives: Resegregation in desegregated schools. *Journal of Social Issues, 41,* 23-43.

Gadsden, V.L. (1991). Trying one more time! Gaining access to literacy. In M. Foster (Ed.), *Readings in equal education, Volume 11: Qualitative investigations into schools and schooling* (pp. 189-201). New York: AMS Press.

Gamoran, A. (1987). The stratification of high school learning opportunities. *Review of Educational Research, 43,* 163-179.

Goodlad, J. (1983). *A place called school.* New York: McGraw-Hill.

Hobson v. Hansen, 269 F. Supp. 401 (1967).

McPartland, J., & Crain, R. (1987). Evaluating the trade-offs in student outcomes from alternative school organization policies. In M. Hallinan (Ed.), *The social organization of schools.* New York: Plenum.

Mitchell, R., Haycock, K., & Navarro, S. (1989). Off the tracks. *Perspective,*

1(3), Council of Basic Education.

National Assessment of Educational Progress. (1985). *The reading report card: Progress towards excellence in our schools; Trends in reading over four national assessments, 1971-84* (Rep. No. 15-R-01). Princeton, NJ: Educational Testing Service.

National Assessment of Educational Progress. (1990). *The reading report card: Progress towards excellence in our schools* (Rep. No. 15-R-01). Princeton, NJ: Educational Testing Service.

Oakes, J. (1983, May). Limiting opportunity: Student race and curricular differences in secondary vocational education. *American Journal of Education*, pp. 328-355.

Oakes, J. (1985). *Keeping track: How schools structure inequality*. New Haven, CT: Yale University Press.

Oakes, J. (1989). Tracking in secondary schools: A contextual perspective. In R. Slavin (Ed.), *School and classroom organization*. Hillsdale, NJ: Erlbaum.

Slavin, R.E. (1987a). Ability grouping and student achievement in elementary schools: A best evidence synthesis. *Review of Educational Research, 57*, 213-236.

Slavin, R.E. (1987b). Grouping for instruction in the elementary school. *Educational Psychologist, 22*, 109-127.

Slavin, R.E. (1989). *Effects of ability grouping on Black, Latino, and White students*. Baltimore, MD: Johns Hopkins University, Center for Research on Effective Schooling for Disadvantaged Students.

Slavin, R., Braddock, J., Hall, C., & Petza, R. (1989). *Alternatives to ability grouping*. Baltimore, MD: Johns Hopkins University, Center for Research on Effective Schooling for Disadvantaged Students.

U.S. Department of Education v. Dillon County School District No.1. (1986). Initial decision in compliance proceeding under Title VI of the Civil Rights Act of 1964, 42 U.S.C. Sec. 200 et seq.

Venezky R., Wagner, D., & Ciliberti, B. (Eds.). (1990). *Toward defining literacy*. Newark, DE: International Reading Association.

9

Teacher Knowledge and Student Learning: Implications for Literacy Development

Linda Darling-Hammond
Teachers College
Columbia University

In "Closing the Divide," Dreeben (1987) describes the results of his study of reading instruction and outcomes for 300 black and white first graders across seven schools in the Chicago area. What he found was that differences in reading outcomes among students were almost entirely explained, not by socioeconomic status or race, but by the quality of instruction the students received:

> Our evidence shows that the level of learning responds strongly to the quality of instruction: having and using enough time, covering a substantial amount of rich curricular material, and matching instruction appropriately to the ability levels of groups. . . . When black and white children of comparable ability experience the same instruction, they do about equally well, and this is true when the instruction is excellent in quality and when it is inadequate. (p. 34)

However, the study also found that the quality of instruction received by black students was, on average, much lower than that received by white students, thus creating a racial gap in aggregate achievement at the end of first grade. In fact, the highest ability group in Dreeben's entire sample was in a school in a low-income black neighborhood. These students learned less during first grade than their lower aptitude white counterparts. Why? Because their teacher was unable to provide the kind of appropriate and challenging instruction this highly talented group deserved.

This example is drawn from a carefully controlled study that confirms what many other studies (e.g., Barr & Dreeben, 1983; College Board, 1985; Darling-Hammond & Snyder, 1992; Dreeben & Barr, 1987; Dreeben & Gamoran, 1986; Oakes, 1990) have suggested. That is, much of the difference in school achievement found between black and white students is due to the effects of substantially different school opportunities, and in particular, greatly disparate access to high-quality teachers and teaching.

The contention of this chapter is that the unequal distribution of educational resources—especially talented and expert teachers able to provide enriched learning opportunities—is a critical obstacle to closing the literacy gap between black and white students. As matters now stand, the students who most need the best teaching are the least likely to get it. Because American investments in teacher quality are inadequate, chronic shortages of talent have created wide disparities in the qualifications and abilities of teachers. In addition, because the distribution of teacher quality is skewed toward those students who reside in affluent, well-endowed schools and districts, poor and minority students are chronically and disproportionately exposed to less well-trained and experienced teachers. From a policy perspective, perhaps the single greatest source of educational inequity is this disparity in the availability and distribution of highly qualified teachers.

Providing equity in the distribution of teacher quality requires changing policies and longstanding incentive structures in education so that shortages of trained teachers are overcome and schools serving black students are not disadvantaged by lower salaries and poorer working conditions in the bidding war for good teachers. Improving instruction for black students also requires improving the capacity of all teachers—their knowledge and their ability to use that knowledge—by professionalizing teaching. This means providing all teachers with a stronger understanding of how children learn and develop, how a variety of curricular and instructional strategies can address their needs, and how changes in school and classroom organization can support their growth and achievement.

Taken together, these propositions argue against policies that indulge bureaucratic impulses to create add-on categorical programs to address the problems that confront black and so-called "at-risk students" or to prescribe simplistic procedures for teachers to follow in classrooms. Instead, this argument begins with a view that schools frequently place students at risk in the manner described at the start of the chapter, and it urges policies that will improve learning by strengthening the preparation of teachers and increasing their chances of teaching effectively. If, in fact, the interaction between teachers and students is the most important aspect of effective teaching, then reducing inequality in learning has to rely on policies that provide equal access to competent, well-supported teachers.

HOW TEACHERS ARE UNEQUALLY DISTRIBUTED

Neither the distribution of students nor the distribution of teachers is random across schools and districts in the United States. Poor and minority children are increasingly concentrated in central-city schools, where teacher shortages are most acute and underqualified entrants to teaching are most numerous.

According to data gathered for a RAND report on urban education (Oakes 1987, p. 2):

- By 1980, 81% of all blacks and 88% of Hispanics resided in metropolitan areas; 71% and 50%, respectively, lived in inner cities.
- In 1980, 80% of low-income blacks and Hispanics were concentrated in the poorest neighborhoods, an increase of 40% since 1970.
- By 1980, "minority" children comprised the majority of students in most large urban districts. By 1984, most Hispanic and black students attended schools with non-white majority enrollments.
- By 1988, only 7 of the nation's 25 largest city school systems maintained a white enrollment of more than 30%.

Meanwhile, as the supply of teachers has dwindled over the past 20 years, teacher shortages have begun to reemerge and, as has been the case over much of the past century, they have affected urban schools most severely. In 1983, the most recent year for which national information is available, shortages of teachers—as measured by unfilled vacancies—were three times greater in central cities than in rural areas or suburbs (NCES, 1985). More than 14% of all newly hired teachers in central-city school districts in 1983 were uncertified in their principal field of assignment, nearly twice the proportion experienced by other types of districts (NCES, 1985a).

In addition, a survey of high school teachers in 1984 found that the schools where uncertified teachers were located were disproportionately central-city schools with higher than average percentages of low-income and minority students (Pascal, 1987, p. 24). In 1985, 5,000 untrained teachers were hired on emergency certificates in New York, Los Angeles, and Houston alone. Many of these districts' vacancies were not filled when schools opened that fall (Darling-Hammond, 1987).

In 1986, shortages stimulated the issuance of over 30,000 emergency and temporary teaching certificates in just the few states that keep records on such matters. The national totals are probably several times this number. The vast majority of these teachers were hired in central-city and poor rural school districts and placed in the most disadvantaged schools. The same is true of teachers recruited through alternative certification routes who have often had only minimal preparation (Darling-Hammond, 1990a).

It is also important to note that the recent decrease in teacher supply has produced an especially acute shortage of minority teachers. Between 1975 and 1985, the numbers of Hispanic and Native American candidates receiving bachelor's degrees in education dropped by 40%, and the number of African-American candidates plummeted by nearly two-thirds (Darling-Hammond, 1990a). Not only do minority teachers provide important role models for black students (along with other students), they are also much more interested in teaching in urban schools than are most newly prepared white candidates (AACTE, 1990).

Teacher shortages subvert the quality of education in a number of ways. They make it hard for districts to be selective in the quality of teachers they hire, and they often result in the hiring of teachers who have not completed (or sometimes even begun) their pedagogical training. In addition, when faced with shortages, districts must often hire short- and long-term substitutes, assign teachers outside their fields of qualification, expand class sizes, or cancel course offerings. No matter what strategies are adopted, the quality of instruction suffers (Darling-Hammond, 1984).

Where shortages are acute and enduring, as they are in central-city schools, many children are taught throughout their school careers by a parade of short-term substitutes, inexperienced teachers who leave before their first year is up, and beginners without training in teaching methods or an understanding of how children learn and how to help them if they do not.

This problem affects all areas of the curriculum, including but not limited to those most associated with traditional literacy, such as reading and language arts. Oakes's (1990) nationwide study of the distribution of mathematics and science opportunities across hundreds of schools found patterns that are pervasive across communities and across school subjects:

Several measures of teacher qualifications make clear that low-income and minority students have less contact with the best-qualified science and mathematics teachers. The frequency with which teaching vacancies occur and the difficulty principals have filling vacancies with qualified teachers vary considerably among different types of schools. Teacher shortages appear most detrimental to low-income and minority students. (p. viii)

Our evidence lends considerable support to the argument that low-income, minority, and inner-city students have fewer opportunities. . . . They have considerably less access to science and mathematics knowledge at school, fewer material resources, less-engaging learning activities in their classrooms, and less-qualified teachers. . . . Moreover, our findings are likely to be equally relevant for subject areas other than mathematics and science. The differences we have observed are likely to reflect more general patterns of educational inequality. (pp. x-xi)

Just as Dreeben found in his study of the teaching of early reading, Oakes (1987) also discovered that "high-ability students at low-socioeconomic status, high-minority schools may actually have fewer opportunities than low-ability students who attend more advantaged schools" (p. vii). The pattern of systematic underexposure to good teaching tends to put all children in high-minority schools at risk.

From a policy viewpoint, then, it is important to investigate how it is that these kinds of widespread inequalities have come to exist and what their potential implications are for the literacy development of black children and youth.

WHY TEACHERS ARE DISTRIBUTED UNEQUALLY

As in most other occupations, the relative attractiveness of salaries, benefits, and other working conditions influence the availability of teaching talent to the occupation as a whole and to various employers within the occupational sector. Teachers are no exception, and the dramatic differences in salaries and working conditions across school districts explain much of the disparity in teacher supply between cities and their generally wealthier suburbs.

In addition, because of the high turnover rates caused by these differentials in salaries and working conditions, most new teachers get hired into the most disadvantaged schools because those are the schools in which most vacancies occur, as many of the more experienced teachers transfer to more desirable schools and districts when they are able.

The new teachers are typically given the most difficult teaching assignments in schools that offer the fewest supports. In large part because of this, attrition rates for new teachers average between 40% and 50% over the first five years of teaching (Grissmer & Kirby, 1987; Wise, Darling-Hammond, & Berry, 1987). This adds additional problems of staff instability to the already difficult circumstances that many black and other central-city youngsters encounter at school.

Teacher shortages like the one that is now growing exacerbate an already serious situation. Furthermore, the same forces that produce the flow of good teachers to advantaged schools, and the ebb of good teachers from disadvantaged schools, are at work within schools wherever tracking persists. Tracking persists in the face of growing evidence that it does not particularly benefit high achievers and tends to put low achievers at a serious disadvantage (Braddock, this volume; Oakes, 1985, 1986), in part because teachers are a scarce resource, and thus must be allocated. The other major reason for the persistence of this practice pertains to the kind and quality of preparation teachers receive generally.

Managing a heterogeneous classroom requires training that relatively few teachers receive and skills that relatively few of them acquire. It requires refined diagnostic ability, a broad repertoire of teaching techniques, and the ability to match techniques to varied learning styles and prior levels of knowledge. It requires skills in classroom management even more considerable than those required in a homogeneous classroom. Because relatively few teachers are prepared to manage heterogeneous classrooms effectively, tracking persists.

The second reason is that very well-prepared, highly skilled teachers are a scarce resource, and scarce resources tend to get allocated to the students whose parents, advocates, or representatives have the most political clout. This results, not entirely but disproportionately, in the most highly qualified teachers teaching the most enriched curricula to the most advantaged students. Evidence suggests that teachers themselves are tracked, with those judged to be the most competent, experienced, or with the highest status assigned to the top tracks (Davis, 1986; Findley, 1984; Oakes, 1986; Rosenbaum, 1976).

The most vocal parents are successful in identifying and requesting the most reputable teachers for their children and in applying pressure for class changes or teacher transfers when teachers do not meet their expectations. Children of other parents are assigned to novices or teachers who have not mastered the teaching techniques that would put them in high demand. As Oakes (1986) notes, these assignments are fairly predictable:

One finding about placements is undisputed: Disproportionate percentages of poor and minority youngsters (principally black and
Hispanic) are placed in tracks for low-ability or non-college-bound
students (NCES, 1985b; Rosenbaum, 1980); further, minority students are consistently underrepresented in programs for the gifted
and talented. (College Board, 1985, p. 136)

A more refined allocation of teaching resources is in part what
has occurred with the recent proliferation of gifted and talented programs across the country. Teachers who are in general the most skilled
are offering rich, challenging curricula to select groups of students, on
the theory that only a few students can benefit from such curricula. Yet,
the distinguishing feature of programs for the talented and gifted frequently turns out to be not their difficulty, but their quality. Students in
these programs are given opportunities to integrate ideas across fields of
study. They have opportunities to think, write, create, and develop projects. They are challenged to explore. Although, arguably, most students
would benefit from being similarly challenged, the opportunity for this
sort of schooling remains acutely restricted. In many instances, the reason for the restriction is simply the scarcity of teachers who can teach in
the fashion such curricula demand.

Even within schools, then, good teaching is too often distributed
unequally. Expert, experienced teachers who are in great demand are
rewarded with opportunities to teach the students who already know a
lot. New teachers, along with those teaching outside their field of preparation, too often get assigned to the students and the classes that nobody
else wants to teach, which leaves them practicing on the students who
would benefit most from the skills of expert, experienced teachers.

In part as a function of the limited skills of their teachers, students placed in the lowest tracks or in remedial reading programs too
often sit at their desks for long periods of the day, matching the picture
in column (a) to the word in column (b), filling in the blanks, and copying off the board. They work at a low cognitive level on fairly boring literacy tasks that are profoundly disconnected from the skills they need to
learn. Rarely are they given the opportunity to talk about what they
know, to read real books, or to construct and solve problems (Davis,
1986; Metz, 1978; Oakes, 1985; Trimble & Sinclair, 1986). If their teachers
know no other ways to teach, what these students learn is quite different
from what students learn in upper tracks or in schools where good
teaching is widespread.

Cooper and Sherk (1989) describe how such worksheet-based
instruction, focusing on discrete "skill" bits, impedes students' progress
toward literacy:

When hundreds of these worksheets, each of which presents a small, low-level skill related to reading, have been completed, children are said to have completed the "mastery" skills program. Often, these children still cannot read very well, if one defines reading as the ability to discern connected prose for comprehension.

[Furthermore], worksheets are devised in such a way, teachers are told, that the material teaches itself. As a result, the amount of oral communication between pupil and teacher and between pupil and pupil is drastically reduced. . . . [Yet] if children are to learn language, a part of which is reading, they must interact and communicate. They must have some opportunity to hear words being spoken, to pose questions, to conjecture, and to hypothesize. (p. 318)

In their discussion of how urban school classrooms must change, Cooper and Sherk go on to describe what teachers should be able to do to support children's literacy development. They identify, among other things, the ability to construct active learning opportunities involving student collaboration and many modes of oral and written language use, the ability to help students access prior knowledge which will help them with the material to be learned, the ability to structure learning tasks so that students have a basis for interpreting the novel experiences they encounter, and the ability to stimulate and engage students' higher order thought processes, including their capacities to hypothesize, predict, evaluate, integrate, and synthesize ideas.

As we discuss below, these kinds of abilities do not emerge as a result of exhortation or mandate. They are a function of teachers' knowledge and preparation. In the long run, improving the teaching that black students receive will require investing much more heavily in the knowledge of their teachers.

HOW TEACHING EXPERTISE MATTERS

American school policy has often started from the assumption that teachers are conduits for policy or curricula rather than active agents in the production of learning. Consequently, many reform initiatives have emphasized improving schools by changing curricula, programs, tests, textbooks, and management processes rather than by improving the knowledge and capacity of teachers. Current literacy policy is no different. Indeed, American policymakers seem to doubt whether there is anything that a teacher brings to the classroom other than the state's or school district's mandated materials, procedures, and regulations. They question whether teacher preparation is necessary and seem to believe that novice teachers are as safe and effective as experienced teachers. These beliefs support the myth that allows teaching expertise to be unequally distributed—the myth that all teachers and classrooms are equal.

Over the past 20 years, educational research has exploded the myths that any teaching is as effective as any other and that unequally trained and experienced teachers are equally advantageous to students. In a study documenting the positive effects of teaching experience on teaching effectiveness, Murnane and Phillips (1981) note:

> The question of whether teachers become more productive as they gain teaching experience has been of interest to policymakers for many years. One reason is that schools serving children from low-income families have typically been staffed with less experienced teachers than schools serving middle-class children. This has led to court tests of whether the uneven distribution of teaching experience constitutes discrimination against low-income children. (pp. 453-454)

Although the correlation between teacher experience and effectiveness is not monotonic over the course of a career, studies consistently find that new teachers—those with fewer than three or four years of experience—tend to be much less effective than more experienced teachers (Moskowitz & Hayman, 1974; Murnane & Phillips, 1981; Rottenberg & Berliner, 1990). Especially in the unsupported environment most encountered, beginning teachers experience a wide range of problems in learning to teach. Problems with classroom management, motivating students, being aware of and dealing appropriately with individual learning needs and differences, and developing a diverse repertoire of instructional strategies to work with a diverse population of students are among the most commonly noted (Johnston & Ryan, 1983; Rottenberg & Berliner, 1990; Veenman, 1984).

Having confirmed that teacher experience does make a difference, researchers are now identifying what it is that expert veterans do in the classroom that distinguishes their teaching from that of novices (e.g., Berliner, 1986; Shulman, 1987). Among other things, expert teachers are much more sensitive to students' needs and individual differences; they are more skilled at engaging and motivating students; and they have a wider repertoire of instructional strategies to call upon for addressing student needs. Much of this research also demonstrates the importance of teacher education for the acquisition of knowledge and skills that, when used in the classroom, improve the caliber of instruction and the success of students' learning (see Berliner, 1984).

This is particularly important in light of the fact that policymakers have nearly always answered the problem of teacher shortages in cities by lowering standards so that people who have had little or no preparation for teaching can be hired. Although this practice is often excused by the presumption that virtually anyone can figure out how to teach, a number of reviews of research summarizing the results of more than 100 studies have concluded that fully prepared and certified teachers are more highly rated and more successful with students than teachers without full preparation (Ashton & Crocker, 1986; Bledsoe, Cox, & Burnham, 1967; Darling-Hammond, 1992; Druva & Anderson, 1983; Evertson, Hawley, & Zlotnik, 1985; Greenberg, 1983).

The extent and kind of teacher preparation are especially important in determining the effectiveness of teachers in "school-based" subjects (those subjects students tend to learn primarily in school rather than through informal learning outside of school), such as early reading, mathematics, and science. Teacher training is also a critical determinant of the use of teaching strategies that encourage higher order learning and that are responsive to students' needs and learning styles.

Strickland (this volume; 1985) stresses that, for early literacy development, elementary school teacher preparation programs must help teachers accommodate a variety of cognitive styles and learning rates with activities that broaden rather than reduce the range of possibilities for learning. They should prepare teachers to understand the nature of language and language development as well as the nature of child growth and development. These understandings should undergird a knowledge of appropriate procedures for fostering language growth at various stages of development. Comer (1988) also stresses the importance of preparing teachers with a strong background in child development as a key to the kind of teaching that has been so successful in his programs for at-risk children. The evidence clearly indicates that such preparation makes a difference in what children learn.

At the elementary level, teachers' background in reading methods courses has been found to be positively related to students' reading achievement (Hice, 1970), whereas teachers' general elementary education training is related to ratings of their instructional effectiveness and to student achievement and interest on a wide range of tasks (LuPone, 1961; McNeil, 1974). A number of studies have found that, compared to teachers who have this kind of training, teachers who enter without full preparation are less able to plan and redirect instruction to meet students' needs (and less aware of the need to do so), less skilled in implementing instruction, less able to anticipate students' knowledge and potential difficulties, and less likely to see it as their job to do so, often blaming students if their teaching is not successful (Allington, 1983; Bents & Bents, 1990; Copley, 1974; Grossman, 1988, 1989; Rottenberg & Berliner, 1990).

These findings are reflected in Gomez and Grobe's (1990) study of the performance of alternate-route candidates hired with only a few weeks of prior training in Dallas. The performance of these candidates was much more uneven than that of trained beginners, with markedly lower ratings on their knowledge of instructional techniques and instructional models, and with a much greater proportion of them (from 2 to 16 times as many) likely to be rated "poor" on each of the teaching factors evaluated. The proportions rated "poor" ranged from 8% on reading instruction to 17% on classroom management. The effects of this unevenness showed up most strongly on students' achievement in language arts, in which students of the alternate-route teachers scored significantly lower than students of fully prepared beginning teachers after controlling for beginning scores.

Furthermore, it seems that appropriate preparation in planning and classroom management is one of the factors that allows teachers to focus on the kind of complex teaching that is needed to develop higher order skills. Because the novel tasks required for complex problem solving are more difficult to manage than the routine tasks associated with learning simple skills, lack of management ability can lead teachers to "dumb down" the curriculum in order to more easily control student work (Carter & Doyle, 1987; Doyle, 1986).

In a striking illustration of how strongly preparation affects a teacher's style and presentation of content, Shulman (1987) tells the story of "Colleen," an active and inventive teacher of literature, which she knew very thoroughly, but a petty tyrant when she had to teach grammar, which she felt she knew poorly. In her literature classes, Colleen adopted a Socratic style that was rich, conceptual, wide-ranging, and responsive to the students. When she shifted to grammar lessons, she adopted a didactic, rote-oriented style of instruction to overcome her lack of self-confidence and her uncertainty about the content. In Admiral Farragut style ("damn the questions, full speed ahead!"), her story illustrates how teaching style changes to become less effective pedagogically when teachers are less prepared.

The differences that teacher preparation makes for student learning are often apparent at the individual level. When school staffing patterns create substantial imbalances in teacher expertise across schools, the effects are startling. When Armour-Thomas and colleagues (Armour-Thomas, Clay, Domanico, Bruno, & Allen, 1989) compared a group of exceptionally effective elementary schools to a group of low-achieving schools with similar demographic characteristics in New York City, they found that differences in teacher qualifications and experience accounted for roughly 90% of the variance in student reading and mathematics scores at grades 3, 6, and 8. Far more than any other factor, teacher expertise made the difference in what children learned.

When the allocation of prepared and experienced teachers is unequal, so is the opportunity for students to learn. The differences in style and content are very real. They are not an abstract proposition.

COROLLARIES

A key corollary to this analysis of inequality is that improved opportunities for black and other minority students will rest, in part, on the professionalization of teaching. There are two reasons for this assertion. First, the professionalization of an occupation raises the floor below which no entrants will be admitted to practice. It eliminates the practice of awarding substandard or irregular licenses that allow untrained entrants to practice disproportionately on underserved and poorly protected clients. Second, professionalization increases the overall knowledge base for the occupation, thus improving the quality of services for all clients, especially those most in need of highly sophisticated teaching.

The students who frequently have the poorest opportunities to learn—those attending the inner-city schools that are compelled by the current incentive structure to hire disproportionate numbers of substitute teachers, uncertified teachers, and inexperienced teachers and that, in general, lack resources for mitigating the uneven distribution of good teaching—are the students who will benefit most from measures that raise the standards of practice of all teachers.

That, in general, the most highly qualified teachers now teach students who are generally successful learners already has another corollary. The standard of practice in a profession is most apt to rise when the structure of the profession encourages the people with the most energy, talent, and experience to tackle the most challenging problems. That structure tends to produce the new knowledge on which the progress of the entire profession depends. The most highly skilled surgeons do not generally perform routine tonsillectomies, for example, just as the ablest lawyers do not generally work on standard wills or contracts. They tend instead to work where the professional challenges are the greatest. Medicine and law are structured so that working on the greatest challenges brings the greatest rewards. The results of work on the most difficult problems in a field extends beyond the experts' immediate clients to the profession at large, which is reinvigorated by each advance in knowledge.

In education, as we have seen, the incentive structure works in reverse. The greatest educational challenges are generally assumed by those least prepared to meet them successfully. There are, however, signs of some change. Although the incentive structure remains firmly in place in most school systems, some systems are experimenting with alternatives. In Charlotte-Mecklenberg, for example, and in Rochester, NY (both systems have set up career ladders), those master teachers who have been recognized for their demonstrated capabilities can be called upon, as part of their privilege and their obligation, to teach children in the schools that most need expert teaching. In such experiments, and in the policy changes they both incorporate and suggest, lie one part of the hope for equalizing opportunities to learn.

BETTER TEACHER PREPARATION

We have never, in the United States, supported teacher preparation very much or very well. In most universities, schools of education get the fewest resources. Even during those periods of intense interest in improving education that seem to occur about once a generation and in which we find ourselves at the moment, neither the federal government nor most states or school systems seem very inclined to spend much money or attention on preparing teachers well. As Berliner (1984) observes:

> It is time for creative thinking on how to revitalize teacher preparation programs. It is also time for budgetary allocations for such programs. Currently, we do not have much of either. At my own institution, the University of Arizona, we have found that it costs the state about $15,000 to educate a liberal arts undergraduate in, say, comparative literature, history, or psychology. To educate an individual for the vitally important profession of teaching, the state pays $2,000 less. . . . I am afraid that Arizona, like the 49 other states engaged in teacher preparation, gets precisely what it pays for. (p. 96)

One reason for this lack of support is a deeply felt ambivalence. Are there things to know about teaching that make teachers more effective? If so, teachers should learn those things. Or, is teaching something that anyone can do, without any special preparation? If so, anything that purports to be preparation is certainly not worth supporting. Clearly, the tension between these two points of view, unresolved for the past 200 years, continues today. In some states, discussions of the importance of professionalizing teaching have led to new requirements for prospective teachers. Meanwhile, however, 23 of these same states have reacted to potential shortages of teachers by setting up alternate routes to certification that bypass standard preparation. Furthermore, almost all states (46) have for many years allowed emergency credentialing: the hiring of untrained teachers to fill vacancies when there are shortages. Teaching is the only licensed occupation in this country that permits this kind of substandard licensing on a regular basis.

For these reasons, teaching currently cannot be considered a full profession. A profession is formed when members of an occupation agree that they have a knowledge base, that what they know relates directly to effective practice, that being prepared is essential to being a responsible practitioner, and that unprepared people will not be permitted to practice. This is not the place for a full-fledged discussion of why and how teaching should become a profession, a topic that has elsewhere begun to receive attention (see Darling-Hammond, 1990b; Wise & Darling-Hammond, 1987). But it is the place to acknowledge that professionalizing teaching would improve the preparation of teachers and also help change many of the other circumstances that now impede the progress of black and other minority students, particularly in the area of literacy.

As far as the students are concerned, ambivalence about whether teachers should be well prepared to teach is a luxury we can no longer afford. Improving literacy and education more broadly for minority students requires policies that improve the preparation of teachers. The institutions that prepare teachers need the investment it will take to produce knowledge about teaching and to create programs that effectively transmit that knowledge to the people who want to teach. Prospective teachers need money to support the cost of their education.

Interestingly, the federal government has used both these policy approaches to build medical education. Through such vehicles as the Health Professions Education Assistance Act and the National Medical Manpower Act, the government has supported the efforts of medical schools to develop the capacity to produce and transmit knowledge. It has provided scholarships and loans for medical students. Now that the United States has perhaps the finest system of medical education in the world, the great debates of 80 or so years ago have lost all but historical interest. But before medicine coalesced into a profession, back when people thought the doctor-to-be might as well learn what he could just by following a doctor around, the debate raged. Was medical education necessary and desirable? Or should medical training be dispensed with in favor of the follow-me-around-in-the-buggy approach? The decision to formalize and strengthen medical education has brought tremendous advances in knowledge. Yet, perhaps the greatest benefit of setting standards of competence in medicine has been that the public is now much better protected from quacks and charlatans. There is a substantial base of knowledge all doctors must acquire.

To the general considerations of improving the preparation of teachers we must add at least one consideration that relates directly, although not exclusively, to improving literacy education for minority students. For various reasons, increasing the supply of well-prepared teachers who are themselves members of minority groups is vital. Teaching should reflect our population, as should all occupations in our society, and the lesser inclination of nonminority teachers to work in inner-city schools makes the flow of minority teachers to those schools essential. Yet, the supply of minority teachers has dwindled even more dramatically over the past two decades than the supply of nonminority teachers.

Whereas the overall supply of newly trained teachers declined by more than half between 1972 and 1985, the number of newly trained black teachers declined by over two-thirds during that period of time. Although a slight increase has been observed for the general teacher pool in recent years, no analogous upswing has yet occurred for prospective black teachers (Darling-Hammond, 1990a). Meanwhile, the schools of education in historically black colleges and universities, from which most black teachers have graduated, are, for various reasons, facing great difficulties. Never well financed for the most part, these institutions and their education programs are in financial jeopardy, in part due to some state policies that tie state educational program approval to candidates' pass rates on teacher certification tests.

A distinction needs to be drawn here that is often ignored: Supporting the institutions that prepare teachers and supplying particular support for the ones that characteristically train mostly minority teachers is one policy and testing teachers is another. Supporting teacher education simply has not been a strategy that policy makers have been willing to adopt. Testing, on the other hand, has proved a popular policy; as currently practiced, it is a low-cost, easily mandated activity with immediate symbolic payoff to elected officials.

Blurring the distinction has some advantages because testing teachers can thereby be seen as a vigorous attack on the problems of preparing teachers. Testing has other advantages. It costs states very little, especially because the people who take the tests pay for the privilege. Just as is true for literacy testing of children, testing teachers or applicants to education schools is also a highly visible policy and clear evidence of a willingness to act.

Testing could ultimately help improve the preparation of teachers, albeit indirectly, if the tests used measured what teachers actually need to know. Then the consequence might be to encourage schools of education to do a more thorough job of preparation. But the tests that are currently available measure only basic skills and general knowledge. Where they treat pedagogy at all, they treat it poorly. Tests like these do little to improve the education of teachers. They can only perform a screening function that is by and large unrelated to the potential effectiveness of the candidates who pass or fail them. In a wide-ranging review of the validity of currently used teacher tests, Haney, Madaus, and Kreitzer (1987, p. 227) conclude:

> These results indicate clearly that current teacher tests, and the manner in which cut-scores are being set on them, are differentiating among candidates far more strongly on the basis of race than they are on the basis of teaching quality. . . . This suggests to us a modest proposal: do not use such tests and cut-scores until it is clearly proven that these tests select among teacher candidates more on the basis of some independent measure of teacher quality than on the basis of race.

It is true that an all-out effort to improve the preparation of teachers would cost far more than simply testing teachers, but discussions of cost would be more usefully discussions of cost-effectiveness. We tend, in education, to see each suggestion for reform as discrete, as a program to add on here, a requirement to add on there, an allocation to add to the already large sums of money being spent. But if we were instead to examine strategies for reform, we would see that the money spent preparing teachers adequately is money that would not need to be spent thereafter to patch up the problems inadequate training creates.

BETTER STANDARDS, MORE OFTEN MET

The implications of innovative literacy instruction are far-reaching and powerful. As the preceding discussion suggests, improving teaching requires not only devoting more resources to the preparation of teachers, but also investing in the development of more meaningful standards for assessing preparation. It does no good, and potentially great harm, to assume that cut-off scores on multiple-choice tests of basic skills or of general knowledge set "standards" that measure teacher preparation in any meaningful way. Much of the content tested by currently available instruments bears so little relationship to what teachers genuinely need to know that we might as well screen teachers on the basis of height (Darling-Hammond, 1986; Haney et al., 1987).

Fortunately, a lot of people are interested in finding more meaningful ways to evaluate teaching and in developing the capacity of the teaching profession to establish fair and useful standards for certification. Promising efforts to develop valid assessments of teaching have been launched by the newly established National Board for Professional Teaching Standards, the Teacher Assessment Project conducted by Shulman and his colleagues at Stanford, the Connecticut and California

State Departments of Education, and the Minnesota Board of Teaching.

Adding urgency to the search for better standards is the fact that current standards so clearly work against the interests of poorly served minority students. The standards we have now measure very little that relates to good teaching, and they screen out large proportions of potential teachers who are likely to staff inner-city classrooms. The standards we need would force a more challenging and knowledge-based curriculum in teacher education and screen teachers on more appropriate bases. The chances are good that the standards that produced both those effects would also produce fewer disparities in test outcomes.

Setting standards is, of course, only half the battle. For whenever there are shortages of teachers, the temptation is to "solve" the shortage by filling classrooms with teachers who do not meet the standards. Too often unresisted in the past, that temptation is apparent today in the fact that 23 states have, in the last few years, set up alternative certification programs. If the myth was true—the myth that in public education all schools are equal, all classrooms are equal, all teachers are equal— then hiring teachers with substandard certification would indeed solve the shortage problem. But, in fact, the effect of lowering standards is to fill only some classrooms in some schools—particularly those that serve minority and low-income children—with less qualified teachers.

Arguing that substandard certification should be eliminated because it reduces the overall qualifications of the teaching corps raises the counterargument: What about shortages? If having too few teachers means canceling courses, increasing class sizes, and so forth, will problems in the inner-city schools be exacerbated as that is where shortages are the most acute?

Without policy intervention, these things would certainly (and already do) happen. Yet there are a variety of feasible solutions.

Financial strategies. Improving school finance formulas so that resources are more evenly distributed would enable the schools that must now pay teachers lower salaries to compete for talent. This strategy, pursued by the state of Connecticut in 1986 through its Excellence in Education Act, invested state funds using an equalizing formula for teacher salary improvements. In a few years it largely eliminated shortages and created teacher surpluses in many fields.

Support for teacher training. Among the incentives designed to make teaching in particular locations more attractive could be offers of especially well-endowed scholarships and loans to prospective teachers who agree to work in those locations.

Locational incentives. Although measures to improve the capacity of all teachers to acquire and use knowledge are central to improving education for disadvantaged minority students, reducing staff turnover in the schools that serve those students remains essential, as does attracting the best teachers to those schools. This will require improving working conditions in the schools where they are now most dismal. Having an office as well as an attractive, well-stocked classroom, being able to make a telephone call in privacy, and using a copying machine that works are accoutrements of work life that are as important to teachers as to anyone else. True, creating good working conditions comes at a cost. But so does failing to create them.

Differentiated staffing. Maintaining standards in the face of shortages would be possible if the need for additional staff were resolved not by hiring unprepared teachers and making them solely responsible for assigned groups of students, but by using instructors, aides, and other sorts of teaching assistants whose responsibilities were more limited than a teacher's. Instructors might be people who have a bachelor's degree, but who have not completed a teacher preparation program. Their job would be to work under the guidance of a master teacher, in a team-teaching situation, for example, teaching students with help and supervision. Aides might, under the supervision of senior teachers, perform some of the more routine tasks of classroom management and record keeping. A senior teacher, like a registered nurse, would have more training and greater responsibilities than the educational equivalents of licensed practical nurses or hospital orderlies.

Differentiating staffing would require changes of other sorts. It would require breaking down the "egg-crate" structure of schools and changing the assumption that a single teacher must be solely responsible for teaching 30-40 children. It would require team teaching, so that the expertise of senior teachers most competent to diagnose, assess, and decide could be more available to the team of adults working with groups of children.

An entirely different, although complementary, approach to solving the problems that shortages present is only now becoming feasible. Consonant with the view that teachers were not all that important to schools, the federal government and state governments for many years collected so little data on the supply of teachers or the demand for them that predicting shortages was virtually impossible. As the realization of the importance of having such data has grown, so has the hope of predicting shortages with some accuracy. Prediction, of course, is a means, not an end. If a state can predict shortages of certain kinds of teachers, it should offer incentives to help underwrite the preparation for those kinds of teachers. It should strengthen the programs that prepare teachers. It should increase the attractions of teaching in the places most likely to suffer shortages of teachers.

Perhaps the biggest problem of all—although it is also perhaps the one most easily solved—has been the failure to recognize that standards and shortages interrelate. Standards are simply not standards in any meaningful sense of the term if they are abrogated at the first signs of shortage; shortages remain shortages, of talent if not of warm bodies, when the people put in charge of classrooms cannot meet standards of good teaching. Once the problem is recognized, solutions can be created. Until it is recognized, the fact that classrooms have been staffed inadequately for some students for quite a long time is apt to remain education's dirty little secret.

MORE HELP FOR NEW TEACHERS

On the first day of school, in the first week of school, throughout the first year of teaching at the very least, even a well-prepared and fully certified new teacher has a lot to learn. Although we all recognize the truth of this assertion—none of us more strongly than new teachers themselves and their students—there has been precious little organized help for beginning teachers. They have been left to sink or swim. As a result, 40% to 50% of beginning teachers leave teaching within five years, most of them in the first two years. Some beginners, through trial and error and luck and maybe a little help from their friends, learn to be effective teachers. The others learn how to get through the day. Needless to say, the results of laissez-faire induction are least satisfactory for the students, for example, who most need teachers who know how to teach them to read, not merely how to cope with their reading problems.

In recent years, the need for supervised clinical experiences—internships and induction supports—for beginning teachers has been increasingly recognized in teaching. (Other professions, such as medicine, nursing, architecture, engineering, and psychology have long recognized that structured, supervised internships, residencies, or apprenticeships are a necessary part of learning how to practice responsibly.) New York State, for example, will require a year-long internship as a prerequisite to teacher licensure. The Minnesota Board of Teaching also has endorsed the concept that beginning teachers go through an internship very much like a residency in medicine.

An idea with great potential that is now moving from the discussion stage toward implementation is the notion of "professional development schools"—schools organized much like teaching hospitals to support the induction of beginning teachers and to provide a center for the more widespread sharing of teaching knowledge through staff development. Over 100 such schools have been established through university school collaborations across the country over the past five years.

The goal of these efforts is to build a teaching force in which every single member has been taught explicitly how to base decisions on the best available knowledge and how to make decisions in the most responsible way. To give beginning teachers such an introduction to the profession, one that equips them with the tools they need thereafter, could cost about $10,000 per teacher (Wise & Darling-Hammond, 1987). Over the course of the teacher's career and over the course of a child's education, that is a very small investment for a very substantial gain.

THE BOTTOM LINE

Until everyone who is in a classroom has a base of knowledge and a well-developed sense of how to use that knowledge to make responsible decisions on behalf of students, there can be no real accountability in public education and no real effort to respond to the needs of black and other minority children. The public education system ought to be able to guarantee that every child who is forced to go to school by public law— no matter what the children's cultural or ethnic history, how poor that child's parents are, nor where that child lives, nor how little or how much he or she has learned at home—is taught by someone who is prepared, knowledgeable, and competent. That is real accountability for all children. As Grant (1989) put it:

> Teachers who perform high-quality work in urban schools know that, despite reform efforts and endless debates, it is meaningful curricula and dedicated and knowledgeable teachers that make the difference in the education of urban students. (p. 770)

When it comes to equalizing opportunities for black and other students to learn, that is the bottom line.

REFERENCES

Allington, R.L. (1983). The reading instruction provided readers of different abilities. *The Elementary Journal, 83*, 454-459.

American Association of Colleges for Teacher Education (AACTE). (1990). *AACTE/Metropolitan Life survey of teacher education students.*

Washington, DC: Author.

Armour-Thomas, E., Clay, C., Domanico, R., Bruno, K., & Allen, B. (1989). *An outlier study of elementary and middle schools in New York City* (Final report). New York: New York City Board of Education.

Ashton, P., & Crocker , L. (1986). Does teacher certification make a difference? *Florida Journal of Teacher Education, 3,* 73-83.

Ashton, P., & Crocker, L. (1987, May-June). Systematic study of planned variations: The essential focus of teacher education reform. *Journal of Teacher Education,* pp. 2-8.

Barr, R., & Dreeben, R. (1983). *How schools work.* Chicago: University of Chicago Press.

Bents, M., & Bents, R. (1990, April). *Perceptions of good teaching among novice, advanced beginner and expert teachers.* Paper presented at the Annual Meeting of the American Educational Research Association, Boston, MA.

Berliner, D.C. (1984, October). Making the right changes in preservice teacher education. *Phi Delta Kappan,* pp. 94-96.

Berliner, D.C. (1986, August/September). In pursuit of the expert pedagogue. *Educational Researcher,* pp. 5-13.

Bledsoe, J.C., Cox, J.V., & Burnham, R. (1967). *Comparison between selected characteristics and performance of provisionally and professionally certified beginning teachers in Georgia.* Washington, DC: U.S. Department of Health, Education, and Welfare.

Carter, K., & Doyle, W. (1987). Teachers' knowledge structures and comprehension processes. In J. Calderhead (Ed.), *Exploring teacher thinking* (pp. 147-160). London: Cassell.

College Board. (1985). *Equality and excellence: The educational status of Black Americans.* New York: College Entrance Examination Board.

Comer, J.P. (1988). Educating poor minority children. *Scientific American, 259,* 42- 48.

Cooper, E., & Sherk, J. (1989). Addressing urban school reform: Issues and alliances. *Journal of Negro Education, 58,* 315-331.

Copley, P.O. (1974). *A study of the effect of professional education courses on beginning teachers.* Springfield: Southwest Missouri State University. (ERIC Document No. ED 098 147).

Darling-Hammond, L. (1984). *Beyond the commission reports: The coming crisis in teaching.* Santa Monica, CA: The RAND Corporation.

Darling-Hammond, L. (1986, Fall). Teaching knowledge: How do we test it? *American Educator,* pp. 18-46.

Darling-Hammond, L. (1987). What constitutes a 'real' shortage of teachers? Commentary. *Education Week, 6*(16), p. 29.

Darling-Hammond, L. (1990a). *Teacher supply, demand, and quality: A mandate for the National Board.* Paper prepared for the National Board for Professional Teaching Standards.

Darling-Hammond, L. (1990b). Teacher professionalism: Why and how. In A. Lieberman (Ed.), *Schools as collaborative cultures: Creating the future now* (pp. 25-50). Philadelphia: Falmer Press.

Darling-Hammond, L. (1992). Teaching and knowledge: Policy issues posed by alternative certification of teachers. *Peabody Journal of Education, 67*(3), 123-154.

Darling-Hammond, L., & Snyder, J. (1992). Traditions of curriculum inquiry: The scientific tradition. In P. Jackson (Ed.), *Handbook of research on curriculum* (p. 41-78). New York: Macmillan.

Davis, D.G. (1986). *A pilot study to assess equity in selected curricular offerings across three diverse schools in a large urban school district: A search for methodology.* Paper presented at the Annual Meeting of the American Educational Research Association, San Francisco, CA.

Doyle, W. (1986). Content representation in teachers' definitions of academic work. *Journal of Curriculum Studies, 18,* 365-379.

Dreeben, R. (1987, Winter). Closing the divide: What teachers and administrators can do to help Black students reach their reading potential, *American Educator,* pp. 28-35.

Dreeben, R., & Gamoran, A. (1986). Race, instruction, and learning. *American Sociological Review, 51*(5), 660-669.

Dreeben, R., & Barr, R. (1987, April). *Class composition and the design of instruction.* Paper presented at the Annual Meeting of the American Education Research Association, Washington, DC.

Druva, C.A., & Anderson, R.D. (1983). Science teacher characteristics by teacher behavior and by student outcome: A meta-analysis of research. *Journal of Research in Science Teaching, 20,* 467-479.

Evertson, C., Hawley, W., & Zlotnick. M. (1985). Making a difference in educational quality through teacher education. *Journal of Teacher Education, 36,* 2-12.

Findley, M.K. (1984). Teachers and tracking in a comprehensive high school. *Sociology of Education, 57,* 233-243.

Gomez, D.L., & Grobe, R.P. (1990, April). *Three years of alternative certification in Dallas: Where are we?* Paper presented at the Annual Meeting of the American Educational Research Association, Boston, MA.

Grant, C.A. (1989, June). Urban teachers: Their new colleagues and curriculum. *Phi Delta Kappan,* pp. 764-770.

Greenberg, J.D. (1983). The case for teacher education: Open and shut. *Journal of Teacher Education, 34*(4), 2-5.

Grissmer, D., & Kirby, S.N. (1987). *Understanding teacher attrition.* Santa Monica, CA: The RAND Corporation.

Grossman, P.L. (1988). *A study in contrast: Sources of pedagogical content knowledge for Secondary English.* Unpublished doctoral dissertation, Stanford University.

Grossman, P.L. (1989). Learning to teach without teacher education. *Teachers College Record, 91*(2), 191-208.

Haney, W., Madaus, G., & Kreitzer, A. (1987). Charms talismanic: Testing teachers for the improvement of American education. *Review of Research in Education, 14,* 169-239.

Hice, J.E.L. (1970). The relationship between teacher characteristics and first-grade achievement. *Dissertation Abstracts International,* 25(1), 190.

Johnston, J.M., & Ryan, K. (1983). Research on the beginning teacher. In K.R. Howie & W.E. Gardner (Eds.), *The education of teachers: A look ahead* (pp.). New York: Longman.

LuPone, L.J. (1961). A comparison of provisionally certified and permanently certified elementary school teachers in selected school districts in New York State. *Journal of Educational Research, 55,* 53-63.

McNeil, J.D. (1974). Who gets better results with young children—experienced teachers or novices? *Elementary School Journal, 74,* 447-451.

Metz, M.H. (1978). *Classrooms and corridors: The crisis of authority in desegregated secondary schools.* Berkeley: University of California Press.

Moskowitz, G., & Hayman , J.L. (1974). Interaction patterns of first year typical and best teachers in inner-city schools. *Journal of Educational Research, 67,* 224-230.

Murnane, R.J., & Phillips, B.R. (1981). Learning by doing, vintage, and selection: Three pieces of the puzzle relating teaching experience and teaching performance. *Economics of Education Review, 1,* 453-465.

National Center for Education Statistics (NCES). (1985a). *The condition of education, 1985.* Washington, DC: U.S. Department of Education.

National Center for Education Statistics (NCES). (1985b). *High school and beyond: An analysis of course-taking patterns in secondary schools as related to student characteristics.* Washington, DC: U.S. Government Printing Office.

Oakes, J. (1985). *Keeping track: How schools structure inequality.* New Haven, CT: Yale University Press.

Oakes, J. (1986). Tracking in secondary schools: A contextual perspective. *Educational Psychologist, 22,* 129-154.

Oakes, J. (1987). *Improving inner-city schools: Current directions in urban district reform* (Center for Policy Research in Education, Joint Note series). Santa Monica, CA: The RAND Corporation.

Oakes, J. (1990). *Multiplying inequalities: The effects of race, social class, and tracking on opportunities to learn mathematics and science.* Santa Monica, CA: The RAND Corporation.

Pascal, A. (1987). *The qualifications of teachers in American high schools.* Santa Monica, CA: The RAND Corporation.

Rosenbaum, J.E. (1976). *Making inequality: The hidden curriculum of high school tracking.* New York: Wiley.

Rosenbaum, J.E. (1980). Social implications of educational grouping. *Review of Research in Education, 8,* 361-401.

Rottenberg, C.J., & Berliner, D.C. (1990). *Expert and novice teachers' conceptions of common classroom activities.* Paper presented at the annual meeting of the American Educational Research Association, Boston.

Shulman, L.S. (1987). Knowledge and teaching: Foundations of the new reform. *Harvard Educational Review, 57,* 1-22.

Strickland, D. (1985). Early childhood development and reading instruction. In C. Brooks (Ed.), *Tapping potential: English and language arts for the Black learner*. Washington, DC: National Council of Teachers of English.

Trimble, K., & Sinclair, R.L. (1986, April). *Ability grouping and differing conditions for learning: An analysis of content and instruction in ability-grouped classes*. Paper presented at the annual meeting of the American Educational Research Association, San Francisco.

Veenman, S. (1984). Perceived problems of beginning teachers. *Review of Educational Research, 54,* 143-178.

Wise, A.E., Darling-Hammond, L., & Berry, B. (1987). *Effective teacher selection: From recruitment to retention.* Santa Monica, CA: The RAND Corporation.

Wise, A.E., & Darling-Hammond, L. (1987). *Licensing teachers: Design for a teaching profession.* Santa Monica, CA: The RAND Corporation.

10

Silencing and Literacy

Michelle Fine
City University of New York

Today's campaigns for literacy, at least in the United States, claim either that literacy will "improve individual employment prospects" or will "empower" the individuals who succeed in acquiring literacy skills. Both stances, from the conservative to the progressive, overstate the consequences of acquiring literacy alone, particularly in a society so blatantly organized through race, class, and gender asymmetries. Yet, both fantasies raise, as they obscure, the question "literacy for what?" In this chapter, I surround the question "literacy for what?" by examining policies and practices of silencing within a low-income public high school in New York City.

The current organization and practices deployed in low-income public high schools ensure that *literacy* will be gained by only a few, and that *literacy for critical consciousness* seems attainable only in resistance to the dominant practices of the school. Through ethnographic work in New York City, qualitative evaluation research in Baltimore, extensive observations and interviewing in Chicago schools, and activist research in Philadelphia's central district and high schools, it appears safe to argue that public schools, as traditionally constituted and practiced,

This is a revision of a chapter which appeared in *Disruptive Voices* by Michelle Fine, University of Michigan Press, 1993. Reprinted with permission of the publisher.

effectively educate toward laminating or papering over power asymmetries in the broader culture. Social problems are justified or taught through primarily individualistic explanations. Subverting literacies for critical consciousness, these schools limit the kinds of literacies that young people can attain from official schooling practices.

The compulsion to silence may be more rigorously patrolled in low-income schools where critical consciousness would be presumed a dangerous (i.e., "political") outcome of education. Throughout public schools, then, discourses of individualism and meritocracy inhibit students' questions and writings, particularly when these students seek to "play with" social and structural explanations of current social problems. Literacies for critical consciousness, as Dubois and Woodson have argued, are terrifying to those in power, particularly when narrated by poor and working-class students, or students who are African American or Latino. So they are not typically taught, suffocated when voiced, or trivialized when argued. This point is made by Woodson who, in the *Mis-Education of the Negro*, wrote:

> Not long ago a measure was introduced in a certain state legislature to have the Constitution of the United States thus printed in school histories, but when the bill was about to pass it was killed by someone who made the point that it would never do to have Negroes study the Constitution of the United States. If the Negroes were granted the opportunity to peruse this document, they might learn to contend for the rights therein granted. . . . They usually say the races are getting along amicably now and we do not want these peaceful relations disturbed by teaching new political thought. . . . What they mean to say with respect to the peaceful relations of the races, then, is that the Negroes have been terrorized to the extent that they are afraid even to discuss political matters publicly. (1972, pp. 84-85)

Low-income students or students of color who voice literacies for critical consciousness are today disproportionately chastised within their schools (coded as *discipline* problems), are pushed out (coded as *dropouts*), and/or, if they are "successful," learn to bend their social critique toward individualistic explanations. At best, they learn to practice what Dubois called "double consciousness." At worst, they forget where they came from. The "I" drops out of their texts. Images of mobility *out* of their communities litter their work. "Rising up" and blaming "them" prevails (see Fine, 1991). Perhaps this is the story of the "successful" acquisition of literacy practices. If it is, the relation of ideology, schooling, and literacy deserves critical examination through the lens of school-based institutional silencing. This is precisely the space carved open in this chapter.

Silencing signifies a terror of words, a fear of talk. This chapter examines such practices as they echoed throughout a comprehensive public high school in New York City, in words and in their absence; these practices emanated from the New York City Board of Education, textbook publishers, corporate "benefactors," religious institutions, administrators, teachers, parents, and even students themselves. The chapter discusses what does not get talked about in schools, and what is not a part of the literacy learning and pedagogy. We examine how educational policies and procedures designed presumably to improve literacy among students in school actually obscure the very social, economic, and cultural conditions of students' daily lives while they expel critical "talk" about these conditions.

SILENCING IN URBAN PUBLIC SCHOOLS

If we believe that city schools are public spheres that promise mobility, equal opportunity, and a forum for participatory democracy (Giroux & McLaren, 1986), indeed one of few such sites instituted on the grounds of equal access to literacy (Carnoy & Levin, 1985); if we recognize the extent to which these institutions nonetheless participate in the very reproduction of class, race, and gender inequities; and if we appreciate that educators working within these schools share a commitment to the former and suffer a disillusionment by the latter, then it can be assumed that the practices of silencing in public schools do the following:

1. Preserve the ideology of equal opportunity and access while obscuring the unequal distribution of resources and outcomes.
2. Create within a system of severe asymmetric power relations the impression of democracy and collaboration among "peers" (e.g., between white, middle-school administrators and low-income African-American and Hispanic parents or guardians).
3. Quiet student voices of difference and dissent so that such voices, when they burst forth, are rendered deviant and dangerous.
4. Remove from public discourse the tensions between (a) promises of mobility and the material realities of students' lives; (b) explicit claims to democracy and implicit reinforcement of power asymmetries; (c) schools as an ostensibly public sphere and the influences wrought on them by private interests, the church, and the military; and (d) the dominant language of equal educational opportunity versus the undeni-

able evidence of failure as a majority experience for low-income adolescents.

Silencing removes any documentation that all is not well with the workings of the U.S. economy, race and gender relations, and with public schooling as the route to class mobility. The following single piece of empirical data provided by the U.S. Department of Labor points out why urban schools might be motivated to silence.

In 1983 the U.S. Department of Labor published evidence that a high school diploma brings with it quite discrepant opportunities based on one's social class, race, and gender, and further that the absence of such a diploma ensures quite disparate costs based on the same demographics. Although public rhetoric has assured that dropping out of high school promotes unemployment, poverty, and dependence on crime or welfare, the national data present a story far more complex. Indeed, only 15% of white male dropouts (age 22-34) live below the poverty level, compared to 28% of white females, 37% of African-American males, and 62% of African-American females (U.S. Department of Labor, 1983). Further, in a city like New York, dropouts from the wealthiest neighborhoods are more likely to be employed than high school graduates from the poorest neighborhoods (Tobier, 1984). Although having a degree corresponds to employment and poverty levels, this relationship is severely mediated by race, class, and gender stratification. Literacy, thus, becomes secondary to issues of race, class, and gender, with "credentialed" African-American youth accruing disproportionately fewer economic or educational advantages than their white counterparts.

In the face of these social realities, many principals and teachers nevertheless continue to preach to African-American and Hispanic students and parents a rhetoric of equal opportunity and outcomes through literacy, the predictive guarantees of a high school diploma, and the invariant economic penalties of dropping out. Although I am no advocate of dropping out of high school, it is clear that silencing, which constitutes the practices by which contradictory evidence, ideologies, and experiences find themselves buried, camouflaged, and discredited, oppresses and insults adolescents and their kin who already "know better." Teachers who refuse to silence also pay a price—this is covered below in more detail.

The press for silencing disproportionately characterizes low-income, African-American, and other students of color in urban schools. In these schools, literacy is bound by politics and the pedagogy of poverty. More often than not in these schools, centralization of public school administration diminishes community involvement; texts are dated (often 10 to 15 years old) and alienating, in omission and commission; curricula and pedagogies are often disempowering for students and for teachers; strategies for discipline frequently result in high suspension and expulsion rates; and calls for parental involvement often invite bake sale ladies and expel "troublemakers" or advocates. These practices constitute the very means by which schools silence and make literacy the *object* of public discourse rather than the *subject* of critical analysis for students and staff.

Silencing more intimately shapes low-income public schools than relatively privileged ones. In such contexts there is more to hide and control. The luxury of examining the contradictory evidence of social mobility associated with literacy may be primarily available to those who continue to benefit from existing social arrangements, but not those who daily pay the price of social stratification. The dangers inherent in questioning from "above" are minor relative to the dangers presumed inherent in questioning from "below." In low-income schools then, the process of inquiring into students' lived experiences and validating those experiences through literacy practices in schools is assumed, a priori, unsafe territory.

Silencing in this chapter is discussed primarily at the level of classroom and school talk in a low-income, "low-skill" school, with a large African-American student population. Surely there are corporate, church, governmental, military, and bureaucratic mandates from which demands for silencing derive. But in the present analysis, these structural demands are assumed, not analyzed. Located primarily within classrooms and with individual teachers, this analysis does not aim to place blame on teachers, but only to retrieve from these interactions the raw material for a critical examination of silencing and literacy. The data derive from a year-long ethnography of a high school in Manhattan, attended by 3,200 students, predominantly low-income African-Americans and Hispanics from Central Harlem, and run primarily by African-American paraprofessionals and aides, white administrators and teachers, and some Hispanic paraprofessionals and teachers (see Fine, 1985a, 1986a).

An analysis of silencing seems important for two reasons. First, substantial evidence has been accumulated which suggests that many students in this school, considered low in skill, income, and motivation, were quite eager to choreograph their own literacy learning, to generate a curriculum of lived experience, and to engage in a participatory pedagogy (Rosen, 1986). Efforts by teachers and administrators which undermined such educational autobiographizing pre-empted opportunities to create dialogue and community—that is, to educate—with students, their kin, and their neighborhoods (Bastian, Fruchter, Gittell, Greer, & Haskins, 1986; Connell, Ashenden, Kessler, & Dawsett, 1982; Lightfoot, 1978). Those administrators, teachers, and paraprofessionals who engaged did generate classrooms of quite magnetic and "alive" participants. More overwhelming to the observer, however, was the collective, structural culture of silencing that engulfed life inside the school.

Second, this loss of connection bears the most significant consequence for low-income students; large numbers of whom are African American. These adolescents are fundamentally ambivalent about the educational process, skeptical about the advantages of engaging in school-like literate behaviors and practices, and appropriately cynical about the "guarantees" of an educational credential (Carnoy & Levin, 1985). The linear correspondence of years of education to income does not conform to their reflections on community life. Most were confident that "you can't get nowhere without a diploma." But most were also mindful that "the richest man in my neighborhood didn't graduate but from 8th grade." And in their lives, both "truths" are defensible. It is precisely by camouflaging such contradictions that we advance adolescents' cynicism about schooling and credentials, thereby eroding any beliefs in social mobility, community organizing, or the pleasures of intellectual engagement.

The silencing process is but one aspect of what is often, for many African-American and low-income students, an impoverished educational tradition. Infiltrating administrative "talk," curriculum development, and pedagogical technique, the means of silencing establish impenetrable barriers between the worlds of school and community life. To unearth the possibility of reclaiming students', teachers', and communities' voices, the practices of silencing must be unpacked.

THE IMPULSE TO SILENCE AS IT SHAPES EDUCATIONAL RESEARCH

Lying is done with words and also with silence.
Adrienne Rich, *On Lies, Secrets and Silence*, 1979, p. 186

In June 1984 I began to lay the groundwork for what I hoped would be an ethnography of a public high school in New York City, to begin in Fall 1984 (see Fine, 1985, 1986). To my request for entree to his school, the principal greeted me as follows:

Mr. Stein: Sure you can do your research on dropouts at this school. With one provision. You cannot mention the words dropping out to the students.
MF: Why not?
Mr. Stein: If you say it, you encourage them to do it.

Even the research began with a warning to silence me and the imaginations of these adolescents. My field notes continue, "When he said this, I thought, adults should be so lucky, that adolescents wait for us to name the words *dropping out,* or *sex,* for them to do it." From September through June, witnessing daily life inside the classrooms, deans' and nurses' offices, the attendance room, and the lunchroom, I was repeatedly bewildered that this principal actually believed that adult talk could compel adolescent compliance.

The year progressed. Field notes mounted. What became apparent was a systemic fear of *naming. Naming* involves those practices that facilitate critical conversation about social and economic arrangements, particularly about inequitable distributions of power and resources by which these students and their kin suffer disproportionately. The practices of the administration, the relationships between school and community, and the forms of pedagogy and curriculum applied were all scarred by the fear of naming, provoking the move to silence.

THE WHITE NOISE CREATED BY ADMINISTRATIVE SILENCING

At the first Parents' Association meeting, Mr. Stein, the principal, boasted an 80% "college-bound" rate. Almost all graduates of this inner-city high school head for college: a comforting claim oft repeated by urban school administrators in the 1980s. Although accurate, this pronouncement fundamentally masked the fact that in this school, as in other comprehensive city high schools, only 20% of incoming 9th graders ever graduate, and statistics on the reading and writing abilities of the students are perhaps even lower. In other words, 16% of the 1,220 9th graders of 1978-1979 were headed for college by 1985. The "white noise" of the administration reverberated silence in the audience. Not named, and therefore not problematized, was the substantial issue of low retention rates.

Not naming is an administrative craft. The New York City Board of Education, for example, had at this time refused to monitor retention, promotion, and educational achievement statistics by race and ethnicity for fear of "appearing racist" (confidential personal communication, February 1984). Huge discrepancies in educational advancement, by race and ethnicity, thereby have been undocumented in board publications. Similarly, dropout estimates included students on the register when they had not been seen for months; they also presumed that students who enrolled in Graduate Equivalency Diploma (GED) programs were not dropouts, and that those who produced "working papers" were actually about to embark on careers (which involves a letter, for example, from a Chicken Delight clerk assuring that Jose has a job so that he can leave school at 16). Such procedures contribute to *not naming* the density of the dropout problem.

Although administrative silencing is unfortunately almost a redundancy, the concerns of this chapter are primarily focused on classroom and school-based activities of silencing. By no means universal, the fear of naming was nevertheless commonplace, applied at this school by conservative and liberal educators alike. Conservative administrators and teachers viewed the bulk of their students as unteachable. It was believed, following the logic of social studies teacher Mr. Rosaldo, that "If we save 2%, that's a miracle. Most of these kids don't have a chance." For these educators, naming social and economic inequities in their classrooms would only expose circumstances they believed to be inevitable and self-imposed. Perhaps these teachers themselves had been silenced over time. It is worth noting that correlational evidence (Fine, 1983b) suggests that educators who feel most disempowered in their institutions are most likely to believe that "these kids can't be helped," and that those who feel relatively empowered are likely to believe that "I can make a difference in the lives of these youths."

Disempowered and alienated themselves, some educators see an enormous and inherent distance between "them" and "us," a distance, whether assumed biologic or social, that cannot not be bridged by the mechanics of public schooling. So when I presented "dropout data" to these faculty, and suggested that the level of involuntary "discharges" processed through this school would never be tolerated in the schools attended by their children, I was rapidly chastised by one senior faculty member: "That's an absurd comparison. The schools my kids go to are nothing like this—the comparison is sensationalist!" Social distance was reified and naturalized.

A more liberal position was held by some other educators, involving a belief in color- and class-neutral meritocracy. These educators dismissed the very empirical data which would have informed the naming process. Here they followed the logic of science teacher Ms. Tannenbaum, "If these students work hard, they can really become something. Especially today with Affirmative Action." They rejected counterevidence, for example, that African-American high school graduates living in Harlem are still far less likely to be employed than white high school dropouts living in more elite sections of New York (Tobier, 1984), for fear that such data would discourage students from hard work and dreams. Enormous energy must be required to sustain beliefs in equal opportunity and the colorblind power of credentials, and to silence nagging losses of faith when evidence to the contrary compels on a daily basis.

Still other educators actively engaged their students in lively, critical discourse about the complexities and inequities of prevailing economic and social relations, and in doing so, expanded restricted notions of literacy to include analysis of the conditions and circumstances that frame their lives Often importing politics from other spheres of their lives, the feminist English teacher, the community activist who taught grammar, or the marxist historian, wove critical analysis into their classrooms, with little effort. These offices and classrooms were permeated with the openness of naming, free of the musty tension that derives from conversations-not-had.

Naming indeed subverts or complicates those beliefs that public schools aim to promote. It is for this very essential reason that naming be inherent in the educational process, in the creation of an empowered and critical constituency of citizens (Aronowitz & Giroux, 1985). It was ironic to note that pedagogic and curricular attempts to not name or to actively avoid such conversation indeed cost teachers control over their classrooms. Efforts to shut down such conversations were usually followed by the counting of money by males, the application of mascara or lipstick by females, and the laying down of heads on desks by students of both genders: the loss of control over the classroom.

To *not name* bears consequence for all students, but most dramatically for low-income, African-American, and other youths of color. To not name systematically alienates, cuts off from home, from heritage, from lived experience, and ultimately severs these students from their educational process. The pedagogical and curricular strategies employed in not naming are examined critically below.

PEDAGOGICAL AND CURRICULAR MUTING OF STUDENTS' VOICES

Constructing Taboo Voices: Conversations Never Had

A mechanistic view of teachers terrorized by naming, and students passively accommodating, could not be further from the daily realities of life inside a public high school. Many teachers name social inequities and critique, although most do not. Some students passively shut down, although most remain alive and even resistant. Classrooms are filled with students wearing walkmen, conversing among themselves and to friends in the halls, and some even persistently challenging the experiences and expertise of their teachers. In some contexts, this behavior constitutes a kind of literacy, but the typical classroom still values control and quiet, as Goodlad (1984), Sizer (1984), Anyon (1983), and others have documented. The insidious push toward silence in low-income schools became most clear sometime after my interview with Eartha, a 16-year-old high school dropout.

Field Note: January 14

MF: Eartha, when you were a kid, did you participate a lot in school?
Eartha: Not me, I was a good kid. Made no trouble.

I asked this question of 55 high school dropouts. After the third responded as Eartha did, I realized that for me, participation had been encouraged, delighted in, a measure of the "good student." Yet, for these adolescents, given their histories of schooling, participation meant poor discipline and rude classroom behavior.

Students learn the dangers of talk, the codes of participating and not, and they learn, in more nuanced ways, which conversations are never to be had. In short, they learn the limitations of official literacies. In Philadelphia, a young high school student explained to me: "We are not allowed to talk about abortion. They tell us we can't discuss it no way." When I asked a School District Administrator about this policy, she qualified: "It's not that they can't *talk* about it. If the topic is raised by a student, the teacher can define abortion, just not discuss it beyond that." The distinction between defining and discussing makes sense only if learning assumes teacher authority, if pedagogy requires single truths, and if classroom control implies silence. Perhaps this is why classroom control often feels so fragile. Control through omission is fragile. Fully contingent on students' willingness to collude, such "control" doubles as a plea for student compliance.

Silencing in public schools comes in many forms. Conversations can be closed by teachers or forestalled by student collusion. But other conversations are expressly withheld, never had. Such a policy of enforced silencing was applied to information about the severe economic and social consequences of dropping out of high school. This information was systematically withheld from students who were being discharged. Few, as a consequence, ever entertained second thoughts.

When students are discharged in New York State they are guaranteed an exit interview, which, in most cases, involves an attendance officer who asks students what they plan to do and then requests a meeting with parent or guardian to sign official documents. The officer hands the student a list of GED and outreach programs. The student leaves, often eager to find work, get a GED, go to a private business school, or join the military. Informed conversations about the consequences of the students' "decision" are not legally mandated. As they leave, these adolescents do not learn the following:

- Over 50% of African-American high school dropouts suffer unemployment in cities like New York City (U.S. Commission on Civil Rights, 1982).
- Forty-eight percent of New Yorkers who sit for the GED test fail (New York State Department of Education, 1985).
- Private trade schools, including cosmetology, beautician, and business schools, have been charged with unethical recruitment practices, exploitation of students, earning more from students who drop out than those who stay, not providing promised jobs and having, on average, a 70% dropout rate (see Fine, 1986a).
- The military, during "peacetime," refuses to accept females without a high school degree, and only reluctantly accepts males who suffer an extreme less than honorable discharge rate within 6 months of enlistment (Militarism Resource Project, 1985).

Students who leave high school prior to graduation are thereby denied informed consent—a fundamental promise of literacy. Conversations-not-had nurtured powerful folk beliefs among adolescents that: "the GED is no sweat, a piece of cake"; "you can get jobs, they promise, after goin' to Sutton or ABI"; or "in the Army I can get me a GED, skills, travel, benefits. . . . " Such is a powerful form of silencing.

Closing Down Conversations

At the level of curriculum, texts, and conversation in classrooms, school talk and knowledge were radically severed from the daily realities of adolescents' lives and more systematically aligned with the lives of teachers (McNeil, 1981). Routinely discouraged from critically examining the conditions of their lives and dissuaded from creating their own curriculum built of what they know, students were often encouraged to disparage the circumstances in which they live, warned by their teachers: "You act like that, and you'll end up on welfare!" (Most were or had been surviving on some form of federal, state, or city assistance.)

"Good students" therefore managed these dual/duel worlds by learning to speak standard English dialect, whether they originally spoke African-American English, Spanish, or Creole. More poignant still, they trained themselves to produce two voices. One's "own" voice alternated with an "academic" voice. The latter denied class, gender, and race conflict; repeated the words of hard work, success, and their "natural" sequence; and stifled any desire to disrupt.

In a study conducted in 1981, it was found that the group of

South Bronx students who were "successes"—those who remained in high school—when compared with dropouts, were significantly more depressed, less politically aware, less likely to be assertive in the classroom if they were undergraded, and more conformist (Fine, 1983b). A moderate level of depression, an absence of political awareness, a persistence of self-blame, low assertiveness, and high conformity may tragically have constituted the "good" urban student at this high school. They learned not to raise, and indeed to help shut down, "dangerous" conversation. The price of "success" may have been muting one's own voice.

Other students from the school in Manhattan resolved the "two voices" tension with creative, if ultimately self-defeating strategies. Cheray reflected on the hegemonic academic voice after she dropped out: "In school we learned Columbus Avenue stuff and I had to translate it into Harlem. They think livin' up here is unsafe and our lives are so bad. That we should want to move out and get away. That's what you're supposed to learn." Tony thoroughly challenged the academic voice as ineffective pedagogy: "I never got math when I was in school. Then I started sellin' dope and runnin' numbers and I picked it up right away. They should teach the way it matters." Alicia accepted the academic voice as the standard, while disparaging with faint praise her own voice: "I'm *wise*, but not *smart*. There's a difference. I can walk into a room and I know what people be thinkin' and what's goin' down. But not what he be talkin' about in history."

Finally, many saw the academic voice as the exclusively legitimate, if inaccessible, mode of social discourse. Monique, after two months out of school, admitted to the limitations of her literacy as practiced in the world outside of school: "I'm scared to go out lookin' for a job. They be usin' words in the interview like in school. Words I don't know. I can't be askin' them for a dictionary. It's like in school. You ask and you feel like a dummy."

By segregating the academic voice from students' own, school literacies from community life, public schools do violence not only linguistic in form (Zorn, 1983). The intellectual, social, and emotional substance which constitutes students' lives was routinely treated as irrelevant, to be displaced and silenced. Their responses, spanning acquiescence to resistance, bore serious consequence.

Contradictions Folded: Excluding "Redundant" Voices

If "lived talk" was actively expelled on the basis of content, contradictory talk was basically rendered impossible. Social contradictions were folded into dichotomous choices. The creation of such dichotomies and the reification of single truths may bolster educators' authority, reinforcing the distance between those who *know* and those who don't; discrediting often those who *think* in complexity (McNeil, 1981).

To illustrate: A social studies teacher structured an in-class debate on Bernard Goetz—New York City's "subway vigilante." She invited "those students who agreed with Goetz to sit on one side of the room, and those who thought he was wrong to sit on the other side." To the large residual group who remained mid-room the teacher remarked, "Don't be lazy. You have to make a decision. Like at work, you can't be passive." A few wandered over to the "pro-Goetz" side. About six remained in the center. Somewhat angry, the teacher continued: "OK, first we'll hear the pro-Goetz side and then the anti-Goetz side. Those of you who have no opinions, who haven't even thought about the issue, you won't get to talk unless we have time."

Deidre, an African-American senior, bright and always quick to raise contradictions otherwise obscured, advocated the legitimacy of the middle group. "It's not that I have no opinions. I don't like Goetz shootin' up people who look like my brother, but I don't like feelin' unsafe in the projects or in my neighborhood either. I got lots of opinions. I ain't bein' quiet cause I can't decide if he's right or wrong. I'm talkin'." Deidre's comment legitimized for herself and others the right to hold complex, perhaps even contradictory, positions on a complex situation. Such legitimacy was rarely granted by faculty—with clear and important exceptions including activist faculty and those paraprofessionals who lived in Central Harlem with the kids, who understood and respected much about their lives.

Among the chorus of voices heard within this high school lay little room for Gramsci's (1971) contradictory consciousness. Artificial dichotomies were delivered as natural: right and wrong answers, appropriate and inappropriate behavior, moral and immoral people, dumb and smart students, responsible and irresponsible parents, good and bad neighborhoods. Contradiction and ambivalence, forced underground, were experienced often, if expressed rarely.

I asked Ronald, a student in a remedial reading class, why he stayed in school. He responded with sophistication and complexity: "Reason I stay in school is 'cause every time I get on the subway I see this drunk and I think 'not me.' But then I think 'bet he has a high school degree.'" The power of his statement lies in its honesty, as well as the infrequency with which such comments were voiced. Ronald explained that he expected support for this position neither in school nor on the street. School talk promised what few believed, but many repeated: that hard work and education breed success and a guarantee against welfare. Street talk belied another reality, described by Shondra: "They be sayin', 'What you doin' in school? Could be out here scramblin' [selling drugs] and makin' money now. That de-gree ain't gonna get you nothing better.'"

When African-American adolescent high school graduates, in

the October following graduation, suffered a 56% unemployment rate and African-American adolescent high school dropouts suffered a 70% unemployment rate, the very contradictions which were amplified in the minds and worries of these young men and women remained unspoken within school (Young, 1983).

DEMOCRACY AND DISCIPLINE: MAINTAINING SILENCE BY APPROPRIATING AND EXPORTING DISSENT

If silencing masks asymmetric power relations, it also insures the "impression" of democracy for parents and students. This strategy has gained popularity in the fashionable times of "empowerment."

At this school the Parents' Association executive board was comprised of 10 parents: 8 African-American women, 1 African-American man, and 1 white woman. Eight no longer had children attending the school. At about mid-year teachers were demanding smaller class size. So too was the President of the Parents' Association at this Executive meeting with the Principal.

President: I'm concerned about class size. Carol Bellamy (City Council President) notified us that you received monies earmarked to reduce class size and yet what have you done?

Mr. Stein: Quinones (Schools Chancellor) promised no high school class greater than 34 by Feb. That's impossible! What he is asking I can't guarantee unless, *you* tell me what to do it. If I reduce class size, I must eliminate all specialized classes, all electives. Even then I can't guarantee. To accede to Quinones, that classes be less than 34, we must eliminate the elective in English, in Social Studies, all art classes, 11th year Math, Physics, accounting, word processing. We were going to offer a Haitian Patois Bilingual program, 4th-year French, a Museums program, Bio-Pre-Med, Health Careers, Coop and Pre-Coop, Choreography, and Advanced Ballet. The nature of the school will be changed fundamentally.

We won't be able to call this an academic high school, only a program for slow learners.

Woman (1): Those are very important classes.

Stein: I am willing to keep these classes. Parents want me to keep these classes. That's where I'm at.

Woman (2): What is the average?

Stein: 33.

Woman (1): Are any classes over 40?

Stein: No, except if its a *Singleton* class—the only one offered. If these courses weren't important, we wouldn't keep them. You know we always work together. If its your feeling we should not eliminate all electives, and maintain things. OK! Any comments?

Woman (1): I think continue. Youngsters aren't getting enough now. And the teachers will not any more.

Woman (3): You have our unanimous consent and support.

Stein: When I talk to the Board of Education, I'll say I'm talk-ing for the parents.

Woman (4): I think it's impossible to teach 40.

Stein: We have a space problem. Any other issues?

An equally conciliatory student council was constituted to determine student activities, prom arrangements, and student fees. They were largely pleased to meet in the principal's office. At the level of critique, silence was guaranteed by the selection and then the "democratic participation" of these parents and students.

Although dissent was pre-empted through mechanisms of democracy, it was also exported. The most effective procedure for silencing was to banish the source of dissent, tallied in the school's dropout rate. As indicated by the South Bronx study referred to above (Fine, 1983a), and the research of others (Elliott, Voss, & Wendling, 1966; Felice, 1981; Fine & Rosenberg, 1983), it is often the academic critic resisting the intellectual and verbal girdles of schooling who "drops out" or is pushed out of low-income schools. Extraordinary rates of suspensions, expulsions, and discharges experienced by African-American and Hispanic youths speak to this form of silencing (Advocates for Children, 1985). Estimates of urban dropout rates range from approximately 42% for New York City, Boston, and Chicago Boards of Education to 68%-80% from Aspira, an educational advocacy organization (1983).

At the school which served as the site for this ethnographic research, a 66% dropout rate was calculated. Two-thirds of the students who began 9th grade in 1978-79 did not receive diplomas or degrees by June 1985. I presented these findings to a collection of deans, advisors, counselors, administrators, and teachers, many of whom were involved in the discharge process. At first I was met with total silence. A dean then explained, "These kids need to be out. It's unfair to the rest. My job is like a pilot on a hijacked plane. My job is to throw the hijacker overboard." The one African-American woman in the room, a guidance counselor, followed: "What Michelle is saying is true. We do throw students out of here and deny them their education. African-American kids especially." Two white male administrators interrupted, chiding what they called the "liberal tendencies" of guidance counselors, who "don't see how really dangerous these kids are." The meeting ended.

Dissent was institutionally "democraticized," exported, and trivialized. These mechanisms made it unlikely for change or challenge to be given a serious hearing.

Whispers of Resistance: The Silenced Speak

In low-income public high schools organized around control and silence, the student, parent, teacher, or paraprofessional who talks, tells, who wants to speak, transforms rapidly into the subversive, the troublemaker. Students, unless they spoke in an honors class or affected the academic mode of imputing nondangerous topics and benign words, if not protected by wealth, influential parents, or an unusual capacity to be critical *and* a good student, emerged as provocateur. Depending on school, circumstances, and style, students' response to such silencing varied. Maria buried herself in mute isolation. Steven organized students against many of his teachers. Most of these youths, for complex reasons, ultimately fled prior to graduation. Some then sought "alternative contexts" in which their strengths, competencies, and voices could flourish on their own terms.

Hector's a subway graffiti artist: "It's like an experience you never get. You're on the subway tracks. It's 3 a.m., dark, cold, and scary. You're trying to create your best. The cops can come to bust you, or you could fall on the electric third rail. My friend died when he dropped his spray paint on that rail. It exploded. He died and I watched. It's awesome, intense. A peak moment when you can't concentrate on nothin', no problems, just creation. And it's like a family. When Michael Stewart [graffiti artist] was killed by cops, you know he was a graffiti man, we all came out of retirement to mourn him. Even me, I stopped 'cause my girl said it was dangerous. We came out and painted funeral scenes and cemeteries on the LL #1 and the N [subway lines]. For Michael. We know each other, you know an artist when you see him. It's a family. Belonging. They want me in, not out like at school."

Carmen pursued the Job Corps when she left school: "You ever try plastering, Michelle? It's great. You see holes in walls. You see a problem and you fix it. Job Corps lost its money when I was in it, in Albany. I had to come home, back to Harlem. I felt better there than ever in my school. Now I do nothin'. It's a shame. Never felt as good as then."

Monique got pregnant and then dropped out: "I wasn't never good at nothing. In school I felt stupid and older than the rest. But I'm a great mother to Chita. Catholic schools for my baby, and maybe a house in New Jersey."

Carlos, who left school at age 20, after five frustrating years since he and his parents exiled illegally from Mexico hopes to join the military: "I don't want to kill nobody. Just, you know how they advertise, the Marines. I never been one of the Few and the Proud. I'm always 'shamed of myself. So I'd like to try it."

In an uninviting economy, these adolescents responded to the silences transmitted through public schooling by pursuing what they considered to be creative alternatives. For such low-income youths, these alternatives generally *replace* formal schooling and fail to help them identify the mechanisms for determining what literacy is and how it is used for multiple purposes. Creative alternatives for middle-class adolescents, an after-school art class, or music lessons privately afforded by parents, generally *supplement* formal schooling.

Whereas school-imposed silence may be *an initiation* to adulthood for the middle-class adolescent about to embark on a life of participation and agency, school-imposed silence more typically represents *the orientation* to adulthood for the low-income or working-class adolescent about to embark on a life of work at McDonalds, in a factory, as a domestic or clerical, and/or on AFDC. For the low-income student, the imposed silences of high school cannot be ignored as a necessary means to an end. They are the present, *and* they are likely to be the future (Ogbu, 1978).

Some teachers, paraprofessionals, parents, and students expressly devoted their time, energy, and classes to exposing silence. One reading teacher prepared original grammar worksheets, including items such as "Most women in Puerto Rico (is, are) oppressed." A history teacher dramatically presented his autobiography to his class, woven with details on the life of Paul Robeson. An English teacher formed a writers' collective of her multilingual "remedial" writing students. A paraprofessional spoke openly with students who decided not to report the prime suspect in a local murder to the police, but to clergy instead. She recognized that their lives would be in jeopardy, despite "what the administrators who go home to the suburbs preach." Yet, these voices of naming were whispers, individual, and isolated.

What if these voices, along with the chorus of dropouts, were allowed expression? If they were not whispered, isolated, or drowned out in disparagement, what would happen if these stories were solicited, celebrated, and woven into a curriculum? What if the history of schooling were written by those high school critics who remained in school and those who dropped out? What if the "dropout problem" was studied in social studies as a collective critique by consumers of public education?

Dropping out, or other forms of critique, are viewed instead by educators, policymakers, teachers, and often students as an individual act, an expression of incompetence and/or self-sabotage. As alive, motivated, and critical as they were at age 17, most of the interviewed dropouts were silenced, withdrawn, and depressed by age 21. They had tried the private trade schools, been in and out of the military, failed the GED exam once or more, had too many children to care for, too many bills to pay, and only self-blaming regrets, seeking private solutions to public problems. Muting, by the larger society, had ultimately succeeded even for those who fled initially with resistance, energy, and vision (Apple, 1982).

I end with an image which occurred throughout the year, repeated across classrooms and across urban public high schools. As familiar as it is haunting, the portrait most dramatically captures the physical embodiment of silencing in urban schools.

Field Note: February 16

> Patrice is a young African-American female, in 11th grade. She says nothing all day in school. She sits perfectly mute. No need to coerce her into silence. She often wears her coat in class. Sometimes she lays her head on her desk. She never disrupts. Never disobeys. Never speaks. And is never identified as a problem. Is she the student who couldn't develop two voices and so silenced both? Is she so filled with anger, she fears to speak? Or so filled with depression she knows not what to say?

Whose problem is Patrice? For Patrice, how do we answer the question—literacy for what?

Nurturing the Possibility of Voice in an Improbable Context

After a year at this public school I left with little but optimism about these youngsters, and little but pessimism about public high schools as currently structured. Yet, it would be inauthentic not to note the repeated ways in which students, communities, and parents were, and the more numerous ways in which they could be, granted voice inside schools. Those teachers who imported politics from elsewhere, who recognized that educational work is political work, that to talk about or not to talk about economic arrangements is to do political work, took as their individual and collective responsibility a curriculum that included critical examination of social and economic issues, and a pedagogy that attended to the multiple perspectives and ideas inside their classrooms. In a vocational education class, Ms. Rodriquez invited students to discuss the conditions of their lives, the relationship of labor market opportunities to their own and their families' survival, and the consequences of giving up, being discouraged, and/or making trouble at work. Although a thorough critique of workplace management was not undertaken, a surface analysis was begun and trust was enabled. Likewise, in a hygiene class, Ms. Wasserman continually probed the lived experiences and diversity among the students. She integrated writing assignments with curricular and social issues, inviting students to author letters to their mothers—alive or dead—about questions "you wish you could or did ask her about sexuality, marriage, and romance." A social studies teacher created a class assignment in which students investigated their communities, conducting oral histories with neighbors, shop owners, and local organizers to map community life historically and currently. These teachers recognized that to *not* mention racism is as political a stance as is a thorough discussion of its dynamics; to *not* examine domestic violence bears consequence for the numerous youths who have witnessed abuse at home and feel alone, alienated in their experience, unable to concentrate, so that the effects of the violence permeate the classroom even—or particularly—if not named.

Students in public high schools, as thoroughly silenced as they may be, nevertheless retain the energy, persistence, and even resistance that fuel a willingness to keep trying to get a hearing. They probe teachers they don't agree with, challenge the lived experiences of these authorities, and they actively spoof the class and race biases that routinely structure classroom activities.

Field Note: September 18

Social studies teacher: A few years ago a journalist went through Kissinger's garbage and learned alot about his life. Let's make believe we are all sanitation men going through rich people's and poor people's garbage. What would we find in rich people's garbage?
Students call out: Golf club! Polo Stick! Empty bottle of Halston! Champagne bottle! Alimony Statements! Leftover caviar! Receipts from Saks, Barney's, Bloomies! Old business and love letters! Rarely worn shoes—"They love to spend money"! Bills from the plastic surgeon—for a tummy tuck! Things that are useful that they just throw out cause they don't like it! Rich people got ulcers, so they have lots of medi-cine bottles!
Teacher: Now, the poor man's garbage. What would you find?

Student (1): Not much, we're using it.
Student (2): Holey shoes.
Others: Tuna cans! Bread Bags!
Student (3): That's right, we eat alot of bread!
Others: USDA cheese boxes! empty no frills cans! Woolworth
        receipts! re-used items from rich man's garbage! *Daily News!*
Student (3): *Daily News* from week before.
Others: Old appliances! Rusty toasters!
Student (4): Yeah, we eat lots of burned toast.
Student (5): You know, poor people aren't unhappy. We like being
        poor.
Teacher: Let's not get into value judgments now. There are peo-ple
        who are eccentric and don't have these things, and poor people
        who have luxuries, so it is hard to make generaliza-tions.
Student (6): That's why we're poor!

Despite attempts to halt the critical talk, these students initiated and persisted. The room for possibility lies with the energy of these adolescents and with those educators who are creative and gutsy enough to see as their job, their passions, and their responsibility the political work of educating toward a voice.

Postscript on Research as Exposing the Practices of Silencing and Literacy

The process of conducting research within schools to identify words that could have been said, talk that should have been nurtured, and information that needed to be announced, suffers from voyeurism and perhaps the worst of post hoc academic arrogance. The researcher's "gottcha" sadistic pleasure in spotting another teacher's collapsed contradiction, aborted analysis, or silencing sentence was moderated only by the ever-present knowledge that similar analytic surgery could easily be performed on my own classes.

Yet, it is the very "naturalness" of not naming, of shutting down, or marginalizing conversations for the "sake of getting on with learning" that demands educators' attention, particularly so for low-income youths highly ambivalent about the worth of a diploma, desperately desirous of and at the same time discouraged from its achievement. If literacy is to enable children, adolescents, and adults to read, write, create, critique, and transform, how can we justify the institutionalizing of silence at the level of policies that obscure systemic problems behind a rhetoric of "excellence" and "progress," a curriculum bereft of the lived experiences of students themselves, a pedagogy organized around control and not conversation, and a thorough psychologizing of social issues which enables Patrice to bury herself in silence and not be noticed? A self-critical analysis must be undertaken so we can make visible the ways in which we teach children to betray their own voices and to reject their own literacies.

REFERENCES

Advocates for Children. (1985). *Report of the New York hearings on the crisis in public education.* New York: Author.

Anyon, J. (1982). Intersections of gender and class: Accommodation and resistance by working-class and affluent females in contradictory sex-role ideologies. In L. Barton & S. Walker (Eds.), *Gender, class and education.* London: Falmer.

Apple, M. (1982). *Cultural and economic reproduction in education.* Boston: Routledge and Kegan Paul.

Aronowitz, S., & Giroux, H. (1985). *Education under siege.* South Hadley, MA: Bergin and Garvey.

Aspira. (1983). *Racial and ethnic high school dropout rates in New York City: A summary report.* New York: Author.

Bastian, A., Fruchter, N., Gittell, M., Greer, C., & Haskins, K. (1986). Choosing equality: *The case for democratic schooling.* Philadelphia: Temple University Press.

Carnoy, M., & Levin, H. (1985). *Schooling and work in the democratic state.* Stanford, CA: Stanford University Press.

Connell, R., & Ashenden, D., Kessler, S., & Dawsett, G. (1982). *Making the difference.* Sydney, Australia: Allen and Unwin.

Elliot, D., Voss, H., & Wendling, A. (1966). Capable dropouts and the milieu of high school. *Journal of Educational Research, 60*(4), 10-186.

Felice, L. (1981). Black student dropout behaviors: Disengagement from school rejection and racial discrimination. *Journal of Negro Education, 50*(4), 415-424.

Fine, M. (1983a). Expert testimony delivered in Newberg v. Board of Public Education. Philadelphia.

Fine, M. (1983b). Perspectives on inequality: Voices from urban schools. In L. Bickman (Ed.), *Applied social psychology annual IV* (pp. 217-246). Beverly Hills, CA: Sage.

Fine, M. (1983c). The social context and a sense of injustice: The option to challenge. *Representative Research in Social Psychology, 13*(1), 15-33.

Fine, M. (1985a). Dropping out of high school: An inside look. *Social Policy, 16,* 43-50.

Fine, M. (1985b). Reflections on a feminist psychology of women: Paradoxes and prospects. *Psychology of Women Quarterly, 9*(2), 167-183.

Fine, M. (1986a). Contextualizing the study of social injustice. In M. Saks and L. Saxe (Eds.), *Advances in applied social psychology* (Vol. 3). Hillsdale, NJ: Erlbaum.

Fine, M. (1986b). Why urban adolescents drop into and out of public high school. *Teachers College Record, 87*(3), 393-409.

Fine, M. (1991). *Framing dropouts: Notes on the politics of an urban high school.* Albany: SUNY Press.

Fine, M., & Rosenberg, P. (1983). Dropping out of high school: The ideology of school and work. *Journal of Education, 165*(3), 257-272.

Giroux, H., & McLaren, P. (Eds.). (1986). Teacher education and the politics of engagement. *Harvard Educational Review, 56*, 213-238.

Goodlad, J. (9184). *A place called school: Prospects for the future.* New York: McGraw-Hill.

Gramsci, A. (1971). *Selections from prison notebooks.* New York: International Publishers.

Lightfoot, S. (1978). *Worlds apart.* New York: Basic Books.

McNeil, L. (1981). Negotiating classroom knowledge: Beyond achievement and socialization. *Curriculum Studies, 13*, 313-328.

Militarism Resource Project. (1985). *High school military recruiting: Recent developments.* Philadelphia: Author.

New York State Department of Education. (1985). Memo from Dennis Hughes, State Administrator on high school equivalency programs, December 4, Albany, NY.

Ogbu, J. (1978). *Minority education and caste: The American system in cross-cultural perspective.* New York: Academic Press.

Rich, A. (1979). *On lies, secrets, and silence.* New York: Norton.

Rosen, H. (1986). The importance of story. *Language Arts, 6*, 226-237.

Sizer, T. (1984). *Horace's compromise: The dilemma of the American high school.* Boston: Houghton Mifflin.

Tobier, E. (1984). *The changing face of poverty: Trends in New York City's population in poverty, 1960-1990.* New York: Community Service Society.

U.S. Commission on Civil Rights. (1982). *Unemployment and underemployment among blacks, Hispanics, and women.* Washington, DC: Government Printing Office.

U.S. Department of Labor. (1983). *Time of change: 1983 handbook of women workers.* Washington, DC: Government Printing Office.

Woodson, C.G. (1972). *The mis-education of the Negro.* New York: AMS Press.

Young, A. (1983). *Youth labor forced marked turning point in 1982.* U.S. Department of Labor, Bureau of Labor Statistics. Washington, DC: U.S. Government Printing Office.

Zorn, J. (1983). *Possible sources of culture bias in the validation of ETS language tests.* Paper presented at the annual meeting of the Conference on College Composition and Communication, Detroit, MI.

Introduction to Part IV
Literacy Curricula and Strategies

Susan L. Lytle
University of Pennsylvania

Developing culturally and socially appropriate curriculum strategies, instructional materials, and assessments for African-American youth is both a critical need and a very complex and demanding task. The profound disjunctions that often exist between home and school, community and school system, and teachers and students make it evident that developing such curricula require new roles and forms of collaboration between and among teachers, researchers, administrators, parents, community members and the students themselves. In turn, the task of reinventing the literacy curriculum so that it fosters learning both in school and out can become a very significant vehicle for building these new relationships and thus for reconstructing literacy learning as a critical dimension of restructuring classrooms and schools. The chapters in Part IV of this volume provide both conceptual frameworks and specific illustrations of ways to envision these much-needed changes.

Over the past decade, a growing literature has focused on various aspects of cultural diversity, examining ways that professionals can work together and with parents and other members of the community in rethinking curriculum and assessment. For example, university-based researchers have explored differences in the ethnicities of teachers and students and the limitations of teachers' knowledge about values and cultures different from their own (Delpit, 1988; Heath, 1982; Michaels & Cook-Gumperz, 1979; Rose, 1989). They have conceived and implemented innovative programs for linking schools with homes and communities (e.g., Comer, 1989; Heath, 1982), and considerable attention has been given to theorizing and inventing culturally relevant and responsive curriculum (Asante, 1991; Foster, 1991; Hale-Benson, 1986; Ladson-Billings, 1990; Ladson-Billings & Henry, 1990; McCarthy, 1990). These studies and others suggest that curriculum development for literacy is a complicated and multifaceted process that requires all participants in the educational community to make problematic their own experiences in teaching and learning to reexamine their assumptions about what is necessary and appropriate for diverse groups of learners.

Drawing from this literature, as well as their daily experiences working with African-American youth, school-based teacher-researchers in urban areas have been using their own classrooms and schools as critical sites of inquiry into curriculum and assessment and have come together in researching communities to share and integrate their observations and analyses (Cochran-Smith & Lytle, 1993). Their research investigates questions about their own diversities—as African-American, white, Latino, and Asian-American teachers—and how these differences create gaps and sometimes complicated bridges between and among them. Some have focused on the ways that tracking denies particular groups of students opportunities for rich and demanding curricula (e.g., Cone, 1990). Others are exploring the various meanings of multiculturalism by finding and using texts that speak to the experiences of different groups and examining what happens when differently positioned students (and teachers) read and respond to this literature (Brown, 1993).

In their studies of daily classroom practice, then, these teacher-researchers are attempting to learn with and from their students how the students themselves construct issues of race and how race is braided with gender, class, and ethnicity. From and with their students, they are learning what students know about literacy and language and about the relationships of language and power (Farmbry, 1993; Joe, 1993). Through these co-investigations, teachers are exploring what happens when literacy is critical, that is, when contexts are created that engage teachers and students at all levels in the co-construction of knowledge by talking, reading, and writing about complex issues of race, ethnicity, culture, and language.

Each of the chapters in Part IV of the volume contributes to this ongoing conversation between and among school and university-based researchers and teachers by addressing some of the central questions in the development of literacy curricula and strategies; the ways that literacy acquisition and development builds on the cultural and linguistic resources of learners; how curricula is co-constructed in specific contexts; the selection of texts appropriate for African-American youth, and the ways that activities may be designed for reading and writing about these texts in culturally meaningful ways; and the various roles of researchers, teachers, parents, community members, and policymakers in the social construction of curriculum and assessment. Explicitly or implicitly, each interrogates current notions of what it means for curriculum and teaching to be relevant, responsive, and/or appropriate for the literacy education of African-American youth and thus opens up new questions and avenues for research and pedagogy.

In Chapter 10, Edwards explores the roles of parents and teachers in children's early literacy development. Focusing on the importance of parent-child book reading as a central dimension of literacy development in and out of school, Edwards presents a case study of the design and implementation of a program intended to enrich parent-child book-reading interactions and to link parents and teachers of kindergarten and first-grade students in ways mutually supportive of children's learning. A key element in the program was a course offered for teachers that explored a wide range of issues related to families and education, home-school communication, and parental involvement in schools. The course was designed to reframe teachers' notions of parental involvement from traditional forms of "cooperation," to services to parents, and eventually to envisioning relationships in which parents and school staff work together as partners. Attracted to the program through grassroots strategies including solicitation by key community leaders, participating parents engaged in book-reading sessions involving researcher and peer modeling, as well as coaching and parent-child interaction. The impact of Edwards's program extended beyond the teachers and parents to include members of the community whose support for children's' literacy learning is not typically enlisted.

In Chapter 11, Harris provides a broad framework for understanding the theoretical issues in using children's literature in the literacy curriculum, arguing for the importance of teachers implementing multiethnic and multicultural curricula that include the history, culture, and experiences of African Americans. Positing the need for a range of instructional strategies, coupled with nontraditional forms of assessment, Harris explores the potential of reader-response theory for investigating types and patterns of student perceptions as they reflect cultural and linguistic differences, as well as relationships between instructional strategies and enhanced discussion and response. Harris argues for African-American children's literature, used in an after-school program, and explores ways to use reading to study issues of race and to elicit even from young children extended and deep responses to literature. Harris's study suggests the advantages that accrue when teachers and researchers form collaborative partnerships to develop curricula and teaching strategies adapted for a local context.

In Chapter 12, the third and final chapter in Part IV, Cooper addresses issues of testing within the context of curriculum reform for African-American and other minority group students. The author raises questions about the effectiveness of textbook and test-driven curriculum, arguing that teaching students how to learn is a radically different task than teaching them to memorize or take tests. Tests need to be aligned with what we know about good instruction, Cooper maintains, and good instruction emphasizes higher order thinking rather than low-level and fragmented skills. His vision for the reform of schools highlights bringing together rather than tracking diverse groups of students, linking home and school in partnerships that support instruction, and reorganizing structures of schooling to make them more interactive, interdisciplinary, and student-centered. School reform, furthermore, links instructional programs with instructional assessments, and traditional, standardized tests pose obstacles for blacks and other minorities rather than measure the collaborative and cognitive nature of learning. The redesign of schooling, Cooper concludes, places responsibility on educators and the community for relating research and practice.

Taken together, the three chapters in Part IV offer provocative images of what may be possible when teachers, researchers, parents, community members, and learners themselves participate in the development of socially and culturally appropriate curricula and teaching strategies for African-American youth. Rather than monolithic solutions in the form of standard curricula or testing programs, they suggest that curriculum development is a function of the local culture and requires educators working with colleagues and others to invent courses of action valid in local contexts and communities.

REFERENCES

Asante, M.K. (1991). The Afro-centric idea in education. *Journal of Negro Education, 62*(2), 170-180.

Brown, S.P. (1993). Lighting fires. In M. Cochran-Smith and S.L. Lytle (Eds.), *Inside/outside: Teacher research and knowledge.* New York: Teachers College Press.

Cochran-Smith, M., & Lytle, S.L. (1993). *Inside/outside: Teacher research and knowledge.* New York: Teachers College Press.

Comer, J.P. (1989). Racism and the education of young children. *Teachers College Record, 90*(3), 352-361.

Cone, J. (1990). Untracking advanced placement English: Creating opportunity is not enough. In *Research in writing:Working papers of teacher researchers.* Berkeley, CA: Bay Area Writing Project.

Delpit, L. (1988). The silenced dialogue: Power and pedagogy in educating other people's children. *Harvard Educational Review, 58,* 280-298.

Farmbry, D.R. (1993). The warriors, the worrier and the word. In M. Cochran-Smith & S.L. Lytle (Eds.), *Inside/outside: Teacher research and knowledge.* New York: Teachers College Press.

Foster, M. (1991). The politics of race through African-American teachers' eyes. *Journal of Education, 172*(3), 123-141.

Hale-Benson, J. (1986). *Black children: Their roots, culture, and learning styles.* Baltimore, MD: Johns Hopkins University Press.

Heath, S.B. (1982). What no bedtime story means: Narrative skills at home and school. *Language in Society, 11*(1), 49-76.

Joe, S. (1993). Rethinking power. In M. Cochran-Smith & S.L. Lytle (Eds.), *Inside/outside: Teacher research and knowledge.* New York: Teachers College Press.

Ladson-Billings, G. (1990, April). *Making a little magic: Teachers talk about successful teaching strategies for black children.* Paper presented at the meeting of the American Educational Research Association, Boston, MA.

Ladson-Billings, G., & Henry, A. (1990). Blurring the borders: Voices of African liberatory pedagogy in the United States and Canada. *Journal of Education, 172*(2), 72-88.

McCarthy, C. (1990). Multicultural education, minority identities, textbooks, and the challenge of curriculum reform. *Journal of Education, 172*(2), 118-129.

Michaels, S., & Cook-Gumperz, J. (1979). A study of sharing time with first grade students: Discourse narratives in the classroom. In C. Chairello et al. (Eds.), *Proceedings of the fifth annual meeting of the Berkeley Linguistic Society* (pp. 647-660). Berkeley, CA: Berkeley Linguistic Society.

Rose, M. (1989). *Lives on the boundary.* New York: Penguin.

11

Using African-American Literature in the Classroom*

Violet Harris
University of Illinois

African-American scholars, educators, and parents seem to perceive literacy in a variety of different ways over time. Three consistent perceptions about literacy emerge when one examines African-American educational historiography, autobiographies, essays, and periodicals. The first persistent theme is the belief that literacy is a valuable commodity and its acquisition involves continuous struggle that has psychological and sociopolitical ramifications. The notion of struggle is evident in written documents throughout the 18th and 19th centuries. For example, in his autobiography, Frederick Douglass (1982) documented the struggles involved in his attempts to acquire literacy while enslaved:

> The most interesting feature of my history here was my learning, under somewhat marked disadvantages, to read and write. In attaining this knowledge I was compelled to indirections by no means

*The work on which this publication was based was supported in part by the Office of Educational Research and Improvement under Cooperative Agreement No. G0087-C1001-90, with the Reading Research and Education Center. The publication does not necessarily reflect the views of the agency supporting the research.

congenial to my nature, and which were really humiliating to my
sense of candor and uprightness. (p. 81)

Douglass also detailed the reactions of those who would limit or deny
African Americans access to literacy. In this instance, it was Douglass's
"slave mistress" who attempted to place strictures on his access to
knowledge:

> Nothing now appeared to make her more angry than seeing me,
> seated in some nook or corner, quietly reading a book or newspaper.
> She would rush at me with the utmost fury, and snatch the book or
> paper from my hand, with something of the wrath and consterna-
> tion which a traitor might be supposed to feel on being discovered
> in a plot by some dangerous spy. (p. 83)

Despite the beatings and other punishments, Douglass became
literate and acquired the conviction that knowledge represented power,
whereas ignorance was equivalent to slavery. African Americans also
acted collectively to determine the type of schooling available to their
children throughout the 19th century. For instance, in the mid-1800s,
parents and interested adults resisted a restructuring of the Free African
Schools in New York City (Rury, 1983). They organized alternative
schools, hired teachers who met the criteria they had established, and
provided the type of education they wished their children to have.
Comparable actions occurred in the the 1960s and 1970s as adults organized Freedom Schools in Boston and independent schools elsewhere.

Anderson (1988), in a major new direction in African-American
educational historiography, detailed the consistent struggles African
Americans waged for literacy in the period between 1865 and 1930. He
documented the relentless battles to acquire funding for school facilities,
books, materials, and teacher salaries as well as the fights to determine
the ideological underpinnings of education for African-American children. Other actions such as the numerous court cases initiated to end segregated schooling, boycotts, and calls for community control of schools
were designed to insure equal access to educational opportunities.

A second consistent theme is the belief that the possession of literacy can be emancipatory or oppressive. Variations of this statement
are apparent in historic and contemporary writings. Literacy is viewed
as emancipatory, because it represents access to a variety of benefits
such as jobs, political and economic power, and individual empowerment (Collins & Tarmakin, 1982; Kunjufu, 1984). The oppressive functions of literacy stem not from its possession, but from the reactions of
those who wish to limit access to it or use literate practices and materials

to inculcate a particular ideology. An explication of this view is found in *Mis-Education of the Negro* (Woodson, 1931, 1969). Woodson argued that curricula designed for most African Americans resulted in enslavement of their minds:

> Looking over the courses of study of the public schools, one finds little to show that the Negro figures in these curricula. In supplementary matter a good deal of some Negro is occasionally referred to, but oftener the race is mentioned only to be held up to ridicule. (p. 134)

Woodson's solution to this dilemma was to restructure the curricula and to publish materials such as *African Myths* (Woodson, 1928) for use in schools.

Similar arguments are found in the contemporary writings of scholars such as Kunjufu (1984, 1985) and Madhubuti (1989). Kunjufu argues that a conspiracy exists which deliberately impedes the intellectual development of African-American males. Madhubuti argues that African Americans should begin developing home libraries comprised of 100 recommended texts written by African Americans such as *The Destruction of Black Civilization* (Williams, 1976). Both believe that education for African Americans as currently constituted is oppressive.

A third theme evident in writings about African-American literacy is the conviction that literacy materials should engender within African-American youth some sense of race pride and identity and commitment to racial uplift. Evaluations of textbooks reveal why these materials were and are needed. According to Elson (1964), schoolbooks-readers, histories, spellers, and geographies published during the 17th, 18th, 19th, and 20th centuries advocated what can be termed *scientific racism*. The typical view advanced in the textbooks about race was that "nature conferred specific characteristics on each member of a racial group throughout historical time; and that . . . races could be classified according to the desirability of their traits" (p. 66). Anderson (1986), although finding that social studies texts did not propagate notions of scientific racism, found that the texts failed to "present and integrate Africans and Afro-Americans into American history during the seventeenth and eighteenth centuries" (p. 265). Further, he asserted that students would not be able to "speak intelligently about any aspect of Afro-American life and culture during slavery" or the post Reconstruction and contemporary periods (pp. 268-274). In addition, others concerned with African-American literacy still battle for more equitable depictions of African Americans in children's literature as evidenced by reactions to books such as *Sounder* and *Amos Fortune, Free Man* (Sims, 1982, 1990).

Although these three themes appear consistently in historical analyses of African-American education, other factors provide some hint of the complex issue of African-American literacy. The purposes of this chapter are fourfold: (a) to discuss the major issues in literacy as they relate to African-American youth; (b) to examine children's literature and its role in literacy education, (c) to describe a preliminary investigation on the use of African-American children's literature with African-American children, and (d) to assess how the results of the preliminary investigation might inform literacy instruction.

THEORETICAL ISSUES IN LITERACY AMONG AFRICAN-AMERICAN YOUTH

Discussions of literacy over the past few years have focused on its social and contextual nature across cultures as well as on numerous pedagogical issues. These discussions have been especially useful in focusing on African-American literacy. Educators have discovered some of the pedagogical, political, and ideological concerns that enable African-American youth to acquire literacy. For example, sociolinguistic studies provide evidence that the verbal interaction patterns many African-American youth employ within their homes and communities differ from those expected by teachers (Foster, 1989; Heath, 1982). As a result, pedagogical concerns have shifted to determine how teachers might help students acquire a range of linguistic forms that enable them to interact in a variety of contexts, including school. Similarly, ethnographic observations of literacy in the homes of poor and working-class African Americans suggest that literacy is valued within these homes, and that family members attempt to develop and nurture an interest in literacy among their children (Taylor & Dorsey-Gaines, 1988). This renewed interest in the role of families contrasts with the perspective that African-American families are deficient in preparing their children for schooling.

There are many interrelated issues in literacy that contribute to discussions about African-American youth's experiences with literacy: (a) the measurement and assessment of literacy (Au, Schew, Kawakami, & Herman, 1990; Johnston, 1984; Lomotey, Master, & Maloney, 1990; Mason & Stewart, 1990; Valencia, 1990); (b) definitions of literacy (Kaestle, 1987); (c) functions of literacy (Heath, 1982; Strickland & Taylor, 1989; Taylor & Dorsey-Gaines, 1988); (d) reading curricula (Applebee, 1978, 1989; Delpit, 1986; 1988); (e) the role of the family in literacy acquisition (Durkin, 1966; Edwards, this volume; Slaughter, 1969; Slaughter Defoe & Richards, this volume; Taylor & Dorsey-Gaines, 1988; Teale & Sulzby, 1986); and (f) sociocultural, historical, and political factors such as differentiated access to literacy based on race, gender, class, or language (Apple, 1982, 1988; Fordham, 1988; Luke, 1988; Ogbu, this volume; Shannon, 1989). Many of these issues overlap; some assume greater prominence than others during different historical periods; yet, each helps determine whether African-American youth acquire literacy. In this section, the discussion focuses on three issues that provide a framework for understanding literacy within this population of learners: (a) definitions and uses of literacy, (b) reading curricula and instructional techniques, and (c) literacy in families. In addition, the section includes a summary of some other interrelated issues that are integral.

Definitions and Uses of Literacy

Definitions and conceptions of literacy vary over time. Literacy or being a literate person has been variously defined as the ability to recognize one's name or write one's name, the ability to read some component of the Bible or catechism lessons, the ability to read text at a particular grade level, and the ability to read, write, and comprehend materials in a critical manner (Kaestle, 1985). African Americans have defined literacy or being literate in similar ways. Documents such as slave narratives, autobiographies, newspapers, and communiques of benevolent societies illustrate the range of definitions and conceptions (Cooper, 1890/1988; Dyer, 1976; Herman, 1984; Kunjufu, 1984; Porter, 1936). For example, Porter determined that 18th-century Negro literary societies sought to instill religious and moral consciousness among free Negroes and advocated the abolition of slavery. Dyer's analysis of an early textbook created for "colored" children revealed that the author attempted to inculcate certain virtues such as thriftiness, modesty, and pride in individual accomplishments. However, a consistent refrain apparent in the writings of political activists, educators, and parents has been that any conceptions of literacy must include some aspects of the recurring themes described in the first pages of this chapter.

The functions of literacy are numerous and tied to the contexts in which literacy is used. They range from the acquisition of information, to the enjoyment of an aesthetic experience, to the inculcation of particular ideologies and values (Luke, 1988). Many of the functions of literacy are the same when examined in terms of race. Where differences in functions exist, they result from differential access and the appropriation of literacy as a tool in sociopolitical reform. The functions of literacy exercised by African Americans are usually examined in terms of school literacy. Typical research results indicate that African-American youth lack many experiences that would enhance their chances for becoming literate.

The research of Taylor and Dorsey-Gaines (1988) broadens our understanding of literacy among poor, urban, African-American families and provides a way of looking at the multiple and multifaceted functions of literacy within some families. They sought to determine the literacy experiences of children who were successfully learning to read and write. Their conclusions are in stark contrast to the traditional descriptions of literacy among poor, urban, African Americans. Traditional research portrays African Americans as inadequate nurturers of their children's cognitive development. Bereiter and Englemann (1966) found that (a) the families used literacy for a multitude of purposes; some 22 in all, including instrumental, recreational, confirmational, autobiographical, and critical-educational, for a variety of audiences and in a variety of contexts; (b) literacy does not necessarily liberate or result in upward mobility for an individual; and (c) education and literacy cannot be used interchangeabley or construed in the same manner (p. 202). The images presented in the book of poor mothers and fathers sharing literature with their children, writing and talking with their children, and nurturing their children's creativity and curiosity contradict the stereotype of African-American homes as intellectually and verbally deficient. Indeed, the image of males engaging in literacy activities with their children contradicts the stereotype of the absent African-American father who does not participate in childrearing.

This body of research is important because of the assumptions underlying the investigations, the questions posed, the research methodologies employed, and the information gleaned from the data collected. First, researchers do not begin with assumptions that African-American children are deficient, or "at-risk," or that African-American youth must acquire all the behaviors and values associated with white, middle-class children in order to succeed in school. Instead, they operate from assumptions that African-American children possess the desire to learn and can learn. Furthermore, they believe that the sociocultural contexts of schooling should incorporate familial and community patterns of interaction, both verbal and behavioral, when these patterns advance learning.

Second, the questions posed reflect these new perspectives. For instance, researchers now generate questions that involve action research. Other researchers want to determine the effects of implementing Afrocentric curricula on student self-esteem and motivation. Still others seek to determine whether placing African-American males in single-sex classes taught by African-American male teachers in order to prevent the fourth-grade failure syndrome works. The emphasis is less on changing the student than on altering or restructuring learning environments and curricula.

Third, many research questions cannot be answered using experimental research designs nor traditional research sites, for example, schools. The researcher must enter into those environments that have been neglected. These include meetings in churches convened to begin tutorial programs, conventions of sororities and fraternities that have education projects, and the meetings of groups such as One Hundred Black Men and One Hundred Black Women. These groups are part of a continuing tradition which began in African-American communities in the 18th century. Yet, traditional literacy research has only recently included an examination of African-American literacy in community contexts.

These insights into African-American literacy will engender new questions, interpretations, and curricula. We might ask how literacy is required to negotiate bureaucratic agencies, to participate in social activities such as religious programs, or to empower oneself through autobiographical writings to be incorporated in schooling? What factors prompt some poor families to cling to literacy as their economic status declines?

Reading Curricula and Instructional Techniques

Despite the availability of a variety of reading instruction methods, for example, skills-centered, basal reader approaches, language experience approaches, and literature-based approaches, the vast majority of students receive a skills-centered approach with a basal reading series as the heart of the instructional unit (Shannon, 1989). With the advent of the 1980s, however, the preeminence of the skills-centered, basal reader approach has been challenged by the emergence of whole language instruction with its emphasis on child-centered instruction, negotiated curricula, and meaningful literate events (Goodman, 1989).

Some would argue that a whole language approach offers the linguistic, ideological, and pedagogical perspectives needed to educate African-American youth in a manner that results in literacy and critically adept, empowered learners (Shannon, 1989). Typically, in whole language approaches, the learner engages in literate events and tasks in which his or her language is accepted and opportunities to acquire a number of linguistic forms are presented. The learner reads and writes about meaningful texts. The learner encounters language as whole units, not as hierarchical skills. The curriculum is driven by the needs of the child and the learning context. The teacher and students share power (Goodman, 1986).

At first glance, whole language approaches would seem to present the ideal literacy curriculum for African-American youth. That is, acceptance of the learner's language would suggest that teachers accept a variety of language forms ranging from Standard English to Black Vernacular English without penalizing the student or negatively evaluating the student's performance. It would also suggest that teachers provide students with opportunities to acquire an expanded linguistic repertoire to enable them to read and write about meaningful texts. At the very least, this would suggest that teachers implement curricula which include the history, culture, and experiences of African Americans, in short, multiethnic and multicultural curricula. In addition, teachers would be expected to use a variety of instructional techniques typically used with average or gifted students such as learning centers, group projects, and problem solving. Finally, the implementation of a whole language curriculum suggests shared power and improved relations with communities and families.

Several instructional programs with varying degrees of success have been designed for and used with African-American youth. For example, Reading Recovery is currently praised as offering literacy for "at-risk" students, a category to which African-American youth are often relegated. According to Pinnell, Fried, and Estice (1990), Reading Recovery is an instructional program designed to identify those students most likely to encounter difficulty in first-grade reading programs. The program is limited, however, to those students who rank at the very bottom in terms of achievement levels on standardized tests. These students receive instruction from a teacher specially trained in Reading Recovery teaching and evaluation methods. In addition, enrichment programs such as Upward Bound and learning strategies such as reciprocal teaching are thought to prepare African-American youth for successful schooling. Although these approaches have been successfully used with "at-risk" African Americans, or other students of color, none of them should be regarded as a panacea to respond to the varied needs of African-American students. It is unrealistic to expect one method or one type of material to meet the literacy needs of African-American youth. As Delpit (1986, 1988) suggests, the development of literacy curricula for African-American youth is not a skills-centered or whole language dichotomy, but rather an issue of curriculum determined by notions of power: who possesses power, how that power is manifested, and the results of that power.

Instructional strategies that may evolve from the application of reader-response theory to literacy instruction may provide new directions for creating literacy curricula and materials for African-American youth. Reader response is what happens in the mind of the reader as he or she reads a literary work (Galda, 1983; Sutherland & Arbuthnot, 1986). Three elements are central in reader response: the text, the reader, and the interactions or transactions that occur between the two. Manifestations of response are found in the reader/listener's remarks, gestures, or literary or creative products. Response can be immediate or delayed, or it may not manifest itself outwardly. Many researchers suggest that the response results from an active, constructive process shaped by the reader's age, experience, cognitive, linguistic, moral, and social development, education, gender, knowledge of text structures, ethnicity, and purposes for reading (Bleich, 1975; Iser, 1972; Rosenblatt, 1978; Squire, 1964). Britton (1970) postulated that readers must assume a "spectator stance" or a reflective posture. Purves and Rippere (1968) asserted that readers' responses could be categorized from simple retellings to evaluative comments about the work's moral significance.

This body of research has implications for literacy instruction (Sutherland & Arbuthnot, 1986). First, forms of response vary, requiring teachers to monitor student response through a number of ways, such as dialogue journals, individual conferences, discussion groups, or dramatic activities. Traditional forms of assessment may not gauge student's understanding fully. Second, different levels of response are discernible based on a number of factors such as genre, author's style, or topic. What needs to be determined is how reader-response theory might apply to African-American children and African-American children's literature. For example, are types and patterns of responses to African-American children's literature influenced by cultural or linguistic differences? What instructional strategies are most conducive to literary discussions? Which contexts impede or enhance African-American children's responses?

CHILDREN'S LITERATURE AND LITERACY

Children's literature has had a role in literacy instruction since the late 18th century. That role is firmly entrenched today through the inclusion of children's literature excerpts in basal readers, family storybook reading, and the availability of children's literature in libraries, bookstores, and general merchandise stores. Literacy experts have detailed the cognitive, linguistic, and aesthetic benefits children derive from interactions with literature (Burke, 1990; Cullinan, 1987). These benefits include improved comprehension, increased vocabulary levels, enhanced critical-thinking skills, enjoyment of the creative uses of language and art, exposure to a variety of linguistic models, increased knowledge about oneself and the world, and models for solving conflicts or problems. In addition, children's literature serves didactic and socialization functions. That is, the literature is used to imbue children with particular values or moral stances (Kelly, 1984).

In a study that determined the role of children's literature in elementary schools, Walmsley and Walp (1989) examined the types and detailed the role of literature used in six schools located in urban, suburban, and rural areas near Albany, NY. They concluded that school personnel, librarians, teachers, and administrators expressed a strong belief in the importance of literature in the elementary school curriculum, that teachers and librarians included read-alouds and opportunities for independent reading in their schedules, and that they focused on children's literature as a method for promoting an interest in reading as a leisure activity. The reading lists obtained from these school personnel contained a number of classics and several authors popular with children. It is probable that school personnel in other parts of the country would express similar beliefs and use children's literature in similar ways. One notable aspect of the reading lists obtained by Walmsley and Walp was that only 7 books out of approximately 112 titles related to the experiences of children of color. The data collected from schools demonstrate how canons are created and perpetuated. Several reasons might account for the limited inclusion of multiethnic literature, for example, a lack of awareness that the books exist or the belief that the books are not as valuable as "classic" literature. Whatever the reasons, the omission of multiethnic cultures reinforces the notion that Euro-American culture is the culture of schooling and the most valued culture and encourages the belief that other cultures have little to contribute to schooling.

African-American children, as well as other children, should have opportunities to engage with African-American children's literature for several reasons. First, many of the works are outstanding examples of literary excellence, for example, *M. C. Higgins, the Great* (Hamilton, 1974). Second, other works focus on popular activities with children, for example, *Hoops* (Myers, 1983). Third, some of the works provide children with opportunities to engage in culturally and historically authentic texts about African-American experiences. Fourth, and just as importantly, many of the works present children with an assortment of aesthetic experiences in a variety of genres.

Some support for the inclusion of African-American children's literature in elementary curricula stems from research in children's reading interests and preferences and learning theory. For example, Purves and Beach (1972) found that students preferred literature that depicted characters similar to themselves and books that reflected their experiential background. This does not suggest, however, that African-American children only need literature that reflects African-American experiences. What it does point to is the importance of African-American children's literature becoming an integral component of any children's literature curriculum intended to expand their knowledge. Children deserve to see images of themselves affirmed in school texts—images that may motivate students to engage with the material in a manner not generally attained with traditional literacy materials.

Recent advances in learning theory also support the inclusion of African-American children's literature in literacy curricula. Anderson and Armbruster (1990) delineated several maxims for learning and instruction, two of which apply here. The first maxim is that "instruction should be rooted in authentic, real-world situations" (p. 398). Many of the books written by African-American authors present authentic, real-world situations which would enable students to use the knowledge they possess, transfer their knowledge to analogous situations, or create new knowledge and understandings. Second, Anderson and Armbruster suggest that "instruction should foster flexibility through multiple perspectives" (p. 398). Often, African-American youth are presented with limited perspectives or interpretations of events (McCarthy, 1988). Imagine, for example, the learning that could result as students wrestled with the varying depictions of slavery in *Two Little Confederates* (Page, 1888/1932) and *Amos Fortune, Free Man* (Yates, 1941), both characterized by some critics as unauthentic. Or, consider the classroom interactions that could result from reading *To Be a Slave* (Lester, 1968) and *Anthony Burns* (Hamilton, 1988), both praised for their first-person accounts, detailed research, and authentic perspectives.

Reconciling disparate literary depictions such as those contained in the four books just mentioned would require a number of cognitive strategies. First, the historical interpretations found in *Two Little Confederates* and *Amos Fortune, Free Man* are the ones perpetuated in schooling, textbooks, and popular culture. Slavery in these books is romanticized and depicted as a benevolent institution necessary for civilizing and humanizing African Americans. These books represent traditional views. In contrast, *To Be a Slave* and *Anthony Burns* depict the reality of slavery: beatings, overwork, murders, slave auctions, and legal battles. These are authentic stories from the perspectives of African Americans. They are oppositional voices infrequently encountered in schooling. Second, students would have to use a variety of cognitive strategies if they were to read these books. They would have to compare and contrast versions, draw conclusions about the veracity of the interpretations, and use critical judgment to determine why a society would perpetuate a romanticized version of a horrific institution. In short, the four books should cause some cognitive dissonance.

Many children do not encounter African-American children's literature, especially literature written from the perspectives of African Americans. The literature has been omitted or has not been made accessible for the almost 100 years of its existence (Harris, 1990). What follows is a discussion of African-American children's literature and its relation to literacy education as articulated by those involved with its creation or dissemination.

AFRICAN-AMERICAN CHILDREN'S LITERATURE

African Americans have long argued for the inclusion of literacy materials that instill race pride, inform children of the historical experiences of their ancestors, and challenge or contradict stereotypical images. For example, in the foreword of *Unsung Heroes* (Haynes, 1921), an anthology of African-American biographies, the author explains why she prepared the biographies:

> telling of the victories in spite of the hardships and struggles of Negroes whom the world has failed to sing about, have so inspired me, even after I am grown, that I pass them on to you, my little friends. May you with all years ahead of you be so inspired by them that you will succeed in spite of all odds. (introduction, unnumbered pages)

Contemporary African-American author/illustrator Tom Feelings (1985) echoes similar sentiments:

> Since I cannot separate art from reality I felt the need to take a long look at Black children and I did just this in the book Daydreamers—the bittersweet portraits of fifty children rendered in many subtle gradations and tones in many levels. The book was meant to pull the reader in below the surface of the paper where a subdued luminous glow lingers even in the darkest faces. I sought to leave room for the subconscious to roam around slowly and freely to stimulate the viewer's deepest senses.

> In short, I hoped to make the reader think seriously about the lives of Black children in this country—past, present, and in the future. (p. 79)

Significantly, most children have not encountered the "culturally conscious" literature described by Feelings and Haynes. Culturally conscious literature reflects, in an authentic manner, the multiplicity of attitudes, beliefs, artifacts, traditions, mores, actions, and cultural knowledge of a particular group (Sims, 1982). *Roll of Thunder, Hear My Cry* (Taylor, 1976), the saga of an African-American family in Mississippi, is an example of culturally conscious literature. In this saga, the family is placed in a context in which family members participate in community activities such as attending church and singing in the choir with other African Americans, the parents and grandmother serve as community leaders who can do so because they are independent landowners, and the father rescues a young male from a lynching by sacrificing some of his cotton crop. In contrast, *Sounder* (Armstrong, 1969) would not be an example of culturally conscious literature. The view of African-American family and community life as positive is absent in this work, which portrays the family as hopeless, unconnected, and marginalized. The unnamed characters in *Sounder* cannot depend on the kindness of neighbors or the support of benevolent organizations. They are isolated and disconnected to other people and institutions in their community. Religion and spirituals, so often sources of succor for African Americans, are presented in this novel as a woeful justification for the family's predicament; it is decidedly noninspirational and culturally unauthentic.

Prior to the mid-1960s, most portrayals of African Americans in textbooks and literature were stereotyped (Broderick, 1973; Sims, 1982). However, several exceptions existed such as the body of literature created by Arna Bontemps, the poetry of Effie Lee Newsome, and the novels of Mary Ovington. If one were to read some of the books published prior to the 1970s, for example, *Little Brown Koko* (Hunt, 1935/1951) or *Epaminondas and His Auntie* (Bryant, 1907/1938), one could perceive the demeaning images of African Americans in children's literature. For instance, Epaminondas's Mammy berates him for behaving in a stupid manner: "Epaminondas, you ain't got the sense you was born with; you never did have the sense you was born with; you never will have the sense you was born with! Now I ain't gwine tell you any more ways to bring truck home" (p. 14). Some would argue that Epaminondas is not necessarily a malicious stereotype, but an example of a "noodle-head" folk tale. That it is a noodlehead tale is quite true, but a certain viciousness pervades the text in descriptions of Epaminondas and his "Mammy." That viscousness paralleled the pejorative images in literature created during the Reconstruction period, which was designed to justify the subordination of African Americans (Brown, 1933). Further, *Epaminondas and His Auntie* is one in a series of storybooks beginning with *The Story of Little Black Sambo* (Bannerman, 1899/1930) and continuing today with *Jake and Honeybunch Go to Heaven* (Zemach, 1982) that depict African-American males as irresponsible, greedy, lazy, and comical. The impact of this pervasive and entrenched stereotype should not be underestimated; many variants exist in all aspects of popular culture.

If African Americans were not depicted in stereotyped ways, then they were omitted altogether. W. E. B. Du Bois published a letter in *The Brownies' Book* that applauded the publication of a periodical for "our children, the children of the sun" (Harris, 1986). Included in the letter from a mother was this expressed desire:

> but I do hope you are going to write a good deal about colored men and women of achievement. My little girl has been studying about

Betsy Ross and George Washington and others, and she says: "Mama, didn't colored folks do anything?" When I tell her as much as I know about our folks, she says: "Well, that's just stories. Didn't they ever do anything in a book? (p. 181)

Implicit in this letter is the child's perception that one's cultural heritage is not important or valuable if it is not validated by inclusion in textbooks. For African-American children possessing this belief, schooling must serve as a constant reminder of their devalued status.

Despite the distortions and omissions, alternative curricula materials that were culturally conscious existed. These materials, textbooks, literature, and periodicals existed as early as the 1890s; they seemed to have, relatively, "flourished" between 1905 and 1944. They formed, quite literally, an "underground curriculum" because of their limited distribution, use, and publication life, and the emancipatory function attached to them. Several African Americans such as Du Bois (1919) and Woodson (1932), who were central in the creation of these materials, argued for their necessity and validity. For example, A. E. Johnson perceived of the need for a periodical for African-American children and published one titled *The Joy* in the 1880s (Fraser, 1973). W. E. B. Du Bois, Augustus Dill, and Jessie Fauset published 24 issues of *The Brownies' Book* during 1920-21 (Harris, 1987). Numerous textbooks such as *Floyd's Flowers* (Floyd, 1905) offered uplifting stories, biographies, and histories that extolled the achievements of African Americans. Arguably, a "renaissance" in curricular materials for African-American literacy occurred during the early 1900s through the 1940s. The apparent decline in materials after the 1940s is explained, in part, by the push for desegregated schooling and the gradual integration of African Americans into "mainstream" culture and institutions. The need for culturally conscious materials did not disappear entirely, however, the need simply went underground only to resurface in the 1960s.

By the 1960s the reemergence of culturally conscious materials was perceptible, perhaps because of the failure of integration and as a result of the burgeoning nationalism among African Americans. Several presses, most notably, Broadside and Third World, gained prominence. These presses, undoubtedly, were bolstered by the ideologies of the Black Power, Black Arts, and Nationalist-Pan Africanist movements. Not only did alternative texts such as *Golden Legacy* appear, but alternative schooling in the form of independent schools known as "shules" also appeared to institutionalize the emerging ideologies. Most of the presses, schools, and curricular materials do not exist currently, but a small coterie of authors, and at least four presses, Third World, Just Us Books, Africa Press, and Associated Publishers, persist as alternative voices.

It should be noted that mainstream publishers now routinely

include African-American children's literature in their texts, basal readers, and anthologies, but only as a result of "canon" wars and changes in the sociocultural milieu. Larrick's (1965) research on the omission of African Americans and their culture in children's books prompted publishers to increase the numbers of books published featuring African Americans. In addition, African-American parents and educators demanded culturally relevant materials and multiethnic curricula. Other factors which prompted the inclusion of African Americans included the emergence of publishing houses under the direction of African Americans, which fulfilled a consumer need unmet by "mainstream" publishers, and the mandates of state and local school districts for multiethnic curricula. The inclusions, although not token, are not overwhelming in number.

Some African-American authors and illustrators of children's books find themselves in an aesthetic and ideological quandary. Few have the luxury of simply creating literature as authors and illustrators who happen to be African American. They must mediate a double consciousness—the African and American aspects of the culture. They are, however, in a unique position to speak to or engage African-American youth in ways not possible with many traditional literacy materials. Unfortunately, the vast majority of African-American youth do not experience the literature on a consistent basis. A variety of reasons account for this situation. Fewer than 2% of the 4,000 to 5,000 children's books published each year are written by African-American authors (Chall, Raschurn, French, & Hall, 1979; Larrick, 1965; Sims, 1990). A perceived lack of demand leads to fewer books published each year, which leads to fewer opportunities for African-American youth to encounter these materials (Roback, 1990). Many parents and teachers are unaware of the existence of the literature. Others who are aware of the literature do not possess the necessary background knowledge to ascertain whether a depiction is culturally authentic. Many others are hesitant to use the literature because they believe that some of it may be too painful for African-American children or that children from other cultures will not want to read African-American children's literature.

Despite these obstacles, African-American children's literature is needed in literacy curricula for all children, but especially for African-American children. Little empirical evidence exists to support this conclusion. However, numerous articles in book review journals and journals of educational organizations advocate for the inclusion of African-American children's literature, for example, the monographs written by librarians in the 1930s and 1940s (Rollins, 1948). Some anecdotal data also exist that suggest that African-American children's literature is a needed component in literacy instruction. For instance, a typical reaction of African-American teachers and many white teachers when shown *Mufaro's Beautiful Daughters* (Steptoe, 1987), a Zimbabwean Cinderella variant, is to utter ohhs and ahhs followed by statements such as "Our children really need books like these. Are there more books like these? Where can we find them?" Clearly, a need for the books is apparent when one conducts workshops on multicultural literature; yet, numerous factors converge to limit access.

Sims (1983) offers some data to support the contention that African-American children's literature benefits children, but there has been no consistent measure of response. Sims conducted a reader-response study with a 10-year-old African-American female named Osula. Osula was given culturally conscious literature to read. She enjoyed the books, identified with some of the characters, and made interpretational and critical judgments about authorial intent and the relationships among the books, contemporary conditions, and her historical knowledge. Bunton-Spears (1990) examined the responses of secondary students enrolled in a honors English class to African-American literature. The responses of African-American students to the literature indicated that they felt as if the literature "spoke" directly to them. The results of Sims's and Bunton-Spears's research suggest the need for similar reader-response studies with more children at different grade levels. What follows next is a discussion of a preliminary investigation to determine African-American children's responses to African-American children's literature.

CHILDREN'S RESPONSES TO AFRICAN-AMERICAN CHILDREN'S LITERATURE: A CASE STUDY

As discussed in the earlier sections of this chapter, the issues associated with literacy development among African-American children have assumed many forms, from discussion about appropriate methods to teach African-American children (Shade & Edwards, 1987) to perceptions of access to literacy by African-American children and their families. In this case study, we focused on a classroom of children, primarily African American, and examined their responses to literature written about and by other African Americans. The study was conducted by the author and a classroom teacher in a small, suburban/rural Illinois city and took place over a period of one academic year. Presented in the sections that follow is a description and discussion of that case study and its implications for promoting literacy development through culturally relevant children's literature. We acknowledge the inherent problems in trying to identify appropriate materials and in presenting them to children in a way that enables them to be analytical and expressive.

The Context of the Study

Although there is ample research on how children and teachers interact around reading within classrooms, comparatively little research focuses on nurturing children's interest in literature, particularly when the literature is matched to the lifestyle, history, and experiences of the primary cultural group of readers. In this study, we were interested in identifying how culturally relevant literature can be used in the classroom and in determining the variety of children's responses to literature—particularly when the characters share the same cultural history as the reader and when the story lines resonate to many of the young readers' lives. By completing dramatic activities with literature as the focal point, we attempted to integrate into the instruction a literature program which provided children with opportunities to hear, read, and write about literature.

The setting of the study was an after-school compensatory program based in a major university and it was conducted in cooperation with the local public schools. The school, described by the principal as an "inner-city" type, is located in a small city in the midwestern region of the United States with a population of approximately 50,000 residents. The school is integrated, and the community in which it is located is predominantly working class. The compensatory program (which was the context of the study) had several goals: (a) to enhance students' potential for academic success through language arts and mathematics instruction; (b) to strive for academic excellence; and (c) to organize enrichment activities which would expand students' experiences with a variety of cultural entities such as museums.

Teachers and administrators represented a broad cross-section of cultural and ethnic groups. Although the sentiments of school administrators, most of whom were African American, reflected the emphasis on literacy as community development (Gadsden, this volume), the principal, an African-American male, specifically expressed sentiments that reflected the messages of struggle for literacy among African Americans. Stating that many of the African-American children in his school needed "lots of help," particularly in the form of enrichment activities, the principal expressed a desire to provide enrichment activities that would prepare the children for mainstream participation and competition. He wanted the children to experience African-American literature, especially the poetry of Paul Laurence Dunbar and Langston Hughes, but he also expressed concern that students interact with classic literature as well and receive moral instruction. His desire for moral instruction, interaction with classic and African-American literature, and preparation for entry into mainstream institutions through education might characterize him as a "race man," a term used extensively in the early 20th century to denote an individual who was committed to the uplifting of the race, who agitated for full participation in societal institutions, and who was a supporter of African-American institutions and benevolent and political organizations. Although used less often today, the terms, "race man and race woman," are valid for describing race-conscious individuals.

Program Participants

The program lasted a full academic year, meeting weekly for two hours per week. At the outset, meetings were conducted with third-, fourth-, and fifth-grade teachers whose comments were similar to those of the principal, that is, that the students needed African-American literature, because they did not receive much of it in school. All teachers expressed enthusiasm for the goals of the investigation, and one teacher agreed to work with me during the year. The teachers also offered several suggestions, among them: that students present an end-of-semester program, that white students have opportunities to participate in the after-school program, that they [teacher] be provided with a list of recommended books for themselves and parents, and that the program focus on oral language activities which would enable them to acquire greater competency with Standard English.

A total of 23 students were selected by their teachers. Students selected for participation included those whose academic performance was average or above average, who were not behavior problems, who would commit to attending the program on a consistent basis, and who needed to have their actual and potential talent nurtured in an enrichment program. The group consisted of 9 African-American females, 11 African-American males, 2 white females, and 1 white male. At the conclusion of the program, the group was reduced in size to 13 with 1 white female, 5 African-American females, and 7 African-American males. Of the original 23 students, 4 were third graders, 10 were fourth graders, and 9 were fifth graders. Of the final group of 13, 4 were fifth graders and 9 were fourth graders. Attrition resulted from the dismissal of four students from the program by teachers and the principal and the voluntary exiting of six other students. No students were dismissed by the researcher.

The researcher, along with one fifth-grade teacher, explored the options for presenting the material to the students. The teacher was an African-American woman with 10 years of teaching experience. The teacher and researcher shared a common philosophy about teaching and were equally committed to using multiple approaches to involving the students in the activities of the program.

The Program: Children's Early Responses to Literature

The study focused on the students' early responses to literature about and by African Americans. Specifically, we were attempting to examine how students would react initially to reading and exploring African-American literature, what specifically they liked or disliked, and how they related the experiences of the story characters to their own lives. The children read, listened to, and wrote more than 13 poems, 6 folk tales, 4 stories, and 1 play. The majority of the literature was African American and was selected on the basis of research in children's interests and preferences. Children in grades three through five preferred literature that contained well-developed characters, adventure, action, positive resolutions, and depictions of familial and peer relationships which were similar to their relationships (Huck, Hepler, & Hickman, 1987; Sutherland & Arbuthnot, 1986). Poetry was included to increase familiarity with a generally neglected genre, to provide situations for dramatic activities, and to offer natural contexts for students to practice a variety of language forms, especially the Standard English forms preferred by the teachers and principal. Other materials used included trade books selected by the students for independent reading, magazines such as *Ebony*, musical instruments, and artwork.

The instructional pattern included several stages. First, students were given opportunities to present and share their prior knowledge of a topic, book, author, or setting. Second, if students possessed limited knowledge, they were presented with new knowledge. Third, the literary work was shared, and students responded orally to the work and/or wrote comments in their journals. Each session was audiotaped, and two sessions—the fall and spring end-of-year performances—were videotaped. The teacher-observer and I maintained journals, and the students' written responses were collected. Brochures and reports describing the school, its students, curriculum, and activities also were collected. Two site visits were conducted in order to develop some sense of day-to-day activities in the school.

There was a narrative discussion of the children's responses to one folk tale, *Mufaro's Beautiful Daughters* (Steptoe, 1987), and a novella, *The Gold Cadillac* (Taylor, 1987). The categories included plot, character, setting, action, style, illustration, and personal engagement. Examples of responses placed in each category were:

Plot: "I didn't like the whole story. I liked the end, because it was weird and it was a happy ending."Character: "I liked Brother Wind, because he is smart."
Setting: "People in the South talk funny."

Action: "It was exciting, funny, and the pictures were good."
Style: "I like it, because it has humor."
Illustrations: "I like it, because it has pretty colorings."
Personal Reaction: [It was] "neat and fun"

The responses of all the students centered primarily on their personal reactions, character, plot, and action. Some students singled out the illustrations as one of the features they liked. One folk tale was presented using an audiotaped version; the responses to that tale, *The People Could Fly* (Hamilton, 1986), focused on the style of the taped presentation. The students' responses demonstrated a high level of similarity in both content and form. Their responses were particularly consistent and forceful for two of the stories, *Mufaro's Beautiful Daughters* and *The Gold Cadillac*.

Mufaro's Beautiful Daughters

Although many children are familiar with the Perrault version of *Cinderella* (Brown, 1954), and a select few recognize the Chinese variant, *Yeh Shin* (Louie, 1982), few children have heard or read fairy tales in which the Prince is, literally, tall, dark, and handsome. The hero in *Mufaro's Beautiful Daughters* (Steptoe, 1987), a variant of Cinderella from Zimbabwe, is tall, dark, and handsome. Steptoe's variant received critical acclaim, most notably the Caldecott Honor Book award of the American Library Association. In an interview, Steptoe spoke of one impetus for writing the book. His reasons reflect some aspects of the three recurring motifs in the history of literacy for African Americans. He stated:

> You know, being a child of the fifties, I was told in white magazines that African's said "ooga booga": they didn't come from a complex society. So I wanted to find out about African culture. And my research took me to southeast Africa where there was trade with China as far back as 500 B. C. The story that I found was a fairy tale recorded by a missionary. It was originally called "The Story of Five Heads." It took me about a year to research the story and about another year and a half to write and illustrate it. (Natov & DeLuca, 1986, pp. 128-29)

The story was introduced with information about southern Africa, Zimbabwe, and the author. Most of the children could recall nothing of Southern Africa, except one student who remembered reports of fighting. With the exception of one student, none of the students had heard the story prior to its presentation in the program. The children were given the names of the characters and the meanings of the names. After hearing the names of the characters, several of the students commented or repeated the names they had heard. The story was read to the group by the researcher, in dramatic fashion. Many of the students indicated through their gestures or asides that they were engaged with the text, especially the segment in which a snake becomes the Prince. The students expressed their preferences by making statements such as : "I liked the end part when it was neat [that] he was all those people. I also like the pictures," or "I liked the part when that one girl was crying and I liked the pictures," or " I just liked it all." On the whole, the transformation of one character from boy to old woman, to snake, to Prince, and the illustrations were the two elements preferred by the majority of the students.

After the oral discussions, the students wrote comments in their journals. Sixteen of the 19 students stated that they liked the story, citing the character's physical transformation, the illustrations, the actions of the characters, the excitement of the story, and the satisfying ending. Two students wrote of their dislikes. One student, a fifth-grade boy, wrote that he did not believe in fantasy. The other, a third-grade girl, wrote that she did not like the story because "I ain't like it. It was boring. Because a tree can't talk." A third student gave an ambiguous response, stating that he liked the pictures, hugging, and kissing, but did not believe the fantasy.

The story contained elements that involved all students at the level of personal engagement. Generally, the engagement was positive. The majority of girls and boys were most affected by the story's characters and action. To a lesser extent, plot and illustration captured their attention. These results reflect general developmental patterns in children's response to literature. Children expressed a preference for stories with well-developed characters with whom they can identify and stories replete with action and a discernible plot.

The Gold Cadillac

Some adults are reluctant to share with children painful historical memories depicted in literature. Others argue that children should encounter accurate depictions, no matter how painful, because many of them are unaware that they occurred, do not perceive how they are affected by the history, or need the truth to inspire them to participate in struggles for equality; this belief harkens to the "never to forget" or "those who do not know their history are doomed to repeat it" perspectives. We hesitated introducing literature such as *Roll of Thunder, Hear My Cry* (Taylor, 1976), a historical examination of racism in the South and one family's triumph, or *A Hero Ain't Nothin But a Sandwich* (Childress, 1973), a fictional depiction of a pre-teen's heroin addiction, because we did not know what the reactions would be. Also, we feared causing pain, disillusionment, or confusion which could not be resolved at the end of the session or in later sessions. Despite our initial reluctance, we selected *The Gold Cadillac* (Taylor, 1987) to share with the students. *The Gold Cadillac*, a part of the continuing saga of the Logan family (circa 1900-1950s), which began with *Song of the Trees* (Taylor, 1975), *Roll of Thunder, Hear My Cry* (Taylor, 1976), and *Let the Circle Be Unbroken* (Taylor, 1981), is an example of historical fiction that presents authentic portrayals of the African-American past.

Ten students wrote their reactions to the story. Eight indicated they liked the story, because "It was 'awesome;' "It was funny, sad, neat story;" "[It was a] great story, good adventure;" and "[The] author has great talent." Three students wrote comments that examined some elements and effects of the text. One girl wrote she liked the book, because the family solved its problems. One boy indicated he liked it, because "its a story about [how] Blacks treated Whites," although he probably meant the reverse. Asked whether they would share the book, most students indicated that they would. However, one third-grade boy indicated that he would not share the book, because it would be his favorite. Two students, a male and female in fourth grade, characterized the book as "okay." The boy indicated that he would share the book, but would not read another book by the same author. The girl indicated it was "not the best, sad because of the arguing, but it turned out good." She stated, however, that she would read another book by the author and would share the book with others.

The responses of the students were particularly interesting to the teacher-assistant. In her notes, she wrote:

> It was so interesting to listen to the children's responses to the book. They responded openly and candidly to the book. It was interesting to hear them say, "He stole the car" [In response to a question about how the father obtained the car] and "He'd better be careful. Someone might hot wire it and steal it." You know they responded from their daily experiences. The children enjoyed the story. It was told simply and from an innocent child's perspective.

The students' predictions during the reading of the story did not suggest that they were totally unaware of African-American history, nor were there any initial indications that they were provided with information that was harmful. Each student responded to the novella at the level of personal engagement, with most children writing about the plot which, according to reviews of the work, was well-developed, fast-paced, and exciting. Students were most affected by the novella's action with its realistic portrayal of racial conflict. Characterization, while not central to the majority of responses, was a factor for some of the children.

General Responses

From the students' responses to the two stories described here, it appears that the literature presented in the program, particularly African-American literature, enriched the children's lives. One example of support is found in the statements of a fourth-grade girl who stated in an interview that she never had poetry in school, but loved poetry now. Other students indicated that they read more, wrote poetry and stories at home, and talked about the books and poetry with family members. Some family members reported they purchased African-American children's literature or checked the literature out of libraries for their children's use at home.

The literature the children read engaged them in ways that paralleled engagement with any literature. The children enjoyed literature with action, adventure, strong characterization, humor, and mystery; these were typical responses. The illustrations of many of the books were especially compelling for many of the children. Music, art, artifacts, or experiences reflective of different aspects of African-American culture elicited extended discussion among the children. For instance, if an *Essence* or *Ebony* magazine was shared in order to provide background knowledge, the students wanted to peruse the entire magazine and talk about its contents. They were eager for information about African-American history, creative artists, famous persons, and current events. In the discussion about Virginia Hamilton and her folk tales, *The People Could Fly* (1986), the students were especially interested and wanted to know where she lived, her marital and parental status, and what she looked liked.

The students' responses to the stories were, generally, at the level of engagement/involvement. Occasionally, a student would discuss or write about specific story elements such as humor or action, but few students analyzed the effectiveness of the author's writing or the value of the work. That would be expected given the students' ages and level of development. Essentially, they responded in a manner that reflected traditional development of a sense of story. Some of the children made moral judgments about a character's actions or the lesson one could extract from a story. Few related the stories or poems to others heard or read in the program, their classes, or the ones they selected for leisure reading. Similarly, few of the children related the literature to their lives.

The types of questions to students resulted in most of their responses being categorized at the engagement/involvement level; they were not conducive to extended responses or discussion. They were "nonliterary and basal-like" (Saul, 1990). That is, the questions paralleled those in some basal readers that require literal responses; many could have been answered without any connections to the work read. For example, a question such as "What do you think about the book?" will not likely elicit extended discussion with third, fourth, and fifth graders. Instead, questions such as "Pretend you are Nyasha walking through the forest, how would you react when the headless woman appears?" would have elicited sustained discussion. In addition, the written responses might have been lengthier and more complex if I had posed this type of question rather than "Tell me if you liked the story and why."

Importance of the Program

Any uniqueness in the after-school program centers on the use of African-American children's literature. Few students engage with a similar number of texts and supplementary materials reflective of African-American experiences; in fact, most children receive limited exposure in their academic careers. Applebee (1989), for example, found that only two African-American authors, Richard Wright and Lorraine Hansberry, appear consistently on high school reading lists. Given that fewer than 5% of children's books published each year relate to African Americans, it is quite probable that lists of books recommended for use in elementary schools are similarly limited.

Another unique element for these children was the incorporation of a modified whole language approach. Most receive skills-centered instruction with limited amounts of literature of any type except what appears in basal readers. The students wrote for a variety of purposes (interview scripts to perform before invited guests, plays because they wanted to write them, and journal responses to share their feelings about the books they read), individually and in small groups. They participated in a number of creative dramatics, they were encouraged to read during leisure time (each selected a book from among the choices I presented based on an interest inventory), and they were given opportunities to make decisions about the activities they wanted to complete (the students suggested writing plays, and I arranged for them to do so).

This program, if modified, has the potential to create contexts for learning which enhance literacy acquisition among African-American youth. Sharing literature, writing about literature, and performing creative dramatics help students perceive the value of literacy and how they might use literacy in their lives. Varied experiences with a range of genre and authors, especially autobiographies and biographies, can inform students of the struggles African Americans have experienced and how these relate to their lives. This goal would fit well within the first recurring theme in African-American educational historiography. The second consistent theme, the emancipatory and repressive functions of literacy, can be made apparent to students as they read African-American literature, discuss the literature, and begin to question, as one fifth grader did, the reasons why they do not have many books about themselves in school libraries. Clearly, a program with African-American literature at its center fulfills the third recurring theme—the need for literacy materials that enhance self-concept, develop race consciousness and race pride, and inspire readers to participate in the struggle for social justice.

Ideally, the person to implement a program comparable to the one described in this chapter would be one who possesses certain beliefs and knowledge. An African-American teacher is not a necessary prerequisite, but a sensitive, informed, and knowledgeable teacher is. A teacher, for example, would have to believe that his or her students deserve to have literature as an integral component of literacy education. The teacher would also have to believe that African-American children's literature is a valuable cultural commodity. The teacher would have to have some knowledge of African-American history and literary traditions or, at the very least, have a willingness to acquire that information. Essential, too, would be the teacher's ability to create learning environments that foster and nurture a variety of literacy events such as the writing of book reviews, plays, scripts, and other texts. Related to this, the teacher should have some knowledge of writing as a process and have the ability to foster discussion that links the literary work to the students and their experiences and understandings. Most importantly, the teacher should have a genuine fondness for literature in order to motivate children to read and value literature. If, however, these attributes seem unrealistic, then a teacher who is caring, who believes that children can benefit from literature, who is willing to explore the literature with children, and who is willing to acquire knowledge about African-American history and culture is probably sufficient.

Some possible hindrances to the implementation of a comparable program include a lack of interest in African-American children's literature among some teachers, limited availability of the literature for purchase, limited budgets for the purchase of children's literature, a reluctance among some adults to use literature that may generate opposition and controversy, and a fear among some teachers that they do not possess the appropriate experiences to share the literature.

ISSUES FOR INVESTIGATION

Literacy among African Americans is a complex issue shaped by a number of pedagogical, ideological, and curricular concerns. Ensuring that each African-American youth becomes literate will necessitate restructuring curricula and schools, involving family and community members, and training teachers in different ways. First, the investigation reported here and other discussions of African-American children's literature (e.g., Sims-Bishop, 1990) affirm and support the idea that three recurring themes—literacy is a valued commodity, literacy can lead to liberation or it can be appropriated for oppressing individuals and groups, and literacy materials should promote race pride, uplift, and respect for one's heritage—are apparent when one examines the history of literacy among African Americans. For example, the educators involved with the after-school enrichment program and those in the schools expressed sentiments parallel to the three themes. Future research and curriculum development should acknowledge these themes and integrate them as much as possible.

A second issue relates to reconciling the expectations of African Americans regarding literacy with those who govern schools. On the one hand, African-American adults want African-American youth to acquire schooling that enables them to mediate all cultural institutions, but not at the cost of total assimilation and alienation from African-American communities.

Third, literacy programs need to provide students with opportunities to engage with meaningful texts and with opportunities to read, discuss, and write about those texts. In addition, new and existing literacy programs should make African-American history, culture, art, music, and literature integral components of those programs. Moreover, new and existing literacy programs should involve family members and other interested community members in their creation and revision.

Finally, teachers' academic preparation should provide them with knowledge of the cultural and linguistic diversity they will confront in the classroom. The courses should emphasis that linguistic uniformity and Standard English are not a prerequisite for becoming literate. Teachers should enroll in courses that apprise them of the history of the students whom they will teach, especially courses that include the perspectives of African Americans. In addition, teachers should enroll in literature courses that expand traditional literary canons.

REFERENCES

Anderson, J. (1986). Secondary school history and textbooks and the treatment of Black History. In D. Hine (Ed.), *The state of Afro-American history* (pp. 253-274). Baton Rouge: Louisiana State University Press.

Anderson, J. (1988). *The education of Blacks in the South, 1865-1930*. Chapel Hill: University of North Carolina Press.

Anderson, R., & Armbruster, B. (1990). Some maxims for learning and instruction. *Teachers College Record, 91*, 396-408.

Apple, M. (1982). *Cultural and economic reproduction in education*. London: Routledge & Kegan Paul.

Apple, M. (1988). *Education and power*. London: Routledge and Kegan Paul.

Applebee, A. (1978). *A child's concept of story*. Chicago: University of Chicago Press.

Applebee, A. (1989). *A study of book-length works taught in high school English courses*. Center for the Learning and Teaching of Literature, University at Albany, State University of New York, Report Series 1. 2.

Au, K., Schew, J., Kawakami, A., & Herman, P. (1990). Assessment and accountability in a whole literacy curriculum. *The Reading Teacher, 43*, 574-578.

Bereiter, C., & Englemann, S. (1966). *Teaching the disadvantaged in the preschool*. Englewood Cliffs, NJ: Prentice-Hall.

Bleich, D. (1975). *Readings and feelings: An introduction to subjective criticism*. Urbana, IL: National Council of Teachers of English.

Britton, J. (1970). *Language and learning*. London: Allen Lane, The Penguin Press.

Broderick, D. (1973). *Image of the black in children's fiction*. New York: R. R. Bowker Co.

Brown, S. (1933). Negro character as seen by white authors. *Journal of Negro Education, 2*, 179-203.

Bunton-Spears, L. (1990). Welcome to my house: African American and European American students responses to Virginia Hamilton's House of Dies Drear. *Journal of Negro Education , 59*, 566-576.

Burke, E. (1990). *Literature for the young child* (2nd ed.). Boston: Allyn and Bacon.

Chall, J., Raschurn, E., French, V., & Hall, C. (1979). Blacks in the world of children's books. *The Reading Teacher, 32*, 527-533.

Collins, M., & Tarmarkin, M. (1982). *The Marva Collins way*. New York: J. P. Tarcher, Inc.

Cooper, A. (1988). *A voice from the South*. New York: Oxford University Press. (Original work published 1890)

Cullinan, B. (1987). *Children's literature in the reading program*. Newark, DE: International Reading Association.

Delpit, L. (1986). Skills and other dilemmas of a progressive Black educator. *Harvard Educational Review, 56*, 379-385.

Delpit, L. (1988). The silenced dialogue: Power and pedagogy in educating other people's children. *Harvard Educational Review, 58*, 280-298.

Douglass, F. (1982). *Life and times of Frederick Douglass*. London: Collier Books.

Du Bois, W. E. B. (1919). The true brownies. *The Crisis, 7*, 285-286.

Durkin, D. (1966). *Children who read early*. New York: Teachers College Press.

Dyer, T. (1976). An early Black textbook: *Floyd's flowers or duty and beauty for Colored children. Phylon, 37*, 359-361.

Elson, R. (1964). *Guardians of tradition.* Lincoln: University of Nebraska Press.

Feelings, T. (1985). Illustration is my form, the Black Experience my story and content. *The Advocate, 4*, 73-82.

Fordham, S. (1988). Racelessness as a factor in black students school success: Pragmatic strategy or Pyrrhic victory? *Harvard Educational Review, 58*, 54-84.

Foster, M. (1989). "It's cookin' now:" A performance analysis of the speech events of a Black teacher in an urban community college. *Language in Society, 18*, 1-29.

Fraser, J. (1973). Black publishing for Black children. *School Library Journal, 20*, 19-24.

Galda, L. (1983). Research in response to literature. *Journal of Research and Development in Education, 16*, 1-7.

Galda, L. (1990). Children's literature as a language experience. *The New Advocate, 3*, 247-260.

Goodman, K. (1986). *What's whole in whole language.* Portsmouth, NH: Heinemann Educational Books.

Harris, V. J. (1986). *The Brownies' Book: Challenge to the selective tradition in children's literature.* Doctoral dissertation, University of Georgia. (Ann Arbor: UMI (AAC8628882), 1987.)

Harris, V. J.(1987). Jessie Fauset's transference of the "New Negro" philosophy to children's literature. *Langston Hughes Review, 6*, 36-43.

Harris, V. J. (1990). African-American children's literature: The first one hundred years. *Journal of Negro History, 59*, 540-555.

Heath, S. (1982). *Ways with words.* New York: Oxford University Press.

Herman, P. (1984). *Southern Blacks accounts of learning to read before 1861* (Tech. Report, Center for the Study of Reading). Champaign, IL: University of Illinois.

Huck, C., Hepler, S., & Hickman, J. (1987). *Children's literature in the elementary school* (4th ed.). New York: Holt, Rinehart and Winston.

Iser, W. (1972). The reading process: A phenomenological approach. *New Literary History, 3*, 279-300.

Johnston, P. (1984). Assessment in reading. In P. D. Pearson (Ed.), *Handbook of reading research* (pp. 147-182). New York: Longman.

Kaestle, C. (1985). The history of literacy and the history of readers. *Review of Research in Education, 12*, 11-53.

Kaestle, C. (1987). Literacy and reading performance in the United States, from 1880 to the present. *Reading Research Quarterly, XXII*, 8-46.

Kelly, R. (1984). Literary and cultural values in the evaluation of books for children. *The Advocate, 4*, 84-99.

Kunjufu, J. (1984). *Developing positive self-images and discipline in Black children.* Chicago: African-American Images.

Kunjufu, J. (1985). *The conspiracy to destroy Black boys* (Vol. 1). Chicago: African-American Images.

Larrick, N. (1965). The all-white world of children's books. *Saturday Review, 48,* 63-65, 84-85.

Lomotey, K., Master, J., & Maloney, C. (1990, April). *The education of African-Americans: An exploratory study of the Buffalo Public Schools.* Unpublished manuscript. Paper presented at the annual meeting of the American Educational Research Association, Boston.

Luke, A. (1988). *Literacy, textbooks and ideology.* London: The Falmer Press.

Madhubuti, H. (1989). *Black men: Obsolete, single, dangerous?* Chicago: Third World Press.

Mason, J., & Stewart, J. (1990). Emergent literacy assessment for instructional use in kindergarten. In L. Morrow & J. Smith (Eds.), *Assessment for instruction in early literacy* (pp. 155-75). Englewood Cliffs, NJ: Prentice-Hall.

McCarthy, C. (1988). Rethinking liberal and radical perspectives on racial inequality in schooling: Making a case for nonsynchrony. *Harvard Educational Review, 58,* 265-79.

Natov, R. & De Luca, G. (1986). An interview with John Steptoe. *The Lion and the Unicorn, 9,* 122-127.

Pinnell, G., Fried, M., & Estice, R. (1990). Reading recovery: Learning how to make a difference. *The Reading Teacher, 43,* 282-295.

Porter, D. (1936). The organized educational activities of Negro literary societies, 1828-1846. *Journal of Negro Education, 5,* 555-576.

Purves, A., & Beach, R. (1972). *Literature and the reader.* Urbana, IL: National Council of Teachers of English.

Purves, A., & Rippere, V. (1968). *Elements of writing about a literary work: A study of response to literature.* Urbana, IL: National Council of Teachers of English.

Roback, D. (1990, November 30). Bookstore survey: Zeroing in. *Publisher's Weekly, 237,* 42-44.

Rollins, C. (1948). *We build together: A reader's guide to Negro life and literature for elementary and high school use* (Rev. ed.). Chicago: National Council of Teachers of English.

Rosenblatt, L. (1978). *The reader, the text, the poem.* Carbondale, IL: Southern Illinois University Press.

Rury, J. (1983). The New York African Free School, 1827-1836: Conflict over community control of Black education. *Phylon, XLIV,* 187-198.

Saul, W. (1990). "What did Leo feed the turtle?" and other nonliterary questions. Language Arts, 66, 295-303.

Shade, B., & Edwards, P. (1987). Ecological correlates of the educative style of Afro-American children. *Journal of Negro Education, 56,* 88-99.

Shannon, P. (1989). *Broken promises: Reading instruction in twentieth-century America.* Granby, MA: Bergin & Garvey Publishers.

Sims, R. (1982). *Shadow and substance: Contemporary Afro-American children's fiction.* Urbana, IL: National Council of Teachers of English.

Sims, R. (1983). Strong Black girls: A ten-year-old responds to Afro-American literature. *Journal of Research and Development in Education, 16,* 23-30.

Sims, R. (1985). Children's books about blacks: A mid-eighties status report. *Literature Review, 8,* 9-13.
Sims-Bishop, R. (1990). Walk tall in the world: African-American literature for today's children. *Journal of Negro Education, 59,* 556-565.
Slaughter, D. (1969). Maternal antecedents of the academic achievement behaviors of Afro-american Head Start children. *Educational Horizons, 46-47,* 24-28.
Squire, J. (1964). *The responses of adolescents while reading four short stories.* Urbana, IL: National Council of Teachers of English.
Strickland, D., & Taylor, D. (1989). Family story book reading: Implications for children, families, and curriculum. In D. Strickland & L. Morrow (Eds.), *Emerging literacy: Young children learn to read and write* (pp. 27-34). Newark, DE: International Reading Association.
Sutherland, Z., & Arbuthnot, M. (1986). *Children and books.* Glenview, IL: Scott, Foresman and Company.
Taylor, D., & Dorsey-Gaines, C. (1988). *Literacy in inner-city families.* Portsmouth, NH: Heinemann Educational Books.
Teale, W., & Sulzby, E. (Eds.). (1986). *Emergent literacy.* Norwood, NJ: Ablex.
Valencia, S. (1990). A portfolio approach to classroom reading assessment: The whys, whats, and hows. *The Reading Teacher, 43,* 338-341.
Walmsley, S.A., & Walp, T.P. (1989). *Teaching literature in elementary school.* Albany, NY: Center for the Teaching and Learning of Literature, State University of New York at Albany.
Williams, C. (1976). *The destruction of Black civilization.* Chicago: Third World Press.
Woodson, C. (1969). *Mis-education of the Negro.* Washington, DC: The Associated Publishers. (Original work published 1931)

CHILDREN'S BOOKS CITED

Folk Tales

Bannerman, H. (1930). *The story of Little Black Sambo.* New York: The Platt & Munk Co., Inc. (Original work published 1899)
Brown, M. (1954). *Cinderella.* New York: Aladdin Books.
Bryant, S. (1938). *Epaminondas and his auntie.* Boston: Houghton Mifflin Co. (Original work published 1907)
Hamilton, V. (1974). *M.C. Higgins the great.* New York: Macmillan.
*Hamilton, V. (1985). *The people could fly.* New York: Alfred A. Knopf.
Hunt, B. (1951). *Little brown Koko.* Chicago: American Colortype. (Originally published 1935)
Louie, A. (1982). *Yeh Shin.* New York: Philomel Books.
Page, T. (1932). *Two little confederates.* New York: Charles A. Scribners

Sons. (Originally published 1888)
*Steptoe, J. (1987). *Mufaro's beautiful daughters.* New York: Lothrop, Lee & Shepard Books.
Woodson, C. (1928). *African myths.* Washington, DC: The Associated Publishers.

Poetry

*Giovanni, N. (1985). *Spin a soft black song.* New York: Farrar, Strauss, Giroux.
*Greenfield, E. (1978). *Honey, I love.* New York: Harper & Row Publishers.
*Greenfield, E. (1981). *Daydreamers.* New York: Dial Books for Young Readers.
*Hughes, L. (1974). *Selected poems.* New York: Vintage Books.
*Johnson, J. (1976). *God's trombones.* New York: Penguin Books.
*Larrick, N. (Ed.). (1968). *Piping down the valleys wild.* New York: Dell Publishing Company.
*Pretlutsky, J. (Ed.). (1983). *The Random House book of poetry for children.* New York: Random House.
*Pretlutsky, J. (1984). *The new kid on the block.* New York: Scholastic.

Stories

Armstrong, W. (1969). *Sounder.* New York: Harper.
Childress, A. (1973). *A hero ain't nothin' but a sandwich.* New York: Coward.
*Childress, A. (1975). *When the rattlesnake dances.* New York: Coward, McCann & Geoghegan.
*Floyd, S. (1905). *Floyd's flowers.* Atlanta: Hertel & Jenkins.
Forbes, E. (1946). *Johnny Tremain.* New York: Houghton Mifflin.
Hamilton, V. (1988). *Anthony Burns.* New York: Knopf.
Haynes, E. (1921). *Unsung heroes.* New York: Du Bois & Dill Publishing Company.
Lester, J. (1968). *To be a slave.* New York: Scholastic.
Myers, W. D. (1983). *Hoops.* New York: Laurel Leaf.
Taylor, M. (1975). *Song of the trees.* New York: Dial Books for Young Readers.
Taylor, M. (1976). *Roll of thunder, hear my cry.* New York: Bantam Books.
Taylor, M. (1981). *Let the circle be unbroken.* New York: Dial Books.
*Taylor, M. (1987). *The gold Cadillac.* New York: Dial Books.
Yates, E. (1941). *Amos Fortune, free man.* New York: Dutton.
Zemach, M. (1982). *Jake and Honeybunch go to heaven.* New York: Farrar, Strauss & Giroux.

*Indicates literature used with students.

12

Connecting African-American Parents and Youth to the School's Reading Curriculum: Its Meaning for School and Community Literacy

Patricia A. Edwards
Michigan State University

HISTORICAL BACKGROUND

In the field of education few topics have received more attention than the failure of African-American children in learning to read. Dummett (1984) laments:

> In spite of the massive effort of educators and researchers, the enormous expenditures in time and money, and the proliferation of remedial reading classes and innovative reading programs, these children are still not learning to read adequately. (p. 31)

Various reasons have been suggested for this persistent reading failure, but as Dummett puts it, "the enigma remains" (p. 31).

Over the years, three views have emerged to explain problems that African-American children experience in learning to read. Two of these explanations center around the language that they speak—Black English. The "deficit" theory was commonly used to explain the reading failure. Some researchers (Bereiter & Englemann, 1966; Deutsch, 1967) suggest that African-American children are linguistically deprived because the language that they speak is unstructured, underdeveloped, and, in general, deficient. This deficient language not only provides an inadequate foundation on which to build language skills in standard English, but also causes cognitive deficiency which leaves these children unequipped for the abstract tasks exacted by the standard English curriculum. However, several researchers provided evidence that successfully disproved this theory (Baratz & Povich, 1967; Gumperz & Hernandez-Chavez, 1972; Labov, 1965). For example, Gumperz and Hernandez-Chavez demonstrated that there is no research evidence to prove that Black English is an inefficient language or that it actually interferes with the reading process.

With many researchers maintaining that the language of black children is not deficient but different, another theory emerged to describe the language of black children—the "difference" theory (Baratz, 1969; Labov, 1965). Proponents of this theory argue that all dialects are equally efficient as systems of communication and that the language of African-American children is highly structured, systematic, and logical. Therefore, although these children speak a "different" language, they are as linguistically capable as those who speak standard English. Although both Baratz and Labov do not minimize the data on the endemic failure of African-American children, they question these data as evidence of language deficiency. They insist that such data indicate that there are differences between the language of these children and the language of the teacher and curriculum. These differences, they suggest, may interfere with learning to read standard English.

There are also various points of view concerning possible significant differences between standard English and Black English. Proponents of the difference theory often disagree on how much interference does occur, where it occurs, and whether it is significant enough to cause the continuing reading failure evidenced among African-American children. According to Labov (1967), the major area of difference between Black English and standard English is the phonology. Baratz (1966) insists that the most significant differences between Black English and standard English are in the syntax. Others, Ruddell (1965), Goodman (1965), and Smith-Dummett (1977), question the significance of these differences in relation to learning to read. Ruddell (1965) suggests that Black English-speaking children show a high degree of language competence when they translate the standard English messages they hear into their own expression, for example, "He will go" to "He go." Goodman came to the same conclusion when he examined samples of African-American inner-city children's reading miscues. Smith-Dummett (1977) studied 300 Black English speakers in Harlem and concluded that a Black English background does not necessarily interfere with receptive competency in standard English. Nonetheless, she found that differences between Black English and standard English may cause reading problems for some children. However, she cautioned educators not to assume that the widespread reading failure of African-American inner-city children is due solely to the dialect they speak.

Goodman, who in 1965 suggested that the differences between Black English and standard English could cause reading problems, later abandoned that theory. In a later article, Goodman and Buck (1973) stated:

> In fact, this writer hypothesized some years ago that there would be a direct relationship between the degree of dialect divergence and success in learning to read. . . .Evidence from several years of miscue research has convinced me that the hypothesis, at least as it applies to the range of dialects spoken by White and Black urban Americans, is untrue. (p. 6)

In the absence of convincing evidence that the reading failure was caused by problems inherent in the language of African-American children, educators began looking into a third area which they believed might provide some answers for the failure of African-American children in learning to read. Several researchers (Cunningham, 1977; Goodman & Buck, 1973; Lamb, 1979; Simons & Johnson 1974; Smith, 1975) suggested that a major cause of reading failure for African-American children was not their language, but their teachers' attitudes toward the language. For example, Goodman and Buck (1973) pointed to the linguistic ignorance of many teachers in the way they characterized the children's language. The researchers noted:

> The only special disadvantage which speakers of low-status dialects suffer in learning to read is one imposed by teachers and schools. Rejection of their dialects and educators' confusion of linguistic difference with linguistic deficiency interferes with the natural process by which reading is acquired and undermines the linguistic self-confidence of divergent speakers. (p. 7)

Other educators believe that teachers need to plan their instructions to accommodate the differences between Black English and standard English. Goodman and Buck (1973) suggest that teachers also know how to analyze the miscues of African-American children during oral reading. Still others argue that teachers' attitudes can not be realistically changed without proposing changes in teacher education (Dummett, 1984). Generally speaking, the message is that teachers need to be educated to understand the language of the children they teach and that teacher training institutions should design programs to increase teachers' knowledge of and sensitivity to the language and needs of African-American children.

Despite the fact that educators and researchers have spent more than 30 years trying to explain why African-American children continue to lag behind white children in reading achievement, the enigma persists—why are large numbers of African-American children not learning to read? Recently, educators and researchers have suggested that the problem may lie in the fact that many economically and educationally disadvantaged children enter school with little or no knowledge of books. In fact, some of these children come from homes in which their parents have never read a book to them. In response to this claim, reading educators have suggested that one way to help these children is by encouraging their parents to read aloud to them. For example, Teale (1981) found:

> Virtually every reading methods book or early childhood education book written and dozens of articles recommend that families read to young children in order to provide a sound foundation for learning to read and write in later years. (p. 902)

The importance of parent-child book reading has been chronicled in reading research. In 1908, Huey advised parents to read to their children. He informed parents that "the secret of it all lies in the parents reading aloud to and with the child" (p. 332). His advice to parents is still reflected in current thinking about the value of this practice. Russell (1984) concluded:

> Reading to your children may be the single, most powerful contribution that you, as a parent, can make toward their success in school. Although teachers and school administrators emphasize the importance of providing quiet study time and space within the home, a child who has difficulty in reading and writing simply will not be able to make productive use of even the most advantageous study conditions. It is only when children enjoy reading and truly appreciate the benefits that artful use of language can have that they pursue their studies with vigor. (p. 3)

Yet another strong argument for reading aloud has been presented by Doake (1986), who argued:

The parents' responsibility for providing a print oriented environment for their children from as early in their lives as possible is obvious. To deny children this experience is similar to and as serious as denying them the opportunity of hearing oral language. All children have the right to be read to! All children have the right to the irreplaceable pleasure of being held in their parents' arms and hearing loved stories again and again. All children have the right to manage the process of learning to read for themselves from the basis of an inner drive created by the countless hours in the company of their books and a loved parent. (p. 6)

In *Becoming a Nation of Readers,* the influential 1984 report, a group of 10 experts agreed that reading aloud to children is the single most important factor in preparing to read (Anderson, Hiebert, Scott, & Wilkinson, 1985). The authors stated:

Parents play roles of inestimable importance in laying the foundation for learning to read. A parent is a child's first guide through a vast and unfamiliar world . . . a child's first mentor on what words mean and how to mean things with words . . . a child's first tutor in unraveling the fascinating puzzle of written language. A parent is a child's one enduring source of faith that somehow, sooner or later, he or she will become a good reader. (p. 57)

Even more recently, Gallimore and Goldenberg (1989) indicated just how important reading to children at home is to children's development as readers in school. They concluded that "children who learn to read in school with minimum difficulty enjoy [a variety of positive experiences, examples and exposure] to simple books, repeated readings of familiar books and stories, and opportunities to read or 'pretend read' favorite books to themselves and to more competent adults and older children" (p. 4).

Few would question the importance of reading aloud to children, but a number of researchers have questioned the feasibility of teachers requesting parents to read to their children when they are unable to read themselves. According to Chall, Heron, and Hilferty (1987), 27 million Americans cannot read a bedtime story to a child. They describe functional illiteracy as an epidemic having reached 1 out of 5 Americans. "It [illiteracy] robs them of a decent living . . . of the simplest of human pleasures, like reading a fairy tale to a child" (p. 190). France and Meeks (1987) also argue that:

Parents, who do not have basic literacy skills are greatly handi-
capped in meeting the challenge of creating a 'curriculum of the
home' to prepare their children to succeed in school. Furthermore,
they can't help their children build a foundation for literacy because
they are unable to read to them. (p. 222)

If it has taken researchers more than 30 years to try to explain
why African-American children continue to lag behind white children in
reading achievement, one can reasonably assume that those children
who were subjects in the early studies are now parents and grandpar-
ents. One could also argue that if the parents' experiences with school
were unsuccessful, there is a strong possibility that their children's experiences with school will be unsuccessful. Consequently, the question
raised by France and Meeks is extremely important: What, then, can be
done to help illiterate and semiliterate parents give their children the
support they need to be successful readers?

The reminder of this chapter provides a case study of the development and implementation of Parents as Partners in Reading, a program
for illiterate and semiliterate parents and their children, and describes
how the Parents as Partners in Reading Program, implemented in
Donaldsonville, LA, affected parents, teachers, children, and the larger
community. The implications of the program for literacy among black
youth are addressed as well as why connecting black parents and youth to
the school's reading curriculum is important. Furthermore, the chapter
highlights the strengths of this program and what is unique or generaliz-
able about it. Last, the chapter discusses what is needed to improve literacy access and opportunities for African-American parents and youth.

DONALDSONVILLE CASE STUDY

In 1985 I volunteered to be a parent consultant at a local Head Start
Center in a rural community located in northern Louisiana. I met with
families once each month for 1-1/2- hour sessions over a period of nine
months, focusing on how parents could become better prepared to support their children's education at the Head Start Center and later in the
public school setting. As I became more familiar with the families, I proposed a book-reading project and solicited volunteers. Five African-
American lower socioeconomic status (SES) mothers were randomly
selected from a total of 18 mothers who volunteered to participate in the
book-reading project. The question addressed was: What does reading
to a child mean to parents for whom book-reading is not a normal part
of their daily lives?

My initial questions were based on the notion that kindergarten and first-grade teachers have assumed that parents have a clear understanding of the skills needed to participate in an effective book-reading interaction with their children. After watching the five mothers interacting with their children over an 8-week period, however, it became obvious that for those who do not normally read to their children, the simple teacher directive "read to your child" is a very complex task (see Edwards, 1989). For example, in the first session the mothers were asked to select a book to read to their preschool child, as I observed and videotaped the book reading. The first mother had difficulty pronouncing almost all of the words in the book and struggled to get through the text. The second mother, a teenager, asked me, "What do I do? Do I point to the pictures? Do I ask questions?" The third mother quickly read the book without stopping and said, "The end." The fourth mother, reading to her two sons, hurriedly moved the book from one child to the other. Distracted, neither child got much from the reading. The fifth mother, frustrated by her child's unresponsiveness, spanked the child.

My interest in parent-child book-reading interactions was guided by previous research in lower SES families (Farron, 1982; Heath, 1982, 1983; Heath & Branscombe, 1986; McCormick & Mason, 1986; Snow & Ninio, 1986). What concerned me about this body of research was that it highlighted lower SES parents' inability to participate successfully during book reading, but did not go on to the next step of recommending strategies for improving parental participation in book reading.

To begin the project, it seemed imperative to help teachers to understand that they need to move from "telling" to "showing" parents what "read to your child" means. It seems that teachers have implicit knowledge of what "reading to your child" really means, but that they encounter difficulty in explaining the concept to parents. Teachers know how to read to their own children at home, but find it awkward to single out specific skills, going from the simple to the complex, in an organized fashion, because they themselves use these skills so well and easily. Therefore, this traditional book-reading pattern leads teachers to say, "Read to your child. You know, open the book and talk about the pictures." However, any global statements teachers make to parents about book-reading interactions "sail right over their heads," making it difficult for parents to translate into practice the much-requested teacher directive, "Read to your child."

Using this information as one basis for discussion, I proposed that assisting parents to participate in book-reading interactions with children would allow the children to benefit more from such interactions. The notion that parents could profit from receiving assistance in book reading has been suggested by other researchers as well (Pflaum, 1986;

Sledge, 1987; Spewock, 1988; Swift, 1970). Spewock proposed that parents who have poor attitudes toward school because of their own negative experiences as students could profit from being trained to teach their preschoolers through children's literature. Sledge proposed supporting mothers in a correctional facility to share books with their infants:

> MILK (Mother-Infant Literacy Knowledge) operated with the conviction that a print rich environment, thick with literacy events, needs not be limited by economics or culture, that a parent's ability and inclination to provide such experiences could be developed through demonstration, discussion, and material support. (p. 2)

Pflaum (1986) suggested that "children with little experience in one-to-one verbal interaction with their parents may profit from instruction that provides such interactive focus. Parents may be able to supplement their interactions through training" (p. 89).

Similarly, Swift argued that training for mothers who are limited in communication skills in the use of preschool books as a vehicle for verbal interaction with their children could have a positive impact on their language and thinking and ultimately on that of their children. He encouraged mothers who had children enrolled in "Get Set," a preschool program in Philadelphia, to join a "mothers' story hour club." He used preschool books to increase mothers' story talk and encouraged them to use what they had learned from these sessions in their reading interactions with their children at home. A variety of methods to involve the mothers was employed. For example, if a mother was unable to read words, she was praised for attempts to describe what she saw in pictures. If a mother could read, she was encouraged to both tell and read the stories.

It became clear there is a major need to help lower SES parents participate in book-reading interactions with their children as evidenced by the large number of low-income children who continue to enter school without having any prior experience with books. Thus, in Fall 1987, the Parents as Partners in Reading Program was organized at Donaldsonville Elementary School, in Donaldsonville, LA.

After I accepted the principal's invitation to implement the book-reading program at Donaldsonville Elementary School (DES), I met with teachers and administrators to discuss the book-reading program and to encourage them to enroll in a course I would be offering through a university extension titled "Parents and Partners in Reading." I provided them with the rationale, objectives, and the content of the course. (The outline of the semester's course activities that were provided is described in the appendix.)

According to Croft (1979), the General Mills survey of parents in

American families reports that families are most likely to turn to teachers for advice rather than to family agencies, social workers, or other such support services. The challenge of meeting that responsibility relies heavily on good parent-teacher relationships. Some schools may be fortunate enough to have a group of sophisticated parents who are experienced in carrying out cooperative programs, but generally, planning and guidance for parent participation rests on the shoulders of the teacher. The teacher, then, is at the hub of parental involvement in the educational process. Teachers' roles include facilitator, teacher, counselor, communicator, program director, interpreter, resource developer, and friend.

Despite the fact that classroom teachers are expected to be active participants in parental involvement efforts, few teachers have had specific training for this. Such training will assist teachers in acquiring strategies for strengthening home and school communication.

Course Objectives
The course included nine objectives. It was designed to assist teachers in:

1. Learning strategies and techniques that can be employed to involve parents in their child's reading program.
2. Becoming more aware of the importance of the role of the family in the education of children.
3. Becoming more aware of materials available to serve families.
4. Becoming more aware of communication approaches with the home and linkages to the community.
5. Planning, implementing, and evaluating parent/school meetings and workshops.
*6. Learning a developmental sequence that progresses from the more traditional types of parent involvement in which parents are asked to cooperate with school staff, to the types of parent involvement in which school staff provide services to parents, and then toward the types of involvement in which parents and school staff work together essentially as partners in education.
*7. Understanding the various models of parent involvement as well as acquiring knowledge about potential costs and benefits to be derived from each model.
*8. Presenting parental involvement to teachers so that it is viewed as a necessary complement to their coursework and not as an optional interest area. As such, teachers will need to learn how working with parents has the potential to improve their work, how to develop better relationships with chil-

dren's parents, and how to help develop more community support for the schools.

*9. Developing a parental involvement teacher-training sequence to address specific knowledge bases related to each specific type of parental involvement. For example, teachers should be taught the differences between teaching children and teaching their adult parents in learning to involve parents as home tutors.

Course Content

The content of the course included a 14-part sequence: (a) the need for parent involvement, (b) historical overview of family life and parent involvement, (c) the parent community, (d) effective home-school-community relationships, (e) the employed/working parent, (f) parental empowerment, (g) organizing a school volunteer program, (h) school-based programs, (i) home-based programs, (j) community-based programs, (k) the art of communicating with parents, (l) parents in the classroom, (m) ideas for parent-teacher meetings, and (n) parent workshops. The course content was centered around five themes—Family Literacy, Effective Home-School-Community Relationships, Parents as Partners in Education, Parents as Partners in the Reading Program, and Parent Practices of Parent Involvement.

The primary teachers were asked to demonstrate on videotape book-reading skills or behaviors from the Resnick et al. (1987) modified checklist. This checklist pertains to four dimensions of parent-child interaction: (a) body management (e.g., sitting opposite the child), (b) management of book (e.g., encouraging child to hold book and to turn pages), (c) variation in the reader's voice and language interactions (e.g., labeling and describing pictures), and (d) affect (e.g., pausing for the child's responses and making approving gestures). Teachers were asked to select skills they felt comfortable modeling and were encouraged to explain as clearly as possible what the skills meant so that parents could understand. Prior to each taping session, I asked the teachers if they had any questions about the skill they were going to model. In many instances, they did have questions. For example, teachers asked, "How long should I model the skill?" "Would you explain a little more about what you want?" and "If I mess up can we do it over?" or "Let me know if I'm doing ok." These interchanges between the teachers and myself usually lasted for approximately 5 to 10 minutes. The interchanges served to assure the teachers that they were considered the experts. At

---

*Objectives 6, 7, 8, and 9 are objectives developed by the Southwest Educational Development Laboratory.

the end of each of the four taping sessions (which lasted for approximately 3 to 4 hours), the teachers and I reviewed the tape. Only in a few instances did we actually retape the skill.

Because 40% of the parents were semiliterate and/or illiterate, it seemed important to solicit community leaders to contact parents who had literacy problems to give them the incentive needed to become willing participants in the book-reading program. Another approach used was to ask parents to contact other parents who would benefit from the program. Both of these grassroots methods were utilized to build strong ties between the home and school.

INTRODUCING THE BOOK-READING PROGRAM TO THE DONALDSONVILLE COMMUNITY

The principal and assistant principal assisted in identifying key community leaders, such as the Ministerial Alliance, business leaders, school board members, and the local superintendent. They also suggested holding a series of meetings at the community center to solicit support from the "ordinary" townspeople (e.g., grandmothers and bus drivers) and contacting people just sitting on street corners about the role they could play in recruiting parents for the book-reading program. Each of these strategies proved to be successful.

The community support was overwhelming. The ministers agreed to preach from their pulpits about the importance of parents helping their children and especially the importance of parents attending the weekly book-reading sessions. After meeting with the ministers, a priest of a predominately African-American Catholic Church echoed the program's message in a sermon the following Sunday to his parishioners. Similar messages were delivered weekly by both African-American and white ministers to parents and children.

A local bar owner surfaced as a strong supporter of the book-reading program, attending all of the book-reading sessions and telling mothers who patronized his establishment that they no longer would be welcome unless they "put as much time into learning how to read to [their] children as [they] spent enjoying [themselves] at [his] bar." He also brought mothers to school to participate in the program and took them back home and worked successfully with the Social Services Department to secure babysitters for parents who otherwise would not come.

INTRODUCING THE BOOK-READING PROGRAM
TO PARENTS AND CHILDREN

The primary reason parents were recommended by the kindergarten and first-grade teachers to participate in the book-reading program was that the teachers feared that the parents' children were at risk of failing kindergarten and/or first grade and that parents who participated could enhance their own children's literacy development. In addition, some students from the 4-year at-risk class and the parent of a third grader participated in the program. The 25 participating mothers had no prior book-reading training and averaged about 9.5 years of formal schooling.

The book-reading sessions lasted for two hours once a week. The overall goal of the book-reading program was to "show" parents how to read effectively with their children. This included learning specific book-reading behaviors to incorporate while reading to their children.

In order to make the parents feel comfortable about participating in the book-reading program, they were provided with a wide list of materials. For example, they were informed that the "Little Books" by Mason and McCormick (1986) and a few wordless picturebooks and picture storybooks would be used in the initial session. As time passed, they could continue to use wordless picture books, picture storybooks, concept books, easy-to-read books, and environmental print books. Parents were then shown the materials to use throughout the year, as well as the phases of the book-reading program—Coaching, Peer Modeling, and Parent-Child Interaction. Each phase lasted for approximately the same length, about 6 or 7 weeks. Parents attended the book-reading program on a weekly basis from October 1987 to May 1988. There were 23 book-reading sessions of approximately two hours each. (It should be noted that not all mothers attended every session.)

During the Coaching Phase, the mothers met with me as a group. I modeled effective book-reading behaviors and introduced a variety of teacher tapes. The mothers watched, listened, waited, responded, and demonstrated what they had learned. The personal demonstrations (which were usually taped) and the teacher tapes served as a type of instructional scaffolding for them. The mothers could stay on after sessions to review tapes and interact with me.

By the end of the 6-week coaching phase, the parents had begun to view book reading as routinized and formatted language events between themselves and their children. They also had begun to adjust their language to their child's level of understanding and were developing an interest and sophistication in book reading. For example, they were able to label and describe pictures, vary their voices, and make motions while interacting with the texts during the sessions. More importantly, parents in their individual ways seemed to be acquiring an internal understanding of what it meant to share books with children.

In the Peer Modeling Phase, parents were helped to manage the book-reading sessions and strategies. This phase was based on Vygotsky's (1978) work, which suggested that the acquisition of skills progresses from a stage in which the teacher and learner jointly collaborate to perform a cognitive task (interpsychological), to a stage in which the learner internalizes and regulates the process him- or herself (intrapsychological). During this phase, I assisted the mothers by (a) guiding their participation in book-reading interactions with each other, (b) finding connections between what they already knew and what they needed to know, (c) modeling effective book-reading behaviors for them when such assistance was needed (encouraging them to review teacher tapes), and (d) providing praise and support for their attempts.

Over the 6-week period, they shared in the book-reading sessions and verbally and nonverbally corrected and guided each other. In addition, they provided for each other the same instructional scaffolding I had provided for them earlier. The mothers displayed the type of adult interactive behavior described by Morrow (1988), such as providing information about the book, relating responses to real-life experiences, inviting their peers to ask questions or comment throughout the story, answering questions and reacting to comments, and providing positive reinforcement for their peers' efforts. The mothers' storytalk increased in complexity, and their shyness about participating in the peer group decreased. Just as importantly, they learned to approach the book-reading sessions with confidence.

In the Parent-Child Interaction Phase, I ceded total control to the parents and functioned primarily as a supportive and sympathetic audience, offering suggestions to the mothers as to what books to use in reading interactions with their children, evaluating the parent-child book-reading interactions, and providing feedback or modeling. In this final phase, the mothers shared books with their own children and implemented book-reading strategies they learned in the previous two phases (Coaching, Peer Modeling). From these interactions, the mothers learned the importance of involving their children in a book-reading interaction and recognized that "the parent holds the key to unlocking the meaning represented by the text" (Chapman, 1986, p. 12). (For transcripts of the interactions during the three phases of the book-reading program—Coaching, Peer Modeling and Parent-Child Interaction—see Edwards, 1991; and Edwards & Garcia, 1991. A fuller description of the topics covered in the book-reading sessions and sample lessons of each of the three phases are provided elsewhere; see Edwards, 1990a.)

THE IMPACT OF THE BOOK-READING PROGRAM ON SCHOOL AND COMMUNITY LITERACY

One of the most important results of the book-reading program was its utilization of a group of unlikely individuals to support literacy learning—a bar owner, bus driver, grandmothers, the Ministerial Alliance, and people sitting on street corners. For all concerned, the book-reading program served as a vehicle for building bridges and mending fences among the home, school, and community. These three groups for the first time were working toward one common goal—"the children." In the past, they had been looking in opposite directions and often blaming each other for the high illiteracy rate that existed in this small rural community.

The book-reading program helped parents, teachers, administrators, and the community realize that family literacy training can make a difference in the lives of illiterate and semiliterate individuals. Chall et al. (1987) justify family literacy training in the following way:

> We need to redouble our efforts to identify and reach those who need to participate in family literacy programs. Solving the literacy problems of the nation [and in a community] will require a multi-level, long-term effort. We must resist the attractiveness of quick fixes and accept only validated and flexible solutions. (p. 196)

The Parents as Partners in Reading Program, which focused on both parents and their children, attempted to provide this type of validated and flexible solution. In assisting parents in how to read to their children and connecting them to the reading program in school, the program also gave them the opportunity to reinforce important learning concepts and skills at home.

In addition, the program changed the attitudes of school personnel toward the parents and children they served. The principal and assistant principal helped to publicize the program in the community, used their personal vehicles to bring parents to the program each week, and created a friendly and warm environment at the school for the parents. The teachers who had feared that children of these parents would fail kindergarten and/or first grade reported that the children's knowledge of written language, directionality, and story grammar had improved because they became a part of the book-reading program. The teachers also reported that the videotaped modeling of effective book-reading behaviors for the parents and enrollment in the family literacy course had broadened their knowledge of literacy development in different family structures.

Several unexpected school results also emerged. For example, the school librarian designed a computer program that listed the names of each child whose parents were participating in the book-reading program so that the parents were able to check out up to five books each week under their child's name. The school librarian also assisted the program each week by selecting books that the parents could understand and that related to the topics that were being addressed in the book-reading sessions. More importantly, the book-reading program changed parental attitudes toward the school. In the past there was little structure to support parental learning. The book-reading program provided such a structure so that parents could help their children with the most frequently requested parent involvement activity—"Read to your child."

SUMMARY

The Parents as Partners in Reading program was developed to answer a particular need: to teach parents how to read effectively to their children and, thereby, to provide the language and reading readiness skills that children need for learning to read and write. Parents as Partners goes to the heart of illiteracy problems: to the home, where the problems stem, and to the parents, from whom the most effective and long-lasting solutions will come. Although the program places the initial responsibility for children's education on the parents, it also connects the parents to two sources that bear that co-responsibility: the school and the community.

The program highlighted in this chapter is one example of how researchers, educators, parents, and community members can ensure literacy access and opportunities for African-American parents and youth. Even though the program was implemented in a small rural Louisiana community, it can be adapted and changed to reflect and keep pace with the literacy needs of a wide variety of parents and children living in diverse environments of our society (see Edwards, 1990a, 1990b).

Schools cannot afford to exclude minority parents as an educational resource. Reaching the family (and especially minority families) is as important as reaching the child (Rich, Van Dien, & Mattox, 1979, p. 37). Regardless of ethnic background or educational levels, parents want to know specific strategies and approaches that they can be involved in with school personnel, and they want more information about their children's educational programs and progress (Edwards, 1987). Kroth (1975) believes that "efforts for involving minority parents should be based on a series of attempts until the right one works" (p. 10). The Parents as Partners in Reading Program was the right choice for parents and children in this small rural Louisiana community. Other paradigms may be equally successful. However, whatever the approach, the model must be developed around the cultural literacy needs and goals of all of the participant groups.

REFERENCES

Anderson, R.C., Hiebert, E., Scott, J.A., & Wilkinson, I.A.G. (1985). *Becoming a nation of readers: The report of the commission of reading.* Washington, DC: The National Institute of Education.

Baratz, J.C. (1969). Teaching reading in an urban negro school system. In J.C. Baratz & R.W. Shuy (Eds.), *Teaching black children to read* (pp. 92-116). Washington, DC: Center for Applied Linguistics.

Baratz, J.C., & Povich, E. (1967, November). *Grammatical constructions in the language of the negro preschool child.* Paper presented at the national meeting of the American Speech and Hearing Association, Washington, DC.

Bereiter, C., & Englemann, S. (1966). *Teaching disadvantaged children in preschool.* Englewood Cliffs, NJ: Prentice-Hall.

Chall, J.S., Heron, E., & Hilferty, A. (1987). Adult literacy: New and enduring problems. *Phi Delta Kappan,* pp. 190-196.

Chapman, D.L. (1986). Let's read another one. In D.R. Tovey & J.E. Kerber (Eds.), *Roles in literacy learning: A new perspective* (pp. 10-25). Newark, DE: International Reading Association.

Croft, D.J. (1979). *Parents and teachers: A resource book for home, school and community relations.* Belmont, CA: Wadsworth.

Cunningham, P.M. (1977). Teachers' correction responses to black-dialect miscues which are non-meaning-changing. *Reading Research Quarterly, 12* (4), 637-653.

Deutsch, M. (1967). *The disadvantaged child.* New York: Basic Books.

Doake, D. B. (1986). Learning to read: It starts in the home. In D. R. Tovey & J. E. Kerber (Eds.), *Roles in literacy learning: A new perspective* (pp. 2-9). Newark, DE: International Reading Association.

Dummett, L. (1984). The enigma—The persistent failure of black children in learning to read. *Reading World, 24,* 31-37.

Edwards, P. A. (1987). Working with families from diverse backgrounds. In D. S. Strickland & E. J. Cooper (Eds.), *Educating black children: America's challenge* (pp. 92-104). Washington, DC: Howard University, Bureau of Educational Research, School of Education.

Edwards, P. A. (1989). Supporting lower SES mothers' attempts to provide scaffolding for bookreading. In J. Allen & J. Mason (Eds.), *Risk makers, risk takers, risk breakers: Reducing the risks for young literacy learners* (pp. 222-250). Portsmouth, NH: Heinemann.

Edwards, P. A. (1990a). *Parents as partners in reading: A family literacy training program.* Chicago: Childrens Press.

Edwards, P. A. (1990b). *Talking your way to literacy: A program to help non-reading parents prepare their children for reading.* Chicago: Childrens Press.

Edwards, P. A. (1991). Fostering early literacy through parent coaching. In E. Hiebert (Ed.), *Literacy for a diverse society: Perspectives, programs, and policies* (pp. 199-213). New York: Teachers College Press.

Edwards, P. A., & Garcia, G. E. (1991). Parental involvement in mainstream schools: An issue of equity. In M. Foster (Ed.), *Readings on equal education, Volume 11, Qualitative investigations into schools and schooling* (pp. 167-187). New York: AMS Press.

Farron, D. C. (1982). Mother-child interaction, language development, and the school performance of poverty children. In L. Feagans & D. C. Farron (Eds.), *The language of children reared in poverty* (pp. 19-52). New York: Academic Press.

France, M. G., & Meeks, J. W. (1987). Parents who can't read: What the schools can do. *Journal of Reading, 31*, 222-227.

Gallimore, R., & Goldenberg, C. N. (1989, March). *School effects on emergent literacy experiences in families of Spanish-speaking children.* Paper prepared for a symposium on Vygotsky and Education at the annual meeting of the American Educational Research Association, San Francisco.

Goodman, K. (1965). Dialect barriers to reading comprehension. *Elementary English, 42*, 853-860.

Goodman, K., & Buck, C. (1973). Dialect barriers to reading comprehension revisited. *The Reading Teacher, 27*, 6-12.

Gumperz, J. J., & Hernandez-Chavez, E. (1972). Bilingualism, bidialectalism, and classroom interaction. In C. Cazden, V. John, & D. Hymes (Eds.), *Function of language in the classroom* (pp. 84-108). New York: Teachers College Press.

Heath, S. B. (1982). What no bedroom story means: Narrative skills at home and school. *Language in Society, 2*, 49-76.

Heath, S. B. (1983). *Ways with words: Language, life, and work in communities and classrooms.* Cambridge, MA: Cambridge University Press.

Heath, S. B., & Branscombe, A. (1986). The book as narrative prop in language acquisition. In B. Schieffelin & P. Gilmore (Eds.), *The acquisition of literacy: Ethnographic perspectives* (pp. 16-34). Norwood, NJ: Ablex.

Huey, E. B. (1908). *The psychology and pedagogy of reading.* New York: Macmillan.

Kroth, R. L. (1975). *Communicating with parents of exceptional children.* Denver: Love Publishing.

Labov, W. A. (1965, April). *Linguistic research on nonstandard English of negro children.* Paper presented to the New York Society for the Experimental Study of Education, New York, NY..

Labov, W.A. (1967). Some sources of reading problems for negro speakers of nonstandard English. In A. Frazer (Ed.), *New directions in elementary\English* (pp. 140-167). Champaign, IL: National Council of the Teachers of English.

Lamb, P. (1979). Dialects and reading. In R. Shafer (Ed.), *Applied linguistics and reading* (pp. 40-50). Newark, DE: International Reading Association.

McCormick, C., & Mason, J. M. (1986). Intervention procedures for increasing preschool children's interest in and knowledge about reading. In W. Teale & E. Sulzby (Eds.), *Emergent literacy: Writing and reading* (pp. 90-115). Norwood, NJ: Ablex.

Morrow, L. M. (1988). Young children's responses to one-to-one story readings in school settings. *Reading Research Quarterly, 23,* 89-107.

Pflaum, S. W. (1986). *The development of language and literacy in young children* (3rd ed.). Columbus, OH: Charles E.Merrill Publishing.

Resnick, M. B., Roth, J., Aaron, P. M., Scott, J., Wolking, W. D., Laren, J. J., & Packer, A. B. (1987). Mothers reading to infants: A new observational tool. *The Reading Teacher, 40,* 888-895.

Rich, D., Van Dien, J., & Mattox, B. (1979). Families as educators of their own children. In R. S. Brandt (Ed.), *Partners: Parents and schools* (pp. 26-40). Alexandria, VA: Association for Supervision and Curriculum Development.

Ruddell, R.B. (1965). The effect of oral and written patterns of language structure on reading comprehension. *The Reading Teacher, 18,* 270-275.

Russell, W.F. (1984). *Classics to read aloud to your child.* New York: Crown Publishers, Inc.

Simons, H.D., & Johnson, K.R. (1974). Black English syntax and reading interference. *Research in the Teaching of English, 8,* 339-358.

Sledge, A.C. (1987, April). *Mother infant literacy knowledge.* Paper presented at the annual meeting of the American Educational Research Association, Washington, DC.

Smith, N. B. (1975). Cultural dialects: Current problems and solutions. *The Reading Teacher, 29,* 137-141.

Smith-Dummett, L. (1977). *Listening comprehension and reading comprehension of black-English-speaking junior high school students black English and in standard English.* Unpublished doctoral dissertation, Teachers College, Columbia University, New York.

Snow, C.E., & Ninio, A. (1986). The contract of literacy: What children learn from learning to read books. In W. H. Teale & E. Sulzby (Eds.), *Emergent literacy: Writing and reading* (pp. 116-138). Norwood, NJ: Ablex.

Spewock, T.S. (1988). Training parents to teach their preschoolers through literature. *The Reading Teacher, 41,* 648-652.

Swift, M.S. (1970). Training poverty mothers in communication skills. *The Reading Teacher, 23,* 360-367.

Teale, W. H. (1981). Parents reading to their children: What we know and need to know. *Language Arts, 58,* 902-911.

Vygotsky, L. S. (1978). *Mind in society.* Cambridge, MA: Harvard University Press.

APPENDIX:

Outline of Fall Semester Course
(the Spring course covered the same content)
EDCI 7107 - Parents as Partners in Reading
Fall 1987
Monday—4:30-7:30 p.m.

August
1   Introduction to class
24   The Need for Parental Involvement
           Historical Overview of Family Life and Parent
           Involvement

September
7   Parents in the Classroom
           The Art of Communicating with Parents
           Effective Home-School-Community Relationships
14   Parental Empowerment
           The Employed/Working Parent
21   Family Literacy
           Parents as Teachers
28   Continue discussion on Family Literacy

October
5   No Class
           (I will be attending a Kellogg Forum in Battle Creek, MI)
12   Organizing a School Volunteer Program
           Models for Parental Involvement
           Ideas for Parent-Teacher Meetings
19   Parent Workshops
26   Parents as Partners in Reading—The Research

November
2   Parents as Partners in Reading discussion continued
           (The Research)
9   Parents as Partners in Reading discussion continued
           (The Research)
16   Parents as Partners in Reading—Practical Applications
23   Parents as Partners in Reading—Practical Applications

December
1   No Class
           (I will be attending the National Reading Conference in
           St. Petersburg, FL)
8   Parents as Partners in Education—Issues and Answers

Have a Happy Holiday Season and Best Wishes in 1988

13

Curriculum Reform and Testing

Eric J. Cooper

National Urban Alliance for Effective Education, Teachers College, Columbia University

It would seem that issues related to testing remain the most prevalent questions to be answered when considering school reform. Article after article in the popular press calls for national school tests (e.g., "The push to consider," 1991; "Congress is told," 1991; "Advisory panel presents," 1991). A focus on improving teaching and learning seems to be given short shrift when national policies are formulated regarding school reform.

The way testing is used remains one of the major hurdles we need to overcome if we are to see the dramatic changes required for meeting the literacy needs of an urban population—and in particular, the needs of African-American students. This chapter addresses testing within the context of curriculum reform and its impact on African-American and other minority group students.

It is assumed by most observers of the American educational system that schools exist to teach students how to learn. Yet, for some observers, this statement is both questionable and controversial (Darling-Hammond, 1985; Linn & Palmer, 1985). For example, in Florida people have argued that schools exist to teach students how to pass a test (the SSAT-1 and SSAT-II). In New York many may argue that instruction is focused on helping students pass the Regents, and in other states it is argued that schools exist to help students pass competency tests or to help students through the equivalent of a Graduate Equivalency Degree (GED) (Linn & Palmer, 1985).

With the growing debate about the expansion of testing in America, one can assume that testing will remain a central issue for those engaged in curriculum reform (Linn, 1991). But it is a premise of this chapter that no matter how good the test, the test is not the same as learning and should not be the primary vehicle used for moving education in the United States or elsewhere towards some semblance of excellence. Teaching students how to learn is essentially different from teaching information, teaching to memorize, teaching to take a test, or teaching any other skill not related to the how of learning.[1]

The question of what should be the central focus for education is one that has increasingly been debated in the United States and in many other nations (Bloom, 1987; Hirsch, 1988; Marton, Hounsell, & Entwistle, 1984). In the 1970s, a general reaction to students' deficiencies led to a renewed public demand for a return to the basics of education (or a focus on the three Rs). It also moved towards what Marton et al. (1984) have called a duality of how one conceives of education, that is, a focus on true and false or right and wrong questions derived from assessment instruments. As interpreted by state legislators, the courts, and school systems in the United States, the decisions resulted in a reversal of the educational trends of the 1960s, a change from open classroom and student-centered instruction to traditional classroom and teacher-centered instruction, and a moving away from scientific inquiry models toward the test-driven curriculum and didactic teaching styles advocated prior to the curriculum revolution of the 1960s (Bussis, 1982; Chall, 1979). The resulting curriculum stresses minimum skills and continues to produce students unable to perform comprehension tasks (Glaser, 1983; Linn, 1991).

Public education in the United States remains under fire from the press, university representatives, business and community leaders, legislators, and parents (Allington, 1991; Cooper, 1987). Kearns (1987) stated that:

> Public education has put this country at a terrible competitive disadvantage. The American workforce is running out of qualified people. If current demographic and economic trends continue, American business will have to hire a million new workers a year who can't read, write, or count. (p. 1)

---

[1]This chapter is adapted from recent articles (Cooper, 1989, Cooper & Sherk, 1989) developed by the author.

Unfortunately, students who may be most in need—African-American and other minority students—are least likely to receive the educational support necessary for success in the 21st century. They, more than other populations, are school-dependent (as opposed to at risk) and as such need access to the best teachers, the best programs, the best assessment instruments, the best material, and the best schools. Poussaint (1987) succinctly states the problem:

> If it is any consolation, it appears that American education is short-changing just about everyone—rich and poor, urban and suburban, advantaged and disadvantaged, black and every other color. Unfortunately, and this is the dilemma, black students are substantially behind a student population that is, as a whole, far behind where current studies say it needs to be. If the goal is only to reach a national average, black kids will be in the no-win situation of trying to play catch-up. [But] playing catch-up will not put black students where the Carnegie Forum on Education and the Economy says all students need to be to make it in the 21st century. (p.44)

To address the implications of why this country does not educate its minority population well, we need to first identify some of the educational drivers that remain as obstacles to literacy development and educational opportunities among African-American and other minority students. The general theme is predicated on the fact that we will not see educational reform until tests are aligned with what we know about good instruction. And, as indicated earlier, it is clearly recognized that tests have become the major tool of policymakers in managing school reform (Linn, 1987, 1991; Madaus, 1987; Pipho, 1985).

DECLINE IN TEACHING THINKING

Over the last two decades, concrete instructional improvement has occurred as we have continued to gain knowledge about the processes of learning through research on time-tested theories (see Dewey, 1933; Glaser, 1978; Harris & Cooper, 1985; Herber, 1978; Kintsch, 1974; Langer, 1980; Marzano et al., 1987; Taba, 1962). Yet, it was also during this period (1972-1980) that, as Darling-Hammond points out, "the use of teaching methods that might encourage the development of higher-order thinking abilities (among minorities) e.g., project or laboratory work, writing tasks, and student-centered discussions, declined in public schools" (Darling-Hammond, 1985, p. vii).

Darling-Hammond (1985) and others suggest that this decline is based on the fact that many tests, textbooks, and curricula have increasingly focused on minimal skills (e.g., literal comprehension, routine computation, and factual recall), rather than the skills that may lead to a higher level of thinking by African-American and minority students, for example, inferential and critical problem solving, comprehension, representation, elaboration, inductive inquiry, synthesis, and evaluation (Strickland & Cooper, 1987).

Allington (1991) suggests that at-risk learners, among whom African-American youth are overrepresented, will not perform well on academic tasks until the educational system recognizes how damaging existing policies have been for this population. In particular, he questions the policies that place students in Chapter 1 programs which in turn teaches them low-level and fragmented skills that continue to affect their ability to perform well.

The consequence of these policies may be illustrated by a national indicator that suggests that African-American and other students are not learning the skills that will enable them to compete well in the workplace. The National Assessment for Educational Progress (NAEP), increasingly accepted as a national indicator of schooling, suggests "there is more cause for concern about the ability of students to solve problems requiring higher-level skills and an understanding of basic principles than about their ability to recall discrete facts or to perform routine operations" (Linn & Palmer, 1985, p. 91).

In spite of the NAEP data, schools continue to focus primarily on low-level skills (Kagan, 1990). Oakes (1989a, 1989b) and Braddock (this volume) provide additional data which indicate that schools serving predominantly poor and minority populations offer fewer advanced and more remedial courses in academic subjects and have smaller academic tracks and larger vocational programs. Darling-Hammond (this volume) also suggests that when African-American and minority students are predominantly grouped in low-ability classes, they obviously will perform only up to those expectations.

It must be understood that students on the whole do not fail; it is the schools that fail students. By offering fragmented instruction to African-American and other minority students and by maintaining low expectations through tracking, schools will often alienate students. The results will be ever-increasing numbers of students dropping out of school (Kagan, 1990).

A VISION FOR SCHOOL REFORM

Due to the diverse needs of students served in the United States and elsewhere, there is a need to refocus on a vision of what should be done in classrooms, rather than focusing on the traditional drivers of instruction. This vision should highlight what students have in common and address the patterns of thinking by which people from different cultures, backgrounds, skill levels, and languages learn to learn in a nourishing atmosphere. I suggest this should be the ultimate goal of education and a source for instructional reform that brings together research on cognition, an understanding of how students engage themselves in the learning process, and the delivery of instruction necessary for diverse student populations. Care must be taken to avoid the abuses of segregation and tracking and an inadvertent separation of African Americans and other minorities into programs that move them away from the mainstream, for example, some special education and Chapter 1 programs (Allington, 1991).

To move towards this vision of school reform, there is an obvious need to recognize that no one approach will be a panacea for addressing the concerns this nation has about education (Slavin, 1988). Yet, there are specific organizational and instructional arrangements that have proven successful in educating disadvantaged and minority students. Sizemore (1985) and Eubanks and Levine (1987), for example, have reported:

> such arrangements emphasize provision of educational assistance to improve reading performance through tutoring before school, during lunch, or after school, utilization of teachers' aides, reduction of nonessential time in art, music, or other subjects, formation of smaller in-class groups for low achievers than for other students. (p. 22)

Other researchers including Bloom (1988) and Comer (1987) have described the importance of linking the home and school in a partnership based on instruction (the use of graded homework is identified as a factor related to improved student achievement). Bloom (1988) also stresses the importance of developing automaticity in reading and an instructional focus on teaching higher order thinking processes as integral factors related to student learning.

Still other educators have stressed the importance of reorganizing schooling as a key to school improvement and student achievement. Bensman (1987) reports on an inner-city school that has reorganized its structure (i.e., physical, instructional and attitudinal) to one that is student-centered. Briefly, the school is one in which teachers and students work under the philosophy that "less is more." Content-area instruction is integrated and focused on three subjects (i.e., math, science, and humanities, including language arts) so that higher order thinking, synthesis, and application are primary goals of classroom activities. Students work in small groups almost exclusively and are taught through such strategies as team teaching, coaching, modeling, and cooperative learning.

The school also does not track students into specific learning streams. In fact, all groups are heterogeneous, whereby students performing on different levels work to support each other's learning. Community involvement of the students is an integral activity of the school; students are allowed opportunities to apply skills learned in the classroom outside of the classroom. High expectations, as well as instructional arrangements that lead to cognitive skill development by students, are the central themes of this highly successful inner-city school.

The need to focus on improving how students are taught to think is well documented. One cannot pick up an education journal without seeing reference to research emerging out of cognitive science (Dewey, 1933; Resnick, 1987). Yet, it is mainly the rhetoric about thinking that has flourished. The application of teaching for thinking to classroom practice still lags far behind (Allington, 1991). Classroom materials in widespread use still emphasize the acquisition of minimal cognitive skills (Raths, Wasserman, Jonas, & Rothstein, 1986). Teachers and administrators continue to purchase material steeped in teaching students low-level basic skills without consideration to what students need to learn to exist as active members of the general society (Cooper & Sherk, 1989). Tests are used that overemphasize approaches to improving students' performance in the "basic" rudimentary skills that are easiest to teach and test (Eubanks & Levine, 1987, p. 24). Resnick (1987) clearly articulates a historical perspective on what may answer the question of why the rhetoric of teaching has flourished, whereas classroom practice has seemingly not followed suit:

> The goal of increasing thinking and reasoning ability are old ones for educators. Such abilities have been the goals of some schools at least since the time of Plato. But these goals were part of the high literacy tradition; they did not, by and large, apply to the more recent schools for the masses. Although it is not new to include thinking, problem solving, and reasoning in someone's school curriculum, it is new to include it in everyone's curriculum. It is new to take seriously the aspiration of making thinking and problem solving a regular part of a school program for all of the population, even minorities, even non-English speakers, even the poor. It is a new challenge to develop educational programs that assume that all individuals, not just an elite, can become competent thinkers. (p. 7)

INTEGRATING EDUCATION DRIVERS

Central to school reform is a recognition that tests and instructional material drive what occurs in school. There is a need to move beyond this restrictive thrust to one that clearly outlines the purposes of instruction. To set a purpose for improved learning involves mobilizing some commitment from students before expecting them to deliver on that commitment. It means sharing the need to comprehend, to think, to understand concepts which cut across subject, grade, age, and school. A way to mobilize this activity is to get both teachers and students to buy into the process of learning—a process in which responsibility for learning is shared by teachers and students (Dewey, 1933; Palincsar & Brown, 1985; Paris, 1985).

How often has a teacher overheard students asking, "Will it be on the test?" in order to find some purpose for some activity which otherwise has little obvious reason. When students ask, "Will it be on the test?" they probably cannot find any other good reason or purpose to learn something. That is the most obvious misapplication of instruction. If it is only the test makers that set purpose in schools, education has left the driving to them, and places in their hands the prerogative for choosing the routes and schedules, the map and destination for the school system.

Rather than using testing as a motivator for learning, teachers might help students develop ownership for the purpose of interactive and interdisciplinary lessons that build on prior knowledge gained from home, community, and school. Activating that background knowledge means making something relevant.

More specifically, as described by Paris (1985), activating background knowledge means building from clearly understood ideas and bridging this knowledge into new areas, motivating interest from curiosity, and celebrating that curiosity with all the reinforcement we can bring to bear. Of course, this does not mean we must always relearn what we already know, but it does return to Plato's observation that knowledge is a continuous rediscovery of our own insights.

School reform will require of teachers, students, and administrators avoidance of inappropriate testing or quizzing, which often follows instruction that lacks a clear purpose and which often stresses basic skills over comprehension and thinking skills. Reform will require instructional programs that are linked to instructional assessments. It will require the use of tests focused on the end result of instruction (i.e., improved comprehension and thinking), as well as knowing how students can be supported to reach the appropriate goals of schooling.

Promising research on new approaches to testing are emerging. Advanced independently by Wise, Resnick, and Wiggins are concepts to testing which when implemented do not distort the instructional process. Authentic measures, as recently described in the literature, are curriculum-driven and are in three parts: performance—student is given a task to be carried out in a limited time; portfolio—examination evaluates a body of work created by the student; and project—how a student works with a group on a particular task ("The push to consider," 1991).

Linn (1991) cautions educators to be aware of the constraints of standardized, paper-and-pencil tests:

> Among the more important constraints (of standardized measures) is the need for efficiency, the desire to represent the test results by a single number that places each test taker on a common scale, and the emphasis on the use of test results for purposes of accountability. The emphasis on accountability limits the domain of the test and, I argue, also reduces the instructional utility. (p. 183)

As Linn suggests, when traditional norm-referenced or objective-referenced tests of educational competencies are required or legislated, they tend to prescribe the nature of instruction in the classroom (Airasian, 1988). Because such tests typically contain specific items that measure discrete skills, teachers drill students on the skills that are tested, even though there may be little or no evidence that such drill and practice leads to improvement in the desired educational outcome (Mehrens & Kaminsky, 1989). Worse, little instructional time is spent on those areas that are important, but not included on the legislated test (Bracey, 1986). There is little question that in such situations teachers end up valuing what they test, rather than testing what they value.

Also troubling is that traditional tests do not adequately prove the measures of the amount of growth or progress that students achieve on such developing competencies. Objective-referenced tests, by definition, are tied to discrete instructional objectives. Because these instructional objectives change across grades, continuity of measurement across grades with objective-referenced tests is rarely if ever feasible.

Traditional norm-referenced tests, which are designed to discriminate among students, are only able to provide information about the performance of students in relation to a norm group. Although standardized tests and normative scores have many limitations (see Cannell, 1987, 1989), two are particularly serious in relation to the concern about setting and assessing higher educational goals and standards for students: (a) normative scores are unable to describe what students are able to do; and (b) normative scores cannot be used to adequately assess student growth over time (for a more complete discussion, see Ivens, 1990).

Given the traditional use of programs designed for disadvantaged students that focus on low-level basic skills to the exclusion of higher order tasks, the obstacles posed by typical standardized measures present a double whammy for African Americans and other minorities. Not only may students be forced into a reductionist program of study, they are often locked into these programs because of poor performance on the tests. Yet, Linn (1991) notes that "a growing body of research indicates that at-risk students perform poorly because of an impoverished or underdeveloped repertoire of learning and study strategies" (p.199).

Clearly, the case continues to be made that assessment influences what is taught and what is learned (Linn, 1991). A response that addresses the educational needs of African-American and other students may be framed by evaluation systems that are both cognitive and interactional, that is, based on an array of instruments derived from cognitive and metacognitive theories of instruction.

But, there are very few tests that are based on comprehension and cognitive constructs. In the area of reading comprehension, work on the state examination used by Michigan (Wixson & Peters, 1987), and Degrees of Reading Power (DRP) used by the states of New York, Connecticut, and Virginia (Koslin, Koslin, & Zeno, 1979), are exceptions. Though quite different in structure, both Michigan and the DRP are based on a definition of reading that is derived from the student actively participating in the construction of meaning through the dynamic interaction of the mind of the reader, the text, and the context of the reading situation. Reading thus is defined as the active participation of the reader with the language of the text and is based on the learner's ability to bridge the gap between the known and unknown.

At the very least, when teaching by the Michigan or the DRP, the teacher finds support for teaching what research suggests is the emerging view of the reading process. Students are thus given extended passages to read and are allowed opportunities for holistic instruction (i.e., instruction is not fragmented into a series of separate skills).

Linn (1991) points to several other emerging trends in testing. Specifically, he notes the dynamic assessment work of Feuerstein (1980) and Campione and Brown (1987) with students at risk. Linn (1991) states:

> It seems that if teachers are to capture the open-ended, iterative process of thinking in their assessments of student performance, they will need to move away from static, paper-and-pencil assessments that stand alone from the learning process and toward the dynamic assessment procedures of Feuerstein and Campione and Brown. Standardized testing does not reveal the process by which a response to a problem or question is constructed and, thus, gives no insight into the student's cognition. In the words of Resnick (1987), standardized test scores and even course grades "do not reveal the

quality of thinking, and they offer no indications of transfer beyond purely academic settings." (pp. 202-203)

Future assessments will be gauged by how well they reflect on the instruction used in classrooms by teachers and students engaged in the collaborative and cognitive nature of learning. Static evaluations that penalize African Americans and other minorities lacking in prior experience of specific skills may begin to lose their luster for educators. Linn (1991) adds in his seminal work on assessment that:

> The case must also be made that thinking skills and processes are essential educational goals that go well beyond the accumulation of factual knowledge . . . the reliance solely on multiple-choice test items distorts the goals and frustrates their achievement. Hence, it is worth the added expense and complexity that such assessment will require. (p. 204)

MATERIALS OF INSTRUCTION

Earlier in this chapter I referred to the "drivers" of curriculum. A discussion on curriculum redesign must also speak to the tools of education that often cloud reform efforts. It is estimated that 80% to 95% of what goes on in the classroom is derived from published instructional material rather than from active processing of knowledge between students and teachers (Osborn & Stein, 1985).

Instructional classroom materials are of two general types: (a) materials for skills development, and (b) materials for instruction in subject matter. Materials for skills development contain little subject matter; a study of one basal reader, for example, indicated that only 13% to 17% of its content was expository in nature (Sherk, 1988). Elementary-level language arts and social studies texts rely heavily on narratives—stories or storylike passages containing characters, setting, plot, and events—to frame the instructional program. In many urban and metropolitan elementary schools, most instructional sessions are spent reading such narrative materials. However, the reading of narratives must be balanced with the reading of expository texts that provide a knowledge base upon which subsequent academic subject knowledge and text comprehension skills can be built (Harris & Cooper, 1985).

Research on reading comprehension casts doubts on the assumption that students can automatically transfer inference skills learned from narrative-based reading lessons to subject-matter text (Sherk, 1988). However, many of the reading comprehension skills that are now taught exclusively in basal reader narratives can be taught in subject-matter lessons from content textbooks. In other words, an elementary-level science text could be used, for example, as the foundation upon which knowledge of the facts of science and the writing patterns of scientific materials are based. By this practice, minority students could be taught early to recognize the patterns of organization and thought relationships (listing, chronological/sequential ordering, and problem-solution relationships) found in expository text, but which are rarely used in basal readers for skills mastery materials.

It is as important for minority students to become familiar with patterns of thought in text as it is for them to develop their subject-matter knowledge base. These thought patterns are essential prior-knowledge concepts students will need in order to handle the more difficult texts they will encounter in later grades. Thus, a shift to the teaching of reading comprehension from expository texts is also needed.

INSTRUCTIONAL FRAMEWORKS

The case has been made for a shift away from traditional testing and instruction based on learning that is fragmented and primarily derived from memorizing factual information. Educators are emerging from a phase in educational history in which test results were viewed as self-fulfilling prophecies. Tests predicted how children would perform certain school tasks, and teachers taught in ways that confirmed those predictions (Shepard, 1989). Research noted in this chapter and elsewhere in the volume have shown that children respond to instruction in the way that is expected of them; if they are expected to be slow, children begin to respond in the way others in the group respond, even though the response pattern and the group they are in may be inappropriate. Children often are relegated to the slow group even though their assignments were based on prediction and not on observed behavior. These children rarely, if ever, get out of the slow groups, and, more often than not, African Americans and other minorities are relegated to the lowest tracks on the basis of test performances.

The problem of the test-driven, self-fulfilling prophecy is particularly difficult for African Americans and other minorities in urban settings (Oakes, 1985). As has been indicated, most standardized tests cannot properly predict performance in these cases, because the assumptions that underlie the tests' construction are often inappropriate for the minority and urban student. Frequently, items in standardized tests present concepts and information that are unfamiliar to many urban children. Additionally, such tests require that children work alone, and urban children often have little interest, experience, tolerance, or incentive for that (Ianni, 1983).

The legacy of research from the 1980s is the conclusion that teachers of African American and urban students must change their teaching practices toward concentrating more time and effort on concept development, cognitive development, reasoning, thinking, and higher order comprehension skills. A strong base of research linking cognitive development to prior knowledge in learning emerged in the late 1970s (Langer, 1982). Those studies concluded that, particularly when reading is the learning mode, those students with much prior knowledge and experience relevant to a subject have less difficulty learning new material and retain more than those who have inadequate or incomplete prior knowledge and experience.

Finding ways to help students relate what they already know to what is to be learned is called *preteaching* or *preparation*. Research has suggested that this is accomplished by teachers in several ways. One way is by encouraging students to make predictions before a reading and/or learning task (Herber, 1985; Ogle, 1988/1989). Predicting, based on the students' prior knowledge of the topic and on what the students think the reading selection will be about, helps them become aware of their knowledge base. It also helps them to focus closely on how the text informs the reader. Another practice is to allow students to examine the structure of textual material before detailed reading takes place (Sardy, 1985). For example, if students can determine that they are going to read a narrative selection, they can review their knowledge of the narrative structure (i.e., a narrative has a setting, characters, plot, beginning, ending, and so forth). If the selection is an expository one, students can be alerted to look for signals that will indicate a particular relationship of ideas (such as cause-effect, comparison-contrast, and/or problem-solution, and chronology or sequence).

For some urban children, growth in vocabulary and word knowledge and in-depth understanding are key factors in the reading comprehension equation. By the time a child is in sixth or seventh grade, he or she should know how to read all of the words encountered in everyday speech. Yet, how do students learn the vast quantity of words that never occur in oral communication and that only occur in text? It is the teacher's role to select those words and to provide students with access to them. In many cases, teachers provide the only access to such words. Teachers must preteach or alert students to pronunciations and discuss word meanings and concepts through informational strategies that provide students with sufficient background knowledge to cope with learning the text in which the words are embedded. Vocabulary/concept preselection is also important, because it offsets the natural tendency of readers to skip unknown words during their search for the overall meaning of text. Students are alerted to look for newly learned words as they read; with word meanings clearly in mind, more precise text comprehension occurs.

LEVELING TEXTS FOR INSTRUCTION

Leveling text in urban classrooms provides learners with added incentives for reading and learning. For those who read less well, the leveling of text provides more practice reading opportunities and more access to knowledge of other subjects in the curriculum, especially when reading independently. For the average child, the current system differs little from what would be in effect if textbooks were leveled. Students who read at levels above and beyond the average are given texts that challenge their best efforts and enable them to move ahead on their own in reading and study situations. For such advanced readers and learners, the challenge to go beyond is a powerful incentive for remaining interested in school, forestalling much of the boredom many of these able learners suffer in urban classrooms (Sherk, 1988). There are many research-based strategies that apply to appropriate leveling and learning from text. They include:

- Activating student prior knowledge before the text is presented for reading (Ogle, 1988/1989; Sardy, 1985);
- Using mapping and graphic organizers to help build schema for students (Sardy, 1985);
- Using questioning strategies (Ogle, 1988/1989);
- Using concept-attainment models for isolating difficult concepts before and after reading/learning assignments (Bruner, Goodnow, & Austin, 1967);
- Matching reading materials through the use of readability and other information related to comprehensibility, that is, motivation, interest, organization, and preferences (Klare, 1985).

CONCLUSION

The instructional challenges proposed within this chapter require teachers who maintain high expectations for all students, administrators with creativity and leadership, restructured classrooms for improved management of instruction, and partnerships forged out of the willingness of all individuals involved in schooling to focus on improving the purposes we set for schools. Cognitive theory as a central theme can be applied with major effect.

Cognitive research has generated a body of knowledge, a library of strategic interventions steeped in a rich reservoir of theories from past decades, that is helping to bring a renaissance to schooling (Presseisen, 1988). Even though this research has provided us with new fuel for accelerating school improvement, it has had remarkably little effect on our nation's urban schools (Allington, 1991). Obstacles such as minimal competency tests and instructional material grounded in lower order objectives need to be removed. Teachers and administrators unwilling to maintain high expectations for all students need to be retrained or removed. Classrooms that are organized primarily for lecturing, in which students, because of their seating arrangements, are forced to engage with the back of their fellow student's heads, need to be restructured. Teachers must avoid delegating passive activities from blackboard cleaning to collecting papers, but retain active learning responsibilities, such as talking, listening, responding, and analyzing, for themselves. Should we so choose to incorporate the process of learning into the management of schools for instruction, cognitive research provides us with an opportunity to do so.

The redesign of schooling needs to be based on an assumption that for meaningful change to occur the responsibility for that change must be placed on the educators and the community—not on the students. Recognizing a need for new testing policies that integrate well with meaningful instruction is central. Most importantly, we need to learn how to extend the implications from research to the community and the local educational agency. All too often research findings never find their way into the school system due to uninformed local policies. In addition to obstacles created by traditional drivers of education, the administrative and community policies that frustrate the implementation of research into practice remain among the important challenges of the 1990s.

REFERENCES

Advisory panel presents national-test plan to Bush. (1991, January 23). *Education Week*, p. 25.

Airasian, P.W. (1988). Measurement driven instruction: A closer look. *Educational Measurement: Issues and Practice, 7*(4), 6-11.

Allington, R.L. (1991). How policy and regulation influence instruction for at-risk learners, or why poor readers rarely comprehend well and probably never will. In L. Idol & B.F. Jones (Eds.), *Educational values and cognitive instruction: Implications for reform* (pp. 273-293). Hillsdale, NJ: Erlbaum.

Bensman, D. (1987). *Quality education in the inner city: The story of Central Park East Schools.* New York: New York Community Trust.

Bloom, A. (1987). *The closing of the American mind.* New York: Simon & Schuster.

Bloom, B.S. (1988). Helping all children learn well in elementary school—and beyond. *Principal, 67*(4), 12-17.

Bracey, G.W. (1986). The impact of testing on the learning process. In *Measures in the college admissions process: A college board colloquium* (pp. 5-12). New York: College Entrance Examination Board.

Bruner, J.S. (1979). *On knowing: Essays for the left hand.* Cambridge, MA: Harvard University Press.

Bussis, A.M. (1982, December). Burn it at the casket: Research, reading instruction and children's learning of the first R. *Phi Delta Kappan,* pp. 327-341.

Campione, J.C., & Brown, A.L. (1987). Linking dynamic assessment with school achievement. In C.S. Lidz (Ed.), *Dynamic assessment: An interactional approach to evaluation learning potential* (pp. 82-115). New York: Guilford.

Cannell, J.J. (1987). *Nationally normed elementary achievement testing in America's public schools: How all 50 states are testing above the national average.* Daniels, WV: Friends for Education.

Cannell, J.J. (1989). *How public educators cheat on standardized achievement tests.* Albuquerque, NM: Friends for Education.

Chall, J. (1979). Minimum competency in reading: An informal survey of the states. *Phi Delta Kappan, 2,* 35-38.

Comer, J. (1987). Black family stress and school achievement. In D.L. Strickland & E.J. Cooper (Eds.), *Educating Black children: America's challenge* (pp. 77-84). Washington, DC: Howard University.

Congress is told a new achievement test for seniors in high school is essential to monitoring reform. (1991, February 6). *The Chronicle of Higher Education,* pp. 22-24.

Cooper, E.J. (1987). Testimony before the Subcommittee on Elementary, Secondary, & Vocational Education at the Committee on Education and Labor, House of Representatives, 100th Congress, 1st session on H.R. 5. *The Reauthorization of Expiring Federal Elementary and Secondary Education Programs* (Serial No. 100-9). Washington, DC: U.S. Congress, 1st session.

Cooper, E.J. (1989). Toward a new mainstream of instruction for American schools. *Journal of Negro Education, 58*(1).

Cooper, E.J., & Sherk, J. (1989). Addressing urban school reform: Issues and alliances. *Journal of Negro Education, 58*(3).

Darling-Hammond, L. (1985). *Equality and excellence: The educational status of Black Americans.* New York: College Board.

Darling-Hammond, L., & Wise, A.E. (1985). Beyond standardization: State standards and school improvement. *Elementary School Journal, 85,* 315-336.

Dewey, J. (1933). *How we think.* Lexington, MA: D.C. Heath.

Eubanks, E.E., & Levine, D.U. (1987). Administrative and organization arrangement and consideration. In D.L. Strickland & E.J. Cooper (Eds.), *Educating Black children: America's challenge* (pp. 19-31). Washington, DC: Howard University.

Feuerstein, R. (1980). *Instrumental enrichment: An intervention program for cognitive modifiability*. Baltimore: University Park Press.

Glaser, R. (1983, June). *Education and thinking: The role of knowledge*. (Tech. Rep. No. PDS-6). Pittsburgh: University of Pittsburgh, Learning Research and Development Center.

Glaser, R. (Ed.). (1978). *Advances in instructional psychology* (Vol. 1). Hillsdale, NJ: Erlbaum.

Harris, T.L., & Cooper, E. (Eds.). (1985). *Reading, thinking and concept development: Strategies for the classroom*. New York: College Board.

Herber, H.L. (1978). *Teaching reading in content areas*. Englewood Cliffs, NJ: Prentice-Hall.

Herber, H.L. (1985). Levels of comprehension. In T.L. Harris & E. Cooper (Eds.), *Reading, thinking and concept development: Strategies for the classroom* (pp. 213-226). New York: College Board.

Hirsch, E.D., Jr. (1988). *Cultural literacy: What every American needs to know*. New York: Random House.

Ianni, F.J. (1983). Home, school, and community. In I. Flaxarow (Ed.), *Adolescent education* (pp. 35-61). New York: Clearinghouse on Urban Education, Teachers College, Columbia University.

Ivens, S.H. (1990). *Assessing educational outcomes*. New York: National Urban Alliance for Effective Education.

Kagan, D.M. (1990). How schools alienate students at-risk: A model for examining proximal classroom variables. *Educational Psychologist*, 25(2), 105-125.

Kearns, D.T. [Chairman and Chief Executive Officer of Xerox Corporation]. (1987, October 26). Speech delivered to Economic Club of Detroit, Detroit, MI.

Kintsch, W. (1974). *The representation of meaning in memory*. Hillsdale, NJ: Holstead Press.

Klare, G. (1985). Matching reading materials to readers: The role of readability estimates in conjunction with other information about comprehensibility. In T.L. Harris & E. Cooper (Eds.), *Reading, thinking and concept development: Strategies for the classroom* (pp. 233-256). New York: College Board.

Koslin, B.L., Koslin, S., & Zeno, S. (1979). Towards an effectiveness measure in reading. In R.W. Tyler & S.H. White (Eds.), *Testing teaching and learning: Report of a conference on research on testing* (pp. 311-334). Washington, DC: National Institute on Education.

Kozol, J. (1988, October). A report card on America's schools after 20 Years. *The School Administrator*, pp. 13-14.

Langer, J.A. (1980). Relation between levels of prior knowledge and the organization of recall. In M. Kamil & A.J. Moe (Eds), *Perspectives in reading research and instruction*. Washington, DC: National

Reading Conference.

Langer, J.A. (1982). Facilitating text processing: The elaboration of prior knowledge. In J.A. Langer & M. Smith-Burke (Eds.), *Reader meets author/bridging the gap* (pp. 76-82). Newark, DE: International Reading Association.

Linn, R.L. (1987). Accountability: The comparison of educational systems and the quality of test results. *Educational Policy, 1*, 181-198.

Linn, R.L. (1991). Dimensions of thinking: Implications for testing. In L. Idol & B.F. Jones (Eds.), *Educational values and cognitive instruction: Implications for reform* (pp. 179-208). Hillsdale, NJ: Erlbaum.

Linn, R.L. (in press). State-by-state comparisons of student achievement: Some reservations and suggestions for enhancing validity. *Educational Research.*

Linn, R., & Palmer, C.J. (1985). Standards and expectations: The role of testing. In *Conference Proceedings on San Francisco Excellence in Education* (pp. 61-89). New York: College Board.

Madaus, G.F. (1987). Public policy and the testing profession—you've never had it so good. *Educational Measurement: Issues and Practice,* 4(4), 5-11.

Marton, F., Hounsell, D., & Entwistle, N. (Eds.). (1984). *The experience of learning.* Edinburgh: Scottish Academic Press.

Marzano, R.J., Brandt, R. S., Hughes, C.S., Jones, B.F., Presseisen, B.Z., Rankin, S.C., & Suhor, C. (1987). *Dimensions of thinking: A framework for curriculum and instruction.* Alexandria, VA: Association for Supervision and Curriculum Development.

Mehrens, W.A., & Kaminski, J. (1989). Methods for improving standardized test scores: Fruitful, fruitless, or fraudulent? *Educational Measurement: Issues and Practice,* 8(1), 14-22.

Oakes, J. (1985). *Keeping track: How schools structure inequality.* New Haven, CT: Yale University Press.

Oakes, J. (1989a). *Allocating opportunities: School and ability-group effects on students' access to science and mathematics.* Santa Monica, CA: RAND Corporation.

Oakes, J. (1989b). *Lost talent: The underparticipation of women, minorities, and disabled students in science.* Santa Monica, CA: RAND Corporation.

Ogle, D. (1988/1989). Implementing strategic teaching. *Educational Leadership, 46,* 47-60.

Osborn, J., & Stein, M. (1985). Textbook adoptions: A process for change. In T.L. Harris & E.J. Cooper (Eds.), *Reading, thinking and concept development: Strategies for the classroom* (pp. 257-273). New York: College Board.

Palincsar, A., & Brown, A. (1985). Reciprocal teaching: Activities to promote reading with your mind. In T.L. Harris & E.J. Cooper (Eds.), *Reading, thinking and concept development: Strategies for the classroom* (pp. 147-160). New York: College Board.

Paris, S.G. (1985). Using classroom dialogues and guided practice to teach comprehension strategies. In T.L. Harris & E.J. Cooper (Eds.), *Reading, thinking and concept development: Strategies for the classroom* (pp.). New York: College Board.

Pipho, C. (1985). Tracking the reforms, Part 5: Testing—Can it measure the success of the reform movement? *Education Week*, p. 19.

Poussaint, A. (1987). It ain't no consolation. In D.L. Strickland & E.J. Cooper (Eds.), *Educating black children: America's challenge* (pp. 44-54). Washington, DC: Howard University.

Presseisen, B.Z. (Ed.). (1988). *At-risk students and thinking: Perspectives from research*. Washington, DC: National Education Association and Research for Better Schools.

The push to consider a once taboo subject: National school tests. (1991, February 3). *New York Times*, p. 5.

Raths, L.E., Wasserman, S., Jonas, A., & Rothstein, A. (1986). *Teaching for thinking*. New York: Teachers College Press.

Resnick, L.B. (1987). *Education & learning to think*. Washington, DC: National Academy Press.

Sardy, S. (1985). Thinking about reading. In T.L. Harris & E.J. Cooper (Eds.), *Reading, thinking and concept development: Strategies for the classroom* (pp. 213-226). New York: College Board.

Shepard, L.A. (1989). Why we need better assessments. *Educational Leadership, 46*, 4-9.

Sherk, J. (1988). *Matching materials to the needs of inner-city students*. Unpublished manuscript, University of Missouri at Kansas City.

Sizemore, B. (1985). Pitfalls and promise of effective schools research. *The Journal of Negro Education, 54*(3), 269-288.

Slavin, R. (1988). On research and school organization: A conversation with Bob Slavin. *Educational Leadership, 46*(2), 22-29.

Strickland, D.L., & Cooper, E.J. (Eds.). (1987). *Educating black children: America's challenge*. Washington, DC: Howard University.

Taba, H. (1962). *Curriculum development: Theory and practice*. New York: Harcourt, Brace, Jovanovich.

Wixson, K.K., & Peters, C.W. (1987). Comprehension assessment: Implementing an integrative view of reading. *Educational Psychologist, 22*, 333-35

Literacy and Cultural Differences: An Afterword

Daniel A. Wagner
University of Pennsylvania

Within the educational research community, social, cultural, and linguistic interpretations of group differences have become increasingly prevalent. Whether one considers infant care, women at work, or IQ scores, there is no shortage of research that describes the various social attributes that "must have" led to such differences. As a number of chapters in this volume have indicated, a cultural explanation seems far more palatable—and allows for more societal intervention—that predecessor biological (read racial) claims. Yet, what do we really know about how societal interventions can take place effectively in a given educational domain or for individuals with different cultural and ethnic experiences? One obvious conclusion from the chapters in this volume is that literacy work across ethnic diversity needs a grounding in both cultural diversity and in-depth cultural understanding. The differences in literacy development within the African-American community, and as contrasted with other ethnic groups in the United States, are becoming increasingly clear.

More generally, it is not uncommon to hear that low levels of literacy are among the chief problems facing contemporary society, particularly school-based literacy programs in urban settings. There are numerous arguments that would support concern for such a point of view, ranging from the economic pressure on the U.S. workplace to the advent of robotics to the major problems endemic in our urban secondary schools. Literacy is a critical part of policy discussions in all of these areas; yet, it has remained difficult to determine whether more literacy or different literacy would help to alleviate the perceived problems. The distinction between "more" versus "different" seems to be at the heart of many educational concerns, especially when cultural differences are the focus of the analysis. Is literacy development among African-American youth a social problem that requires new models of understanding, a better tailoring, or greater sensitivity to the social, cultural, and linguistic dimensions inherent within that community of learners? The chapters in this volume suggest, as does much of the discourse in this area, that the more/different distinction is not new in education but that it needs to be addressed more effectively as we become aware of the important differences in literacy that exist across ethnic boundaries.

In an attempt to explore these issues in a different context (Wagner, 1991), I came to the conclusion that the cultural difference argument in literacy is particularly salient because literacy is so tightly linked to the total social lives of individuals (as distinct from their "school lives"). In this critical sense, literacy needs to be seen not only as affected *by* culture but also *as* culture. Literacy in contemporary society—regardless of one's level of demonstrable skill—is so much a part of life that it is inherent in the culture. This simple assertion goes a long way to explaining why it is so difficult to intervene in school-based and nonschool (i.e., adult) literacy learning. Literacy, like language and dialect use, is deeply embedded in social life, personal experience, and community expectations.

If accepted, the above argument leads to a nettlesome conclusion. Any attempt to intervene in order to change an individual's literacy status means change not only in a set of skills as measured by most tests and taught in schools but also in the behaviors, attitudes, and beliefs that define each individual, the rest of his or her community, and, ultimately, the structure of communities and societies themselves. Resistance to individual and cultural change, not a new topic in African-American studies, has remained relatively unexplored in current conversations about literacy. We may need to ask whether the very high dropout rate from school and adult literacy programs is related to such a cultural *decalage* between recipients and providers. As various policy options toward trying to improve literacy are considered, the issue of its cultural roles and attributes needs to be better understood as well. As we have seen in this volume, literacy as a cultural entity needs to be examined carefully and understood within the African-American community by individuals who study and work in the community. Efforts to change literacy within that community will likely require integrating current uses of literacy and community identity into learning and instruction so that literacy efforts may be valued, useful, and achievable for African-American learners.

REFERENCE

Wagner, D.A. (1991). Literacy as culture: Emic and etic perspectives. In E.M. Jennings and & A.C. Purves (Eds.), *Literate systems and individual lives: Perspectives on literacy and schooling.* Albany: SUNY Press.

Author Index

Subject Index